The Banat of Temesvar

Stanford Studies on Central and Eastern Europe
Edited by Norman Naimark and Larry Wolff

The Banat of Temesvar
Borderland Colonization in the Habsburg Monarchy

Timothy Olin

Stanford University Press
Stanford, California

Stanford University Press
Stanford, California

© 2025 by Timothy John Olin. All rights reserved.

No part of this book may be reproduced or transmitted in any form or by any means, electronic or mechanical, including photocopying and recording, or in any information storage or retrieval system, without the prior written permission of Stanford University Press.

Printed in the United States of America on acid-free, archival-quality paper

Library of Congress Cataloging-in-Publication Data available on request.

Library of Congress Control Number: 2024033987

ISBN 9781503639942 (cloth)
ISBN 9781503641754 (ebook)

Cover design: Susan Zucker
Cover art: Gabriel Bodenehr, *Lithography of Timisoara* (Temesvar), 1716, Wikimedia Commons

Contents

Acknowledgments		vii
A Note on Archives, Sources, and Names		ix
	Introduction	1
1	Conquest and Construction *Development in the European Borderlands*	23
2	Security and Loyalty *Colonial Settlement from 1718 to 1829*	50
3	The Religious and Ethnic (Re-) Construction of the Banat	88
4	Expectations Fulfilled? *Colonists and the Government*	120
5	Settler Culture *Frontier Problems and Solutions*	144
6	Local Responses to Habsburg Rule I *Migration and Unrest*	171
7	Local Responses to Habsburg Rule II *The Making of Serbs out of Rascians*	191
	Epilogue: The Banat Germans *1848 to the Present*	209
	Notes	233
	Bibliography	291
	Index	311

Acknowledgments

AS ANYONE WHO HAS undertaken one knows, projects like this are both solitary and collaborative endeavors.

I would like to thank everyone who read, commented on, or otherwise helped me complete the book manuscript, including Charles Ingrao, Rebekah Klein-Pejšová, Michael G. Smith, Karl Roider, Rita Krueger, Howard Louthan, Scott Berg, Jonathan Kwan, Larry Wolff, Gary Cohen, Sanket Desai, Chris Walsh, Lori Witt, Mark Barloon, Michael Hochedlinger, the participants in the "History and Culture in Central Europe during the Long 18th Century" workshop at the Center for Austrian Studies at the University of Minnesota, the anonymous reviewers, and the many (and in some cases, very few) people who heard and commented on my presentations at conferences over the years. As noted in the footnotes, small portions of this material appeared previously in the *Austrian History Yearbook* 48 (2017): 159–72. I want to thank the editors there for giving me space to work out some of these ideas.

Of course, I take full responsibility for any errors and omissions.

Further, I want to thank and praise the library staff at Purdue University and Central College for tracking down obscure works from faraway places. I would also like to thank the archivists and staff at the archives in Vienna, Budapest, Timișoara, Novi Sad, Kikinda, Pančevo, and Zrenjanin for their hospitality and support.

Along the way, several institutions and groups have financially supported my research. I would like to thank the Purdue History Department (Paul and Reed Benhamou Scholarship, Woodman Travel Grant), Purdue Graduate School (Research Grants), the Purdue Research Foundation (PRF), the Central European History Society, and Central College (R&D grants, IPD money).

Most importantly, I would like to thank my family. My parents, Tom and Judy, have been supportive of my education from the start. My children, Emmerich and Abraham, have always kept me grounded and reminded me of what is truly important in life. Finally, I need to thank my wife, Tana, for her love and patience over the more than thirteen years it has taken to complete this project. Without her support, it would have been an impossible task. This book is dedicated to her.

A Note on Archives, Sources, and Names

Archives and Sources

Throughout this book, I have privileged primary documents found directly at Austrian, Serbian, and Romanian archives as evidence wherever possible. To verify and expand on these sources, I have used published primary sources that reproduce archival documents, contemporary travel journals, and newspaper accounts. I will discuss the relative merits and deficiencies of these source bases in the introduction and throughout the work. Two important published collections of documents have helped underpin the archival work and have in themselves led to important insights. These sources deserve a short introduction that will also serve to highlight the effects of World War I and II on the archival evidence available in the region.

Lajos Baróti's *Adattár délmagyarország XVIII századi történetéhez* (Repository of eighteenth-century south Hungarian history) is a collection of local administrative registries from the eighteenth century. It is arranged by location and date. Dispatches are short and range from the mundane (collection of taxes) to the bizarre (the disinterment of suspected witches by government officials). Baróti collected these dispatches around the turn of the nineteenth century from the government archive in Temesvár (Timișoara, Romania). Interestingly, a number of eighteenth-century documents in the archive today are copies of documents from Vienna made by Baróti in the 1890s. According to Josef Wolf, another collector and publisher of primary documents on the Banat's German-speaking colonists, the archive lost many documents following the First World War, and Baróti's transcriptions are thus invaluable.

My own experience in the Timișoara branch of the Romanian National Archives confirms this rather pessimistic appraisal of the eighteenth-century documents housed there. While there are many interesting documents there from the period, the lack of a large collection of official government documents is conspicuous. This was not an isolated case. While doing research in Novi Sad, Serbia, I discovered, rather unsurprisingly, that many of the documents housed there fell victim to the Second World War. At this archive, as well, there was a surprising dearth of any documents on the Habsburg administration of the Banat before 1780. I was told that the Germans took many of the documents to Berlin during the Nazi occupation, and they are now lost. Additionally, I heard stories of earlier archivists finding documents for sale in the local bazaar, where they were rescued from an unknown future. In other archives in Serbia, I heard stories of archives used as detention centers and documents burned by prisoners to keep warm. Dealing with such losses is a regrettable but ultimately unavoidable part of working in an area that has experienced such violent upheaval over the past century.

Anton Tafferner's *Quellenbuch zur donauschwäbischen Geschichte* is a five-volume set of primary documents collected and transcribed over the course of twenty-one years. The documents come primarily from the Austrian, Hungarian, and German state archives, though there are a number of documents that he sourced from other published works. Tafferner's documents cover the whole settlement area and thus many documents are only of tangential interest to the current study. Due to the depth and breadth of his materials, this collection has been an invaluable resource that has both helped in understanding the Banat as well as how it fit in the larger Habsburg Danube.

While I used other published primary sources in the research conducted for this book, including Josef Wolf's enlightening *Quellen zur Wirtschafts-, Sozial- und Verwaltungsgeschichte des Banats im 18. Jahrhundert*, the prevalence and importance of the two proceeding works in the text merited further explanation.

Names

Names and naming are a dangerous business when talking about Central Europe. No matter what naming scheme one chooses, there will inevitably be questions. This is understandable. In a region that has seen multiple imperial and ethnoreligious groups pass hegemony between one another, not to mention the experiences of fascism and communism, names can betray political ideology and long-held grudges. Such debates go back at least to the early 1900s if not earlier. In the United States, we are just starting to publicly reckon with names and naming, from reasserting Native American names for lakes in places like Minneapolis, Minnesota, to the names attached to counties and university buildings.

In order to avoid these political disputes, in which I have no wish to take part, I have used the language of the sources whenever possible. There are a few exceptions. In order to ensure consistency, I have altered some names (e.g., Lippa, Lipova) and have used the name more prominent in the sources.

German-speaking settlers are sometimes referred to as "Swabians" in the literature; this shorthand is deceiving. Much as the "Palatines" who settled North America or the "Saxons" in Transylvania, the "Swabians" were in fact an amalgam of many different groups from the German- and at times French-speaking world. I will refer to these groups as German-speakers, Germans, colonists, or settlers. I provide more rationale for this choice in the introduction.

As for local people, I will refer to them by the names prominent in the eighteenth-century sources. With the advent of nationalism in the region, Romanian nationalists claimed the "Wallachs" while Serbian nationalists claimed the "Rascians." What Wallachs and Rascians themselves would have thought of this, especially in the earlier periods, is naturally unknown. I only use the national names in the nineteenth century when they start to appear more heavily in the sources and when at least some of the people begin self-identifying as such. Of course, I recognize that many, perhaps most, people remained a-national ("nationally indifferent"). Some will be happy with this choice, others will not. I believe that by choosing to follow the language of the sources, I am on solid ground.

Similarly, I will use the place names found in the sources, except where there is a widely used English version (e.g., Vienna). For instance, the Habsburg sources, and the archives, almost exclusively use the name

Temesvar (without the á) or Temeswar for the region and the largest city in the Banat. For the sake of consistency, I have chosen to use Temesvar, without the á, for the period before 1778, and Temesvár, with the á, for the period afterward when the Hungarians gained control. With citations, I followed the document as best as possible. The use of a more "Hungarian" variant for the earlier period might strike some readers as odd, given that until 1778 the Banat was ruled directly from Vienna. I can only respond that it is very rare to see the German Temeschburg, generally only in the earliest documents. Similar thought was put into the use of other place names in both the map and throughout the manuscript.

I will refer to Greek Catholicism as Uniatism and the Uniate Church. Again, this is following the sources.

The Banat of Temesvar

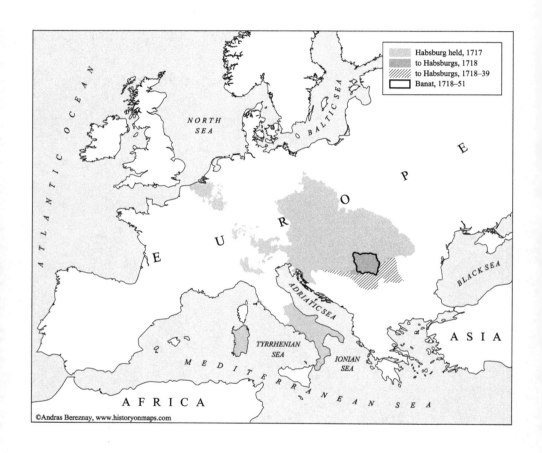

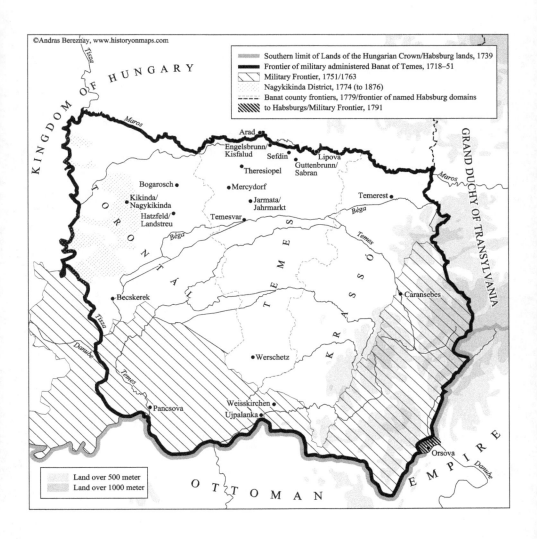

Introduction

THE BANAT OF TEMESVAR was a Habsburg creation. Known to the Ottomans as the Eyalet of Temesvar, the region was bounded to the north by the Mureș (Maros, Marosch) River, to the west by the Tisza (Tisa, Theiss) River, to the south by the Danube River, and to the east by the Carpathian Mountains. It was only when the region was under Viennese control from 1718 until 1778 that it officially had the name of "Banat."[1] During this time, the Banat's plains and mountains became a sandbox in which imperial administrators could play. Grand projects to improve production and to reshape the swampy landscape changed the region economically and physically. Alongside these material changes, and oftentimes in support of them, the Habsburgs sponsored the infusion of a colonial element in the Banat as tens of thousands of Western and Central Europeans descended on the region, adding dynamic ethnic, linguistic, and religious elements.

When the court in Vienna ceded control to the Hungarians in 1778, the "Banat" ceased to exist, officially, if not colloquially. The handover was the first of three major dissolutions of the short-lived region: territorial, political, and demographic. The territorial dissolution occurred when the Hungarians dismembered the Banat and incorporated it into their county system creating Torontál, Temes, and Krassó-Szörény counties. The political dissolution came in 1920 when the Treaty of Trianon ended Habsburg control and divided the historical Banat between three states: Romania; the Kingdom of Serbs, Croats, and Slovenes; and a small portion to Hungary. The demographic dissolution of the region's long-standing multiethnicity began in 1918 and was mostly complete following World War II. A region that had once boasted a German-speaking minority approaching one-quarter of the population both suddenly (in Yugoslavia) and more slowly (in Romania) lost this population to flight, expulsion, and emigration in the aftermath of the Nazi defeat. Currently, the vast majority of inhabitants of the historical Banat belong to the dominant ethnic group of their state, be that Romanian, Serbian, or Hungarian. In this way, it resembles other "backward" multiethnic borderlands that no longer exist. As Kate Brown put it when discussing the history of the Kresy in today's Ukraine, this work is "a biography of no place and the people who no longer live there."[2]

Despite this upheaval, the history of the Banat is neither solely a rousing history of increasing national self-determination nor a lamentable history of the loss of a multicultural society. The story is, in fact, much more intriguing, and complicated, than either teleological perspective implies. The Banat in the eighteenth century was a space where different peoples and cultures met and interacted. It was a frontier, a borderland, a latter-day march of European culture. Postcolonial historians have extensively studied such areas. Mary Louise Pratt called them "contact zones."[3] Richard White referred to them as "the middle ground."[4] The Banat was a "transborder" region that linked populations in the Habsburg, Holy Roman, and Ottoman Empires who shared "a common history, common economic integration and common cultural features."[5] Rather than simply creation or loss, movement and interaction are the keys to understanding the region and its broader significance.

These interactions were not always peaceful. There was violence and dispossession as the Habsburgs and their proxies sought to secure their claims to the borderland and pull it politically and economically into Europe. A complicated ethnoreligious situation threatened the actualization of these goals. War and confrontation with the Ottomans, colonization by hitherto largely alien elements, and local resistance to Habsburg rule were consistent problems throughout the eighteenth and into the nineteenth century. Habsburg policies, at least until Joseph II, privileged Western and Central European colonists to the detriment of local people. The Habsburgs, much like later nationalists, sought to compartmentalize and physically separate different ethnoreligious groups even as their policies added to the diversity of the region. Using a variety of methods, the authorities sought to create monoreligious, and to a certain extent monoethnic, islands of settlement throughout the Banat from the early eighteenth through the first quarter of the nineteenth century. They wanted to implant a population that they could trust to help secure the region against anticipated Ottoman aggression and internal threats to their rule. They further believed that different groups were incapable of living near each other without strife. They sought to protect the more privileged groups, like the colonists, from the local inhabitants, like the Romani and Wallachs. While the violence was not on the scale that became common in the twentieth century, the Habsburg administration did use force to achieve their ends. They expelled all Muslims from the Banat following conquest. They attempted to convert local people to Roman or Greek Catholicism (the "Uniate" Church). They dispossessed and relocated groups to make way for colonists.

These policies, and their consequences, led to periods of ethnic tension and violence as local people reacted to the imposition of a foreign, colonial culture. This tension had long-term effects. Almost any time there was war in the region (1737–1739, 1788–1790, 1848–1849, 1939–1945, though notably not 1914–1918) local people targeted colonists and their descendants for violence and disappropriation. While the expulsion and often outright destruction of German communities following the Second World War was certainly sparked by Nazi policies and aggression, the roots of this ethnoreligious conflict go back to the eighteenth century and the initial settlement.

This work explores the creation of a settler society and culture as well as the impact it had on the surrounding standing population. It charts the development of a Central European settler culture in the region, exploring its ecology, architecture, material culture, written records, and interactions with local people in a unique map of settlement. It argues that the colonists faced a variety of challenges in their new homes and used both practical and spiritual means to deal with them. Furthermore, it demonstrates that colonists, in particular German speakers who had and continue to have a reputation as a "cultured" influence in Eastern Europe, were not the modernizing force desired by the Habsburg authorities, especially in the early years of the colonial movement. Comparing the colonial experiment in the

Banat with contemporary experiences of German-speaking colonists elsewhere (Russia, Spain, and North America) will further highlight his fact. We will then shift perspective and explore what the standing population thought of the change and how they engaged both official policy and the settlers themselves. The conclusion illustrates that the memory of this colonial history has affected, and continues to affect, interethnic relations in the region.

Investigating popular culture, especially that of rural people in the eighteenth and nineteenth centuries, is fraught with difficulties.[6] In the settler case, I try to understand the "everyday life" of a settler. Who were they? What did they do? Where did they live? What were their fears? What did they believe? It is important to remember that there was not a uniform settler culture, no more than there was a uniform Wallach or Rascian culture. Instead, culture varied, especially between rural and urban, flatland and mountain. While there were differences in the "popular cultures," some aspects were shared among most colonists. Investigating this world is not an easy task. It can be hard for people in industrial and postindustrial societies to access the mental and physical world inhabited by early modern people.

Additionally, sources on popular culture and daily life are rare. Peasants and artisans in the early modern period rarely left written evidence behind. What one commonly does see are official petitions, pleas, and stylized court and judicial proceedings that were often focused more on form than substance. Those commoners who did produce unique written materials were exceptional and unlikely to be "normal" individuals with representative experiences. Thus, the "authentic" voice of common people is extremely difficult to find in the eighteenth and even in the early nineteenth centuries. Similarly, investigating cultural borders and colonial encounters is a difficult endeavor. When the authentic voice fades, I use official documents created by the elite (travelers, scientists, government administrators, etc.) to help reconstruct how peasants and commoners lived in the Banat throughout the eighteenth and early nineteenth centuries.

Sources describing popular culture or colonial people created by the elite need to be approached with caution. Government sources are not inherently neutral and often betray official or personal biases.[7] Likewise, travelers and their descriptions, which were crucial to contemporary and current notions of the frontier, are filled with suspect interpretations. According to

Pratt, travel writers were "advanced scouts for capitalist 'improvement.' "[8] As such, they often portrayed the lands they visited as empty or misused. Such tropes were extremely common in elite descriptions of the Banat. The perceived emptiness or misuse of land justified European conquest and the reordering of society in both the Banat and in the wider colonial world. Travelogues also "gave European reading publics a sense of ownership, entitlement, and familiarity" with faraway lands.[9] In the Banat, travel writers and other scholars assisted and justified Habsburg control and their developmental policies initiated shortly after conquest.

This is not to say that all of their observations are worthless. As Maria Todorova points out, speaking specifically of the French and German literature on the Balkans:

> Despite professed and internalized reservations about objectivity, reading some of the nineteenth-century products of the great descriptive effort aimed at the collection and accumulation of positive knowledge cannot fail to fill one with enormous respect for the broad endeavor, immense erudition, and tireless labor that went into these works. This is not to say that there are not occasional flashes of preconceived ideas or outright prejudice but the amount of disciplined and critical observation vastly superseded the minor faults one is bound to discover.[10]

Thus, while this literature can be biased and reproduce prejudices, it can also be effectively used as a historical source.[11] The key is to read travelogues and official documents looking for information that the author may not have intended to include, or may not have found very important, but that nevertheless can provide important insights into the often-hidden world of peasant life. Critically, historians need to verify and corroborate information, as much as is possible for the eighteenth and nineteenth centuries, across multiple source bases.

The Utility of the Banat's History

The Banat has had a potent historical and political influence vastly outstripping its small size and short existence. As Larry Wolff said of Galicia, another artificial Habsburg creation, the Banat "acquired meaning over the course of its historical existence . . . it accumulated multiple and shifting layers of meaning . . . [and] meant different things to its diverse populations, and acquired complex significance in the observations of statesmen and the imaginations of writers."[12] Both the memory and the amnesia of the Banat's history have been powerful propaganda tools.[13] Since the eighteenth century, scholars and observers have used both the historic and modern region as an exemplar of everything from the socioeconomic theory of cameralism to Nazism to multiculturalism. Early work on the territory extolled the virtues of the Habsburg monarchy and especially the work of the early administration under Florimund Mercy in developing the region along European lines.[14]

Following the rise of nationalism in the nineteenth century, travelers and observers changed the object of the praise. Rather than solely the intelligence of the Habsburg regime, it was the industriousness of the colonists (now described as "Germans") that made the Banat great.[15] This line of argumentation, that is, the Germans as "cultural beacons" (*Kulturträger*) in the East, has continued up to today, even in otherwise excellent histories.[16] In an echo of this tendency, modern Romanian tourist literature and some scholarship tout the German contribution to Timișoara to the local culture while downplaying or outright ignoring other ethnic groups.[17] Banat Germans themselves, and their supporters in the wider German-speaking world, used this laudatory, often imagined history as a national rallying point, first against Magyarization and later as a means to preserve their heritage in the newly created states of Romania and the Kingdom of the Yugoslavs.[18] Adherents of Nazism and its accompanying German ultranationalist world view took the praise for the German element in the region to a horrifying end.[19] To be clear, Germans were not the only group to use the Banat to showcase a nationalist viewpoint, especially in the interwar period. Hungarians, Romanians, and Serbs also co-opted the Banat's history to bolster their own national myths and make explicit claims to territory. Though occurring largely after World War I, such pieces appeared as late as the turn of the twenty-first century.[20] After the expulsion and flight of many of the Germans of the Banat following the end of World War II, a number of books looked back on their tenure in the region with longing.[21] Others were more explicitly apologetic texts that sought to minimize the Banat German role in the atrocities of the war or focus solely on the crimes committed against them in the aftermath, especially in Yugoslavia, giving very little context with which to judge the chaos and violence that followed the war.[22]

There are, of course, numerous monographs and articles on the region written by professional historians, generally in German, with longer works appearing especially in the interwar period or shortly after World War II.[23] One potential problem with many of these scholarly treatises is that their authors were Banat Germans or their progeny. Many of the publishers of these works were and are likewise groups closely tied to the Banat German community in Austria and Germany. Neither factor is in and of itself a problem, but it does give these authors an "insider" perspective which can be both a blessing and a curse. Also potentially problematic is the fact that many of the seminal works on the subject were written in the 1930s. While the authors themselves may not have been associated with the Nazis (and some of the scholars of the Germans of the East *were* unabashed Nazis), the climate in which they wrote was especially toxic.[24]

More recently, scholars and politicians have used the Banat as a showpiece for multiculturalism.[25] According to this vision, the region is a template for greater Europe, a region where different ethnic constituencies live, and have lived, in relative harmony. Such contentions ignore the earlier history of the Banat and especially the migration and ethnic cleansing (the Holocaust, anti-Roma violence, German expulsion, Yugoslav Wars) that since the end of World War I has rendered the wider region ever more homogenous and thus less likely to exhibit interethnic conflict. While there were certainly extensive periods in which Wallachs, Rascians, and colonists were not engaged in violent confrontation, the consistency with which problems did arise is indicative of underlying tension, a tension that only increased as national movements gained prominence in the nineteenth century. While cooperation among individuals assuredly did occur, in a broad sense, competition was the norm.[26]

The treatment of the Banat in the English literature on the Habsburg monarchy is limited. Aside from one general monograph, most articles have used the Banat as a vehicle to comment on broader imperial policy.[27] As Judy Batt noted, there was no "systematic history of Banat in English to which to refer the reader."[28] In recent treatments of the history of the Habsburg monarchy, the Banat is, perhaps naturally, relegated to the periphery. Oftentimes, these works misrepresent small, but potentially vital aspects of the region, such as who was allowed to colonize or who had sovereignty over the region. These mistakes generally make the Habsburgs (Maria Theresia in particular) look more tolerant than they were.[29] Quite often, the Banat seems to be shorthand for "somewhere far away on the frontier," set up in comparison with more "central," generally urban areas. This book fills this lacuna and provides an in-depth history of the region and its peoples, using the colonial endeavor there as a framework for understanding the broader history. This will put the Banat more firmly on the mental map of Habsburgists and provide a basis for comparison to other colonial ventures around the world, an effort I begin in this work as well.

Germanization, Catholicization, Europeanization

Much as in other colonial ventures throughout the world, the Habsburgs brought different types of colonists to the Banat. There were military colonists whose job was to secure the southern border of the monarchy, and thus of "Christian Europe," against the threat of the Muslim Ottomans. The Banat was a place to send deactivated and incapacitated soldiers, like Spanish military pensioners in the 1730s, soldiers following the Seven Years' War, or numerous other "invalids" who were placed there throughout the eighteenth century. Some were administrative colonists. Educated men, they came to the Banat to set up and monitor the emperor-king's domains. There were also specialized colonists. For instance, a small contingent of Italians brought their knowledge of silk, hemp, and rice cultivation to the region.[30] These migrants were to actively teach other colonists and local people how to do novel forms of cash-crop agriculture. That said, the most numerous, most durable, and most important for the future demographic makeup of the Banat were the agricultural settler-colonists.

The majority of these colonists were German speaking. The use of the term "Germans" as a catchall for the Western and Central European colonists recruited to settle in the Banat in the eighteenth century is a problematic but ultimately useful and largely accurate shorthand used by contemporary colonial officials as well as later scholars. That said, not all colonists were German speakers. In addition to colonists from purely German-speaking areas, other migrants came from Alsace and Luxembourg.[31] Lorraine was likewise a major source of migrants. After 1766, when the French took formal control of the region, the migrants were French subjects, whatever language they spoke. It is important to note that these geographical terms, as used by authorities at the time, do not match the current borders of the regions and include areas, for example, that are currently in Rheinland-Pfalz and

Saarland, adding an additional layer of complexity.[32] Thus, in addition to the German-speaking colonists, there were also some French-speaking colonists who migrated to the Banat from these regions.[33] Unfortunately, there are no solid numbers for how many French speakers migrated, though they appear to have been a small, though not insignificant, minority of colonists. There were villages with "French" names like St. Hubert, Charleville, and Seultour (as well as other villages with German names) that contained numerous Lorrainers and Alsatians, but as historian Friedrich Lotz pointed out, not even these "French" villages were "purely French."[34] To try to quantify how many "French" migrants were French speakers would be exceedingly difficult.[35] One would have to go through the lists of migrants and attempt to identify those with "French" names and use this as a basis for counting French speakers. This would obviously be a highly problematic way to determine one's mother tongue, and ultimately there is no reliable way to know how these people self-identified, or how they would have understood the categories ("German" or "French") in the first place. Those with "French" names may have been more culturally "German" and vice versa. Additionally, German scribes in Vienna and elsewhere may have Germanized "French" names, further obscuring an individual's origins and possible mother tongue.

Given the absence of concrete numbers and the inherent uncertain nature of ethnic belonging especially evident in the early modern period, I will use the term "German" throughout the work to describe *all* Western and Central European colonists. There are several reasons for this. First, all sources agree that German speakers *were* a significant majority of the colonists who came over the course of the eighteenth century, both from the Holy Roman Empire (henceforth, the Reich) and later from France as well. Secondly, the authorities themselves often referred to the colonists as "Germans" when making statements about them or when trying to recruit them.[36] There is significantly less mention of "French" colonists in the archival record (though the Italian colonists were more often noted due to their centrality in the silk industry).[37] Travelers also generally referred to the colonists in the Banat as "Germans." Effectively, for the authorities, any migrants who came from Western and Central Europe and fulfilled the Habsburg government's mission of populating and securing the region were colonists and *Germans*.[38] Thirdly, whatever their origins, the vast majority of the colonial, nonlocal population was "German" in language and culture by 1848 at the latest.[39] Thus the historical remembrance of the region focuses on the Germans to the detriment of the French and other groups who assimilated with the Germans.[40] In this work, "German" denotes the linguistic group of the majority of colonists, a general governmental designation for Western and Central European colonists, and by the nineteenth century, at the latest, an identifiable ethnolinguistic group.

One of the main disputes in the study of German migration to the East, whether to the Banat or to Russia, regards the preference, or lack thereof, for German colonists and the perception that the authorities wanted to "Germanize" the region.[41] This question divides historians because it is central to understanding the migration as well as understanding and interpreting the later development and importance of the colonies. According to one narrative, Germans were prized for their industriousness and thrift, making them an ideal population to use as colonists. They were recruited to help bring the benighted population of a region into the European mainstream.[42] The preponderance of German settlers seems to support this position. Some historical evidence does as well. Writing to Emperor Charles shortly after his capture of the Banat's capital Temesvar in October 1716, Prince Eugene of Savoy informed him that he had "ordered the Interim-Command to take only German inhabitants . . . in the newly conquered place [i.e., Temesvar], some of whom have already applied, and quarter the Rascians and others in the *palanka*."[43] Historians of the opposing narrative explain the overwhelming predominance of Germans in the colonization of the East by arguing that it was easier to recruit Germans in the Holy Roman Empire than other ethnicities in other places.[44] Though, as we will see, many German states resisted the recruitment of their people for colonization projects, and these efforts did work to some degree.[45] These scholars further point to the fact that other groups (French, Spanish, Italians, Armenians, Bulgarians, Slovaks, Cossacks, among others) served as colonists, and for them, this indicates that the Habsburgs were willing to take any ethnicity in service of populationist goals. This openness made the Banat one of the most ethnically (and with Joseph II's Acts of Toleration, religiously) diverse areas of European settlement, rivaled only by the mid-Atlantic in British North America.[46] While both positions have some merit, the question itself misses a crucial aspect of settler recruitment throughout the period. As we will see, it appears that

"Europeanness" and trustworthiness (often defined by religion) of the colonists were ultimately more important than their "Germanness," though Germanness often served as a marker of both. In other words, all Catholic Germans were trustworthy but not all trustworthy people were necessarily Catholic Germans.

In the end, although the recruitment of settlers was neither focused solely on Germans nor an open-door policy, Germans did make up a majority of colonists. The Holy Roman Empire was a prime recruiting ground for colonists. Localized overpopulation, war, famine, and disease throughout the eighteenth century often, though importantly not always, combined with administrations too weak to prevent larger states from recruiting in their lands led tens of thousands of Germans to abandon their homes for the prospect of a better life elsewhere. Germans themselves may have sought out settlement in the Banat because of the political connection between the western German (and later French) lands, the Banat, and the Habsburg monarchy. Males tied to the House of Habsburg were, with one exception, the titular heads of the Holy Roman Empire from 1452 until 1806. Franz Albert Crausen, the first man tasked with bringing colonists to the region in the early 1720s, was a German speaker. The most important representative of the government in the Banat from conquest into the 1730s, Graf Claudius Florimund Mercy, was from Lorraine. Maria Theresia's husband and later Holy Roman Emperor, Franz, was Duke of Lorraine. Whatever the importance of these connections, Lorraine proved to be a prolific and reliable recruiting ground for settlers.

In addition to the sheer number of Germans who came to the Banat during the eighteenth century, which already indicates a measure of official encouragement not extended to other potential colonizers, the privileges and incentives offered to them and other Western and Central Europeans were generally better than those offered other groups, such as the Bulgarians or the Rascians. Some groups of migrants, such as the Wallachs, were apparently only rarely offered privileges. The authorities responsible for early migration to reconquered Hungary, for instance, overlooked the "spontaneous South Slav and Wallach migration out of the Ottoman domains" in favor of recruiting migrants from Upper Hungary and in particular the German-speaking hereditary lands.[47] While German speakers were welcomed as colonists, the authorities often hesitated to allow other groups entrance to the Banat. This, of course, ebbed and flowed over the century, and some officials were more pro-German than others, but generally speaking, there was a desire among the administration to specifically recruit and settle Germans. The sources are clear that the authorities believed that Catholic Germans were more loyal and reliable (and perhaps more industrious and knowledgeable) than the local Orthodox Wallachs and Rascians, who, in their estimation, possessed many vices and potentially divided loyalties.

Whatever the expectations of the administrators were, without governmental help and continual repopulation the German communities would likely not have survived. The less governmental support they received, the more likely it was that they collapsed. As we will see, between the intermittent warfare that led to attacks on their colonies by Ottomans and Wallachs alike and (perhaps most destructively) a novel disease regime, the German communities were on tenuous ground throughout the eighteenth century. It is hard to imagine that the later success the German colonists enjoyed in the nineteenth and twentieth centuries could have been achieved without the early support provided by the Habsburg administration. In the end, the German agricultural colonists should only be seen as tangentially involved in many of the major development projects of the eighteenth century in the Banat. In typically absolutist fashion, most of the development of the region (the draining of swampland, the creation of roads, the design of towns and villages, the reestablishment of mines, etc.) was a top-down rather than a bottom-up phenomenon, with Vienna as the driver of change rather than any local nonelite population. Admittedly, many of the civil servants who oversaw this development were Germans, but they were different from the rural, farming Germans who made up most of the settlers.

In addition to the question of Germanization, there are similar debates about the authorities' desire to both Catholicize and Westernize the region. Once again, the answer is not at all transparent. According to the sources, the Habsburgs did entertain dreams, from conquest through the end of Maria Theresa's reign and the incorporation of the Banat into Hungary, of Catholicizing the region. Officials hoped that by placing Catholics in the Banat and by encouraging local inhabitants to convert to Roman or Greek Catholicism, they could make the region into a Catholic space. That was the dream. The reality was much different as there was little chance of realizing this goal. The failure to make the Banat Catholic does not mean that it was not a goal of the Habsburg administration. As we will see, they certainly Catholicized the official migration to the Banat, one aspect of the region over which they had, in theory, total control.

The question of Westernization, or as I will refer to it, Europeanization, is trickier to answer. By Europeanization, I mean both the creation of manufactories and industry in towns and cities and the transfer of rural land from subsistence agriculture and herding to intensive, settled grain farming. This process also involved the remaking of space, for instance, the construction of villages and houses along geometric, rational lines and the creation of canals and roads. In addition, Europeanization meant something more intellectual, ethereal, and thus harder to pinpoint. This aspect of Europeanization was the promotion of certain values (thrift, industriousness, order, rationality) and the open attack on others (superstition, backwardness, criminality, laziness) that accompanied the creation of the more physical and visible manifestations of Enlightened Western European culture.[48] In sum, this represented the incorporation of a region into the European economic and social system.

This drive was not limited to the Banat nor only to the Habsburgs. Larry Wolff's comments about Galicia could easily apply to the Banat as well. "Galician barbarism was to be reformed, and Galician backwardness was to be ameliorated."[49] These values were, of course, defined by the colonizers, as order or superstition or backwardness are doubtless cultural constructs. As Kate Brown highlights, "the trope of backwardness" was also used in the Russian Empire and later USSR to justify assimilation and government intervention.[50] As we will see, given the Habsburg policy of ethnoreligious separation, practiced until the reign of Joseph II, and the official and scholarly views of local people, especially the numerically superior Wallachs, there is little doubt that the Habsburg authorities wanted to Europeanize, that is, develop, improve, rationalize, the Banat, and they often viewed the local people as an impediment. In essence, the Habsburgs brought people from the European heartland to protect and improve the European periphery. The drive to Catholicize and Europeanize varied from time to time and administrator to administrator but these values helped shape the Banat.

Europeanization was, in the end, a "civilizing mission," the kind practiced throughout the colonized world. Accurate or not, the idea that it was a "Turkish yoke" that caused the underdevelopment of the region was a long-lived one and mirrored similar narratives in other areas of former Ottoman rule. According to this perspective, Ottoman Turkish rule was responsible for degrading the land and "ruining" the local people, causing them to embrace ignorance, sloth, and vice. Writing shortly after his victory at Temesvar, Savoy reported that the "Tatars and Turks notwithstanding [the imperial presence], sneak, camp, burn, and destroy and even where they do not go, they chase away the inhabitants with the fear captivity."[51] Lady Mary Wortley Montagu described the Rascians in imperial employ as "rather plunderers than soldiers" in a letter written in 1717 from Belgrade. She further stated that they "look[ed] more like Vagabond Gypsies or stout beggars than regular Troops," and their priests resembled "Indian Brahmins." For her, they were a "race of Creatures."[52] Joseph II lamented in 1768 after a trip to the region, that "the Turkish form of government in the Banat continues."[53] Francesco Griselini, the region's first historian, brought the idea of the Turkish yoke into the popular literature on the region.[54] It had staying power. In a newspaper article on the history of the Banat written in 1827, the author bemoaned the "ruinous influence of Turkish slavery" on the "self-esteem, morality, religion, liturgy, even the spoken and written language" of local people. They "became raw barbarians" because of the "Turkish yoke."[55] He claimed that these ruinous results were "even today unmistakable in the character of the Nationalists" (i.e., Rascians and Wallachs).[56] According to Joseph von Dorner, a traveler in the mid-nineteenth century, Ottoman rule and the intermittent warfare were the reasons why the people of the Banat, and especially the Wallachs, were so far "behind" other Europeans.[57] One hundred and sixty years later, even historian R. J. W. Evans described the Wallachs as "indeed a socially and economically oppressed and wild, serf-like people."[58]

The belief in the detrimental effect of Ottoman rule made it very easy for local officials and observers to dismiss and denigrate the local people and their culture. Furthermore, it gave a historical, almost (pseudo-)scientific reason for the superiority of Western, and in this case German, culture, which had never been subjected to Ottoman rule. Importantly, the interpretation also took their agency away and made them passive participants in the creation of their culture, perhaps opening the door for redemption through example. In other words, it justified a program of Europeanization.

As we will see, Europeanization was an ongoing process that continued well into the nineteenth century. A perpetual attempt to raise the level of the frontier to the level of the heartland, it could never reach completion. Writing almost 140 years after conquest, traveler A. A. Paton highlighted the perpetual nature of the process, stating that "in a quarter of a century, Steam and German civilization will entirely alter the aspect of these still semi-barbarous regions."[59] Following World War II, the concepts of socialism and Europeanization (or modernization as it became known) became entangled. The process of Europeanizing the region continues to this day, with attempts by the European Union to raise standards (in meat-packing and distilling alongside environment and governance) in Romania to EU levels. The situation in Serbia—still on the outside of modern "Europe" looking in—demonstrates how the process of Europeanizing the Banat, and southeastern Europe in general, though started by the Habsburgs, continues to this day.

The attempt to Europeanize and civilize the region helps firmly place the Banat's history into a global colonial one. As one official there put it, "I borrowed much from the Spanish and Portuguese, what they set as laws in India."[60] While most officials were not as blunt (or perhaps as aware) as he, many undoubtedly saw the Banat as the Habsburg's colonial domain. As we have seen, Habsburg officials and travelers disparaged local people and their culture, a trend observable in overseas colonial situations as well. The tropes of "idleness and sloth," found in accounts of Khoikhoi of South Africa (the disparagingly named "Hottentots"), can also be found in accounts of the Wallachs of the Banat. According to one official, they "by far surpassed even the Indians in laziness and indolence" because of the lack of agricultural development.[61] Observers of America complained that Spanish Americans neither wanted to improve their lands nor take advantage of the abundance around them. They failed to "rationalize, specialize, and maximize production."[62] Griselini compared the local people at the time of conquest to "Arabians and other pastoral peoples" in their "love of roaming, tendency to steal, treachery and savagery." He further compared them to animals.[63] Similarly, as historian Klemens Kaps noted, nineteenth-century "statisticians Demián and Martin Schwartner saw Vlachs, Croats and Serbs as 'wild people' and 'natural men' who had to be 'civilized' before they could partake of social and economic progress."[64] Such complaints served similar purposes regardless of where they were made: to denigrate a subsistence lifestyle that was incomprehensible to the more "enlightened" Europeans and less compatible with their designs.[65]

Scholars debate to what degree these instances are comparable. Alison Frank, echoing Pieter Judson, argues that at least in the nineteenth and twentieth centuries, overseas and continental European rule was different enough that the comparison does not hold.[66] Others disagree. Andrea Komlosy contends that "border regions played a role for the continental empire that was provided by colonial acquisitions for overseas empires," a sentiment with which I agree.[67] Despite, or perhaps because of, such debates, the settler-colonial perspective has exerted an important influence on my thinking about the ways in which the German experience in the Banat relates to the wider settlement of Europeans throughout the world. While no attempt was made in the eighteenth century to physically eliminate the inhabitants of the region, as occurred in other settler-colonial instances, there was a denigration of local culture and an attempt to replace it with something more acceptable to authorities (German-speaking migrants, Uniate/Greek Catholic Church, settled agriculture in place of more migratory lifestyles).[68]

To place the Banat in a world-colonial framework is beyond the scope of this work. Instead, I will seek throughout the book to show how the colonialism in the Banat compares to contemporary examples of colonialism involving German speakers at the frontiers of European culture, both in Europe itself (particularly Spain and Russia) and North America. In all cases, the German colonists were, unwittingly, at the vanguard of Europeanization, changing landscapes and theoretically, culture. Echoing my characterization of the Banat, Bernard Bailyn has described North America as a "marchland ... of the European cultural system" and Russia as an "*Eastern* Marchland of European civilization."[69] The comparison will highlight both the ways in which the colonial experience in the Banat was unique as well as how the region was part of a larger movement of German speakers that occurred in the eighteenth century.

Perhaps the most accurate way to look at the issues of Germanization, Catholicization, and Europeanization in the Banat is to take a more limited view. Regarding the first two concepts, the Habsburg authorities were not delusional. They may have *talked* about a pure Catholic space in the initial heady time following reconquest, but they quickly realized this was not a realistic endeavor. They *never* talked about the complete displacement of local people in favor of Germans. Such a maximalist plan would have been the product of radical nationalist, not imperialist, thought. The central goal, visible in all periods before 1780, was to place a loyal population on the border. Loyal in this case meant Catholic and, to a more limited extent, German. The question of Europeanization is trickier. In this case, the Habsburg authorities truly did want to change the nature of the Banat and make it more economically productive. They wanted to settle nomadic and seminomadic peoples like the Wallachs and the Roma. They wanted peasants to practice agriculture with an eye toward the market, rather than only subsistence. They wanted to change the landscape from wild and swampy to settled and geometric. This was a lofty goal but one that they had arguably largely accomplished by the middle of the nineteenth century.

Religion, Ethnicity, and the State

This work is not only about the infusion of a German colonial element into the Banat but also about how this demographic change radically altered the ethnic and religious balance in the region. The Germans can be seen as the Habsburgs' representatives in the Banat. Habsburg officials and learned travelers distrusted and demeaned the standing population. The Wallachs had a reputation as poor farmers and criminals. They also had coethnics in Ottoman Wallachia. The Rascians likewise had coethnics in Ottoman Serbia with whom they maintained a bond. They also flirted with the Russian Empire throughout the eighteenth and nineteenth centuries based on their common religious and ethnic ties. From the government's perspective, German-speaking colonists were there to fulfill the needs of the state and provide a loyal population in case of upheaval.

When discussing the other two major groups in the region, I have generally used the term "Wallach" to describe the group later claimed by Romanian nationalists and the term "Rascian" for the group claimed by the Serbians, though there may have been overlap between the two groups. To do otherwise seems anachronistic, ascribing to them aspirations and a world view that may have been foreign to them. In the seventeenth century, the term "Wallach" did not have any protonational connotations and was sometimes used to describe any emigrant from Ottoman lands, though by the eighteenth century, more specific connotations were emerging.[70] These are also two of the terms used by the government itself in describing local people. Much as with the term "German," the use of these signifiers (e.g., Wallach, Rascian, etc.) in this work lacks modern nationalist over- and undertones and describes linguistic and an assumed cultural belonging and follows the lead of the sources from the period, which used them in an analogous fashion. In this same vein, I will use the term "ethnicity" as opposed to "nation" to describe the various peoples of the Banat. Again, the term "ethnicity" appears to me to be less teleological and less presumptuous of supposed national feeling that many in the Banat did not likely have.[71]

In light of their goals, the authorities in the Banat enforced an ethnoreligious hierarchy until at least the time of Joseph II, some remnants of which are still noticeable into the nineteenth century. Joseph II's religious toleration dampened the religious component of the hierarchy, after which the ethnolinguistic component became ever more important.[72] At the pinnacle of this hierarchy in the eighteenth century were the Catholic, and after the 1780s also Protestant German colonists. After 1778 and the transfer of the lands to Hungarian control, Magyars were also part of this group and took an increasingly leading role. After them were other Catholics, such as Bulgarian migrants. Greek Catholics or Uniate Rascians and Romanians, that is, those people who kept Orthodox ritual while accepting Catholic hierarchy, were next. The Orthodox Rascians also enjoyed a level of privilege due to their importance in populating and defending the military border, though they were occasionally resettled to make way for Germans and had to contend with Hungarian distrust after 1778. The numerically superior Orthodox Wallachs were in the middle ground and were often discriminated against in favor of the Germans and other privileged groups.[73] Jews and Roma occupied the lowest levels of the hierarchy, though Jews were often more tolerated because of their real and assumed economic value.

The language of the administration, while a logical reaction to the existence of the diverse groups in the region, gave away their preferences for Catholics and nonlocals. Germans from outside the Banat were "colonists" or "settlers." Wallachs or Rascians from outside the Banat were generally "Turkish emigrants" or simply "emigrants." Complicating matters, the Banat was the site of a variety of types of migration, from nomadism (transhumance) and urbanization to colonization and marriage migration.[74] Historians of migration recognize the contested nature of terminology used to describe people on the move. "Migrant," "immigrant," "refugee," "colonist," etc., are historically contingent terms, and their meanings, and the values attached to them, are unstable.[75] This is especially true the further one gets from the present and when working in a foreign language or across disciplines. For instance, while "emigrant" in eighteenth-century English had a positive connotation, the connotation in eighteenth-century Austrian-German cited above appears neutral, if not slightly negative.[76] We will examine this topic in more depth in chapter 2.

Due to this hierarchy and the plethora of ethnoreligious groups in the Banat, this work also tangentially addresses questions of "identity," a term and idea popular and contentious among historians and social scientists. I will say little about how individual residents of the Banat "identified." Given the nature of the impersonal sources, such an attempt would be largely speculation, if individuals can ever be truly said to have a stable identity at all. What I can talk about with more confidence is how the government *identified* people and how it used these imposed identities to order the region intellectually. In general, the government identified *communities* most often using ethnicity (Wallach, Rascian, Illyrian, German), an ethnoreligious combination (e.g., nonunited Rascians, Uniate Wallachs), or the blanket term "Nationalist," which in Habsburg parlance throughout the eighteenth century referred to the combined Rascian and Wallach community. Importantly, the term did not carry the modern connotations of nationalism.[77] Individuals were identified differently. Throughout the period leading up to 1848, the government used a person's religious affiliation more often than ethnicity as an identifier in documents designed to help officials identify a specific individual. In fact, religion (Greek nonunited, Uniate, Catholic, Evangelical, Jew) was often *the* major nonphysical identifying characteristic. In these documents, there are sometimes more muted references to ethnicity, for instance, birthplace, the languages spoken by the individual,[78] or descriptions of their clothes ("is dressed like a Wallach").[79] In an 1842 Contumaz certificate (which proved a person had completed quarantine on the border), there was a specific place designated for clothing.[80] A typical example of this form was a printed "travel pass" from 1828 that listed attributes that an investigator would then fill in by hand. In it, physical attributes such as height, nose, and hair color were listed. There was no space for "ethnicity/race" nor was there a space for "languages." There *was* a place to list religion.[81] At this point, the government did not yet see ethnicity, or even language, as the key identifier.

As this highlights, religion was an important identifier in the Banat, especially given the government's policy of settling people of similar ethnoreligious backgrounds in relatively closed communities. Within the hierarchy of the Banat, religious affiliation also clued observers (both internal and external) into one's relative standing. That said, sometimes references to ethnicity were blatant, especially in documents describing an event that had occurred rather than in a document meant for identification. One document described Pava Lasin and Pavel Ristin as of "the Rascian Nation" (*der Nationer Raÿz*).[82] Another described the "Rascian Krümer Thodor Russ."[83] Thirty military deserters were "Wallachs."[84]

The government imposed special titles on Jews and German colonists in documents of the eighteenth century that reflected their diametrically opposed positions in the Banat's hierarchy. Generally, the title *Jud* accompanied the Jews whenever they were mentioned.[85] One never sees simply the name Mayer Amigo, a leading businessman in the Banat. He is always referred to as *Handelsjud* (trade Jew) Mayer Amigo. If not given as a title like *Handelsjud*, *Bettlerjud* (beggar Jew), or *Dienstjuden* (servant Jews), the designation was often paired with a place of residence, *Jud zu Mako* (Jew from Mako) or *Jud zu Werschetz* (Jew from Werschetz). Almost any time a Jew was mentioned in official correspondence in the eighteenth century, their religion was immediately tied to their person and indicated their social position. In a similar way, German colonists were also identified as "Colonist" in official documents, though unlike the German colonists, for whom the title brought incentives and assistance, the title "Jud" conferred disincentives and discrimination. By the nineteenth century, this was changing. For instance, when Jacob Weisz, a Jewish merchant from Kikinda, sued two Rascians over payment for tobacco, a religious title was not given.[86]

It is tempting to say that as we move through the period up to 1848 we see more descriptions based on ethnicity and that religiosity was losing ground as a major identifying characteristic, but as the above example from 1828 showed, this was not necessarily the case. In fact, religion and ethnicity became increasingly intertwined as certain religions became markers, along with language, of certain ethnicities. For instance, while there were Catholic Rascians/Serbs in the Banat, Serbianness and Orthodoxy were often inseparable. While often confusing, the interplay between religion, language, and ethnicity is crucial to understanding the region and its dynamism. These labels, and government favor, played key roles when destabilization brought violence to the region. In these instances, groups seen as lesser would use the chaos to attack and dispossess those held in higher esteem by the government. Thus, how the government identified and organized people is a constant theme of this work.

After an overview of the history of the Habsburg Banat, we will take an in-depth look at the business of recruiting settlers from the 1710s through the beginning of the nineteenth century, when a major change in the Habsburg policy regarding populationism occurred. Already in the 1810s, the government was ordering border commands to discourage immigrants from the Ottoman lands. In 1822, they were ordered to turn away any immigrants who did not have means.[87] In 1829, this policy, a means test, was extended to potential immigrants from the German lands. Though not the first attempt to limit German migration to individuals of some wealth, these policies marked the end of an era. From the government's perspective, the lands were effectively "full." Chapters 3 and 4 will explore the creation of German settler culture and the degree to which the colonists achieved the government's goals. While by the later nineteenth century, the Germans of the region were prosperous, that outcome was not guaranteed. In fact, early government support was key to their later success. We will then explore the local reactions, particularly Wallach and Rascian, to that society until the early nineteenth century. While interactions were often peaceful, they became violent when the status quo of the region was disturbed, such as in times of war. The epilogue will explore the Revolution of 1848 into the twentieth century, following the trends identified in the work.

There are several reasons that make 1829 an ideal stopping point. The means test effectively ended officially sanctioned German migration to the region. It was during this time that Magyarization noticeably intensified. Hungarian became the official language, much to the dismay of the local people. This development led to nationalist responses among the other ethnicities of the Banat, in particular, the Rascians, some of whom were adopting a Serbian nationalism in tandem with Ottoman Serbs and were recognized as a threat by the Habsburg government. The story ends at the point when the colonial populating of the Banat concluded and nationalist ideologies began to rise in earnest. Those ideologies and the revolution itself, while certainly rooted in the history we will explore in this work, represented a departure from the top-down, governmental definitions of ethnicity and loyalty that had existed previously. While the architects of nationalism in the region were often educated and privileged, thus in many ways "top-down" as well, they claimed to speak in the name of the "nation," something the previous Habsburg government did not do.

1 Conquest and Construction

Development in the European Borderlands

Wer Ofen eingenommen, der habe nur eine Statt erhalten,
Wer aber Temeswar weggenommen, der habe
    ein ganztes Land bekommen.

[*He who took Ofen got only a city,
He who took Temesvar got an entire land.*][1]

WHEN MONARCHS AND THEIR administrations surveyed their holdings in the eighteenth century, they often saw undeveloped, depopulated lands. Frederick William of Prussia had East Prussia, devastated by the Great Northern War, famine, and disease which dropped the population by more than one-third. His son, Frederick II, faced similar problems after the Seven Years' War.[2] Since the sixteenth century, the Russian Empire had driven the Ottoman Empire and its proxies from the northern littoral of the Black Sea, opening up the steppe for settlement. Both Peter I and Catherine II looked to German colonists for help developing those lands.[3] Bourbon Charles III of Spain, in keeping with other enlightened rulers of the time, wanted to settle depopulated lands and "create a 'modern' peasant community in Andalusia."[4] Great Britain had lands in Ireland and in North America that, from the perspective of the government, needed improvement and population.[5] All these states recruited and settled German-speaking colonists in response to their needs.

The Habsburgs were no exception. The conquest of Ottoman holdings, begun in 1683 and continuing into the eighteenth century, supplied them with lands depopulated and underdeveloped, at least in their eyes. This drive to secure and develop was not solely about rote populationism or economics. The Banat was the most militarily active border of the Habsburg monarchy in the eighteenth century until the French Revolution. The Habsburgs and Ottomans fought three wars largely in the Banat (1716–1718, 1737–1739, and 1787–1791). In light of this, a loyal and stable population working productively was key to the defense of the monarchy as a whole.

At the time of conquest, for the Habsburgs and other observers, the region was *not* perceived as Europe nor were its people European. The land was filled with bogs and marshes breeding terrible diseases, the flora "closely related" to "Asian" varieties.[6] The local people were likewise "oriental" or "Eastern" in their religion, clothes, and manners.[7] What is striking about this language is that it describes people and landscapes *within* the monarchy itself. This leads to the conclusion that the Banat, even into the nineteenth century, was seen differently, closer to a colony in the overseas sense of the word than the other Habsburg lands. As elsewhere in the colonized world, the Habsburgs believed the land and the people were desperately in need of development and Europeanization to bring them into line with the other crown lands, making them stable, secure, and profitable.

Settlers were central to the plan to Europeanize the Banat. They were to be the trusted population that would help not only defend the region in times of conflict but also actualize its economic and social transformation in times of peace. The sociopolitical theory of cameralism, with its policy prescriptions from populationism to autarky, formed the intellectual backbone of the regional development plan. The ventures undertaken in service of development varied between highly successful and complete failures. War twice interrupted and destroyed the development work. These dichotomies, war and peace, development and destruction, West and East, highlight the tense, unsettled atmosphere that prevailed in the Banat throughout the eighteenth and into the nineteenth century.

Conquest: 1683–1718

The history of the Habsburg Banat began at the gates of Vienna in 1683.[8] After a two-month siege, troops commanded by Jan Sobieski and Charles of Lorraine were able to break the impasse and push the Ottomans out of the Austrian lands. Starting in 1684, the Holy League, which included Habsburg Austria, Poland-Lithuania, Venice, the papacy, and from 1686, Muscovy, advanced into the Ottoman Empire. Aided by rebellion and political turmoil there, the Holy League was able to make great gains in the late 1680s, capturing Buda in 1686 and Belgrade in 1688. What ultimately saved the Ottomans from potential collapse was the outbreak of war between France and the Habsburgs in 1688 that opened up a new front for the Habsburg armies in Western Europe. In 1690, the Ottoman line finally began to solidify. They quit hemorrhaging territory and even managed to take a few fortresses back, including Belgrade. The next several years were largely a stalemate with no major advances made by either side. While the Habsburgs besieged Temesvar, the capital of the Banat, in 1696, they were unable to capture the fortress.[9]

The brutal war between the Ottomans and the Austrians that raged in and around the Banat in the 1680s and 1690s marked the beginning of a hundred-year period during which the Banat periodically hosted violent conflicts (1716–1718, 1737–1739, 1787–1790). Contrary to the stories at the time and later, it was not only the Ottomans who employed wanton violence. The Austrians were likewise guilty of a number of atrocities. Habsburg troops killed all of the inhabitants of the town of Arad.[10] Serb irregulars, allied with the Austrians, wreaked havoc around Temesvar, robbing, plundering, and abducting travelers and even gardeners to hold for ransom. The Austrian siege of Lipova was particularly brutal. The Ottomans agreed to surrender the town if they and their goods were allowed safe passage to Temesvar. Graf Caraffa, then in command of the imperial armies, countered that for the offer to be acceptable, they needed to relinquish their weapons and that he still retained the right to detain whom he wished.[11] As they left the city, imperial soldiers beat and robbed them. They even killed a number of them, disemboweling them in search of hidden gold and silver and leaving their corpses on the roadside. German officers attempted to quell this behavior, even shooting their own men, but to no avail. Caraffa then ordered all men and women from the town, except for one hundred indigent people, detained for ransom, dividing this valuable booty among his soldiers. If captives could not make their ransom, they were either kept as domestic slaves or sold into international slavery. Conversion to Christianity, much like conversion to Islam for Christians captured by the Ottomans, could ease the burdens of captivity.[12] Such "faith slavery," as historian Robert Davis calls it, was common throughout the Mediterranean Basin.[13] For many in the region, their first interaction with Habsburg power was defined by violence; such violent interactions between the local population and the government recurred regularly for the next hundred years, as we will see.

The humiliating and costly defeat of the Ottoman army at Zenta by Prince Eugene of Savoy in 1697 spurred along the peace process. The threat of renewed war with the French encouraged the Austrians to negotiate.[14] In 1699, the Treaty of Karlowitz ended the first stage of the Habsburgs' march into the Balkans. The treaty confirmed Habsburg possession of Hungary and Transylvania. Importantly, though, the Eyalet of Temesvar, as it was then known, was still held by the Ottomans, as it had been since 1552. After Karlowitz, the Ottomans fully expected a renewed Habsburg assault. They attempted to prepare for it, rebuilding the fortress at Temesvar and reopening the gunpowder factory in the town. By 1716, there were around eight thousand Ottoman troops in the region, far fewer than the 16,000 estimated by Habsburg authorities.[15] The Habsburgs, for their part, had several problems that distracted them from further conquests in the Balkans. Between rebellion in newly conquered Hungary and two major outside international conflicts that demanded their attention (the Great Northern War and the War of Spanish Succession), the Habsburgs were content with an uneventful southern border. With peace concluded with the Hungarian rebels in 1711 and the end of the War of Spanish Succession in 1714, the possibility of an aggressive Austrian policy vis-à-vis the Ottomans re-opened.[16]

The spark that ignited the next Austro-Ottoman War was the Ottoman attack on Venice in 1714. The Ottoman Porte wanted to recover the territory of Morea, ceded to the Venetians in the Treaty of Karlowitz. While there were many compelling reasons not to aid the Venetians, Prince Eugene, hero of Zenta, was a powerful advocate for war. Eugene won a major victory at Petrovaradin and by October 13, 1716, was in possession of Temesvar. Belgrade fell again on August 18, 1717. As before, international events worked against the Habsburgs. In late 1717, the Spanish, despite promises to the contrary, invaded Habsburg Sardinia. This made a peace treaty with the Ottomans even more desirable. The Treaty of Passarowitz, concluded in 1718, was based on the principle of *uti possidetis*, or the possession of what each army controlled at the time of the negotiations.[17] Thus, the Banat became a Habsburg prize of war.

Highlighting the strategic importance of the region, the Ottomans worked continuously, though unsuccessfully, to recover it, both through diplomatic and military means, throughout the eighteenth century. In 1726, for example, the Porte offered one million florins for the return of the "Town and Bannat of Temeswaer." This proposal was "absolutely rejected."[18] Following the next war from 1737 to 1739, they raised their offer to four million crowns.[19] Another offer of a "considerable Sum of Money" was apparently made not long after.[20] The same newspaper reported in October 1741 that the Porte intended to demand the return of Banat as a requirement for the "Continuance of Peace between the Grand Signor and the Queen of Hungary."[21] At this time, Maria Theresia was embroiled in a struggle with the Prussians over Silesia, and the Ottomans calculated that she could not afford another conflict. The next month, they reported that the Sultan had declared that far from having any intentions of taking the Banat, he would rather send troops to support the queen if the religious differences were not so great.[22] Rumors of a possible attack continued into 1743 but never materialized.[23] A final war in the late 1780s also was not able to regain the territory for the Ottomans. Neither money nor war was enough to dislodge the Austrians after the Treaty of Passarowitz.

Cameralism and Development

By the time this treaty legalized Habsburg possession of the Banat, they already had nearly thirty-five years of experience in integrating former Ottoman domains. One of the crucial documents to understanding Habsburg policy in these new territories was the *Einrichtungswerk des Königreichs Ungarn* created under Cardinal Leopold Kollonich. Issued in August 1689, it represented the collective knowledge of the previous five years of administration in Hungary. The recommendations were wide-ranging, covering everything from the military (supply and quartering issues) and the economy (taxation) to religion (Catholicization where possible) and repopulation (immigration from outside).[24] These migrants, both Hungarian speaking and German speaking, were to be lured to the area through tax exemptions, much as later settlers to the Banat were.[25] While many of the policies in the document were never undertaken, it represents an early snapshot of what Habsburg policies in these territories might be, and we will see echoes of these policies in later ones undertaken in the Banat.

Who administered the land was a crucial factor in the pace and scope of development. Much of Hungary was initially thought of and treated as a *neo acquistica*, a new acquisition to be ruled from Vienna rather than Buda. The estates and nobility in Hungary resisted this imposition and put forward their own *Einrichtungswerk*, which highlighted their stature and importance. With certain important exceptions, like the military border constructed along the Habsburg-Ottoman frontier, they were largely successful in maintaining or regaining their power in much of reconquered Hungary, codified in the Treaty of Szatmár in 1711.[26] In the Banat, the Habsburgs decided neither to return the land to Hungarian rule nor work with the existing local power brokers (many of whom had fled with the retreating Ottoman army), instead placing the entire region under the auspices of the Hofkriegsrat (the royal military council) and later the Hofkammer (the royal treasury).[27] Championed by Prince Eugene, this was in part done to separate the Protestant Magyars from their possible Ottoman allies. Prince Eugene argued that keeping the Banat under the direct rule of the emperor, much like Transylvania, would benefit the royal finances, allow for the creation of good management, and would aid in security.[28] The administration in Vienna also hoped to see increased revenue from land under their direct control. In the Banat, the emperor was both ruler and lord (*Herrscher und Grundherr*).[29] Thus, Charles VI and, later, Maria Theresia were able to rule absolutely, without having to seek the input or approval of any body of nobles. This made the Banat an ideal place to experiment with economic and social policy, an opportunity that the Habsburgs made use of throughout the eighteenth century.

The bureaucratic framework used to govern the Banat changed over the course of the eighteenth century. Until 1745, oversight from Vienna was provided by the Neoacquistische Subdelegation with membership drawn from the Court Chamber (Hofkammer) and the War Council (Hofkriegsrat). Reporting to this body from the region itself, the Banat Land Administration (Landesadministration) was responsible for executing the decrees from Vienna and handling the day-to-day affairs. A presidium composed of two civilians, the commanding general (who also served as governor), the fortress commander, and the high commissioner for supplies headed the organization. In the field, each district had an administrator (*Distriktsverwalter*), under whom served finance clerks (*Gegenschreiber*) and subordinate administrators (*Unterverwalter*).[30] Villages were headed by a mayor (*Schulz* in colonial villages, *Knez* in local ones). Between 1745 and 1747, the region was under the auspices of the Hofkommission in Banaticis, Transylvanicis et Illyricis. This body changed from a *Hofkommission* to a *Hofdeputation* in 1747.[31] In the early 1750s, the Landesadministration became purely a civilian-led and oriented organization. Highlighting this change was the retirement of the governor and *Generalfeldwachtmeister* Engelshofen in favor of a civilian leader.[32] As the archival record shows, many major decisions, like overarching colonial policy or the resettlement of existing populations, were made in Vienna but executed by the administration in Temesvar. This could lead to tension if the local administration delayed implementing directives they received from Vienna.

Most of the officials brought in to administer the Banat, especially in the early days after conquest, were not native to the region, though some had military experience there. Military men, especially invalids, inhabited both military and civil administrative positions in the Banat. When hiring new or replacement administrators, the Banat Land Administration would send a ranked list of potential candidates to the Subdelegation in Vienna, who, in turn, would produce a report for Charles VI or Maria Theresia. Candidates with connections in the administration or who spoke the local languages naturally fared better. They were also supposed to be loyal and honest, though as we will see, this was not always the case.[33] Many administrators also brought family with them when they took up their positions. Administrators were generally awarded annual salaries and were given accommodations. Sabine Jesner notes that the sources portray the salaries as "extraordinarily high," though officials also often sought increases. Accommodation was either in state-owned buildings or officials received a subsidy to support private housing.[34]

The administration of the region was a constant thorn in Vienna's side. Throughout the eighteenth century, the government issued ordinances regarding the proper way for officials to conduct their business. In 1733, the authorities issued a patent regarding toll collectors, providing rules to prevent abuse and encourage transparency in their actions.[35] In 1754, the government released an "Ordinance against the Untrue and Dishonest Officials in the Temesvar Banat" threatening untrue and thieving officials with corporal punishment and the death penalty. Those who under Austrian law could not be hanged were to be beheaded.[36] In another ordinance, officials were told never to conduct searches alone. They were to bring another representative with them, like a mayor. This was likely to prevent any hint of impropriety.[37] This situation continued at least until the end of the eighteenth century. According to Joseph II, the officials were "despots in their districts" and were characterized by "hatred, envy, enmity, bias, self-interest, prejudice, melancholy, [and] slowness."[38]

Whatever their capabilities, these officials were tasked with reconstructing the region. The sources, at least those written from the Habsburg perspective, are universally negative about the state of the Banat at the time of conquest. Reports complained about abandoned villages along with unused estates and fields that showed promise should they be cultivated correctly. They also cited the extensive swamps and marshes of the region as an impediment to development.[39] In the early 1720s, a complete map of the Banat was made, allowing for a fuller picture of the problems and potential of the region. In addition to the geography, which included lots of swamps and sand, the maps showed the demography. Many areas were shown as uninhabited. Around Pancsova, for example, there were twenty-two inhabited villages versus thirty uninhabited.[40] Much as in other colonial instances (e.g., Russia, the Americas), these initial impressions of depopulation and destruction became part of the enduring history of the Banat.[41] Griselini, the traveler and early historian of the region, was particularly harsh in his assessment of the pre-Habsburg Banat. In his opinion, the Turks had been terrible stewards of the land, allowing once-prosperous towns to be swallowed by the swamps. For him, this was especially distressing because of the fertility and economic potential available in the Banat.[42]

Both during and after the conquest, there were naturally questions about what to do with the conquered land. In the Habsburg decision-making process, cameralism played a crucial role. The term "cameralism" encompasses both an economic and sociopolitical theory as well as guidelines on the practical administration and maintenance of the state.[43] The two strands of cameralism, the theoretical and the practical, sometimes intersected and sometimes did not. Recently, the degree to which cameralist theory became state practice has been called into question.[44] The effectiveness of cameralism is also debated: Were the ordinances and patents followed? Were officials corrupt, or did they have the best interests of the people in mind? Whether or not many of the cameralist theoreticians were simply ladder climbers who used their ideas to gain favor and money, the ideas they championed appear to have influenced the development plans of the Habsburg government.

Cameralism had an early and later stage that differed in some important ways. The early cameralists were concerned, first and foremost, with the increase in the supply of money and thus the increase of the ruler's (or state's) power. This could be done by limiting expenditures or increasing revenue or creating wealth through mining. Later cameralists were also concerned with the power of the state but with a new twist. Like the earlier cameralists, they saw that the power of the state lay in its population and its productive capacity and that increasing the population was one way to augment state power. Importantly, they also saw that a happy population was a more productive population and thus, unlike the earlier proponents, they urged the ruler to take the happiness of his subjects into account.

While establishing a direct link between cameralists and projects undertaken by the Habsburg state is extremely difficult, the influence of the former on the latter can be imperfectly gleaned by looking at the circles in which the theorists found themselves (i.e., did they even have access to policymakers?) and by comparing the theories to the practices used in the Banat. Published only one year after the successful defense of Vienna, one of the earliest treatises on the newly emerging economic and social situation was Philipp Wilhelm von Hörnigk's *Österreich über alles, wann es nur will* (Austria above all, when only it will). As the title implies, Hörnigk's goal was to instruct the Habsburg administration on the methods required to become a great European power. His work became one of the three foundational texts of "early cameralism."[45] Hörnigk was a lawyer and civil servant who plied his trade throughout the German lands, at one time working as an attendant to Christoph Roya von Spinola, a confessor in the Viennese court who ended his career in the employ of the Bishop of Passau.[46] He was thus intimate with political affairs and the court and had at least some access to policymakers.

Hörnigk was primarily concerned with countering French influence in Europe through the development of the Austrian lands. He advocated many different ways to improve and strengthen the economy and the state. Mining was central to his system, as was the exploitation of other natural resources. Precious metals were to be kept in the country. He borrowed the idea of a complete import ban from the French economic system of mercantilism. As the Austrians were large importers of French goods, this would simultaneously weaken French production while strengthening Austrian. He believed that autarky was a sign of a strong state and encouraged the Austrian authorities to make this their goal. In particular, he argued that the state should promote the creation of luxury goods to lessen its dependence on expensive imports and stimulate the export economy. Several products he suggested were tried in the Banat, including silk, tobacco, olives, and rice. He also strongly promoted manufacturing. He argued that a good worked within the country gained in value over simply exporting the raw material. If a good needed to be imported, like spices that could not be grown in Austria, then the government should pay for this in exports, not in precious metals. He encouraged increasing the population within the realm. In fact, he argued that of all his proposals, this one was the most important issue ("höchste ... Angelegenheit"), if the most ignored.[47] More people meant more production and consumption, and thus more revenue. Foreign experts could teach Austrian subjects profitable skills. This revenue could then be used to improve the army or to fund further development projects, such as colonization.[48] Johann Joachim Becher, another of cameralism's foundational thinkers, agreed. He argued that "the more populous a state is, the more powerful it is."[49]

Increasing population was one of the most important characteristics of cameralist thought and one that was practiced in the Banat throughout the eighteenth century. The number of people in a state was seen as indicative of its power. This aspect is what separated German cameralism from other strands of mercantilism.[50] The depopulation of the Thirty Years' War (1618–1648) highlighted the importance of human capital in the German-speaking world. By the eighteenth century, the populationist impulse had developed and spread further, eventually reaching Spain and Russia. Populationism involved both the increase in population through immigration as well as the maintenance of population through restrictions on emigration.[51] Theorists often discussed why people emigrated as well as whether emigration was legal. Christian Wolff, for example, argued that people emigrated for a number of reasons: high taxes, oppression, loss of liberty, the expectation of a better life elsewhere, bad governance. Becher likewise argued that tyranny caused people to emigrate while good governance attracted people. In his estimation, people were justified in emigrating away from a tyrannical government.[52] Such populationist ideas became a centerpiece of the administration of the Banat throughout the eighteenth century.

These ideas were retained by later cameralist thinkers. Perhaps the most notable theorist of the later cameralists was Johann Heinrich Gottlob von Justi. Justi held several administrative positions throughout the Reich and in Austria. He was granted a professorship at the Collegium Theresianum in 1750. He was the author of the first cameralist textbook based on the "Prussian model." If Justi represented a new school of thought, many of his foundational beliefs were the same as those of the earlier theoreticians. For instance, he believed that good government would prevent emigration and that a ruler should not prevent his subjects from emigrating. He differed from earlier thinkers in a few important ways, though.[53] For Justi, gold and silver were not as important as they were to earlier theorists. He believed that wealth emanated from commerce and industry rather than precious metal reserves. He believed that the industriousness of subjects could be encouraged by intelligent rule. The happiness, *Glückseligkeit*, of the subject should be the paramount concern of the ruler. Happy subjects were more productive subjects, and more productive subjects led to a stronger state. Justi defined happiness materially as the ability of subjects to live above the line necessary for subsistence. The government's responsibility was to create the conditions for a subject's material success. Justi left the moral questions of happiness, like religion, to the conscience of the individual.[54]

This belief further informed his populationist theories. He believed that religiously intolerant policies only hurt states, especially when they caused economically productive populations to emigrate. Toleration attracted populations and helped the overall economic development of the state. Unlike earlier cameralists, who put an upper limit on immigration relative to the size of the area in question, Justi believed there was no limit, so long as the migrants made the state *glücklich*. He believed that the ability to produce and feed these migrants could grow unceasingly.[55]

Another later cameralist, Josef Sonnenfels, summed up the benefits population increase offered for the state: a larger population increased the number of potential soldiers, making the state more internationally and internally secure. More people led to greater production and more variety in production. Finally, an increased population had the potential to raise tax revenue while simultaneously lowering the individual's tax burden. Thus, populationist policy served state *and* subject.[56] For the cameralists, living in a pre-Malthusian world, increasing populations led only to increasing wealth and power for the state and its ruler.

Although we can see numerous examples of projects in the Banat from colonization to economic development that would have pleased these cameralists, it is hard to determine the extent to which theory informed practice. In the nearly twenty years of peace that reigned in the Banat following conquest (from 1718 to 1737), Claudius Mercy, the first military governor, and his successors were able to accomplish many development projects designed to strengthen the area militarily and economically. Improving the infrastructure was crucial to both goals. Controlling the vast quantities of water in the region was another major undertaking that lasted until at least the 1770s and was one of the Habsburg administration's major achievements. The government constructed breweries and mills.[57] The *Fabrik Vorstadt* (the "Factory Suburb") was cameralism in action. This suburb of the capital was a hive of manufacturing, including oil pressing, textiles, and woodworking.[58] Many of the manufactories, such as the textile manufactory, were built using government funds and then later leased to private individuals.

The cameralists must have been pleased with the possibilities for mineral extraction in the Banat. Mining had been an important part of the Banat's economy for centuries. German-speaking miners had been invited to neighboring regions, specifically to the Banat of Severin and Transylvania, as early as the thirteenth century, for both mining and security reasons. While German villages and culture in Transylvania managed to weather the Ottoman onslaught, the others perished.[59] Many of the mines taken over by the Austrians had previously been used by the Turks. According to one contemporary expert, gold mining in the region went back to Roman times. The authorities rehabilitated abandoned mines and established new ones. Some of the first German migrants to the region in the eighteenth century were miners. The mountains of the eastern Banat was rich in iron, copper, gold, silver, and lead. The iron ore from Dognazka was eventually used to make shells and bullets for the Austrian army.[60] By 1733, the Banat was responsible for half of all the copper mined in the Habsburg crownlands.[61]

Just as Hörnigk had suggested, the authorities also invited foreigners to the Banat to help set up novel agricultural projects throughout the eighteenth century. This was part of a broader movement of skilled workers and agriculturalists within Europe helping to build canals or improve milk production.[62] Born in the Austrian Netherlands, Maximillian Fremaut was recruited to drain the Banat's swamps and create arable land. He later brought his "Dutch style" to Triest, Aquileja, Hungary, and the German Reich.[63] Italians were crucial to the construction of several of the new enterprises encouraged by the cameralists, such as sericulture. Many in the government hoped that silk production would become a major source of income. Before this period, the Austrians were forced to buy large amounts of this textile from outside the empire. In keeping with cameralist thought, the government wanted to create domestic production for this luxury good to prevent the outflow of capital. Administrators sought to make the Banat into a silk region since shortly after conquest, though it was not especially successful until the later part of the century. The administration used diverse means to promote the project. In addition to bringing in Italian experts, the government also promoted the planting of mulberry trees as early as 1719, a necessity in raising silkworms.[64] Anyone caught cutting one down faced the possibility of the death penalty. The first short-lived local newspaper of the early 1770s, the *Temeswarer Nachrichten*, contained a series of articles on silk as well as instructions on how to raise silkworms.[65]

Italians also spearheaded hemp and rice production. Hemp was an important natural resource in the eighteenth century and key to shipbuilding. Production in the Banat was slated to support the sail-making manufactories in Trieste.[66] Increasing hemp production was a major goal of many governments around the world. In the Americas, the British were especially interested in growing hemp to support their navy and reduce its dependence on their traditional Swedish suppliers.[67] Rice had become popular among the upper classes, and once again, the Banat seemed the ideal place to encourage domestic cultivation to replace imports.[68] Already in the 1740s, the government was trying to encourage this project.[69] This endeavor brought the most Italians to the Banat. In 1774, for instance, the administration gave

Secundo Limony land provided he used one-third of it to experiment with rice. He brought twelve Mantuan families with him. The families were given land for their subsistence and ten years of tax freedom. In 1777, 5,500 fl. were earmarked to bring additional families. In 1782, the workers were excused from robot in order to focus on rice cultivation.[70] Limony was apparently of such importance in the region that Johann Caspar Steube, a cobbler turned soldier from the Holy Roman Empire who served in the military in the Banat in the 1770s and 1780s, specifically mentioned him in his memoirs. He claimed that Limony's experiment in rice cultivation was a failure and that, in the end, his creditors came after him.[71]

What separated these technical migrants from the German agricultural migrants was their smaller numbers and their impermanence. They were not expected to stay. When two Italians contracted to oversee the hemp project asked to leave Habsburg service, the government allowed them to, noting that since the subjects in the Banat now knew how to grow hemp, there was no reason to incur any further costs relating to their work.[72] Similarly, in 1750, the director of silk and rice production, Canonicus Rossi, informed the court that the rice planter Rovano Sarino and the rice miller Paolo Garaboldi were no longer integral parts to the success of the rice-growing project. Maria Theresia herself responded and agreed that there was already enough local knowledge to keep the project alive. They were given remuneration and grain for their return trip to Italy as compensation for the early termination of their contracts.[73] Unlike Germans, who were recruited en masse, the Italians were recruited in small numbers as experts.

Renewed Conflict and the Creation of the Military Border

The development of the Banat under Mercy was impressive. Unfortunately for the region's development, renewed conflict with the Ottomans led to the destruction of much of the work he had spearheaded. The Austro-Turkish War from 1737 to 1739 ravaged the Banat. It was the product of Russian aggressiveness and Austrian obligations. The Russians and Austrians had a defensive alliance that obligated the Austrians to attack anyone who attacked the Russians. This pact was further complicated by Russian military assistance during the War of Polish Succession that virtually guaranteed Austrian participation in any future war against the Turks, at least in the Russian's estimation. For their part, the Russians wanted to gain control of the northern Black Sea littoral and in 1735 began taking martial steps toward achieving this goal. The Austrians initially withheld support, as technically, it was Russian aggression, not Turkish, which sparked the war. They eventually joined the war in 1737 in an effort both to maintain the alliance with Russia, discover their war aims (!), and to prevent them from winning too much territory in the Balkans.[74]

The conflict was a disaster for the Austrians. Although they did manage to retain possession of the Banat, they lost Belgrade, the kingdom of Serbia, and Little Wallachia to the Ottomans.[75] This was another brutal war with atrocities committed by both sides. There were reports of Ottoman troops desecrating altars in Christian churches and digging up bodies in cemeteries in Caransebes.[76] In Ujpalanka (also Neupalanka), Ottoman troops murdered monks.[77] In Werschetz (today's Vršac), they killed many of the inhabitants, took the rest as slaves, and set fire to the town.[78] In June 1738, the local administration estimated the number of subjects from the Banat in Ottoman captivity at 3,070. They could buy their freedom, but it was very expensive.[79] Armies loyal to the Habsburgs drove the population away through "committed excesses [*Excessen*]."[80] They also resorted to collective punishment and torture to deal with rebellious Wallachs who turned on Vienna during the war.[81] Habsburg officials reported "perjurious" mayors (*Knesen*) and rebellious inhabitants who "murdered at will." Some majors who stayed loyal were hanged by the Ottomans.[82] Treachery was not limited to the Habsburg subjects. British newspapers reported that some imperial troops deserted to the Turks in exchange for one-third more in pay than the Janissaries.[83] A region that had recently been a testament to the power of development and cutting-edge economic theory had quickly devolved into the site of brutal interimperial, interconfessional, and interethnic violence.

The Banat was now in need of reconstruction and development, much as it had been following its capture in 1716. Depopulation was again an issue. Reports of displaced or fleeing subjects were common. As one administrator noted in late 1738, in "usually such populated areas [around Ujpalanka], there is hardly a person to be found."[84] In 1739, one Prince Lobkowitz found the region "entirely ruin'd, the Country defeated, and [he] met with only three Peasants in his March, who ran away as soon as they perceiv'd him."[85] For years after the war, escaped slaves made their way to the Banat. In April 1757, for example, five individuals who had been slaves in Turkey wanted to settle in Werschetz. The last Turkish War had ended in 1739, indicating that many of these people had likely been in captivity for more than eighteen years. They all had incredibly sad stories. Some were like Catharina Baurin, whose husband and daughters were still in Turkish captivity. Others' families had died during the last Turkish war and the concurrent plague outbreak. These individuals had been residents of the Banat before their capture and sought to start their lives anew in the region.[86] They were the lucky ones. Many subjects taken as slaves never made it back.[87]

Despite the obvious need, the outlay of money for reconstruction had become a riskier proposition. Whereas before 1739, a buffer had existed between the Ottoman Empire and the bulk of the Banat, the Turkish gains from the peace treaty made it the southern boundary between the two states. This fact alone made the region vastly more geopolitically important. Before any thought could be given to further development projects, the area needed to be made secure. All manner of administrative outposts needed to be built to control the flow of people and goods over what was now an imperial borderland. To protect the Banat, and the Habsburg domains as a whole, the authorities began erecting a formal military border along the southern frontier.[88]

Local peasants had been utilized as soldiers long before Habsburg occupation. The Hungarians had a similar system in the fifteenth and sixteenth centuries, though one not as strictly regimented as Grenzer, or border guard, society became. The earlier peasant-soldiers generally exploited the remaining peasants to subsist rather than establishing themselves in the organized fashion that became common in the Habsburg military border. Other even less formally organized peasants created "self-protection associations" that sought to protect their "fatherland" from both the sultan and the kaiser, though they tied this sense of solidarity to their immediate surroundings rather than in some protonational sense.[89] The Ottomans also used local Wallachs and Rascians in their military, performing some of the same functions (like manning fortresses and watch posts) that they later performed for the Habsburgs. Some were even Spahis and given Timars in "wasted or dangerous places" to develop. Overall, the region was "overabundant" in "combat-ready serfs."[90] Once under Habsburg control in 1726, the emperor accepted a proposal by Mercy to create an unpaid *Landmiliz* (militia) to help protect the region. Thus, a militia made up of 4,200 soldiers was created entirely from former Ottoman subjects.[91]

This forerunner to the later Grenzer regiments gained importance after 1739. Given the propensity for the local population to side with and perform military duties for whoever seemed to offer the best deal, the role of ethnicity and religion in these units became a focal point for administrators, underlining the government's attentiveness to these aspects in determining loyalty and potential disloyalty. After the Wallachs had to a large degree sided with the Turks during the war (or at the very least were perceived as having done so), administrators discussed both how to subdue them and how to secure the new border.

A number of plans were put forward to secure the border. Initially, there was a plan to remove the Wallachs from the border around Orsova and replace them with more trustworthy settlers.[92] One military advisor, Koch, had a more ambitious scheme. He proposed the resettlement of all the peasants then currently living along the southern border, including those in Caransebes, Orsova, Ujpalanka, and Pancsova Districts. The farmers in these districts would be moved north, their places on the border taken by Grenzer. Although the government in Vienna appeared to be supporting the less drastic measure, that is, the expulsion of Wallachs from Orsova only and the use of the regular military along the border, the military commander at the time, Engelshofen, actually instituted a *third* plan. In 1740, he created a military group out of the existing Rascian militia (whom Engelshofen feared would desert to Ottoman service [!]), partisans from Transylvania, Catholic Bulgarians, and Albanians to perform many of the duties the later Grenzers would, including guarding the border and manning the quarantine stations.[93] To what extent this motley group of soldiers displaced local Wallachs is unclear, though it highlights the importance of ethnic belonging among administrators.

The creation of a more formal border proceeded despite internal disagreements on how to staff and manage it. In 1742, authorities erected a line of watchhouses staffed by Rascians along the border.[94] The border took even more formal shape in the 1760s with the creation of the Illyrian and German Banat Regiments with headquarters in Weisskirchen and Pancsova, respectively. They had a combined strength of around 7,700 men.[95] In addition to being soldiers, the Grenzer also worked the land. While the military initially owned all of the land and provided it to the Grenzer as a loan (*Militärlehen*), by 1812, in Weisskirchen, at least, the government gave the ownership rights to the colonist-soldiers themselves.[96]

The militarization of the frontier and its population was not the only sign highlighting the new geopolitical reality in the southern Banat. In addition, there were the *Contumaz*, or quarantine, stations along the border in Schuppaneck, Ujpalanka, Kubin, Pancsova, and Semlin.[97] While other European states created sanitary cordons during times of crisis, Charles VI oversaw the construction of a permanent cordon along the entire Ottoman-Habsburg border in 1728. The plague cordon lasted until 1857.[98] The quarantine stations served both practically to prevent a real danger (the potential spread of the plague) and intellectually to demarcate the boundary between the West and the East. The creation of these stations was directly connected with the overall Habsburg mentality that drove the settlement of the Banat. One government report highlighted the connection between the Ottomans and the plague in the minds of many Habsburg subjects when it stated that the plague was emanating from the "Sultanischen Residenz Stad" (the sultan's residential city), though a later report uses the much less descriptive Constantinople.[99] In the minds of this official, the feared plague came from the seat of Ottoman power. The connection between contamination and the East could not be clearer. The Banat, its institutions and its colonists were meant to act as a barrier to Ottoman, oriental, Eastern incursions and diseases.

The connection between dirt, disease, and the "East" has been noted by scholars.[100] The quarantine stations tangibly represented this connection, straddling the border with one gate on Ottoman soil, one on Habsburg. Items passing through quarantine from the Ottoman lands needed to be decontaminated before coming into the Habsburg domains but goods passing the other direction did not. For example, when Ottoman subjects in quarantine needed to buy food from the Habsburg border guards, they would put their money in vinegar, thinking it would kill the plague. Like people, larger shipments of items were also quarantined, usually for twenty-one days. Certain items, such as wine, milk, vinegar, and fruit, were not subject to quarantine and were simply required to be cleaned with vinegar by a "cleaning boy."[101] During one outbreak of the plague in 1738, all letters bound for Vienna were required to be treated with a special smoke in an effort to sanitize them.[102] After Ottoman subjects completed quarantine, they were given a certificate to prove that they were healthy. These were standardized, printed forms with blank spaces to fill in personal information. These documents contained the person's origin, destination, age, duration of stay, description (both physical and of clothing), the number of days spent in quarantine, and, most importantly, a statement attesting to their health ("fresh and healthy").[103] Such certificates were issued until at least 1842, around the same time the quarantine cordon ended.[104] Many people, especially smugglers, tried to avoid these stations. If caught, they faced criminal charges for bypassing quarantine.[105] They could be sentenced to hard labor, such as building fortresses or caserns.[106] They also faced possible corporal punishment. In early 1759, for instance, twenty-one individuals from Wallachia attempted to sneak past a quarantine station. When caught, they were caned and expelled back over the border.[107]

Throughout most of the eighteenth century, these stations were hives of activity. There were consistent reports of plague outbreaks in the Ottoman domains and an almost equally consistent stream of instructions from the central government to the stations. Often, reports of plague outbreaks came from travelers and merchants arriving in the quarantine stations. The instructions on how to handle a possible outbreak of the plague often came from the highest authorities. In 1754, an outbreak occurred in Bulgaria and Wallachia. Maria Theresia herself ordered tighter restrictions at the border. She also allowed the officials there to act without waiting for instructions, if need be.[108]

One the Grenzer's duties was to staff these outposts, and thus the quarantine stations and the military border shared much of a common history. The military frontier and the quarantine system (or perhaps blind luck) worked for a number of years in keeping disease, if not Ottoman armies, from crossing into the Habsburg domains.[109] The last widespread outbreak of the plague in the Banat was 1738–1740, though there was an outbreak in Pancsova in 1743.[110] There were reports of plague in the Ottoman domains well into the nineteenth century. In 1818, news from Wallachia and Moldavia indicated a possible plague outbreak. The Austrian government then ordered that the border "enforce the quarantine regulations with the utmost rigour."[111]

Transfer of Sovereignty: The Hungarian Crown Gains the Banat

The impetus behind the military border and the quarantine line had come from Vienna. Since the conquest, political decisions in the Banat had been subject only to the Habsburg emperor and his or her administration. This changed in the late 1770s. In early 1778, Empress Maria Theresia agreed to turn over domestic political control of the Banat to the Hungarian crown. In a note dated January 23, 1778, the empress ordered the Bohemian-Austrian Chancellery to turn over whatever material the Hungarian Chancellery might request on the Banat.[112] Thus, one of the first orders of business in the transference of sovereignty was the transference of documents (specifically the "Banat Acts") from one Chancellery to the other.[113] The Hungarians also specifically requested documents relating to privileged areas like Kikinda, the Jewish toleration tax, and maps, both of the land in general and those on which the land parcels were demarcated.[114] The requested documents clearly show that the authorities at the Hungarian Chancellery were trying to understand what they were about to gain, especially where the anomalies were.

Although the Hungarians legally took control on June 22, 1778, they were not in actual control of the region until April 23, 1779.[115] This transition fulfilled a promise Maria Theresia made to the Hungarian Diet in 1741.[116] Although many Hungarians had demanded control over the Banat since its conquest, there was no tangible movement on the issue until the late 1760s. Interestingly, it was Joseph II's musings that provided the impetus that eventually led to Hungarian rule. After his 1768 trip to the region, Joseph made suggestions regarding its improvement, one of which was the sale of land and the imposition of lord-peasant relations. Importantly, he did not suggest the incorporation of the Banat into Hungary; it was to still be administered from Vienna. Leading Habsburg administrators, including State Chancellor Kaunitz, seized on his suggestion as a possible solution to the administrative and financial problems plaguing the region.[117]

The Hungarians initially resisted this plan. They demanded that the pre-Ottoman lords receive "their" land back even though they had not been in possession of the land for more than two centuries. They eventually agreed to a compromise. While the Hofkammer would sell the land itself to the highest bidder, political control of the Banat would be returned to the Hungarians. While Joseph never explicitly endorsed the reincorporation, his earlier plans and later silence on the matter suggest at least his tacit approval. An advertisement from 1782 showed the base prices of a number of cameral villages and towns that were to be auctioned off. The lowest price was 5,363 fl. for Toba while the highest up for auction was Neusina at 404,645 fl. According to the advertisement, bidding was open to all subjects of the king *and all foreigners* (!), whatever their religion, including Greek Orthodox and Protestants. They were free to buy as much as they wanted so long as the total worth did not exceed 400,000 fl. Non-Habsburg subjects were required to pay assessed taxes. Non-nobles were required to pay the noble taxes (*Nobilitartaxe*). The government allowed buyers to pay only a percentage of the purchase price. It appears at least 50 percent was required. The remainder was due within ten years, and the principal was assessed 4.5 percent interest.[118]

Having only paid part of the purchase price, many new landowners wanted to get as much money out of the land in as short a period as possible. This led to numerous abuses and in 1784, Joseph halted the sale of the land. Why Joseph supported a project so seemly inimical to his larger goal of neutering the nobility and supporting the peasantry provides insight into his world view. According to historian Antal Hegedüs, Joseph never wanted to eliminate the lord-peasant relationship, which he saw as natural, but rather wanted to make it fairer, more just. He saw the Banat as a corrupt money pit and believed it was in the best interests of the state to liquidate its holdings there.[119] Despite the abuses, Joseph allowed sales to recommence in 1789, now even allowing Jews to purchase land.[120] Sales continued into the nineteenth century with the Hofkammer also retaining control over some areas. In 1806, there was still talk in government circles about how best to use the remaining empty lands in the Banat, some of which were leased but uninhabited.[121]

After the transfer, the Banat became subject to Hungarian laws and social organization. In Hungary, nobles (around 5 percent of the population in 1820) reigned supreme. They paid no taxes, though some of the lowest nobility were taxed from time to time. They had the right to habeas corpus and were subject to no one but the king, to whom they only owed armed service. They could own their personal domains. Peasants were the direct subjects of these nobles. They owed taxes and performed military duty at the pleasure of the king or the noble Diet. They could be arrested at will.[122] For a land that had from its conquest until this point been solely the domain of the Austrian monarch, this was a shocking and abrupt change for its inhabitants. The German colonists, in particular, felt that the transfer in sovereignty violated the promises that had induced them to migrate, and in this, they were correct.[123]

In addition to losing the relative political autonomy they enjoyed, the colonists were also subjected to the imposition of Hungarian culture (Magyarization). Initially beginning partly as a reaction and resistance to Joseph's perceived "Germanizing" of the bureaucracy in the 1780s, by the early nineteenth century, the promotion of Hungarian language and culture had become an end in and of itself.[124] The Hungarians feared not only the influence of German culture but also the prominence of Slavs and Slavic culture. Proponents of Magyarization found intellectual backing for the expansion of Hungarian language and culture among the French *philosophes* and later among the German Romantics.[125]

Slowly, Magyar dominance in Hungary became codified. Beginning in 1805, there were language laws. The Hungarian Academy of the Sciences and a National Museum appeared in 1825.[126] Also in 1825, the Hungarian Diet pushed for the increased use of Magyar over Latin in government business. The Diet of 1830 renewed the demand. The king, more concerned that the Diet agreed to his proposals on taxes and the army, allowed concessions. At the Diet of 1832, Hungarian became the primary language both in the government and the church. The prominent position afforded Hungarian was further solidified when a later gathering decreed that all petitions by the Diet and the counties had to be in Hungarian. Birth, marriage, and death certificates were likewise to be in Hungarian. Bureaucrats, priests, and ministers needed to be proficient in the language. They even attempted to extend the requirements to the military. Regiments from Hungary were to communicate with the crown's counties in Magyar.[127]

It is important to reiterate that not all of the Banat was placed under Hungarian control in 1778, leading to a mishmash of sovereignties. The military border remained under the control of the Military Council in Vienna until its dissolution in 1871–1872.[128] Also, the "Banat Mountain District" remained under the control of the Orawitzer Oberbergverwaltung (Orawitza High Mountain Administration), which answered to the treasury. This changed in the early nineteenth century as the Hungarian authorities received the right to govern there.[129] By 1830, the beginnings of the policy of Magyarization were visible in this remote, mountainous region.[130] As late as the 1840s, there were "fiscal estates" in the Banat. These estates were under the direct control of the emperor, though unlike crown domains, they could be liquidated.[131] For example, Emperor Franz gave the crown village of Deutschbentschek to Fieldmarshal Karl Schwarzenberg for his service in the Napoleonic Wars.[132] Perhaps most interesting was the Gross-Kikinda Crown-District. Created by Maria Theresia in 1774, it consisted of ten villages (*Ortschaften*) for Rascians who did not want to serve in the Grenzer regiments and who wanted some form of self-administration. This "privileged" area remained outside Hungarian control until 1876, when it was subsumed by the Torontal Komitat.[133]

Even though much of the Banat was now controlled by the Hungarians, it remained a place for agricultural experimentation well into the nineteenth century. In 1789, there was even a "bee inspector" in Habsburg employ.[134] Likewise, silk production and manufacturing remained a central goal of the authorities. Even in the late 1780s, the emperor requested that any orphans in the royal free cities who wanted to learn to make silk should report to Pest to two silk manufacturers who were willing to provide four years of training. The state was even willing to help support these children: 40 fl. for a boy, 24 for a girl, plus 12 fl. yearly for clothes.[135] A newspaper article in 1827 pitched silk cultivation as a use for "children and other people incapable of working."[136] When the French Revolutionary Wars caused cotton prices to skyrocket, there were moderately successful attempts to grow it in the Banat starting in 1795. These efforts were redoubled in 1808–1809. Though ultimately a failure, its cultivation was especially promoted among German regiments in the military frontier.[137] Other potential cash crops were also tried. Using a suggestion by Ludovico Maria de la Lena, Johann v. Klaniczay, the royal prefect in Werschetz, attempted to grow olives in the Banat starting in 1809. Using three hundred small plants and twenty-five pounds of seeds from Fiume (today's Rijeka, Croatia), he grew these plants on public lands in his district. In addition to this experiment, Klaniczay suggested using the crown's lands in the Banat to grow plants to create dyes, thus minimizing the outflow of Austrian money for this luxury.[138] Cameralists back to Hörnigk would have been pleased with the suggestion.

The Last Austro-Ottoman War and Political Developments into the Nineteenth Century

The last major incursion by the Ottomans into the Banat occurred at the end of the 1780s. Once again, the Austrians' relationship with the Russians dragged them into a destructive and violent conflict. In 1787, a series of small problems and diplomatic disagreements led the Ottomans and Russians to declare war.[139] Despite high hopes for a successful conclusion, given the state of the Austrian military and the favorable international situation, the war was not a resounding victory for the Austrians. When the Russians delayed their attacks, and chose to attack only a very specific target, the Ottomans were able to redirect their forces against the Austrians. In 1788, 147 communities in the Banat fell victim to invading Ottoman forces.[140] In 1789, the Austrians and Russians scored some major victories, capturing Bucharest and Bendery, respectively. The next year, the weight of international and domestic affairs forced the Austrians to sue for peace. The Treaty of Sistova, finalized in early 1791, was based on each state's position at the start of the war.[141] In the end, very little territory changed hands, but war had once again disrupted the government's plans for the region.

As in the earlier wars, both sides ravaged the Banat. The Austrians, specifically, the Brechainville and Lilien Corps, were responsible for destroying forty-two villages to prevent them from falling into Ottoman hands.[142] Imperial troops also set fire to Weisskirchen as they fled.[143] In comparison to earlier conflicts, reports of Austrian misdeeds were few. As always, there were numerous reports of Ottoman destruction.[144] They burned villages, disemboweled the colonel of a Wallachian regiment, and beheaded the sick along with their surgeons.[145] Given that Ottoman soldiers were "generally paid for each enemy head they collected," decapitation should perhaps not surprise us. In fact, a French POW described how his captors had decapitated two sick soldiers to ensure they would receive their payment. Live slaves were also valuable, especially to the perennially underpaid Ottoman soldiers.[146]

Thus, it is not surprising that Ottoman soldiers took thousands of Habsburg subjects for the slave markets. According to the press, the total number of all "prisoners and other persons taken in the Bannat of Temeswar and other places" was "very considerable." In 1789, for instance, the sultan promised 50,000 individuals that they would not be sold as slaves, while at the same time "numbers daily" were sent on to Asia to be sold.[147] While the reported numbers may be viewed with some suspicion, they were large enough to warrant attention in the Treaty of Peace signed at Sistova in 1791. In it, the treaty makers noted that a "considerable number of them [i.e., imperial and royal subjects and soldiers] still remain in domestic slavery in

Turkey," having not yet been released by the Ottomans. Thus, "in the space of two months . . . all the prisoners of war and slaves, of whatever age, sex, or condition, wherever they may be found, or to what persons soever they may belong" were to be returned, free of charge, to the Habsburg lands.[148] The Ottoman authorities offered one hundred piasters to their current masters to return them, though many were completely missing or had converted to Islam.[149] As noted by historian Will Smiley, the Ottoman archival record contains "few traces" of these civilian captives, unlike the military captives who enjoyed some amount of official protection and were generally not enslaved.[150] That records about such slaves, and other acts of cruelty, are scattered and often found in unofficial sources should not surprise us.

The enslavement of German colonists became a part of the settler cultural memory and undoubtedly fed ill will toward local people well into the nineteenth century. In his history of the Banat published in 1861, Lénert Böhm recalled a story told to him by his grandfather. He told Böhm that *his* grandmother (i.e., Böhm's great-great-grandmother) had been enslaved during the 1737–1739 Austro-Ottoman War despite being "fairly old." The Ottomans had used dogs to find hidden Germans, and one of these dogs had found his grandmother hidden in a bush near Weisskirchen. She was carried off to the Ottoman domains, where she was sold as a slave, spending thirteen years as a nanny in the harem of her master. A group of Trinitarians, known as the "White Spaniards," bought her out of slavery and helped her return home to the Banat.[151] This story rings true given the many similarities (working in the harem, emancipation by religious orders) that it shares with other "captive narratives" told in the wider Mediterranean.[152] Such stories and memories, whatever their truth, persisted within families for generations and likely did little to improve interethnic understanding in the Banat.

Interestingly, there were also stories of Ottoman civility. For example, the *General Evening Post* reported that the Turks "behaved with the greatest humanity" during their retreat. According to this report, it was the Habsburg troops, not the Ottomans, who set fire to Pancsova. In fact, the Ottomans tried to help extinguish the fire.[153] It appears they were also trying to build some good will in the region. They apparently told residents that if they shaved their heads, this would be a sign that they supported the Ottoman cause.[154] Despite Ottoman attempts to win over the local population, they were unable to displace the Austrians and recapture the region. With the end of the war, the Banat was once again in need of rebuilding. Unlike after previous wars, there was no major government-led initiative to reconstruct the region. Events in France quickly put any other plans on hold.

This was the last Austro-Ottoman war. From this point until 1848, the Banat ceased to be the grounds for major geopolitical events, though as we shall see, there were important domestic conflagrations in the early 1800s. Of course, this statement benefits from hindsight. Observers throughout Europe did not know that the Austrians would not be involved in another war with the Turks. The Habsburg administration itself saw renewed conflict as a definite possibility and prepared for it. In 1801, for example, fear of a renewed war with the Turks led the imperial government to increase grain stores in the Banat and Croatia and prepare the border regiments.[155] In the early 1820s, with unrest in Ottoman Wallachia, the government again increased troop strength on the border.[156] The minor international incidents that did occur in the early nineteenth century were generally limited and did not explode into open interstate conflict.

Throughout the eighteenth century, the Banat was always an important region for the Habsburg authorities, though the reasons for its importance transformed as domestic and international issues evolved. While it had been the site of numerous interstate conflicts in the eighteenth century, by the early nineteenth century, its importance as a military bastion against Turkish aggression had largely faded. A constant throughout the period was the region's role as a place of experimentation: social, agricultural, economic, and as we will now begin to explore, demographic. These experiments were meant to pull what had been to Habsburg eyes a backward, barbaric, "Eastern" region in the early eighteenth century into the modern Western world, to Europeanize it.

As the next chapters will highlight, the Habsburg administration intended German colonists to play a major role in all phases of its transformation from an Ottoman backwater into a modern European space, much as the Russian, Spanish, and British did. They were seen as an industrious, loyal population who would assist the Habsburgs in their development plans and in securing the Banat against the external Turkish threat and the internal indigenous one. The transplantation of tens of thousands of Germans to the

Banat was no easy task and severely disrupted local traditions and customs while at the same time creating new ones.

In order to encourage colonists to settle and develop the land, the Habsburgs needed to create conditions that would attract migrants and then advertise them. Helping them in their efforts, the difficulties of life in the Holy Roman Empire throughout the eighteenth century induced at least part of the population to consider leaving. By the mid-eighteenth century, the Habsburgs were not alone in their colonial efforts. Prussians, Russians, Spaniards, and Brits all competed to bring German-speaking migrants to their lands. In this competition, the Banat fared well as a destination. As the next chapter will show, successive Habsburg administrations constructed and maintained, both on the ground and in the minds of prospective migrants, the conditions necessary to bring thousands of German-speaking migrants to the frontier of Europe.

2   Security and Loyalty

Colonial Settlement from 1718 to 1829

> At Marxheim, which is a village two hours below Donauwörth, where the embarkation is, we had to wait eight entire days because of the indescribable mass of people that were there. Like a small army, although people departed from there daily, one little noticed it, as when a drop of water is taken from a river.
>
> —*A migrant's description of the people leaving the Reich for the Banat and Hungary in 1724*[1]

ON JUNE 9, 1752, a group of recruiting agents presented one hundred German Catholic Lorrainers for settlement in the Banat.[2] In an enlightening petition to the government, the prospective colonists detailed their understanding of what incentives they expected for settling. They explained that it had been brought to their attention that there were areas in the kingdom of Hungary (*sic*) where the government was offering three free years for settlement. In addition, they had heard that the government was also proffering materials to build "a little house." They made clear that they recognized that after the passing of the free years, they would be required to pay taxes. They wrote essentially to confirm that their understanding of the privileges would be respected and honored by the government.[3] In response to this plea, the government in Vienna issued a statement in Empress Maria Theresia's name directed at these prospective colonists, using the names of the agents to identify the group. The authorities ordered that all who came in contact with this group were to respect their passes and give them free travel to the Banat.[4]

The centrality of the Banat to the security of the Habsburg domains and its potential as an incubator for novel economic and social experimentation led the administration to initiate and support the migration of colonists to the region. From relatively simple origins, the project became progressively more complex. By the 1760s and 1770s, a whole administrative apparatus existed to handle the movement and settlement of tens of thousands of migrants. While the early settlers experienced harsh conditions and often lacked extensive material support from the government, the colonial machine eventually doled out significant benefits and advantages to the incoming migrants.

A German-speaking peasant in the eighteenth century had no shortage of options if they wished (and were able) to emigrate.[5] Much like the Habsburg administration, other governments were influenced by the idea that increased population would mean increased power. Additionally, these states wanted to bring Europeans to their peripheries in order to make them more productive, to "Europeanize" them. Larger states, importantly, Prussia, Russia, Spain, and Great Britain, mirrored the Habsburgs in their efforts to use the German lands as a source of manpower for population projects in their own states and colonies. There were other smaller efforts as well. In 1739, for instance, there was an attempt to settle parts of Tuscany (Maremma) with colonists from Lorraine. The colonists were offered inducements to settle, but desertion and death doomed the endeavor. It appears that this effort was led by Maria Theresia's husband, Franz-Stephan, who at the time was both Duke of Lorraine and Duke of Tuscany.[6]

As we will see both in this and in later chapters, the recruitment of a specific type of colonist, their promotion through material goods and aid, the redistribution of already-occupied land to their benefit, and their separation from the undesirable elements of the society were all actions in service of larger goals. Most immediately, the colonists were to help authorities secure the region by establishing a loyal population. In the long term, the migrants were to help with the Europeanization of the Banat. Some authorities specifically hoped that the colonists would help transform the Banat from subsistence agriculture and herding to high-yield farming. The government even expected "colonists" forced into migrating to the Banat to do their part in populating and settling the region. Over the long term, the privileges proffered by the government enabled the colonists to take a dominant social and economic position in the region. While this ascension to prominence did not occur until the nineteenth and early twentieth centuries, the Habsburg administration laid the groundwork in the eighteenth.

Migration in Eighteenth-Century Central Europe

Migration in any era is a daunting undertaking. There are plenty of factors that encourage a potential migrant to stay put. A restricted world view might limit one's capacity to see beyond the borders of home. Laws might prevent legal migration. Costs associated with migration, from transportation and food to the loss of income on the journey to the cost of creating a new life, may dissuade an individual. Familial, religious, or cultural obligations may tie one to a homeland. Travel to a new place, perhaps hundreds or even thousands of miles away, was particularly difficult in the eighteenth century.

Despite the mental, physical, and material barriers to migration, there have always been people who have decided to migrate.[7] To help understand why, research on migration often talks about "push" and "pull" factors. Here, I am not referring to a straightforward economic model where people move from "less developed" places to those with "higher wages and standards of living."[8] When examining migrants, especially migrants in the eighteenth century, economics was not the sole explanatory cause of migration, and it is impossible to know the exact convergence of factors that caused them to pull up stakes. At a basic level, migrants must have calculated that the place they were going to was in some way better than the place that they were, either initially or eventually.

Despite the potential limitations of the model, push-pull factors provide a handy way to think about the reasons why people migrate. Push factors are reasons why a migrant would want to leave their current home. In the eighteenth century (and later as well), factors such as restricted freedom (religious and/or political), inclement weather, famine, war, crime, disease, high taxes, feudal dues, right to marriage, localized overpopulation, and debt led people to migrate. The Rhine lands, the source of many of the German-speaking colonists, experienced many of these problems.[9] Pull factors, which draw a migrant to a particular place, naturally included solutions to the push factors (e.g., lower taxes, no feudalism, good land, etc.) alongside the work of already existing communities of coethnic/religious migrants or recruiters (both potentially touting the benefits of migration). Distance to the destination and the cost to get there were also important pull factors.

In trying to recruit settlers, states had to not only determine what might induce a peasant to migrate (i.e., create the "pull") but also to make sure that their pull factors were better than their rivals'. When the authorities in Trier tried to discover the reasons for the migration of their subjects in the 1720s, pull factors were central.[10] According to investigators, the migrants likely wanted to take advantage of the "fertility" and supposed ease of agriculture in Hungary. Additionally, investigators felt that the peasants wanted the "great freedoms" that they had heard about there.[11] Creating enticing pull factors was especially important for the Russian, Spanish, and British governments as they had to deal with both remoteness from the Reich alongside cultural foreignness when attempting to attract migrants. It took the longest to get to Russia (approximately a year) and was the most expensive to get to the Americas. It was so expensive that many migrants had to sell themselves, or their children, for a set number of years to pay for their passage (the "Redemptioner System").[12] Hungary and the Banat were the closest, cheapest options (not accounting for the Russian subsidization of travel).[13] For the migrants, particularly in the 1760s, this situation was a positive one. The competition meant that potential migrants had, in theory, a choice of privileges and destinations. As we will see, the competitors were keenly aware of each other's presence and sought to match or exceed what was on offer from their rivals. This likewise benefitted the potential colonists.

In addition to "push and pull" factors, there were also forces devoted to preventing or hindering migration, what we think of as "binding factors." Many of these would have been personal and thus often hidden in the historical record: personal (age, sickness, temperament), familial (elderly parents, infant children, sick relatives), social (position of communal importance), or economic (business ties, lack of funds). Governments also acted as "binders." The polities of the Holy Roman Empire, and even France, attempted to resist the draining of their population for others' colonial projects. The small states of the Holy Roman Empire felt particular demographic pressure because of the larger states' seemingly insatiable need for settlers. Local authorities passed laws designed to discourage migrants from leaving. For instance, in 1724 authorities in the Archbishopric of Trier issued an ordinance against the migration to "Hungary." In it, they threatened migrants with a loss of rights should they decide to return home. Specifically, it stated that if migrants came back they would be treated as "vagabonds" and expelled (!).[14] Similarly, the Bishop of Constanz and the Duke of Württemberg issued a joint resolution regarding migration in 1724. They ordered that only migrants with valid passes were to be allowed to migrate. Others were to be stopped at the border and returned home. At times, there were "emigration taxes." In late eighteenth-century Bavaria and the Palatinate, this was 3 percent of a migrant's taxable property.[15]

When such measures failed to stem the tide of emigration, authorities took more drastic actions. The strictest was the *Auswanderungsverbot* or emigration ban. Every time there was a major movement of people (the 1720s–30s, 1760s, 1780s), the authorities in some of the affected states issued such bans. The Archbishopric of Trier issued one in 1731 and in so doing referenced a similar ban issued by authorities in Mainz. No one, "rich or poor," was allowed to leave Trier for the "Hungarian colonies." Those who attempted to or did in fact emigrate were subject to confiscation of property and corporal punishment.[16] The authorities intended these ordinances to control not only migrants within Europe but also to the Americas. In one from Saarbrücken in 1764, the authorities even specifically mentioned the recruiters for the "so-called 'New Land.'"[17] In the 1760s, polities again forbade emigration. To remain with the example of Trier, they issued another emigration ban in 1763. In the 1764 reiteration of the ban, central authorities tasked local authorities with preventing emigration.[18]

Again in 1786, the authorities in Trier attempted to prevent emigration through legislation. Authorities complained that although they tried to warn their subjects about the "falsity of the perception" under which they emigrated, people were still going, some returning after a "sad experience." They further tried to undercut some of the promises of the recruiters by stating that "inactivity and idleness" led to "misery" in foreign lands in the same way that it did at home. In other words, there was no earthly paradise in which they would not have to toil for their bread. Those who were hardworking could find success without emigrating. This cut to the heart of some recruiters' promises about the amazing fecundity of the lands to which they sought to bring migrants. This ordinance once again banned unapproved migration. Illegal migrants were to have their property confiscated, including that of their wives and children who accompanied them. They were also to be placed in prison or a workhouse for a year then faced the possibility of expulsion from the polity. Both legal and illegal migrants were forbidden from returning. Illegal migrants who returned were to be beaten with a rod then expelled. Those who had migrated legally were told to leave and faced the same punishment as illegal migrants if they tried to return a second time. Recruiters faced arrest, corporal punishment, confiscation of their property, expulsion, and in certain cases, the death penalty.[19] As historian Anton Tafferner pointed out, the sheer volume of these petitions is a sign that, despite the often-harsh consequences that faced both recruiters and migrants, they did little to stem the tide of subjects out of the Holy Roman Empire.[20] The push factors were able to overcome the binding ones.

The Habsburgs were both facilitators and impediments to the migration of Germans throughout Europe. While on the one hand encouraging migration to their lands, they also issued emigration bans in the 1750s and 1760s.[21] The fact that the Habsburg ruler was also the Holy Roman Emperor could lead to interesting conflicts of interest. After Joseph became Holy Roman Emperor in 1765, he apparently worked at cross-purposes to his mother, who remained archduchess in Austria and queen in Hungary. In September 1768, Joseph issued an edict as Holy Roman Emperor banning emigration at the same time that his mother was trying to use Reich colonists to populate the Banat. According to the decree, emigration had led to the loss of "many service-capable people" and caused depopulation. The decree banned emigration to "other lands that have no connection to the Reich outside the boundaries of the Holy Roman Empire."[22] There was a renewed call for corporal or capital punishment for foreign recruiting agents.[23] To what extent the authorities intended this to limit migration to the Banat, as opposed to the Russian Empire or the British colonies, is debatable. In fact, in another emigration ban issued a month before this one, the authorities specifically exempted migrants headed to Hungary.[24] The September decree itself focused more on sea travel for migrants, citing specifically Lübeck, Bremen, and Hamburg as main points of interest. Considering that migration to the Banat continued into the 1770s, Habsburg agents and the emigrants themselves obviously found ways around the ban.[25]

While the British only considered a ban in 1773, the French, like the leaders of the German states, actively sought to enforce a migration ban.[26] They were keen to recruit colonists for their own possessions and maintain manpower for the economy and the military.[27] They also had lands that were hotbeds of emigration, such as Alsace and, after 1766, Lorraine. Emigration even occurred from more westerly regions. When major movements to the East began occurring in the late 1760s, the French threatened migrants with forced galley service and the confiscation of their property. French authorities in Vienna also sought to use diplomatic channels to fight emigration. Furthermore, they authored unflattering descriptions of Hungary and the Banat to be spread in Lorraine to dissuade people from migration.[28]

Antecedents and Early Efforts at Populating the Banat

Despite these states' efforts, they were unable to prevent people from leaving and seeking their fortunes elsewhere. No matter how many patents they enacted or how judiciously they policed foreign agents, they could not address the underlying causes of people's desire to migrate and prevent foreign governments' encouragement of resettlement. As the Habsburg armies pushed the Ottomans out of the traditional Hungarian lands starting in 1683, they resettled their newly won territory. Although the settlement outlined in the *Einrichtungswerk* took no account of ethnicity, German speakers were already preferred to solidify Habsburg control of the region and ensure a loyal population, much as they were expected to in the Banat and elsewhere. Similarly, while Protestants could settle the land, only German-speaking Catholics were to be allowed in the towns and fortresses.[29] Tolerance only went so far, even in Hungary. The first *Impopulationspatent*, or decree relating to the re-peopling of the conquered regions, was issued in 1689. In this first call for settlers in Hungary, the author (Cardinal Kollonich) explicitly invited all comers regardless of their "rank, nation or religion," an open-door policy that would not hold in the Banat. The patent offered three free years from "taxes and robot" (*Gaaben und Robathen*) for "domestic" settlers and five for foreign. Such "free year" concessions became a central piece of all further immigration patents and contracts.[30]

Settlement in Hungary took place not only on royal lands but also on the lands of various nobles. Unlike the Banat, which was declared a "new acquisition" and thus all crown land, the Habsburgs returned much of the rest of historic Hungary to the nobility, provided they could prove ownership prior to the Ottoman conquest. These Hungarian nobles, new and old, also tried to recruit German speakers to settle their lands. In the early years of colonization, private landowners granted privileges on an ad hoc basis. Each group of settlers had their own specific concessions granted to them by their new lord. Many groups were given very similar privileges and over time this developed into a more systemized, standardized approach. A number of the contracts signed between the lords and their peasants survived and seem likely to have served as the template for later, imperial settlement patents.[31] Given this context, the mass settlement of the Banat based on a contractual agreement was not a novel idea but rather the understandable culmination of existing processes.

Even at this early date, the Habsburgs were not the only state looking to recruit German speakers to settle their marginally populated lands. In the same year as the Siege of Vienna (1683), ethnic Germans led by Franz Daniel Pastorius arrived in Philadelphia in the British North American colonies.[32] By the early eighteenth century, recruiters combed the German Reich looking to entice peasants away from their homes with promises of work, land, and tax freedom in Britain's North American colonies.[33] The influx of German-speaking colonists overwhelmed the British ability to deal with them. After the Dutch shipped a large group to England to relieve themselves of the nuisance of their presence in Dutch ports, British officials scrambled to accommodate them. Officials proposed a number of possible places to settle them: Rio de Plata, various islands in the Caribbean, the Canary Islands, or small islands off the English coast, as well as North America. In 1709, the government transferred 794 Protestant Palatine families, consisting of around 3,073 individuals, to Ireland. By 1711, 188 families were on the lands allotted them. In 1712, 254 families were settled "in the country," with 130 of them on the estate of Sir Thomas Southwell in the County of Limerick. As the region was rumored to be the staging ground for a Catholic army, the government used Germans, in this case, Protestant Germans, as a means of securing an unstable frontier much as they did later in the Banat, Russia, or Spain.[34] In North America, colonists were likewise viewed as a potential loyal frontier force to help resist Native Americans or foreign enemies and "populate the exposed border areas."[35] British competition for settlers continued throughout the eighteenth century. Between 1683 and 1783, an estimated 120,000 German-speaking migrants arrived in North America.[36]

The first colonists in the Banat arrived shortly after the conquest of Temesvar in 1716. They were, for the most part, soldiers and government officials. Soon thereafter, the need for merchants, artisans, and masons in the capital and for miners in the mountains forced authorities to seek outsiders to help fill the labor gaps. In 1722, for example, 450 individuals came from Tyrol to work in the mines in the eastern Banat.[37] The authorities also sought to bring in more German merchants, hoping to displace the "Greek" and Jewish ones who at the time dominated trade in the region.[38] The nature of the migration changed by the early 1720s. As field agents reported that the lands were depopulated and destroyed and that there were no sedentary people to cultivate them, the authorities realized that they needed to encourage more rural agricultural migration.[39]

In the earliest large-scale movement of such colonists, the Hofkriegsrat approved the settlement of 600 families near Arad and in the Banat in 1721–1722. The administration tasked Lieutenant Johann Franz Alberth von Crausen with scouting the region for potential settlement sites. In addition to this duty, he proposed privileges he felt should be offered to prospective colonists, most of which were accepted by the central government. First, migrants received land to settle. Crausen had located areas he felt were most suitable for habitation, and this was where authorities placed the incoming migrants. Secondly, the government provided them with "Imperial Free Passes" which enabled them to leave their current homes in the Reich and cross the maze of administrative boundaries that led to the Banat. They were given wood with which to build and to use as fuel for three years. They were also given bricks and lime to build in areas where wood was scarce. Interestingly, they were not allowed to make their own bricks nor were they allowed to brew beer or spirits. The government tightly regulated these activities. They were given three "free years," which freed them from all obligations to the crown including the *Contribution* (a tax) and the quartering of soldiers. The fourth year, they were required to pay one-third of their taxes, and in the fifth, two-thirds. After that, they were to pay as all other residents of the region. They were free to trade but were subjected to the same tolls and taxes as everyone else. Another concession regarding trade was the banishment of Jewish residents from colonial towns, markets, and villages. This seems to have been a means to protect or encourage colonial merchants and consumers. The final point concerned religious matters. The government provided for a priest or pastor for the colonists.[40]

Almost as interesting as what the government offered prospective colonists at this early stage is what they did not offer. With the exception of land and building materials, the government did not offer the colonists any material goods. They were not given livestock or seed to start their farms. They were not given the tools of their trade, if they possessed one. They were not given furniture, cooking utensils, or any other household items. In fact, they were not even given the supplies, including food, that were necessary to make the journey from the Reich to the Banat. The government expected the colonists to bring everything they needed from their current homes. They allowed all of these goods to pass through borders toll free, an important concession, but they did not provide the necessary tools for survival once the settlers reached the region. In hindsight, this was a mistake. It made the lives of these early German settlers difficult as they tried to adapt their old tools and practices to new conditions, hindering their ability to take root. The administrators of the later, significantly larger movements of colonists to the Banat seemed to have learned from this early mistake and provided much more in the way of material concessions to the incoming settlers, things that both helped them survive the lean early years and gave them a distinct economic and material advantage over the other peoples of the region.

German colonists recruited by Crausen recognized very quickly that this deal left a lot to be desired and petitioned to have it improved. In late 1722, early 1723, a group of German colonists wrote the government to ask them to cover the cost of the trip. They praised the current "prerogatives and freedoms" for giving them hope and courage as they left their old homes for their new ones in the Banat, but they wanted more. They complained that they were required to pay their lords not only to free themselves from serfdom but also to leave their homeland. Furthermore, it was fifty miles to Regensburg (where a boat would pick them up) and then a "quite a long trip by water" to the Banat, all of which they were expected to pay for themselves. The potential colonists argued that there were hundreds, if not thousands, of additional settlers in their home regions if only the costs were less. They went on to promise that if they were given the funds to help them in their move, they would be the "truest subjects," and that, furthermore, they would encourage their friends and neighbors back home to become colonists.[41]

Crausen himself echoed these sentiments in his own letter to the administration. He also complained about the transportation costs, though for different reasons. He indicated that he had already recruited and sent three hundred families from the Reich but that only forty families had made it all the way to the Banat. According to him, most of the families had disembarked along the way in Hungary and stayed there, poached by Hungarian recruiters and lords. Like the potential colonists above, he went on to say that there were many people left in the Reich who would like to emigrate, but if the government did not better provide for the trip, these people might not make it to the Banat. At the very least, the government needed to cover the costs of travel from Regensburg to Temesvar to ensure that they made it and did not get off the transports earlier. The government agreed that this was indeed a problem and authorized that potential colonists be paid a stipend based on age. All men and women over fifteen years old received a Thaler or 1 fl. 30 kr., paid *upon arrival* in the Banat.[42] This payment scheme forced them to make the journey and likely encouraged people not to abandon the migration early. The government also requested that this concession be made public, hoping to attract the "thousands" of families promised by the colonists and Crausen. This did not solve all of the problems, though. Population loss to Hungarian lords and recruiters remained an issue for Habsburg authorities throughout the eighteenth century.

From an early date, the Banat itself produced its own recruiters and the migration became self-sustaining, at least to a degree. Historian Dirk Hoerder has noted that personal testimonies and invitations from known individuals were more powerful than government recruiters in encouraging migration throughout history.[43] In January 1724, the administration in Temesvar sent three recent migrants (Johann Kasper Mehrberg from Bavaria, Reinhard Niebel, and Wendel Ackermann) back to the Reich to recruit additional colonists. In addition, they also carried letters from colonists. One official there, the *Amtsvogt* Vock from Neustetten, openly opposed their mission. He wrote that he would not recommend anyone migrating to the Banat. He said that "Nibel [sic] is a dumb, spoiled, drunk fellow and debtor, both have been hardly a quarter of a year there (in the Banat) and know nothing of the reality [*Haubtwesen*]; they blather in a way anyone likes to hear." He went on that "Christianity lies and remains buried in the Banat."[44] Perhaps because of the personal testimonies, this official resistance did not stop them from securing three hundred settlers.[45]

By the mid-1720s, the government sought to standardize and widely publicize the colonial privileges to further encourage such movements of Germans to the Banat. In 1726, the government released a printed settlement patent that listed the "imperial prerogatives and freedoms" available to "German families" who took part in the peopling of the Banat.[46] These privileges were much the same as the ones offered to the colonists in 1722: free land, free building material, freedom to trade as long as they paid the typical fees, four free years,[47] etc. Again, the government did not provide much in the way of material goods, explicitly reminding the colonists to bring food for the journey and artisans to bring the tools of their trades. Interestingly, Jews were again forbidden to settle among the incoming Germans unless the inhabitants of the colonial village wanted to allow them in their communities, perhaps a tacit recognition that Jews may have a societal role to fill. Germans were also allowed to settle in groups. If forty to fifty families wanted to leave the Reich and settle together in the Banat, the government promised to facilitate this movement. The government also sought to introduce some manner of quality control. They explicitly stated that vagabonds, beggars, spendthrifts, and other "unrealistic souls" were not wanted.

The most interesting new privileges enumerated in this document regarded the relationship between the peasant farmer and the government. Whereas in the Reich peasants were beholden to a lord, this document clearly stated that peasants were subject to the emperor alone.[48] This must have been an attractive offer to people who had long labored under a system that could allow lords to act with impunity. This privilege became a cornerstone of all future settlement patents, at least in the minds of the peasants, as reflected in their later reminiscences. When the Banat was "returned" to Hungarian rule in the late 1770s, and the court began to sell villages and other areas to the nobility, a return to a serf-like existence occurred. The settlers felt betrayed and looked back to this settlement patent as legal precedence for the freedoms they had enjoyed.

Compared to many other settlement opportunities available at the time, the Banat appears to have offered a better overall deal for prospective colonists from the Reich. The 1724 settlement contract between Graf Paul Ráday and his peasant-colonists in Hartau an der Donau (in reconquered Hungary) provides a good basis for comparison. Other than the four free years, a standard concession in most contracts, the terms offered by Ráday differed from those offered by the emperor and were more explicitly geared to exploit the peasants. After the conclusion of the free years, his total yearly taxes were higher than in the Banat. Peasants were allowed to have a pub for only half the year while the one owned by the lord was open year-round, another way to get into the peasants' pockets. This was a common tactic in feudal societies, including in Russia.[49] Whereas peasants in the Banat were freed from obligations to a lord, the ones on noble Hungarian estates were not. Ráday required his peasants to plow in fall and spring, to mow and stack hay, and to cut grain. They were to give him a pair of chickens and a pound of butter per year as well as the tongue of any animal they slaughtered for sale. One ninth of their harvest went to the lord, and they were required to transport it if necessary.[50] For colonists seeking to escape serfdom, Hungary offered little refuge.

While the terms of settlement in the Banat were better, the land provided its own difficulties. The combination of a harsh climate and a novel disease regime decimated the early colonists. The difficulties the German settlers faced, as well as their hardiness and perseverance, were alluded to in 1734 during discussions surrounding the possible settlement of Spanish military pensioners.[51] Graf Hamilton, the second governor of the Banat, was skeptical of the ability of the Spanish pensioners to deal with the conditions there. As evidence, he referred to families "from the Reich" who had struggled through adversity to settle the region. All family members including children had to work in order to sustain themselves and their livelihood. According to Hamilton, they were largely successful because Germans had been raised to work hard from a young age.[52] If even these Germans had to work extremely hard to survive, Hamilton questioned whether the Spanish pensioners would have to ability and wherewithal to become successful farmers. The difficulty the Germans experienced adapting to their new environment encouraged the government to expand the privileges in a bid to make their lives easier and to preserve their numbers.

This expansion was visible in settlement patent of 1736. This time, travel costs were explicitly covered. In addition to free land (which the author of the patent mentioned was very difficult to come by in Germany), they were also given five "free years," one more than offered in 1726.[53] They also sought to attract a better sort of colonist. To this end, all families had to prove they had 200 fl. This money would help them buy a house, a wagon and plow, draft animals, cows and calves, pigs, and enough food to get them through until their first harvest.[54] Though recruitment under this patent was curtailed by the outbreak of another Austro-Ottoman War (1738–1739), later patents reflected a similar attempt to save the government money while also ensuring that the colonists would become prosperous, tax-paying subjects.

Migrants against Their Will: The *Wasserschub* and the Hauensteiner

While most colonists migrate of their own free will, there are always some who are not given a choice.[55] The 1740s–1760s was a period of forced migration from Vienna to the Banat. This movement was known as the *Temeswarer Wasserschub* (Temesvar water transport) and involved the deportation of hundreds of petty criminals to the Banat. The movement of criminals and other undesirable people to the frontier has been a common tactic throughout history. The British were especially keen to move criminals and POWs to their overseas colonies. In the seventeenth and into the eighteenth century, such people were sent to the British North American colonies.[56] From the late eighteenth century, Australia was the destination of choice.

One aspect that separates the *Wasserschub* from other forced movements of criminals is the predominance of women.[57] These women were often cited for leading a "wanton or dissolute life" (often *liederlich*), likely a euphemism for prostitution, though this word is never used. The government's stated goals for the "incarcerated women" were simple. First, they would benefit from the chance at starting a new productive life on the frontier away from their old criminal one in the central Austrian domains. Secondly, their work as spinners in the manufactories of the Banat would benefit the government financially. In essence, they were going to literally "pay" for their crimes and detention. In addition, officials also felt that their presence helped the larger goal of populating the region. Both increasing the population and rebuilding manufacturing were major concerns following the Turkish War from 1737 to 1739 that had once again severely damaged the region socially and economically. The first two movements occurred in September 1744 and December 1744. These early forced migrations were deadly for the participants. Of the seventy-seven women sent, thirty-three had died by 1746. A further six had deserted.[58] Desertion was a constant problem and later manifests of prisoners sent to the Banat showed that deserters who had fled earlier sentences often were caught again in Vienna and sent back to finish their terms.

Even when men were later sentenced to serve time in the Banat, there was still a predominance of women. In 1752, a memorandum discussing the tenth shipment again stressed that the nature of the *Wasserschub* was partly punishment, partly to increase the population of the Banat. Of the eighty-nine convicts sent on two ships in early 1752, eighty were women. The overwhelming majority (55/80) were twenty-five or younger. The youngest were fifteen (2/80). There were only seven older than thirty years. The oldest was forty-three. All were Catholic. Most were single (74/80), and those who were married tended to be older than average (all married women were older than twenty-five). There was one married couple, Anna Maria Stenglin and Anton Stengl, sentenced to the Banat for vagabondism and theft. There were five widows.[59]

One of the most common crimes was "hanging around/roaming with soldiers" or a variation, again presumably a euphemism for prostitution. Such women were seen as a particular threat because of the potential for venereal disease to sap military strength.[60] Another common crime was leading a "dissolute life," which also may be a euphemism for prostitution, though this is more unclear. Other crimes included vagabondism, theft, burglary, begging, extortion, smuggling, and even one woman sent to the Banat for child murder, potentially abortion. Two women were convicted of inappropriate contact with a married man, presumably adultery. Two more were convicted of blasphemy, including a baptized Jew. For many, this was not their first time in the Banat as their rap sheets contained convictions for *Revertierung*, or coming back to the Austrian lands after being sentenced to the Banat. A typical case was twenty-five-year-old Catharina Wolfin. Born in Pressburg, she had been arrested five times, most recently for *Revertierung* and "hanging around with soldiers." For these crimes, she was sentenced to six years.[61] It is interesting that the authorities populated the Banat not only with criminals from Vienna but also from the German hereditary lands, Hungary, and even 104 people from Milan. Intriguingly, the authorities sent *only women* from Vienna in this instance.[62]

Women were an integral part of any colonization and population plan, which helps explain why the government sent young, single women to the Banat. While a number of German families settled in the 1730s and 1740s, there were still large numbers of single men in the region, soldiers, for example. Additionally, given the high mortality rate among colonists, and the dangers of childbirth, German women were likely scarce. While there were local women, the authorities wanted to keep sharp divisions between people of different languages and religions, thus bringing German women to the Banat helped prevent the mixing of Germans and local people.[63] By bringing women to these single men, the government hoped to solve a two-pronged problem. First, the women were given the chance to marry and work and thereby lead "respectable" lives in the Banat. Secondly, the men of the region could also become "respectable" by marrying Germans and settling down in the surrounding countryside. There are a number of corollaries for such an action throughout history. The English, for example, brought petty criminal women to Australia in an attempt to deal with the large single-male population there.[64] Similarly, the Portuguese imported women to their colonies to serve as wives for colonial officials.[65]

If the Habsburg authorities had similar goals, there is little explicit archival evidence of their success. As indicated in her criminal record, Anna Maria Griessbacherin married Ignaz Griessbacher, a shopkeeper in Temesvar. The marriage must not have been a happy one, as she was under arrest in the Austrian domains for vagabondism and was to be shipped back to the Banat.[66] In 1752, a Catholic widower originally from Bavaria, Franz Heuber, petitioned the government to be allowed to marry the Roma Regina Theberin who had come to the Banat on the ninth shipment of people. Her crimes were not mentioned, and the authorities could not establish her marital status. This holdup is the likely reason why this story made it to the archives. In the end, officials left it up to the court security committee to decide whether or not this marriage should be allowed.[67] While there are few documented cases of women from the *Wasserschub* marrying men in the Banat, it seems likely that this was a regular occurrence, if only for the fact that marriage would have removed these young women from the custody of the state and put them in the custody of their new husbands. Such matches would have supported the overall Habsburg mission of populating the region and would likely have been encouraged.

By 1754, the gender discrepancy began to even out. In that year, one shipment had thirty-one men and thirty-seven women. By this time, the authorities had also refined their methods. They divided the people in this shipment between those who were to work in the Banat as punishment for their crimes and those who were to be allowed to go free once in the region. Who was allowed to go free and who had to work in the "prison and workhouse" was largely determined by age, marital status, and criminal history. This divide was much more noticeable among men. Men who were older and married were more likely to be released than those who were younger and single. Among both men and women, individuals who had escaped from earlier sentences in the Banat or had multiple convictions on their records were much more likely to be required to work than those who were first-time criminals. The crimes committed generally mirrored those of the earlier groups: vagabondism, begging, premarital sex, and escape. Again, all convicts in both groups were Catholic, and most were single. Interestingly, there were more older, married men than older women, who were still predominantly single and under thirty.[68] This indicates the difference in official thinking regarding who would best further the government's goals in the Banat. Married men, like other noncriminal colonists, could be expected to either farm or seek gainful employment to support their wives and, later, hopefully, families. Women were sent to the Banat to provide wives to men who were either single or widowed, thus they were in prime childbearing years and single. Even as more men took part in the forced migration through the later 1750s and into the 1760s, the need for women in the Banat did not decrease and was part of the official thinking about the *Wasserschub* until the end.[69] In 1763, noticing the disparity between men and women in the Banat, the administration hoped to use the *Wasserschub* to bring more women to the region and restore the gender balance. Further, there was hope that these people would create families and become (re)productive members of society. This desire did not generally conform to reality.

From the limited view available, life as a convict in the Banat could be difficult and dangerous, especially for the women. Although they were supposed to work in prison or the workhouse, they were generally simply let free on arrival due to limited space in these facilities. In fact, many of the incoming migrants had difficulty finding work. After one group arrived in 1753, an official in Weisskirchen complained that the convicts were not only "poorly clothed" but also that they were also lacking provisions. The official suggested providing these individuals with three kr. per day from the

"Population Fund" until they found work, at the very least for eight to fourteen days.[70] Some lucky ones may have been able to find work as servants, but some unfortunate young women were likely trafficked as prostitutes. In 1756, authorities arrested the "vexing pimp from foreign lands and dangerous human seducer" Peter Rotini in the Banat. Although his arrest did not mention any interactions with the convicted women, it is not hard to imagine that he took advantage of this population.[71] In a particularly disturbing dispatch, authorities noted that "many unemployed wanton women" were being seized at night and that two were recently found dead. In response, the municipal authorities demanded that all of the unemployed women be rounded up, confined, and identified. Further, householders were to be notified not to allow such people in their homes or face stiff penalties.[72] Given the conditions and the dangers, many tried their best to escape and made their way back to Vienna, often only to be caught again and shipped back.

Although it continued until 1768, official views on the forced migration differed and eventually led to its demise. While officials in Vienna, including a very enthusiastic Empress Maria Theresia, were supporters, others, like her son Joseph and many officials in charge of administering the Banat, were not. For the former, the *Wasserschub* was a fantastic way of ridding Vienna, and other Habsburg lands, of their problem populations and perhaps was useful in reforming them. For the latter, the incoming people were not "of quality" and thus were of minimal help in settling and improving the land. The end to the forced migration came following Joseph's inspection tour of the region. He noticed that none of the goals of the *Wasserschub* had been achieved; the people neither helped populate the region in any meaningful sense nor were they important to its economic development. In his mind, it was a travesty of justice and as such to be ended. Joseph's opposition to the *Wasserschub* is interesting, especially in light of his own propensity for creative and horrific punishments. He believed in cruelty to dissuade crime. For example, under his watch, criminals sentenced to *Schiffziehen*, the pulling of ships up the Danube, died in great numbers after long, agonizing work. Regardless, he found an ally in State Chancellor Wenzel Anton Kaunitz, and they forced the discontinuation of *Wasserschub*. The last group of convicts arrived in 1768.[73]

This was not the only forced migration to the Banat in the 1750s. As a result of ongoing peasant unrest in Hauenstein (located in the Black Forest region of the Holy Roman Empire), the authorities banished several peasant leaders to the Banat. Hauenstein was part of Outer Austria, thus the inhabitants were Habsburg subjects. This peasant uprising had been an ongoing headache for the Austrian authorities since the early eighteenth century. It had characteristics of both a rebellion and a civil war, as peasants fought both the civil authorities and each other. The main dispute involved the encroachment of the abbey of St. Blasien on the rights of local peasants. The other dispute occurred *between* peasants as they disagreed on the best way to deal with the situation. As the abbey tried to exert more control, the peasants resisted, and the conflict at times became violent. The most explosive part of the conflict was the "Salpeter Wars" in the 1740s.[74]

Vienna worked hard to put down this rebellious behavior using both the carrot and the stick. When attempts at a negotiated settlement failed, the authorities resorted to hard labor, exile, and executions, especially for high-ranking rebels. They imprisoned some in Freiburg; they forced others to perform hard labor on the fortress there. In 1738, authorities sentenced Joseph Mayer, one of the ringleaders in the most recent uprising, to hard labor in Raab.[75] Before 1739, another place of punishment was the fortress in Belgrade where exiles performed forced labor. After the loss of Habsburg Serbia, Komorn (today's Komárom on the border between Hungary and Slovakia) hosted many of these rebels.[76] Conditions at the fortress were terrible. They were often forced to make do with bread and water. They requested that their families send them goods such as clothes.[77] They were eventually granted six kr. per day to meet their immediate needs, money which likely helped alleviate some of their misery.[78]

Starting in the 1750s, the rebels were sent to the Banat.[79] In 1752, authorities were surveying land on which to settle eighty Hauensteiner families.[80] In 1755, the authorities exiled several "restless" families to the Banat to prevent the outbreak of further violence.[81] Authorities had initially discussed sending the families to Transylvania. In the end, they decided on the Banat because the Hauensteiners were Catholic, and Transylvania had only been used as a land of exile for Lutherans up to this point.[82] Some of the migrants had resources; others were poor.[83] They were not to be settled with one another but rather in different districts or at least different villages.[84] Much like the "dissolute women," the "restless" Hauensteiners were to further the interests of the state through their punishment.

The High Point: The Theresian Migration

As we have seen, there were a number of private ventures starting as early as 1726 alongside officially sanctioned and forced migration.[85] These continued into the 1750s. Settlers Johann Adam Schmid (or Schmin) and Nikolaus Christ received travel passes to return to the Electorate of Mainz and other locations to bring settlers back to the Banat in 1750.[86] Similarly, Mathias Vischbach and Mathias Plesies, both born in the Electorate Trier though residents of Beschenova in the Banat, received passes to return home and bring more colonists. They were returning to Trier to handle some inheritance issues. They were given a "promotional letter" that outlined what potential colonists could expect for privileges in the Banat. These were very similar to the ones we have seen thus far.[87] It is completely possible that they recruited other family members or neighbors from their old residence in Trier to come with them to the Banat, as earlier colonists had promised to do. The temporary return of settlers to their former homelands was a perhaps surprisingly common feature of eighteenth-century migration. Even "Newlanders," German-speaking migrants to North America, returned to their places of birth to settle accounts, retrieve inheritances, or recruit settlers.[88] By traveling between the place of colonization and their former homelands, these migrants strengthened "migratory networks" that sustained the settlement of the frontier.[89]

In addition to people from the region returning home to recruit and bring back settlers, there were also professional agents who made a living through recruiting Germans and bringing them to the Banat.[90] Johann Oswald, for example, was a resident of Temesvar who, when called back to his home in Honzrath, Saarland, asked for and received permission to bring settlers back to the Banat with him.[91] The government later agreed to send him back to the Reich to recruit more colonists.[92] After his death in 1752, his widow Anna Marie wrote the government in Temesvar asking for the money promised him for bringing colonists to the Banat. She claimed he was personally responsible for the recruitment of 1,600 settlers. Although an investigation into the matter could only confirm 720 of the 1,600, the government in Vienna agreed to pay her the 200 fl. for which she had asked with the addendum that this payout was the most she was going to get.[93] While the government was responsible for creating the conditions for settlement, private individuals could undertake recruitment, often for no more reason than personal gain.

During the early 1750s, there was another officially sanctioned movement of Germans to the Banat that was largely driven by this public-private synergy. In 1752, Empress Maria Theresia issued another settlement patent. As we saw in the introduction to this chapter, settlers and their agents wrote the government to outline their understanding of the colonial privileges and asked the government to respect them. This type of petition was a common feature of this period of colonization (early 1750s). In fact, some petitions were so similar that it seems likely that the same people were writing them or that agents were sharing a template of what to write.[94] Why the colonists felt the need to reiterate their privileges is unclear. Perhaps they wanted a more explicit recognition of their status before they arrived. They may not have trusted the hand billets or the agents' promises and wanted an official government response to their fears. It may have also been a ploy on the part of the agents, who almost undoubtedly helped author these petitions, to receive a document that told toll and tax collectors that the people they were leading enjoyed imperial protection. This would speed up the process of movement and lower the chances that they would be delayed or have to bribe their way through borders. Whatever the reason, these types of petitions do not appear in the records of the other large movements of people to the Banat.

By the later 1750s, the number of Germans entering the Banat waned, largely due to war. The Seven Years' War (1756–1763) diverted the Habsburgs' attention from colonization projects and focused it squarely on the Prussians and the opportunity to recover Silesia, lost during the War of Austrian Succession (1740–1748). In 1757, Austria and France signed the Second Treaty of Versailles, an offensive alliance against Frederick II's Prussia, bringing the Habsburg lands into the war. Such a massive undertaking left little blood and treasure to support the colonization of the imperial borderlands. In 1763, the Habsburgs signed a peace treaty in Hubertusburg, Saxony, which recognized the borders that prevailed at the start of the war.[95] They now accepted that Silesia was permanently lost, a fact that made improving the Banat much more pressing.

While the war disrupted the German settlement of the Banat for its duration, its conclusion inaugurated an unprecedented drive to populate the region. One of the main impetuses in the beginning of this phase of colonial movement was the reintegration of deactivated soldiers into peacetime society. Soldiers or POWs becoming colonists was a common occurrence in Prussia, Sweden, and British North America, among other places, throughout the eighteenth and into the nineteenth century.[96] Getting these men out of the Reich and the Austrian domains, and placing them on the periphery, was a great means to diffuse a potentially volatile and expensive situation. There was a sense of urgency. The peace treaty was signed on February 15, 1763, and a settlement patent, which directly addressed soldiers, was promulgated only ten days later on the twenty-fifth of the same month. It was addressed to both soldiers made "duty-less and other 'followers' " who were hanging around in the Habsburg domains. The privileges enumerated here were similar, though marginally better, than the previous patents. In addition to land and building materials, the government offered six years of tax and *Contribution* freedom for farmers, ten years for artisans and professionals.[97] A less detailed announcement inviting colonists to the Banat appeared in the *Wienerisches Diarium*, the forerunner to the *Wiener Zeitung*, on March 31, 1764.[98]

While the administration was inviting colonists to the civil Banat, they were also more formally erecting the military border. This also involved the settlement of so-call "invalids" (those injured while in the military) and veterans on the border. By 1766, 1,800 men, 949 women (wives of the soldiers), and 487 children from "invalid houses" in Vienna, Prague, Pettau, and Pest had settled in the emerging border. Most were older men (forty to sixty years old). All were Catholic. The number of German speakers among them is hard to discern, with many listing their birthplace as "Bohemia." Most were either too old or did not have the requisite skills to effectively work the land. Others felt that they had already worked enough, and this was their retirement.[99]

There was no "means test" associated with this proclamation. In fact, although not explicitly offered in the 1763 settlement patent, the authorities did provision incoming settlers with the necessities of creating of farmstead. That help was not free, at least in the long run. Animals and material were provided to them in expectation of repayment at a later date (*Anticipation*). In the military border, housing was also part of the *Anticipation*.[100] By giving the colonists what they needed to be successful farmers, and by receiving reimbursement for it at a later date, the authorities hoped to both assist the settlers *and* keep costs down. Colonists with means were expected to provide animals and equipment for themselves, while poor ones received more help. For instance, the author of one document urged colonist overseers to provide "hardworking" but poor colonists with whatever they needed to be successful, including colonists who asked for "advances."[101] Colonists received a book into which their debts, and their repayments, were entered. Negligent colonists whose animals died or were stolen were not only hurting themselves but also hurting the government's chances of being compensated for its outlay. It is hard to tell how much of the money was actually repaid, though it appears collection was a major problem both because of the state of the account books and the lateness of colonists' repayment. In 1773, there were apparently 300,000 fl. in outstanding loans.[102]

The authorities had to balance fiscal prudence with the generosity needed to "pull" colonists to the Banat. The 1760s was a high time for colonial projects in Europe, and Habsburg administrators were keenly aware of this competition. The Russian Empire issued two calls for settlers almost concurrently with the Habsburg efforts (1762, 1763). The Manifesto of 1763 promised "very advantageous and convenient Places for the settlement and Habitation of Mankind" that contained "unexhaustible Treasures."[103] There was money for travel. As in the Banat, colonists were offered loans to set up their farmsteads. Rural settlers were promised thirty years of tax freedom, exemption from military service, and religious freedom.[104] This manifesto ignited a major movement of settlers. By 1774, 30,623 colonists had migrated to the Russian Empire.[105]

The Spanish crown was likewise active in recruiting colonists. The patent issued on April 15, 1767, announced that "for the comfort and use of all German and Dutch peasants, day laborers and artisans, youths and journeymen, young and old, single and married men and women, and small children" one of the "richest" kings of Europe had opened his "treasure chest," including money, animals, tools, and land, if only the people followed the instructions contained in the patent.[106] Here, colonists likewise received travel money and ten years of tax freedom alongside the land, a house, and the necessities for a homestead. Artisans were also invited provided they were Catholic, mirroring the religious exclusion practiced by the Habsburgs in the Banat.

The Habsburg authorities were acutely aware of both the Russian and the Spanish efforts to recruit settlers. In fact, a copy of the Spanish call for settlers is held in the archival fonds on the Banat. Both efforts put colonial administrators on edge. They banned the publication of the Russian 1763 Manifesto within their realms.[107] A report from Moscow dated March 19, 1767, noted that there were "more than 15,000 German colonists" in Tver on the Volga who were waiting for the ice to break on the river to continue their journey to Saratov where they were to settle.[108] They kept track of recruiters and advertisements.[109] Officials in the Reich noted that they had obtained copies of the advertisements used by the Spanish recruiters from Günzburg, Altdorf, Stockach, and Basel. The patents led to a discussion among ministers in Vienna and the Reich (including State Chancellor Kaunitz-Rietberg), the bulk of which revolved around the question of matching the privileges offered by the Spanish. An official from Basel was particularly interested in the travel money offered by the Spanish and Russians. A group of officials from Freiburg claimed the privileges offered by the Habsburg government were "almost [the] same" as the ones offered by the Spanish. Due to this, the officials hoped that the departure of people to Hungary would not be affected by the Spanish offer. As of December 1768, the Banco-Deputat, who apparently had jurisdiction over such matters, had made no definite decision regarding these issues.[110]

Local officials in Donaueschingen also noted the Spanish recruiters with dismay. One official complained in late February 1768 that because of them, there were numerous subjects asking to be released from serfdom and allowed to migrate. The authorities found this movement "alarming" and ordered that no subject be given the permissions necessary to take part.[111] A note from early March indicates that the Austrians were winning the contest to attract settlers, at least at this point and at this location. In it, the official said that although he had received word that he was not to allow subjects to emigrate to Spain, he had not yet encountered such subjects. Rather, the subjects who contacted him all wanted to migrate to Hungary (under which designation the Banat would likely, if erroneously, have fallen). He was writing to ask whether these subjects should be allowed to migrate or not.[112]

Despite the competition, the movement of migrants to the Banat that began in 1763 was very successful. In fact, it was too successful. By the early 1770s, the Habsburg administration was looking for a way to staunch the flow of settlers. There were two main reasons why this occurred, one political and the other environmental. First, there had always been tension surrounding the colonization plans. While many supported them, some opposed them, arguing that there was more money to be made through herding than through settlement. Others, like the future emperor Joseph II, thought the money spent on migrants, for instance, the huge outstanding debt in 1773, was out of proportion to their worth. By the early 1770s, the opposition to state-sponsored settlement was more forcefully advocating their position and gained the upper hand in policymaking. Aiding them was the second reason: a famine in Western and Central Europe in the late 1760s and early 1770s that unleashed a massive migration. The call for migrants had been so successful in the late 1760s that there were already more colonists in the Banat than could be adequately accommodated even before the famine. Older, more established colonists were forced to quarter incoming colonists, while some were placed in temporary settlements in the military border.[113] The death and desertion rate was staggering. More than one thousand families either expired or otherwise disappeared within the first year.[114] In 1770, Maria Theresia personally addressed the problem. She privately ordered that no more colonists were to be recruited. Germans in the Banat were not to be allowed to write friends and relatives in their homelands and encourage them to migrate. In a stark reversal of previous policy, migrants on their way should be *directed* and *allowed* to settle in Hungary on either crown or noble estates.[115]

Her measures did not staunch the flow and more public measures were undertaken. Newspapers were used to discourage people from migration. On February 11, 1771, Karl Franz Leutner, an official in charge of emigration/immigration, placed a notice in the *Carlsruher Zeitung* (newspaper). Leutner made clear that there were some serious problems in the settlement of people in the Banat. There were simply not enough houses or equipment to provide for the "large numbers" of colonists. According to Leutner, the government was going to be concerned with the settlement of people who were already there for some time to come. Therefore, the recruitment of more colonists needed to be discontinued. To this end, only those individuals who arrived at collection points, presumably in the Reich, by the end of March 1771 were to be provided with the typical travel money and passes. Those who arrived after this date were not to be transported to the region until the situation there had improved.[116]

This did not stop individuals from asking for money to migrate. Shortly after the release of this notice, potential colonists asking for assistance were being told that they had to cover the costs themselves.[117] The government even denied soldiers and invalids who wanted to migrate (the original impetus for this wave of migration). Michael Schmalmüller, who had served over nine years as a gunsmith or master gunner (*Büchsenmeister*) and was now an invalid wished to settle in the Banat. He was told that although he would be given land, he needed to pay for his travel costs, his house, his animals, and any tools he would need.[118] A soldier with twenty years of service was likewise deprived of the money necessary to settle.[119] There were few exceptions. Authorities even denied Susanne Junkherin and her two children from Lorraine. She requested travel money in order to be reunited with her husband who had been in the Banat for two years.[120]

The notice in 1771 was followed up a year later with a much more definitive one that effectively announced the end of all colonization in the region. On January 13, 1772, an article entitled "News for the Public" about colonization in the Banat appeared in the *Marggräflich=Burgowisches Wochenblatt*. Indicating that the message came from "high places," the paper bemoaned the state of the colonists in the Banat who had come of their own volition, having paid their own way after the suspension of government support for travel over a year earlier. These people were unable to establish themselves and instead had to be supported by the government to prevent their demise. The author went on to say that the Habsburgs were no longer supporting settlement in the Banat, and that while potential settlers would still be given land when they arrived in the Banat, they were expected to pay for their own transport and the costs associated with setting up a farm.[121] Perhaps even more tellingly, colonists who came to the Banat were no longer exempt from tolls on the goods they brought with them; they were taxed.[122] This represented a sharp change in government policy that had, up until this point, supported almost unfettered German migration. Unfortunately for the administration and their plans, the number of colonists outpaced the government's ability to deal with them.

Even this dire warning did not staunch the flow of people for quite a while. The archival records from this period are filled with petitions from individuals who wanted money to move to the Banat. They were invariably denied. Between January and March of 1772, an additional 791 families, 3,055 people in all, settled the Banat.[123] By September, an additional 592 families, comprising 2,506 people, migrated and settled in the region on their own volition and, importantly, using their own money.[124] This was the last significant movement of the late Theresian migration. By fall 1772, the migration died off. In 1773, very few people petitioned the government for travel money, and few were reported entering the Banat. Large-scale migration took a ten-year hiatus.

Regional Settlers: Migrants, Refugees, Colonists?

Thus far, this chapter has focused on the migration of German-speaking colonists. They were not, though, the only groups of migrants who arrived in the Banat during the eighteenth century. Wallachs and Rascians from the Ottoman lands had been moving north and west into Hungary for hundreds of years by the time of Habsburg conquest.[125] As we saw in the introduction, classifying migrants can be difficult. Meanings change across languages and time. When discussing the movement of local people the authorities chose to use different terms than they used with migrants from Western and Central Europe. Unlike the colonists, who clearly left one home for another at the invitation of the government, classifying and understanding local settlement patterns is more difficult. Were the people refugees? Colonists? Economic migrants?

Throughout the 1720s, there were reports of subjects both fleeing and returning to their villages in the Banat. In the immediate aftermath of the war of conquest, even as the government privileged incoming German-speaking colonists, it still issued calls for those Wallachs and Rascians displaced by the conflict to return to their homes. From the official perspective, they may not have thought that they were particularly good farmers or possibly even good subjects, but when faced with the prospect of having *fewer* subjects in the Banat or having the Wallachs, the choice was clear. Income and manpower trumped any other concerns. The calls also seem to have been directed at Ottoman subjects who might want to flee the empire, though this is a bit unclear.[126] In addition to attracting people, the authorities also sought to prevent the flight of their new subjects. In 1723, the central administration lauded the local administrators in Ujpalanka for their efforts in preventing local people from fleeing. In fact, they were further charged with tracking down and bringing back from Ottoman Serbia any "deserters" from the region. At times, the government even tasked military units with such retrieval operations, though sometimes these people returned of their own volition.[127] These efforts largely succeeded in settling the local population and tying them to the land, though the idea of local people as "wanderers" persisted. After the mid-1730s, reports of large movements of people out of the Banat decline, though, as we shall see, do not disappear entirely.[128]

Any time there was a war in the region, though, population shifts occurred. In 1737, five hundred "Catholic Clementiner" and Rascians wanted to leave Bosnia and settle in the Banat. In 1738, as we have already seen, Germans and some local subjects fled the southern Banat in front of the Ottoman onslaught. Habsburg subjects from Transylvania also made their way to the Banat in the years during and shortly after the war.[129] In those same years, there were also a number of Bulgarian Catholic families coming to the Banat and Transylvania from Austrian Wallachia. The bishop of Nicopoli and a Habsburg advisor in Austrian Wallachia, Stanislavich, petitioned the government to provide grain and salt to help support the recent immigrants and prevent starvation. He related that the most recent Turkish invasion forced these Catholic subjects to flee their homes, leaving many of their possessions behind.[130] Even wars involving neighboring states could be opportunities to increase the population. Writing in 1769, Maria Theresia noted that if war broke out in Poland, the Habsburgs stood to gain a number of migrants ("many thousands") who would flee the conflict between Russia and Turkey in search of "security." Accordingly, it would represent a "major advancement of the population business." She asked that her ministers devise plans for how to handle such a development in order to "best profit from these circumstances."[131] Essentially she saw "refugees," to use the modern term, as a possible boon to the state, a very different notion from the modern one that often frames refugees as a burden.

The next war in Banat, from 1787 to 1790, unleashed a similar flood of migrants in all directions. In 1788, six hundred Rascians crossed the border from Ottoman Serbia to the Banat. Their fate highlights the government favor given to the Germans. Unlike the colonists, these Rascians were given little. They initially worked as harvesters and farm hands near Becskerek, though when the harvest was over, they sank into poverty. They sent four emissaries to the emperor with a petition begging him to provide them with both shelter and provisions to make it through the winter.[132] The emperor's answer is unknown. This is not to say that the authorities treated such refugees without compassion. When the administration ordered the movement of a group of Ottoman migrants out of the military border to a place near Arad, they debated how best to provision them for the journey, whether in grain or in money. The author argued that money would be better because, among other reasons, the people would have neither time nor a way to grind the grain for bread, especially if the places that were lacking a mill.[133] While officials treated these individuals humanely, they did not treat them as lavishly as they had the German settlers.

In 1789, even more Rascians fled over the border. By May, 13,859 "mostly Serbs" had entered the Habsburg realms, in particular the military border. Monks from the Studenica monastery in Ottoman Serbia brought the bones of Stefan Nemanja the "First-Crowned," an important medieval Serbian ruler, with them over the border to Pancsova. These were later brought to Syrmia, then back to Studenica. More Serbs fled after the failure of Karadjordje's Revolt in 1813.[134] In 1821, Turkish refugees, fleeing attacks from Arnauts (generally Albanians) and Wallachs who were engaged in an uprising against their Ottoman rulers, appeared at the Banat's border. Officials, still fearing plague, refused to allow them to enter the state, and they remained at the custom house "like heaps of merchandise."[135] Such movements, especially of such a highly sacred object, reflect the fluid nature of the border. They further show how the Rascians on both sides of the frontier shared a transimperial culture and history, one that continually concerned the Austrian authorities, as we shall see.

Beyond people returning to their homes or crossing the border as refugees fleeing war or persecution, the use of foreign Wallachs and Rascians to populate the region had occurred since conquest. For instance, in 1718 Mercy extended the offer of two free years to any inhabitants of Wallachia or other parts of the Ottoman Empire who wanted to settle in the Banat. The government talked about extending free years to incoming migrants from Transylvania who planned to settle in Arad. Some emigrants from Wallachia were extended free years occasionally, as well. There is evidence of this trend in a document from 1752. It appears that emigrants "from the Turkish territory" were given three free years. The document seems to indicate that such emigrants who came "from time to time" were given such free years. It also admonished officials to be careful to keep track of these people so that at the end of their free years, they would begin to pay their share in taxes. This highlights the point that any inhabitant who could pay taxes and provide soldiers was better than no inhabitant.[136] Some Wallachs and Rascians were also given free years when they were transferred in the 1760s to make way for Germans. That said, they could also be turned away. In one case, the Ujpalanka administration reported that there was no land on which to settle incoming migrants. Some were even skilled workers, specifically in the production of charcoal.[137]

The settlement of local people differed from the settlement of Western and Central European colonists in crucial ways. Importantly, there is no evidence of large-scale recruitment efforts involving active methods of recruitment (pamphlets, newspapers, agents, etc.). Relatedly, while both the German and regional colonists were at times offered free years, German colonists were offered substantially more assistance beyond the free years (material, animals, etc.), even if that assistance was often in the form of loans. In other words, the government provided more "pull factors" for German colonists than others. In addition, the language of the sources is telling. In the documents, "colonist" invariably refers to Western and Central Europeans. Regional people were referred to by their regional name. This highlights that for the government, there was something special, something different about the German migration. While regional people might be stopped at the border and sent back home, Germans were seemingly always allowed to settle and colonize, if at times on less favorable terms.[138] German migration was only halted because of war (1737, 1788) and famine (early 1770s). As we will see in later chapters, there were developmental and security reasons that the Habsburg administrators wanted what was, at least in their minds, a more advanced and loyal population on the southern border.

The Beginning of the End: The Josephian Migration through the Early Nineteenth Century

One leader who did not think German colonists were key to the success and stability of the region was Emperor Joseph II. As we saw in chapter 1, the transfer of the Banat to the Hungarian crown in 1778 and Empress Maria Theresia's death in 1780 were watersheds. Joseph, unlike his mother, was not as interested in recruiting specifically German speakers or Catholics.[139] He believed that local people were cheaper and more likely to be able to survive the climate in the Banat. He claimed that "one of the land's own children, especially of the Rascian nation and the emigrants from Turkey or Wallachia will certainly be much cheaper and more successful in the goal of population increase than all foreigners."[140] He further lamented that "never has 900,000 fl. been more poorly spent than in service to this colonial endeavor. This money has brought few people, created poor villages and almost unusable houses, has not advanced culture, had led to deforestation, discouraged and discontented settlers, and finally has driven Nationalists [i.e., Wallachs and Rascians] from their house and home, making them disgusted and sullen."[141]

Despite his misgivings, some in the government continued to focus on recruiting Germans. In 1782, Joseph's government released a settlement patent that was much more heavily infused with Enlightenment values and material benefits for settlers than anything previous. Referencing the uninhabited, wasted nature of the region, the patent was designed to attract settlers to the Banat, the Batschka (the territory to the west, now part of northern Serbia), Galicia, and Lodomeria (both in today's Poland). In addition to a house and land, religious freedom was guaranteed to settlers of the Banat for the first time. The oldest son was exempted from military service. The length of tax freedom was extended to ten years. Transport from Vienna and sustenance until they were able to provide for themselves was guaranteed. Health care was provided. Importantly for their future success, farmers were provided with draft animals and farm implements while artisans and professionals were provided with the tools of their trades.[142] These concessions (goods, freedom from taxes and conscription) gave them an instant technological and economic advantage and unleashed another large migration of German speakers, the Josephian migration.

In addition to a better set of privileges, the Germans who came were subjected to a more rigorous selection process. The government wanted to ensure that only potentially prosperous migrants made the trek. There were three specific qualifications a potential migrant had to meet to be recruited. First, the migrant needed to have a pass from the authorities. Second, they needed proof from local authorities that they were good farmers, that is, that they cultivated their fields and understood agriculture. If they were artisans, they needed proof that they practiced the trade they claimed. Finally, farmers needed to prove that they had 200 fl. in cash. Artisans were not subjected to the means test.[143] How effective these provisions were in ensuring a certain level of competence among incoming migrants is unclear. Surely, some unscrupulous agents recruited anyone. Some migrants may have traveled on their own to the Banat, especially those who did not qualify. That notwithstanding, those who did meet the qualifications were well poised to take a leading role in the agricultural development of the region, especially when their competence was paired with generous government support.

While most Germans benefitted and prospered due to the terms offered in the patent, some did not. There were dishonest private landowners in the Banat who used the flow of migrants generated by the settlement patent to colonize their lands while disregarding the terms that had brought them there. The Temesvar administration directed one unlucky group to the estate of Lukas Lazar. According to the settlers, he only gave them one year of tax freedom and demanded that they repay him in cash for everything they received within three years. They requested placement in a crown village (i.e., a village still under the direct control of the crown rather than a private lord) where they could receive the benefits and privileges to which they felt they were entitled. Such complaints were apparently not rare and contributed to the image of the Germans as a quarrelsome lot, focused on their rights and privileges.[144]

The Josephian migration of Germans from the Holy Roman Empire was the last large-scale movement of Germans to the Banat. It officially ended in 1787 when the government declared that all "advantages and advances [of money]" were no longer on offer and that no more colonists would be allowed to settle government property. The government made this announcement in *Reichs-Oberpost-Amtszeitung* (an imperial newspaper) on March 13. The article declared that there were no more open places in the "Hungarian Cameral properties" and thus the emperor had decided to completely halt migration. It did say, though, that anyone was free to come to the Banat, provided they undertake the journey with their own money. They were then free to settle on private lands with the understanding that the government would not provide them with any further monetary assistance.[145]

After this announcement, no other major government-sponsored movements of people to the region were attempted. Although there were colonists still coming to the Banat or resettling within the region, the volume dropped precipitously. The land was now largely held by the nobility, a consequence of the return to Hungarian rule. As such, individual nobles could and did fund private colonization projects of their own estates well into the 1800s. For example, the owners of the village of Kleinschemlak, the Croatian Ostojić family, settled Württemberger families on their lands in the 1810s.[146] In 1828, Bohemian Germans settled in Lindenfeld to escape the "oppressive hardship" of their homeland.[147] The imposition of a 500 fl. means test on prospective colonists in 1829 effectively ended any noteworthy migration from the Reich.[148]

There was another type of migration in the post-Josephian period. This was the migration of the sons and daughters of the earlier settlers to other less exploited areas of the region. This resulted in *Binnenmigration*, or migration between established villages, as well as the founding of so-called "daughter colonies." This had been going on since the eighteenth century but became more common around the turn of the nineteenth century. In 1780, for instance, eighteen couples moved from Hatzfeld to Gerdyanus (Gertianosch). Two years later, fifteen additional couples came.[149] In 1807, Rittmeister Johannes Nepomuk von Rauth leased vacated land from the Hofkammer and reestablished a village there, Deutschsanktmichael, recruiting colonists from nearby areas. In Aliosch, there were no German residents until 1840, when Germans from surrounding communities began moving to what had been a predominantly Romanian (Wallach) village. There were also cases of Germans coming to the Banat from the Batschka or Zips (in today's Slovakia).[150]

While immigration to the former civil Banat largely ended after the Josephian migration, the Hofkriegsrat continued to encourage German migration to the military border, which was still under Vienna's control. In 1790, the military looked to replace population losses incurred in the Austro-Turkish War through renewed colonization from the Reich, among other places. Initially, no colonists were to be accepted from the Austrian lands, the goal being a general population increase from outside. Many of the new colonists were Evangelicals, allowed to settle in the Banat following Joseph's Patent of Toleration. They were given three free years, support until the first harvest, and travel money. In 1791, there were 725 new families consisting of 4,091 people in the Banat military border. For the Evangelicals, a new village, Franzfeld, was built in keeping with the principle of religious separation.[151] In 1799, Border Inspector Graf Colloredo called for renewed colonization with Germans. He further proposed to offer them ten free years. Both suggestions were accepted. This offer was so successful (about four hundred families came), that they had to halt migration in late 1801 and early 1802 because of a lack of housing. In keeping with Habsburg policy, Catholics were settled with Catholics, Protestants with Protestants. In 1821, thirty-five Protestant German families from Württemberg and Hessen settled in Mramorak. By this point, the authorities were no longer very enthused with the cost of bringing German families to the Banat.[152] After this date, no meaningful migration of such families occurred to the military border. Some migration of German miners also continued in the Banat's mountains into the early nineteenth century. In 1793, following the destruction of the Austro-Ottoman War, 140 mountain Germans were settled in the Banat. In 1799, an additional seventy families from the Alpine lands came due to a dearth of qualified professionals.[153] Interestingly, both the military border and the mountains remained under Vienna's control, which likely explains why they were still apt to use Germans in their settlement plans.

In a muted repeat of the forced migration of the Theresian era, the Banat became a dumping ground for French POWs during the French Revolutionary and Napoleonic Wars. In 1793, when captured French soldiers reneged on their vows to change sides and fight against their state, they were shipped to the Banat to be held as bargaining chips.[154] The administrators there used them to dig the Theiss-Danube canal, though those who took an oath of loyalty to the emperor were allowed to settle.[155] Those who decided to settle were to be treated "with humanity" and were to "become Colonists and Inhabitants of those uncultivated provinces."[156] The administration was even concerned with their spiritual well-being and brought in "French Emigrant Ecclesiastics" to minister to the soldiers-turned-colonists in "reason and Christianity."[157] This experiment had some nasty consequences. Disease ravaged the POWs en route. They were blamed for epidemics in Vienna, where hospitals were established to treat them. In one shipment, five hundred died at Eberdorff. Of the remaining 226, only seven made it to Peterwardein in the Batschka alive.[158] Once in the Banat, there were reports of "the most virulent contagion" being spread by the French, owing to the "strong liquors" they were given to prepare them for battle.[159] Other victims of the French and Napoleonic Wars ended up as colonists in the Banat. Tyrolean "freedom fighters" led by Josef Speckbacher took refuge in Königsgnad in the Banat in 1809–1810. Almost half died of disease. Some of the rest returned to Tyrol when the Austrians recaptured it in 1814. Others moved to Temesvár. A testament to the harshness of the region, of the twenty-two families that remained in the village, only one survived into the twentieth century.[160]

By the nineteenth century, the Banat had ceased to be a place of immigration and slowly became a place of emigration, a trend that increased over the course of the century. In August of 1806, a report came to the Hungarian treasury that sixty German colonists had left with "wagon and horses" for the Russian Empire. The colonists were reportedly leaving because they felt "extremely oppressed/dejected" (*bedrückt*). It went on to say that most colonists felt the same and were poised to follow their example. There was apparently discontent among the inhabitants of the Banat's remaining crown possessions. Individuals from these had requested transfer to the military border and were likely the same who left for Russia. The authorities ordered an investigation and further suggested that the border and toll offices forestall the emigrants. They also ordered local officials to report possible emigration attempts to higher authorities. One official stated that, although he had not heard of the recent attempt to leave for Odessa or some other foreign place, occasionally colonists tried to transfer within the Banat because of an overbearing lord or simply to seek out better land. He further stated that to the best of his knowledge, there had been no foreign agents in the region recruiting colonists.[161]

Such individuals took part in the settlement of the Black Sea region. In 1807, for instance, the Russian government welcomed thirteen Protestant families from Temesvár and Kula (in today's Serbia and part of the Batschka region). They named their community Franzfeld after the one they had left in the Banat (the Evangelical community in the military border), even though they were not the first colonists there (there were at least two men who preceded them).[162] Franzfeld in Russia was twenty-three miles west of Odessa, near the mouth on the Dniester River. Of the thirteen Protestant families, the authorities resettled eight to other Lutheran villages. Additional migrants from Alsace and the Palatinate bolstered the remaining families.[163] In the later nineteenth century, the focus of migration switched from Russia to the Americas, but the results were the same. The Banat was no longer a site of immigration but of emigration.

By the 1840s, some observers saw this movement as not only weakening German states but also as benefitting rival colonial powers. One such critic, Hans von Gagern, suggested to Habsburg State Chancellor Klemens von Metternich that a new round of southeastern colonization be undertaken. What this meant geographically is a bit unclear. Gagern himself implied that it would be in the lands vacated by the Turks following the anticipated breakup of the Ottoman Empire. Around the same time, Helmuth von Moltke suggested establishing more German colonies along the Danube, so that German culture would exist "from the Swabian mountains to the Sulina mouth." Such notions continued up until the Revolution of 1848. Anton von Schmerling said that the pacification of Hungary made large areas of land available for German colonization on the Hungarian plain. He further mentioned "the blessed Banat." Unfortunately for the viability of such a plan, it was seen as self-serving for the Habsburgs and as anti-Magyar and anti-Prussian.[164] All of these later plans came to naught.

The number of Central and Northern European colonists who settled in the Banat over the course of the eighteenth century is hard to estimate. Most of the numbers that one finds were based on counts done in Vienna as colonists made their way through the city. These numbers are problematic. First, as we have seen, not all colonists who went through Vienna ended up in the Banat. Some settled in other parts of Hungary or took their money and went back to their homelands. Second, not all colonists went through Vienna. As we have also seen, informal networks, like regional or familial ties, encouraged some people to migrate, and these individuals may have bypassed Vienna on their way to the region or may not have registered with authorities there for any number of reasons.[165] Also, after the erection of the military border, it is hard to determine whether the numbers given account for migration to both places or simply to the civil, later Hungarian county, domains. That said, some educated guesses have been put forward. In the early stages of Habsburg rule, between 1722 and 1725, an estimated 12,000 to 15,000 colonists arrived in the Banat.[166] There were approximately 24,000 Germans living in the Banat by 1760.[167] From 1763 to 1776, around 11,130 families, consisting of 42,000 individuals arrived.[168] A newspaper article on the region, published in the *Temeswarer Nachrichten* in May 1771, estimated the German population at around 45,000.[169] The population in 1792 was 90,000.[170] One hundred years later, in 1890, this number had ballooned to 430,644, or 24.2 percent of the total population of the region, largely through natural population growth.[171]

As we have seen, various push-pull forces encouraged an individual to migrate: the government, recruiters, neighbors, relatives, and perhaps most importantly, their own individual situation. Habsburg encouragement of migration varied over the course of the eighteenth century, though the level of material support continually rose in an attempt to ensure the success of the settlers. Despite the fits and starts, the migration succeeded in implanting a German-speaking element in the region that by the early twentieth century made up 25 percent of the population. In that respect, the populationist experiment in the region can be seen as a dramatic success.

Other aspects of the plan to colonize the Banat were less successful in hindsight, despite the authorities' best efforts. They had a vision for what the Banat should look like, religiously and culturally. They wanted a strong

Dates	Number of Migrants	Estimated Population
1722–1725	12–15,000	
1760		24,000
1763–1776	11,130 families or 42,000 individuals	
1771		45,000
1780		43,201 Germans/French/Italians[a]
1784	"6,000 souls"[b]	
1785–1787	3,000 families[c]	
1792		90,000
1890		430,644

a. These non-Balkan Europeans existed alongside 181,639 Wallachians, 78,780 Rascians, 8,683 Bulgarians, 5,272 Roma, and 353 Jews. Griselini, *Aus dem Versuch*, 45.

b. *St. James's Chronicle or the British Evening Post* (London, England), July 16, 1785 – July 19, 1785. "Last year 6000 souls settled in this Bannat.... These serve to replace the Wallachians who are quitting the Country."

c. *General Evening Post* (London, England), April 14, 1787 – April 17, 1787. This led to the creation of eleven new villages and 1,904 houses. It cost one million florins.

Catholic presence where ethnoreligious groups lived in isolation from each other. To achieve these goals, they ensured colonists were exclusively Catholic, expelled Protestants, and engaged in population transfers of local peoples. While initially successful, we will see that the advent of Joseph's sole rule in 1780 and the transfer of the Banat to Hungary at around the same time undercut earlier efforts at Catholicization and separation.

3 The Religious and Ethnic (Re-) Construction of the Banat

> With the exception of the existing population [landes-nation], no others but Catholic residents should be allowed in and to occupy the lands of the neo acquistica [neoacquistischen Landen].
>
> —*Protocoll: 15 May 1724: Response to presence of Evangelicals in the Banat*[1]

IN MARCH 1753, NINE LUTHERANS from Upper Austria, having been in custody for a year in Komorn[2] and the fortress in Buda, requested to convert to Catholicism. Detained for their faith, they were awaiting transfer to Transylvania, a part of the monarchy where their religious beliefs were tolerated. In Komorn, several of them had experienced personal tragedies. Maria Feichtberger's father died, as did Catharina Eleiger's, leaving her with 15 fl. 7 kr. Another woman's husband had died. They could not, and interestingly did not want to, be allowed back to their former homes. A return to their previous faith seemed too great a risk. The best idea therefore seemed to be to settle them in a Catholic community in the Banat, one "where there is good air and water." The authorities also hoped this would encourage other families, already in Transylvania, to see the errors of their ways and convert "back" to Catholicism.[3] If they did, then they, too, would be allowed to live in exclusively Catholic areas like the Banat.[4]

Though pleased at the prospect of converting some Protestants, the authorities in Vienna were a bit suspicious of the whole affair. They charged the administration in Temesvar with tasks designed to protect the religious integrity of the Banat should the recent converts be crypto-Protestants. For example, they ordered that these people not be allowed near the border with Transylvania, presumably to prevent any possible interaction between the new Catholics and their old coreligionists. They further asked that the pastor of the community in which they were settled take a special interest in them for the sake of the Catholic religion.[5] Both of these stipulations indicate that the government, while happy to (re)convert Protestants to Catholicism, recognized that such conversions were tentative. Exposure to their old friends or community, or not being sufficiently educated in their new faith, put them in danger of renewed apostasy.

Religion, and to a lesser degree, ethnicity, were crucial in determining who could settle in the Banat. In fact, potential religious conflict was one of the main reasons why the Banat was to be repopulated in the first place. From the Habsburg's perspective, the region needed a strong Christian population to act as a "bulwark" against the Muslim Ottomans.[6] Not just any Christians were acceptable. They also wanted a loyal population to act as a buffer between the Ottomans and the Protestant Hungarians.[7] The Habsburgs felt that Catholic subjects were more reliable and thus sought to "Catholicize" the region to some degree, at least until the reign of Joseph II. They hoped that a line of Catholic settlement would disrupt the possibility of collusion between their Ottoman Muslim enemies and a Hungarian Protestant group whose loyalty, given their rebellions and religion, was suspect.

In addition to controlling the influx of colonists, the authorities also sought to control the demographic layout and settlement patterns in the land itself. Throughout the eighteenth century, even after Joseph's more tolerant policies, colonial administrators were already thinking like later nationalists, separating people by religion and ethnicity ostensibly to preserve calm. Each "people" or religion had a village, town, or region to which they belonged, and mixture of these groups was to be avoided as much as possible. Though, as we shall see, sometimes religious affiliation trumped ethnolinguistic differences. Authorities feared that contact could lead to strife and unrest. In the official mindset, one of the jobs of the government was to mediate these problems and doing so often involved using the power of the state to separate people. To this end, the authorities often placed incoming settlers on lands that they had cleared of their local inhabitants, including some of the best land in the region.

What made the Banat unique was the amount of control the imperial authorities could exercise there. As a *neo acquistica* controlled from Vienna until 1778, they had a level of influence over policy and implementation unrivaled in the rest of the monarchy. This control extended not only over economic but also demographic questions. Much as the Habsburgs expelled Lutherans from the Austrian crownlands, but tolerated them in Hungary and Transylvania, so, too, did the Habsburgs police religious belonging in the Banat. It is no coincidence that such policies largely ended when the civil Banat was placed under Hungarian control.

Security I: Controlling the Religious Makeup through Migration and Conversion

At the time of conquest, the capriciousness of the Hungarians worried the Habsburg administration and led them to use demographic engineering in an attempt to mitigate the perceived threat. Already in the late 1660s and early 1670s, Hungarian magnates had attempted to disrupt Habsburg rule with the collusion of the French and Ottomans. Some of the rebels fled to Ottoman Hungary and began to arrange attacks from this stronghold. This led the Habsburgs to enforce an even stronger policy of Catholicization and centralization on their Hungarian lands. In 1678, the rebels united behind Imre Tököli.[8] One historian has described the conflict as a "war of religion" between the "counter-reform[ing]" Habsburgs and the Protestant Hungarians. This rebellion, and the short-lived state it created, enjoyed Ottoman support, and Tölöki even worked with the Ottomans as they prepared to siege Vienna in 1683. He remained loyal to them even when it was clear that Hungary was lost and in 1690, sought to conquer and reestablish Transylvania as an Ottoman vassal.[9]

A more sustained uprising occurred in the early 1700s. Ferenc II Rákóczi's rebellion (1703–1711) was still in the minds of the Habsburg administrators as they thought about how best to incorporate and develop the Banat. The uprising was in response to several grievances. Though he was Catholic, he exploited resistance to the Catholicization of Hungarian territory and the settlement of Germans in Hungary. He looked to the Habsburg's inveterate enemy, France's King Louis XIV, the Sun King, for assistance. He appealed to the Russians, and like Tököli before him, Rákóczi was willing to enlist the help of the Ottoman sultan in his rebellion.[10] Similarly frightening for Vienna was the willingness of some Orthodox subjects to support him. The Treaty of Szatmár on May 1, 1711, in which Charles VI received peace for an agreement to rule by Hungarian law, ended the aggressive attempts at Catholicizing Hungary and made it safe for Protestants.[11] It may also have made ruling the Banat as a "new acquisition" much more desirable. Ruling in this way, the Habsburgs could still enforce a Counter-Reforming mentality without having to answer to the Hungarian elite.

This was not the end of the threat from the Rákóczi family. After the collapse of the rebellion, Habsburg authorities brought Josef Rákóczi, son of Ferenc, to Vienna and attempted to instill him with loyalty to the Habsburg monarch. This did not work, as Josef fled for the Ottoman domains in 1736. After initially being ignored by the Ottoman authorities, his potential for rabble-rousing became useful during the 1737–1739 war. He and the sultan concluded an alliance that promised him control over a buffer state including Hungary and Transylvania. Rákóczi tried to rally the Magyars to his cause, offering eighty gulden to any soldier who would fight for him. The Habsburgs declared him a rebel, anyone who joined him a traitor, and offered a reward for him dead or alive. His intended rebellion was a failure, as few Magyar nobles had a desire to follow him.[12] Thus the *perceived* threat of an Ottoman-Hungarian alliance lasted well into the eighteenth century even if the chances of a successful partnership were low. This fact undoubtedly influenced Habsburg policy in the region.

Facing external threats from the Muslim Ottomans, outlined in chapter 1, and internal threats from the Protestant Hungarians who allied with them, the Habsburgs looked to their Catholic subjects as a source of loyalty and stability. Shortly after the conquest of Temesvar, the newly formed Banat Land Administration expelled all the non-Catholics from the city. This included "heathens, Jews, Turks, Lutherans, and Calvinists . . . all heretics."[13] There were even plans to expel the Orthodox from the city.[14] According to the Habsburg world view, none of them could be trusted as they were enemies of the Catholic faith.[15] Only Catholic Germans enjoyed "civil rights" (*Bürgerrechte*) in Temesvar and only they could sit on the municipal council (*Magistrat*).[16] As early as 1717, some imperial administrators were already planning on bolstering the Catholic population of the region. They hoped that through "exemplary living and gentle ardor" the Orthodox inhabitants of the Banat would receive "inspiration" and join the "true belief" of Catholicism. They further stated that the conquests, still taking place at the time of their writing, should be used to introduce Catholicism and help it grow. Such advances were aimed squarely at Orthodox inhabitants. Those locals whose churches kept Greek ritual but submitted themselves to the authority of the pope and Rome, hereafter Greek Catholics or Uniates, were largely left alone. In fact, the administrators ordered that one or two "Turkish mosques" in Temesvar should be given to the Greek Catholics to set up churches.[17]

The foundation of the Romanian Uniate, or Greek Catholic, Church happened as a result of Habsburg expansion into Transylvania in the late seventeenth century. The authorities saw the Romanians as possible allies against the Magyar nobility there. Before the Habsburgs took control of the region, the constitution did not recognize the Romanians or Romanian Orthodoxy as equal to the other "nations" of Transylvania (the Magyars, Szeklers, and Saxons). Such poor treatment made them particularly open to Habsburg overtures. By 1700, the Jesuits and Cardinal Leopold Kollonich were able to convince the Romanian Orthodox Bishop Atanasie and a number of clergy to accept the pope as the "visible head" of the church. In addition, Uniates had to use unleavened bread in ceremonies, acknowledge the existence of Purgatory, and accept the doctrine of the Holy Trinity. In exchange, the Orthodox clergy were put on a level equal to that of the Catholic clergy. In 1701, Bishop Atanasie formally cut all ties with the Romanian Orthodox hierarchy in Bucharest. He was then named the "Bishop of the Uniate Church in Transylvania," a position for which the emperor reserved the right of appointment after consultation. The union benefitted the Romanians by allowing them access to Catholic education, something that helped invigorate the movement toward Romanian equality and later nationalism. In the early eighteenth century, there was resistance to the establishment of the union among both noble and common Orthodox in Transylvania.[18] With the conquest of the Banat, the Uniate Church gained a potentially fertile recruiting ground. Uniates occupied a privileged "middle ground" between the Catholics and Orthodox. By accepting the pope, and thus Catholicizing to a degree, the Uniates were able to enjoy more benefits from the Habsburg largesse.[19] The Habsburgs, for their part, got a population that they could consider more reliable, at least from an ideological, if not a practical standpoint. It is also an example of the law of unintended consequences. In trying to solidify loyalties through religion, the Habsburgs helped sow one of the seeds of their own destruction, nationalism.

While conversion to the Greek Catholic Church was welcomed, Catholicism was the gold standard for loyalty. In order to promote the "implantation and propagation of the sole sanctifying Catholic belief in this land," there were plans to bring in Jesuits and Franciscan monks as missionaries in and around Temesvar. They specifically requested that they know how to speak Rascian.[20] In 1734, there was still discussion about how best to bring "schismatics" into the "true faith."[21] How seriously authorities took these plans is debatable.[22] It seems likely that most realized that the complete Catholicization of the Banat was unrealistic but felt it was necessary to pay lip service to such a lofty and pious goal. Even if this is the case, it is instructive of the ethnoreligious mental map by which some authorities viewed the Banat. Ideally, it would be a totally Catholic region: Muslims would be driven out, Protestants would be kept out, Orthodox and Jews would convert or leave, and Catholic Germans would control and colonize.

Empress Maria Theresia reinvigorated the effort to convert Orthodox believers. In her own words, she wanted "to plant the Catholic religion in all districts as well as promote the union [between the Orthodox and Roman Catholic Churches] as much as possible." Though this was to be done without "violence and compulsion," it shows where her priorities lay. It is especially telling that these orders were in response to some of her councilors advising *against* German colonization and the further promotion of the church union. They argued, as Joseph would later, that the Orthodox Wallachs and Rascians would make the best (and cheapest) colonists. According to their perspective, the discharged soldiers would be better used in colonizing the "German crown lands." As for the promotion of the union, they pointed out that a similar strategy in Transylvania had upset local hierarchies and led to unrest. They warned that a comparable project in the Banat could lead to similar results. They were further unsettled by the possibility that locals in both regions, the Banat and Transylvania, could make common cause against the Habsburg regime under the guise of resisting the church union.[23]

While the Habsburg authorities were never successful in converting large numbers of local Orthodox people to either Catholicism or the Uniate

Church in the Banat, they could claim at least some minor victories.[24] A 1734 report on the state of the region related the existence of a number of Catholic Wallach and Rascian villages, holdovers, in the author's opinion, from old Hungarian rule.[25] In Carrasova, for example, both the Rascians and the Wallachs were Roman Catholic. They built a church and got a Jesuit missionary. According to the report, this caused the "zealous propagation" of the religion. Given their Catholicism, these Rascians were considered loyal subjects and enjoyed the favor of the administration. There was even a proposal to exempt twenty to twenty-four Catholic Rascians in Caraschova and Szlatina from the *Contribution* in exchange for their help in combating the endemic robbery in the region.[26] In the village of Bekasch, the administration resettled the local Wallachs to make room for fifty incoming German families but left the Catholic Rascians to live with old and new German settlers.[27]

When prolific traveler Johann Kohl visited Bekasch (he called it Rekas, today's Recaş, Romania) in 1840, the Catholic Rascians were known as *Shokatzes*, and their origins were disputed. In fact, locals denied that they were "Rascians or Servians." Kohl heard three theories: that they were Roman Catholics from Illyria, baptized Turks, or Dalmatians.[28] According to statistics collected by Elek Fényes, there were 429,868 "Schokatzen (katholische Serben)" along with 828,365 "'Raitzen' (Serben)" in Hungary in 1840.[29] Macartney also mentioned a group of "Crassovans" near Reşiţa, a mountain town that had a similarly obscure Catholic Slav population, as a "transition people, neither pure Bulgar nor pure Serb." He further referred to a town in the "Western Banat" that had a similar population "now Germanized," perhaps referring to Recaş (though Recaş is more north-central than western). He mentioned two other theories for their origins put forward by other scholars: that they were Croats or that they were Catholic Bulgars.[30]

Despite these small pockets of Catholicism, authorities faced a difficult task in converting local people. Investigators complained that people in certain villages did not go to church unless forced and did not even know what Christians believed.[31] In July 1750, the Lippa administration reported that the inhabitants of Sabran were in no way inclined to join the Uniate Church. The local Uniate priest, Nedelkovits, cited them for denying the church. Similarly, the residents of Temerest expressed their desire to remain Orthodox.[32] Then in 1752, a report noted that Uniates in both Temerest and Sabran were apostatizing and rejoining the Orthodox Church (though likely many of these people had never considered themselves Uniates). The author urged the resettlement of Catholics to this area in order to bolster their numbers. He further said that twelve to fourteen Catholic families from Guttenbrunn could be moved to Sabran. In his opinion, this would settle the long-standing religious differences there.[33]

Whatever action was taken, this issue did not go away. In Temerest, the Uniate preacher there said he did not always feel safe given the unrest. People were no longer going to church. They were either not baptizing their children or having a midwife do it. Couples were sneaking off to Transylvania to be married by Orthodox priests there. They were burying their own dead.[34] In all the major life events where religion played an exceptional role, these people were shunning the Uniate Church. In response to the unrest in Orthodox and Uniate villages, Vienna ordered the Banat Land Administration neither to install any Uniate preachers nor build any new Uniate churches without the "highest consent."[35] The problems persisted. In 1755, another report on the situation told a similar story. One hundred people in Temerest, who had been in the union, now wanted to use Orthodox pastors from surrounding villages for their "spiritual necessities." The investigating official agreed to allow this but further ordered the inhabitants not to hinder the Uniate pastors in any way.[36]

Most local people were happy to keep their beliefs and proved quite resistant to the authorities' efforts to convert them. For instance, between 1750 and 1766, fewer than 150 Orthodox believers converted to Catholicism in the Banat, around the same number as Protestants.[37] With the failure of major conversion efforts, the dreams of a pure Catholic region died. The new plan was much more realistic and recognized the reality that local beliefs were not easy to change. By the 1750s, the area was to be the exclusive domain of Catholic *and* Orthodox religions. That is not to say that attempts to bring Orthodox believers to the Uniate Church completely disappeared. In 1769, Philippides de Gaya, a Habsburg adviser, suggested that further government intervention would help lead Orthodox to convert to Uniatism and thus make them more loyal. He proposed the creation of a press for Cyrillic materials, which Maria Theresia approved. In the 1770s, Maria Theresia twice tried to "Catholicize" the Serbian Orthodox catechism. Some church officials felt the official publisher of Cyrillic material, Joseph von Kurzböck, was also trying to encourage conversion to the Uniate Church.[38]

While attempts to change local religious beliefs were fitfully conducted, the exclusion of Protestants quickly became a central issue for the government. Initially, this was not the case. Some of the first settlers in the Banat were Protestant. Even Cardinal Kollonich, an important figure in the reconquest and rebuilding of Hungary, advocated bringing Protestants to the region. In the 1720s, Charles VI wrote personal letters to some of the rulers of the Holy Roman Empire asking for their assistance in populating the southern boundary of his domains to make it a "bulwark of Christianity" (*eine Vormauer der Christenheit*). While he focused on Catholic lands, he also sent letters to friendly Protestant rulers. He specifically asked that peasants be freed from their duties without having to pay. For their part, some of the rulers were suspicious. They thought that the request might infringe on their rights granted by the Peace of Westphalia. They feared (often rightly as it turned out) that their subjects might face persecution for their religious beliefs. Additionally, stories of the rough conditions in "Hungary," especially disease, had made it to the Reich, and authorities did not want sick, poor subjects to return home and burden the state.[39] Some Protestant villages, especially in the military border near Ujpalanka, were founded in this early period.

Protestant German-speaking miners from Upper Hungary, Austria, and later the Reich came to the mountains to reinvigorate copper, lead, silver, and iron mines there as well as found agricultural settlements. In 1724, Protestant leaders in Langenfeld sent a letter requesting a pastor with colonists headed back to the Reich to recruit more settlers. They promised him a better salary than he could receive in the Reich and further promised to cover his transportation costs. With what appears to have been at least the tacit understanding, if not outright acceptance of Governor Mercy, Johann Karl Reichard came from Adelsheim to take the job.[40] His tenure as pastor coincided with the increased persecution and eventual complete rejection of Protestants as colonists in the Banat. By the mid-1720s, the authorities were attempting to prevent these beliefs from spreading and rid the region of the Protestants who were there. In 1724, the Viennese government wrote the authorities in Temesvar that they had information that there were a number of Lutherans among the Germans who had come as migrants, including a Lutheran preacher and the secretary of the mountain director in Oravitza who also acted as a pastor.[41] They made clear that this was unacceptable. Any Lutherans who appeared for settlement in the Banat were to be turned away. Any Lutherans already resident in the Banat were to be expelled and sent to Transylvania or "somewhere, where their religion is tolerated."[42] In the spring of 1725, nine months after his arrival, Pastor Reichard fled first to Belgrade, then to Mercy's estate in Varsád and Kalazno, Tolna County, Hungary. Facing ever more persecution in Hungary (among other personal issues), he returned to the Reich in 1731.[43]

His departure did not eliminate Protestantism in and around Ujpalanka. In 1726, an administrator reported that two Lutherans in Petrilova, the schoolmaster and the mayor (*Schultz*), openly, and repeatedly, practiced their "heretical religion." While the administration decided not to punish them this time, they reminded local authorities that in the future they could face corporal punishment or even the death penalty. In Ujpalanka, a lower-level administrator, N. Unrein, and his wife were either crypto-Protestants who hid their religion from the authorities or perhaps were tolerated out of apathy or necessity. The upper administration accused Unrein of preaching a Lutheran sermon to buoy up his followers.[44] In the 1734 report on the Banat, the author admitted that "many Acatholics" had been among the colonists who came in 1723–1724. He assured his audience that by the time he wrote, "almost all" had converted to Catholicism.[45]

The discriminatory policies against Protestants that crystallized in the mid-1720s had economic as well as social consequences. In May 1724, Governor Mercy wrote the Hofkammer in Vienna regarding a group of Evangelical miners. Barred from practicing their religion, they had informed the administration that they were leaving in September for their homeland. To make matters worse, they were not Habsburg subjects (they were "from foreign places") and thus the authorities were unable to force them to stay "with violence and against their will." Mercy had to concede that these miners were of central importance to the success of that venture. He claimed that they mined as much in four months as others did in twelve. For this reason, their loss would be an economic blow. To prevent this from happening, Mercy suggested that these Protestants be granted *exercitium religionis* (the right to practice their religion) at certain times of the year but only in the privacy of their own homes. He further suggested that they be allowed to bring in a pastor from Transylvania to preside over the ceremonies. Importantly, Mercy was not advocating tolerance in any modern sense of the word. In exchange for these privileges, the Protestant miners would be required to train Catholics. Mercy believed that with this training, Catholics would be able to take over leadership of the mining operations within three years, allowing the Protestants to be evicted with no loss of income for the government.[46]

The Neoacquistische Subdelegation, the body in charge of administering the Banat, agreed.[47] While reiterating the official government policy that the Banat was to be home to only Catholics and Orthodox people, they conceded that in this case, the Protestants should be afforded special treatment given the economics of the situation. Their first suggestion was to try to convince the Protestants to go to Transylvania once or twice a year and conduct their religious affairs there. If this was resisted, then they could be allowed to bring in a pastor from Transylvania to attend to their spiritual needs but only under certain conditions. It would be allowed only once or twice a year. The ceremonies could not take place in the open. The pastor must have no contact with nearby Catholics. He could not minister to other Evangelicals from the Reich who may be in the region. They could also not speak ill of Catholicism.[48] In this case, the economic development and stability of the emerging region trumped the religious goals of the Habsburg authorities.

With the succession of Empress Maria Theresia in 1740, the official position on Protestants did not significantly change. Despite the pleas of her advisors that intolerance was economically destructive, she continued to oppose any loosening of restrictions on Protestant settlement, much like her father.[49] Under her rule, the position of most non-Catholics in the Habsburg domains, especially Jews and Protestants, deteriorated.[50] Renowned for her piety, she was a product of the Counter-Reforming tradition and sought to make the Banat, and the Austrian domains in general, ever more Catholic.[51] Under Maria Theresia's rule, even the "dissolute women" brought in the Temeswarer *Wasserschub* were all Catholic.[52]

The treatment of the "Bulgarian"[53] Catholics highlights the importance of religion in the minds of colonial officials under Maria Theresia. In this case, religion played the deciding role in the privileges granted to what were, in the modern vernacular, refugees. Many of these individuals were not what one would understand as ethnic or cultural Bulgarians. The Habsburg administrators referred to them as Bulgarian Catholics and Paulichaner. Although by the late seventeenth century, both groups of Catholics had lived in and around Chiprovsti for centuries, their origins were very different. The "Bulgarian" Catholics were the Bulgarized descendants of Catholic

Saxon miners who came to the region in the Late Middle Ages but who had never adopted Orthodoxy. The Paulichaner, originally from Armenia, were also known as *pavlikyani* and were originally followers of a heretical dualist theology. The Byzantines had transferred them to the Bulgar lands in the eighth century, where they formed one of the earliest Christian communities. In the early seventeenth century, Bishop Salinat of Chiprovsti began efforts to convert them to Catholicism. Although the Orthodox religious establishment as well as local Muslims eventually attempted to counter the Catholic missionary works through conversion efforts of their own, "the Catholic missionaries scored a clear victory."[54]

Catholic conversion efforts only worsened the Paulichaners' already poor relations with local Orthodox peoples, though the contempt in which their neighbors held them was a valuable tool for the missionaries. Also helpful was the fact that, although many of them still practiced various non-Christian rites and rejected some common Christian symbols like the cross and baptism by water, they did see themselves as Christians and did revere the pope as a "legendary, almost mythical figure." While the *pavlikyani* were receptive to the missionaries' advances, they proved resistant to the wholesale adoption of Catholicism. The missionaries decided that education was the path to complete conversion and to this end, opened schools and distributed books among the converting "heretics." Interestingly, the language used by the missionaries in their educational effort was a Croatian dialect, a fact that may have, though unintentionally, helped them communicate when they finally migrated to the Banat.[55]

The collapse of the Ottoman forces at the gates of Vienna and their subsequent territorial losses through the 1680s shattered the relatively peaceful coexistence between Catholics, Orthodox, and Muslims in the Bulgarian lands. Bulgarian Catholics, who, though ethnically and culturally different from the converted Paulichaners who lived in the same area, were at the forefront of a rebellion against the Ottomans. In September 1688, with Habsburg armies having captured Belgrade, the Bulgarian Catholics of Chiprovsti rebelled under Georgi Peyachevich. The Ottomans violently repressed this uprising, killing one-third of the region's population and enslaving others. Many fled north, seeking protection under the Catholic Habsburgs. The position of Catholics in Bulgarian lands was irreparably damaged and contributed to the later movement of Catholics to the Banat.[56]

Many fled their traditional lands in 1689 following the repressed uprising. Many of these eventually came to the Banat in the late 1730s and early 1740s. One aspect that made these people so attractive to the Habsburg state was their Catholicism. By allowing them to settle in the Banat, the state was populating the region with settlers who were seen as religiously loyal. In February 1740, the central government ordered the Temesvar Land Administration to allow the Catholic Bulgarians, who enjoyed imperial protection, to settle in the Banat. They were to be offered both free land and free years.[57] By 1745, the government had codified these privileges. Although there were several iterations, an important example was the document issued to the Bulgarians in Wincka (Vinka, Vinga, Theresiopel) in 1745. The colonists of Vinka were to pay a 5 fl. yearly head tax. They were given a certain amount of control over the local judiciary alongside the ability to elect judges and juries, though certain cases remained out of their purview. Interestingly, all correspondence with the government was to be in German while contracts and other documents written in the name of the community were required to be translated into either German or Latin. As most of these people had been in the Banat for a number of years, and thus had exhausted their free years, the document did not extend them this privilege. In fact, it warned possible migrants to Vinka from another Bulgaro-Paulichaner area of settlement within the Banat, the Pradium Beschenova, that they would not be extended any more free years should they choose to move. It further warned the town officials not to extend any privileges or "other conditions" to newly arriving individuals that were not being offered throughout the region.[58]

Although the Habsburgs often viewed the two communities as one and the same, as we have seen, the Paulichaner and Catholic Bulgarians were in fact very different. By the 1750s, the Paulichaner on the Pradium Beschenova were doing well enough to request an administrative separation from the Bulgarians in Theresiopel/Vinka. They also requested the propagation of a new set of privileges for another group of Paulichaner they wanted to bring in from Wallachia. They asked for many of the typical concessions. For those individuals coming "ex Turcico" (from the Ottoman lands), they requested five free years. Others, presumably from other parts of the Habsburg realms, would receive only three years. As always, wood, both to build and burn, was an important concession to seek. They asked to be excused from quartering soldiers in perpetuity, except during wartime. They asked for certain concessions regarding their civil administration, including the ability in certain situations to use, in the words of the official, their "foreign Oriental manners to judge, [which are] very different from those in the Banat."[59] These were apparently granted, and the separation of the Paulichaner from the Bulgaro-Catholics hurt the community at Theresiopel. The loss of the Paulichaner heralded a significant population decline. Where there had been 140 families living in Theresiopel in 1748, by 1751 this number had shrunk to 118, a 16 percent drop in population in only three years.[60] This began a long slide into decay. According to the author of a description of the Banat in 1789, the only difference between Theresiopel and "a common [*gemeinen*] Wallach village" was the name.[61]

The privileges extended to the Paulichaner and Bulgarian migrants were similar in many ways to those extended to the Western and Central European colonists. For instance, both were given initial free years in which to build their communities without having to worry about taxes and obligations to the government. There were, of course, many differences. Crucially, the patents involving the Bulgarian Catholics were "stop-gap" or "one-off" patents. They largely dealt with the situation on the ground rather than attempting to create pull factors for a more sustained migratory movement. The reality was that Bulgarian Catholics were coming to the region, they enjoyed imperial protection, and they could be made colonists. By this point, the government was already helping the German colonists financially with moving costs and the costs associated with setting up a farmstead or a workshop. This assistance does not appear to have been extended to the Bulgarians.

While the authorities under Maria Theresia welcomed Bulgarian Catholics, they continued the earlier policy of forbidding Lutheran colonists in the Banat, even potentially useful ones.[62] Protestants were forbidden to serve the Habsburgs in any capacity (civil or military) there.[63] Authorities issued a resolution in the early 1750s that all non-Catholic civil servants were to lose their positions in the government. *Feldscherer* (army surgeon) Johann Wolfgang Burkhart of the Orsova District was a victim of this policy.[64] Despite five years of recognized excellent service in the army, he was outed as a Lutheran and given the choice to resign his position and leave the Banat altogether or to declare himself a Catholic and reject his former beliefs. In a letter to the administration, he renounced his former beliefs in favor of the "sole salvatory Christ-Catholic belief." Recognizing that some may question his conversion, he explained that he did not merely become Catholic to save his job but rather it was something he felt deep in his heart. Despite the explanation, the authorities were suspicious of his sudden turn to Catholicism and had his beliefs confirmed by a priest, Calestin Jelinek, who confirmed Burkhart's change of heart. Now a Catholic, the administration in Vienna ordered him to be reinstalled in his old position or given one of equal standing.[65] He was not the only non-Catholic in the Banat to convert. Between 1750 and 1766, over a hundred Lutherans and forty-three Calvinists in the Banat converted.[66] While the Banat might not be a pure Catholic domain, it was at least to be free of any and all Protestants.

The prohibition of Protestant colonization in the Banat did not mean that the authorities completely shunned them as potential colonists within the Habsburg domains as a whole. In Austria, primarily in Upper Austria, Carinthia, and Styria, there were several Protestant cells. The government initially sought to convince them to convert and even sent missionaries to preach among them, often to no avail.[67] Perhaps learning from the experience of the Salzburg expulsions in the 1730s, in which their Prussian rival gained 12,000 colonists, Habsburg officials in the 1750s instead decided to transfer this population within their own holdings.[68] Protestants in Austrian lands were sent to live among the Transylvanian Saxons, their ostensible Lutheran brethren. This plan had the advantage of retaining them as subjects while banishing them to a place where they could do no spiritual harm to their Catholic neighbors. What the government euphemistically described as "free emigration,"[69] looked in practice more like forced migration.[70]

It was a quite clever solution to the "problem" of multiconfessionalism in the Austrian lands and mirrored what the Habsburg state was doing in the Banat. Authorities wanted a compartmentalized state where each village, town, region, or crown land was as uniform as possible. In this case, the Austrian lands were to be Catholic, the Banat was to be Catholic (and by necessity Orthodox as well), and Transylvania could be Orthodox and Protestant, whether Austrian-Protestant or Lutheran-Transylvanian Saxon. By sectioning off parts of their domains for nonconforming groups, they were able to achieve a level of homogeneity, especially in regions deemed important for stability and security, while avoiding the loss of the population that would have accompanied outright expulsion.

The Catholic Banat played a central role in the movement of Protestants to Transylvania. In the best-case scenario, the Austrian Protestants were put on ships in Klosterneuburg, a town just north of Vienna and traveled down the Danube to the Theiss River. From there, they were taken by canal to Temesvar, then overland to Transylvania. The authorities worried about the religious integrity of the Catholic population along the route. And perhaps they were right to fret. In mid-1752, for example, a group of four men, seven women, and three children from Styria appeared at the border of the Banat, when they were supposed to be in the fortress at Komorn. The Temesvar administration wrote to Vienna asking for advice, which replied in no uncertain terms that Protestants would not be tolerated there. They demanded that the local authorities track these people down. From the authorities' perspective, they belonged in Transylvania.[71] To prevent potential problems in the future, they ordered that the Lutherans be brought across the Banat as quickly as possible and given over to the Saxon authorities in Müllenbach (today's Sebes, Romania). They were under no circumstance to allow *any* Lutherans to remain in the Banat.[72]

It is important to note that although these people may have been forced into moving to Transylvania, the government did not wish them any overt harm. They saw the "migration" to Hungary as good for the Protestants as well. They would be able to practice their religion freely and openly. They would be able to help each other as coreligionists.[73] While perhaps unintentional, the process did lead to many deaths. Of the 677 heads of family recorded as having made the trek from Upper Austria to Transylvania from 1752–1756, 234 died before 1760, a loss of 35 percent of the migrants in the first years.[74] Konrad Schünemann put the losses even higher. He claimed that of the 2,724 Protestants brought to Transylvania between 1752 and 1756, 1,208 died (44 percent).[75] Forced migration was devastating for the Protestants.

The enforced religious uniformity in the Banat did not change in 1763 with the new call for settlement that coincided with the conclusion of the Seven Years' War.[76] In the settlement patent, the religious rules separating Catholic and Protestant regions were maintained. In it, the authorities allowed settlement of people of the "Augsburg confession and Reformed religion" as well as free exercise of religion in Hungary and Transylvania but *not* the Banat. The requirements to settle in the military border regions of the Banat were the same. Only Catholics had the right to settle in these sensitive areas because they were seen as more reliable and loyal. Those who chose to would enjoy the same benefits the Habsburgs had extended to the current residents in the military border.[77] There were also tentative plans to settle Prussian POWs in the Banat, but they never came to fruition. The Prussians' Protestantism made them undesirable colonists.[78] This crucial settlement decree, which began the movement of tens of thousands to the Banat and Hungary, reaffirmed the exclusive Catholic nature of the Banat and the desire to use Hungary and Transylvania as a destination for religious dissidents. In 1768, Empress Maria Theresia herself reiterated that no Protestants could settle in the Banat in a resolution on settlement in the Banat and Hungary.[79]

Though they desperately wanted settlers, they were also desperate to prevent Protestant penetration. As we saw in the introduction to the chapter, the outcome of these often-contradictory impulses was to offer potential Protestant colonists the option of conversion. When a retired soldier, Johann Peiser, and his wife sought to settle in the region, the government responded that if they converted to Catholicism, they would receive permission.[80] In at least one case, the authorities floated the idea of removing children "out of Christian love" from an Evangelical mother and placing them with Catholic parents.[81] Whether the individuals themselves truly discarded their old beliefs and embraced Catholicism, or whether they made a tactical decision based on the options they were presented, is unknowable. In either case, it shows the extent to which religion remained a deciding factor in the colonization of the Banat before the succession of the more tolerant Emperor Joseph II.

The combination of Joseph's succession and the transfer of the Banat to the Hungarian crown completely upended the religious order that had predominated there since 1716. The Patent of Toleration issued in 1781 publicized the end of discrimination against Lutheran, Calvinist, and Orthodox subjects. In December 1781, another patent allowed Protestants previously displaced by Habsburg authorities to return to their former homes in Austrian crown lands without fear of penalty.[82] The settlement patent of 1782 guaranteed religious freedom to colonists of tolerated faiths. While not included in the patent, restrictions and official discrimination against Jews also lessened. Uniates faced a unique set of circumstances. In Transylvania, many Uniates took the opportunity offered by the Patent of Toleration to convert to Orthodoxy. Joseph responded in a decree on August 20, 1782, by threatening to punish anyone who tried to convert a Roman Catholic or Uniate to Orthodoxy. The decree further stipulated that anyone who wished to convert out of the Catholic or Uniate Church complete a six-week course of instruction.[83] Thus while an important step toward toleration, Joseph's patents were not an open-ended invitation to practice religion in any way one might choose.

In addition to Joseph's policy changes, the Banat was now under Hungarian sovereignty, and Hungary, including Transylvania, was a place where Protestants had been more or less tolerated since 1711. After 1778, the Banat became part of this cultural sphere, distancing it from the former anti-Protestant policies that had emanated from Maria Theresia's Vienna. It also ceased to exist as a distinct political entity and was absorbed into the political and geographical structure of Hungary, further undermining its uniqueness as a potential compact Catholic space within a sea of Orthodoxy. This combination of Joseph's tolerance and the Banat's administrative handover opened the region to settlement by Lutherans and other Protestants.

They responded to the opening. As we saw, the movement of Protestants was particularly pronounced in the military border. By the nineteenth century, there were Evangelical communities of varying sizes throughout the Banat. To this day, their churches stand in the Serbian towns of Kikinda, Pancsova, and Zrenjanin (Becskerek), though the community of believers no longer exists. In Kikinda, for instance, a list of the births/marriages/deaths in 1853 can give us an idea of the relative size of each community there in the mid-nineteenth century. For Catholics, the numbers were 198/59/118, for Orthodox: 594/160/335, and for Evangelicals: 9/2/5. Perhaps most interestingly is the language in which the communities reported their numbers: Catholics in Hungarian, Orthodox in Serbian, Evangelicals in German.[84]

The idea that Catholics and non-Catholics had to be kept separated persisted despite the changes in policy under Joseph II. In 1798, for instance, Kameralpräfekt Johann Kovats suggested bringing in only Roman Catholic settlers to the village of Gyapju (a village located between Szalonta and Grosswardein).[85] Kovats justified his suggestion by arguing that having two religions in the community would make life difficult for the people there. They would have to fund two churches instead of one and the land allocated to the current church would have to be split. He further believed that this would lead to "disputes" between the two communities. The government, in turn, would be required to intervene in these disputes, costing it time and money.[86] Thus, even with the increased toleration under Joseph, ideas about separation and peacefulness remained.

Security II: Land Transfers and Mono-Ethno-Religious Settlement

The Habsburgs were attempting to remake the region into an integral part of their empire, a Catholic space, and a strong defensive border against a hostile enemy. Given these goals, the movement of certain populations and the promotion of others was an unavoidable part of this transformation. In general, this meant the expulsion or transfer of "Eastern" peoples (Muslims, Wallachs, and to a lesser extent, Rascians) in favor of "Western" peoples (mostly Germans and northern European colonists and to a lesser extent Spaniards and Italians). As one official stated, it was "against the highest ethos . . . to mix Wallachs and Germans."[87] Though there were some notable exceptions to this rule, especially when religious considerations trumped ethnic ones, the maxim held sway from conquest until the ascension of Joseph II.

The capture of the land itself was violent and initiated the first, though by no means last, dispossession of a standing population. One of Prince Eugene's first acts upon capturing the fortress of Temesvar was to expel all "*Turks, Jews*, and other Inhabitants" (emphasis in original).[88] For Savoy, Jews were Eastern and were fonder of the Turks than the Christians.[89] Christians who had adopted Islam freely in the past were free to go with the expelled Muslim army. Perhaps fearing recent forcible conversion, those who had only recently converted could be prevented from leaving. The newly arrived German Bürger asked to turn the mosques into churches and the Turkish baths into a Rathaus. They also asked for permission to dispose of the property of the non-Catholic Rascians expelled from the city.[90] Muslims throughout the Banat either fled with the Ottoman armies or were expelled.[91] Osman Ağa, a diplomat and translator for the Pasha of Temesvar, related all the tragedy that befell him when the Habsburgs gained control of the region. He lost everything, including the fief he had received from the pasha for his services. Even more tragic, his wife and family died in an explosion in Belgrade. In the end, with nothing left for him in the region, he moved to Istanbul, where he lived until his death.[92] Many other Muslim Ottomans shared similar fates.

While Muslims faced outright expulsion, Orthodox Christians confronted intraregional displacement to make room for incoming Catholic settlers.[93] Despite the fact that the administration described the region as "sparsely inhabited" and "depopulated," Wallachs, and occasionally Rascians, were forced from their homes and lands and replaced with colonists. In 1722, Crausen, the Banat's first major recruiter, pushed hard for land confiscation and redistribution to incoming settlers. In Lippa, he suggested that all the Wallach and Rascian residents should be rounded up and concentrated in a certain area of the city, their former property then divided among incoming migrants. While Mercy and the Hofkriegsrat rejected this proposal as impractical, they ordered that the Germans be settled on the former lands of the Turkish fiscal wine gardens and fields there. While they did not take over lands from current inhabitants, they were settled on lands that had enormous potential and that gave them an agricultural head start. The settlement of colonists on some of the best land or, at least, land that had already been broken and tamed, became a pattern observable throughout the whole of the eighteenth century.

While the plan to resettle Lippa was scuttled, the government did approve of other large-scale dispossessions proposed by Crausen. The Moldova area (today's Moldova Nouă in Romania), including the villages of Radima, Bohseschena, and Pohmak, was to be cleared of its inhabitants. German colonists were to take possession of the farmlands, fields, and wineries.[94] The local people were to be resettled in Biel Breska. In the area around Oravitza, where Crausen had indicated that around three hundred families could be settled, Mercy ordered any Wallachs who had not yet vacated the fiscal wineries there be removed and again the land was to go to Germans. In Jarmatha (or Jahrmarkt, a village near Temesvar), a place that also saw later displacement during the Theresian settlement, the government ordered that, to protect their well-being, the Germans who settled there were to be separated from the Rascians who currently inhabited the area. There were some areas that were considered sufficiently populated and thus not good candidates for settlement, for example, Facset, Lugoj, and Caransebes. Why the administration chose to clear some areas of their current inhabitants and not others is unclear. Later evidence indicates that there was likely a dual desire to settle Germans in areas deemed important for the security of the Banat as a whole and to create monoethnic communities. This facilitated both ease of administration as one language and religion simplified the implementation of the government's will and also hindered interethnic and interconfessional violence. The government in Vienna recognized this could be a problem, especially given the disruptive nature of the colonial settlement. In fact, they advised against moving local people in Oravitza and Prostain precisely for the fact that this could stir up resentment (*Odium*) against the incoming Germans, who, speaking German and wearing German clothes, would be easy targets. Additionally, while Mercy said he would like to move these people, they had a strong connection to the land through their ancestors and would likely prove very troublesome. These two facts combined to save the locals from dislocation.[95]

The fear that the extant population would target Germans and their settlements was not unfounded and ultimately led to the consideration of grander dislocation plans. During the Austro-Turkish War of 1737–1739, some of the Wallach population participated in the decimation of Habsburg mines and German settlements in the southern Banat.[96] In and around Oravitza, precisely the spot that worried earlier Habsburg administrators, the destruction caused by the combined efforts of the Ottomans and the Wallachs had been particularly widespread. Wallach dissidents were also active in Orsova. After the war, given the apparent anti-Austrian leanings of the Wallach population, and the fact that Orsova was now on the front line with the Ottoman domains, elements within the government suggested their wholesale dispossession and replacement with German Catholic, or at the very least Catholic, settlers. One even suggested the expulsion of peasants (which would have been mostly Wallachs) from the whole southern border. Although it is unclear to what extent these plans were put into action, they do indicate the government's thinking vis-à-vis German settlement and local displacement. Locals were untrustworthy subjects and, given the volatile geopolitical situation in the southern reaches of the Habsburg realms, could at any time side with the Ottoman enemy.[97]

As with the German settlements, the local Orthodox population experienced the power of the state to disrupt their lives with the establishment of Bulgaro-Catholic settlement at Vinka (Theresiopel). The government ordered the land currently occupied by the Callugian (Orthodox) Monastery of Hodos vacated and the land turned over to the Bulgarians. In 1745, the Temesvar administration informed the Orthodox patriarch of the situation.[98] The monks were transferred from a monastery that they had inhabited for a hundred years. Shortly thereafter, they wrote to the government to complain that the land they received in compensation for their old monastery was insufficient. The government's response was direct and dismissive: the land they were given had been surveyed and was fine. According to the administration, the reason the brothers were complaining was because their new land was not near a village. Therefore, the six monks who lived there were unable to exploit the villagers for money and labor and thus were angry.[99] In this case, the Bulgarians' religion gave them precedence over the Orthodox monks. While resettlement was almost exclusively intended to support German colonists, it could also support other religiously acceptable populations.

When the religious unrest in Temerest and Sabran broke out in the early 1750s, authorities devised a potential plan to mediate the problem based on population transfers. In Temerest, the church saw no path forward for the union there and suggested displacing all the residents and resettling the village with adherents of either the Catholic or the Uniate Church. In Sabran, one author suggested moving both the Uniate and Orthodox families and giving the land to the *German* community of Guttenbrunn.[100] At the same time, the Roma of Sabran complained to the Banat administration about land taken away from them by the local Lippa administration and given to incoming German settlers of Guttenbrunn. The administration ordered the Roma placed in the villages of Kisfalud or Sefdin.[101] This problem was persistent. In 1785, after the succession of Joseph II, the government ordered the Greek Catholic residents of Sabran *not* to be moved to Temesvár or Arad. Instead, they were to be left in Sabran and urged to make better use of the land.[102] While it is unclear whether or to what extent any of these population transfers took place, and in some cases it appears they did not, it highlights the government's stance that displacement was a potential solution to discontent. The situation also shows the change in policy that accompanied Joseph's succession.

Such dispossessions and the forced movement of local people became a tactic in accommodating the incoming German settlers. In the late 1740s, Wallach migrants from Transylvania were relocated, with some refusing to leave. The reason given for the displacement was the authority's desire to have the Germans near mulberry trees, a key component of the silk production they were to help create.[103] In addition, the government felt that the Germans would be better able to exploit the fruit and grapevines they planned to have there. Finally, the authorities hoped that in case of hostilities with the Turks, the Germans could be armed and brought to help defend Temesvar. The remaining Wallach families wrote to Vienna to protest their movement, but their pleas were denied. If they persisted in their obstinacy, Maria Theresia threatened them with deportation to Transylvania.[104] In this situation, the government calculated that the presence of colonists would bring more economic and security benefits than harm. Though much as with the authorities' anti-Protestant plans, economic concerns could trump the forced migration of local people, especially those who were paying taxes.[105]

The same impulse to strengthen border defenses that drove the dispossession and resettlement of Wallachs and Rascians along the border following the 1737–1739 war was visible in further movements of people in the 1760s. In Transylvania, for example, officials gave Orthodox Wallach residents of the border region a choice. They could either convert to the Uniate Church or they would be expelled and replaced with Catholic settlers. While Rascian residents in the Banat were not proselytized, they, too, were slated for removal from the area's southern border that had been designated for incoming Catholic military veterans. Only the intervention of the empress saved them from complete removal. Instead, they, too, were given a choice. They could either become Grenzer and remain or choose to retain civilian status and be removed. Initially, even those who chose to take on Grenzer status, artisans and traders excepted, were to be removed from areas settled by Germans but, in practice, they were allowed to remain in the "German border." Those who moved were given uninhabited land and free years and were paid for the houses they left behind.[106]

In the early years of the late Theresian migration in the civil Banat, there was again a lot of discussion about the best way to accommodate the predicted large numbers of colonists. When local officials asked permission to investigate where to settle colonists, they specifically mentioned that they wanted to explore with which local villages colonists would have to compete and explore the option of removing them and replacing them with German communities.[107] In July 1765, the government in Vienna authorized the Land Administration to carry out forced resettlement but only on a case-by-case basis. The central government was particularly keen to settle Germans in the area between the Marosch, Theiss, and Bega Rivers. The reasons for the transfer, explicitly enumerated by the government, were two-fold. First, the replacement of the local population with German settlers was meant to help staunch smuggling (especially of salt), animal theft, and robberies. Secondly, authorities believed that in case of renewed war with the Ottomans, a resident German population in the region would help ensure that important lines of communication—between Arad, Segedin, Peterwardein, and Temesvar—would remain open.[108] All of this was part of a larger Habsburg plan to delineate lines of settlement and habitation that separated one religious or ethnic group from another. As we have seen, the Banat was to be Catholic (and Orthodox) while Transylvania was to be Protestant (and Orthodox).

Although they were dispossessing these people, some of whose behavior had been traitorous during the last war, the government in Vienna cautioned the Banat administration to be careful and to transfer people only when necessary. Care was also to be taken that the people were comfortable and treated well. They were subjects, after all, and the authorities did not want them to develop additional hard feelings toward the government.[109] The goal was not so much elimination (a later nationalist goal) as it was separation. Thus while the authorities were transferring local populations to make way for German settlers, they were also planning the creation of new villages for local people. For example, in March 1764, the Pancsova administration asked for permission to create new villages exclusively for local people. They argued that such villages would be useful in connecting Pancsova with the outlying areas.[110]

It is important to note that there was never complete agreement on the policy toward the displacement of the local people. While both the central government in Vienna and the local administration in Temesvar agreed that some areas needed to be ethnically engineered, in general, it appears that the Temesvar administration advocated for more widespread displacement than the Hofkammer was willing to contemplate. Within the Hofkammer itself, there was disagreement. Especially in the late 1750s and early 1760s, there was a faction that did not support any sort of colonization and settlement. This group wanted to protect the herding and animal husbandry interests that had thrived since the cessation of the earlier colonial efforts. According to their logic, leasing the lands to herders guaranteed the biggest profits at the least risk to the government.[111] While their efforts to hinder colonization were largely in vain there was never complete agreement on anything regarding the Banat and its administration.

While many of the affected locals were Wallachs, in Jarmatha, the local Rascians also experienced the power of the state to remake the ethnic composition of the Banat.[112] The reasons for this transfer differed from the more security-oriented ones that justified the displacement of the Wallachs in the area between the rivers. Here, there was already a community of German colonists from earlier migrations known as "Deutsch Jarmatha" that had been separated from the preexisting community of Rascians, "Rascian Jarmatha," by Mercy's order.[113] In accordance with the central government's wishes, German colonists were to be placed in areas with existing German communities. Unable to secure any additional land from other surrounding areas, the authorities deemed it necessary to confiscate land from the Rascians to distribute among the incoming Germans. The government settled 192 families on properties that had held ninety.[114] The land was not simply confiscated without remuneration, in keeping with the expressed ideal that the displaced were to be treated well. The authorities estimated its worth at 5,422 fl. 48 kr. Payment for the confiscated wineries, homes, and gardens was to be delayed until the Rascians were settled in their new homes.[115] Not that the government paid a fair price. This was only half of what the land was actually worth.[116]

There was some resistance to this underpayment. At least one local tried to use the Habsburg court system to receive what he felt was fair compensation for his land. In 1770, the Temesvar administration reported that Bogosav Stanko filed a lawsuit regarding his "vineyard in Jarmatha which was taken away and given to the colonists."[117] He claimed the government never compensated him for the loss of his vineyard.[118] The Temesvar administration responded that they did indeed offer Stanko 245 fl. in compensation, but he refused, hoping for more money.[119] It also appears as if he sued the current owners. A "Stancsu Bosesku" sued Susana Karabelin over a "disputed vineyard and house plot" around the same time as these other lawsuits.[120] The case unfortunately disappears from the records before the outcome is clear, but it does provide an interesting example of the contested nature of the dispossessions.[121]

The authorities planned to move Jarmatha's Rascians to the Pradio Peterda. Like the confiscation of the Rascians' land, this, too, was more easily said than done. At the time of the proposed transfer, the Pradio was leased to a herder named Lajos. Despite the fact that he had been told several times that he would have to vacate the area, the "agitated ox trader" never resigned himself to the fact that he was going to have to take his animals elsewhere. The government even resorted to threats when it appeared he was not going to move. Unlike the land the Rascians had been forced to leave, the land to which they were going was largely undeveloped. It had simply been an area on which herders had grazed their animals. The incoming people would have to build houses, break ground to plant crops, and generally create an agricultural region out of an undeveloped area. The government recognized the enormity of this task and sent several officials to the region to scout out the best places for settlement. In this case, it was not the Germans who were to be the "pioneers," winning virgin land for agriculture. In fact, they were placed in a region already largely converted to agriculture and viticulture, on the properties of people who were removed. On the Pradio Peterda, it was the Rascians who were to be the true pioneers, transforming pasture to cropland.[122]

This was the plan. The actual outcome differed. The Rascians of Jaramata did not want to leave their homes. Without the approval of the *Knes* (mayor), and with the people, led by their religious leaders, actively refusing, the local government resorted to pressure to get them to move. That was not all. Instead of settling the people on virgin lands, authorities instead forced them into an already inhabited village, Checea. This was done to preserve the Pradio for grazing (!). This created a tense situation between the old residents and the newcomers. Another problem arose as central authorities had already earmarked some of the land on which the incoming Rascians settled for settlement by German colonists from the nearby villages of Landstreu and Hatzfeld. This led to conflicts between the colonists and the displaced locals. The goal of moving people without upsetting them and their surroundings had failed miserably, and the local authorities incurred the ire of Vienna for their terrible mishandling of the situation.[123]

The following year (1766), more resettlements took place, though they were considerably more organized. What made this round of dispossession particularly interesting was the negotiated nature of the locals' departure. While local people could not resist the power of the state to displace them, the state nonetheless did want them to be loyal and productive in their new homes. This gave the local people a bit of agency that allowed them to attempt to ease their burdens. When the authorities ordered the residents of Sefdin and Kisfalud to vacate their lands to make way for colonists, inhabitants of both villages negotiated separate, though remarkably similar, deals outlining the conditions for their transfer.[124] The locals received a three-year adjustment period, during which time certain obligations were dismissed or lowered (like the colonists but three years fewer). For instance, they were allowed to pay only part of their *Contribution* during this period. In addition to a lower tax burden, they were also able to negotiate freedom from traditional work obligations in order to prepare their new lands for settlement. Interestingly, they had to help the local government collect wood for the incoming settlers until they had left the village completely. They were able to negotiate government-funded transport for the poor or those who did not have draft animals. While they could not take their old fruit trees with them, they were allowed to take the young ones and to sell the old ones, with colonists given preference.[125] After the government had debated the intricacies of the concessions, they were then presented to the locals whose presence at such meetings was recorded.[126] The government hoped that such concessions would ameliorate hard feelings caused by the movement itself. For the villagers, they simply tried to make the best out of a bad situation.

As the number of famine-stricken colonists arriving in the Banat peaked around 1770, land was again at a premium. Officials floated a number of plans. Herr Neumann von Buchholt proposed to resettle the inhabitants of the "small village" of Monorat and replace them with German Catholics. A Calugier (Orthodox) monastery currently possessed the village, but Buchholt was undeterred. He said that the government should demand proof that the monastery had a right to the village. If they could not prove ownership, then the government could move the inhabitants of the village and replace them with German colonists. The village's proximity to the German community and Catholic church in St. Peter made the location especially advantageous. The committee to which he presented his plan agreed to investigate the village to see if it was suitable for settlement.[127] The investigation revealed that there were forty-eight Wallach families, one "new Banater" (Roma), nineteen Orthodox monks, and three widows living on over 2,540 yokes of land.[128] While it is unclear if the government confiscated the land for incoming colonists, it is yet another example of the privilege the migrants enjoyed. Not only was the government willing to dispossess local people, but they were also willing to dispossess local religious orders, much as they had done for the Bulgarian Catholics, to satisfy the land needs of the colonists.

Treasury advisor (*Hofkammerrat*) Paul Festetics proposed another plan. He suggested buying twelve to fifteen houses in the local villages in the Batschka and slating them for Germans who were unable to find accommodation in the Banat. His plan was quickly scuttled. First, there was no guarantee such people would willingly sell their houses. If they did not, then physical violence would be needed to remove them, and this went against Maria Theresia's desires. Secondly, even if they could get the houses, they would be settling Germans among Wallachs and Rascians, and this was something to be avoided at all costs, as we have seen. Officials feared that such mixing would lead to unrest and rebellion, and they cited cases where it had.[129]

The "Central Population Instruction for the Banat," interestingly released two days after the newspapers declared the end of government-supported migration in 1772, appears to reiterate the possibility of forced migration to accommodate settlers. The authors state that already existing German areas were expected to absorb a set number of incoming colonists based on their available land and ability to do so. It further states that Wallach or Rascian villages that the government had not slated for movement would be required to absorb inhabitants from villages that were moved.[130] Whether or not this policy was put into practice is unclear, but it shows the continuity of colonial policy from the 1720s to the end of Maria Theresia's reign.

In the military border, the officials had even stronger reasons to be concerned with the ethnic makeup of villages. Between 1770 and 1774, the authorities maintained the separation between Rascians and Germans when constructing new towns. The military administration wanted to settle Germans between the Rascians and the border to hinder communication between coethnic communities on the Habsburg and Ottoman sides of the frontier. The initial plan to settle the Rascians behind the Germans was scrapped when officials realized that this would have burdened them in getting to their fields. In the end, they were settled next to the Germans. When settling the area around the existing village Sefkerin, a completely new village, Glogonj, was built for the Germans. Another plan had the Germans in the center of Opovo with the Rascians surrounding them, where an earlier plan had them living in separate districts. Although the military finally said it wanted to have the communities living side by side, too much preparation for the new village had already been done to change its design. They wanted to have the communities together so that the Rascians could be watched. In the military border, this policy of separation lasted well into the nineteenth century. The first time the authorities did not separate people based on religion or ethnicity in the military border was in the village of Mrmanorak in 1818–1821.[131] For over one hundred years, the government had insisted on keeping different groups apart on order to promote peace among them and to keep potentially disloyal subjects under observation. Interestingly, nationalists began coming to the same conclusion later in the century, first on local, then on a countrywide scale.

As in so many other aspects of government, the succession of Joseph II completely changed the resettlement policy. Though highly critical of the Wallachs and their society, Joseph recognized the history of resettlement for what it was: a naked grab at the best land in the region. He lamented that "it is also true that, in order to make room for settlers, their best land was taken, their villages moved, and many more vexations added to them, even though they are the oldest inhabitants of the land."[132] The authorities in charge of the Josephian migration instituted a policy of *no* population transfer. For instance, in 1784 the administration in Temesvár asked the government in Vienna to authorize the transfer of seventy Wallach families to make way for anticipated German settlers. The government's response was an unequivocal no. The Wallachs were to be left alone.[133] Crucially, Joseph himself openly opposed the forced resettlement of Rascians and Wallachs, or as he called them the "older colonists." While conceding that the settlement of Germans had been useful, he complained that it had cost a lot of money. Furthermore, he argued that "every such family [i.e., local family] is to be more esteemed than three German families" because of their acclimation to the land and their inner strength. For this reason, he ordered that no land be taken away from any local people in order to settle Germans.[134]

Some in the government tried other tactics to turn Wallach into German space. In a number of cases, the government confiscated sections of Wallach districts and used them as the basis for new German colonial villages.[135] Despite these machinations, with the emperor opposed to transferring local people, the period of Habsburg population manipulation through forced migration came to an end.

While there was no forced migration, the old mindset that dictated that Germans needed to live separately from other peoples continued through Joseph's reign. In 1784, Crown Administrator Baron Ladislaus von Orczy reiterated the old belief that Germans and others, because of their different values, religions, and languages, needed to be separated to prevent disorder and discord. According to Orczy, this was not only his belief; the German colonists themselves would refuse to live near Wallachs. This is an interesting opinion given the fact that the government ordered locals to house, for payment, several German families while their own homes were being prepared. Or perhaps this was the reason that Germans would then later refuse to live with them.[136]

While there is no indication that the administration in Vienna initiated any more orders for transference after the succession of Joseph, there is evidence for at least one smaller transfer instigated by the local administrators. In 1785, the first Germans arrived in Morawitza, which to that point had been a village of Wallachs and Rascians. The colonists did not get along with the other groups. When the Ottomans invaded in 1787, the Germans fled, while the local people remained in the village. After the war, the Germans returned to find their homes decimated. They blamed the local Wallachs for the destruction. Then there were high-profile murders. One German leader, Stefan Waldmann, was found in his field dead and mutilated. Robbers murdered Anton Storinger and his son in their home during the day. Finally, in 1790, the government transferred the Wallachs of Morawaitza to Radovantz (Deschanfalva).[137] While most of the forced transfers ended with Joseph II, there was still a desire by the local administration to remake the demographics of the Banat in order to maintain calm.

By the early nineteenth century, and especially as the century went on, the economic position of the colonists continued to improve, especially vis-à-vis the Wallachs (some of whom now began embracing a Romanian identity). The Germans were able to leverage this economic advantage, one which the Habsburg government helped to create through incentives and privileges, into land and power in the rural economy. Germans, especially the sons and daughters of colonists, used this money to purchase land in what had been Romanian and Serbian areas of settlement as in Aliosch. Increasingly, Germans were landowners while many Romanians were reduced to laborers.[138] Importantly, and what separated this round of land transfer from the earlier ones, was that it was not government run and was done through private commerce, conducted either by lords on their lands or by individual German families.[139] That said, the fact remains that Germans and colonists continued the process of remaking the demographic and physical landscape in a way that was very consistent with the Habsburg vision that had been in place since the early eighteenth century.

The importance of religion for other eighteenth-century recruiting states was mixed, with Catholic regimes being the most restrictive. The Spanish, for instance, specified that they only wanted Catholic craftsmen in the Sierra Morena.[140] They also strongly encouraged marriage ("according to the Christ-Catholic manner") among young people anywhere along the journey.[141] The Prussians accepted Huguenots and other Protestants as well as Jews (at least in Berlin).[142] Similarly, among the German-speaking settlers who arrived in British North America between 1683 and 1783, "the majority" were Lutheran.[143] After the death of her German Lutheran husband, Queen Anne had wanted to help the "poor German Protestants."[144] The Russians were by far the most tolerant. In fact, they promised religious freedom "without hindrance or molestation." In exchange for this privilege, migrants agreed not to proselytize or attempt to convert others. The exception to this rule was Muslims who could be converted or enserfed ("made band-men to anyone").[145]

As we have seen, the Habsburg authorities were also very restrictive in terms of tolerated ethnicities and religions from the 1720s forward. It was not a static policy. What under Charles and Maria Theresia was to be a Catholic space, was largely deconfessionalized under Joseph. Though he was no friend of the Wallachs, especially in his later years, as we shall see, he likewise ended the Habsburg policy of displacing local people to benefit incoming settlers. This did not end land transfers. Government-sponsored transfer gave way to noble-driven then market-driven exchanges as the Germans used their budding economic advantage to purchase land.

As will become even clearer in later chapters, while most locals adhered to their traditional subsistence lifestyles, the settlers, with a lot of help from the administration, took control of the economic and agricultural life of the region. Violence, from both sides, was an unfortunate side effect of this process. In the next two chapters, we will explore what that colonial culture looked like and how the colonists interacted with the government, each other, and the landscape. Far from being a runaway success, the implantation of a prosperous colonial culture in the region proceeded in fits and starts and did not really gain traction until the nineteenth century.

4 Expectations Fulfilled?

Colonists and the Government

> Magyar jobbagy perlö tars, svab jobbagy pénzes zacskó.
> Ungarischer Fronbauer ist ein Streithansel, der schwäbische ein Geldsack.
> [A Magyar serf is a pack of trouble, a Swabian a moneybag.]
> —*An eighteenth-century Hungarian saying from Satu Mare (Sathmar, Szatmár)*[1]

THE ROAD TO THE BANAT was a long and weary one for many colonists. One group who left the "Fatherland" with passports and no money wandered through Hungary for two years. They often did not know whether they were "in the Panat (*sic*) or not." On their journey, local notables who wanted them to settle their lands courted them. Circumstance and unhelpful government officials forced the forty families, which included 106 children, to work as day laborers to support themselves. Even once they made it to the Banat, their troubles were not over. After seeing the new village of Grabaz, where they noted good land and houses, they petitioned the government in Temesvar to allow them to settle there. They argued that given such an opportunity, they could become contributing members of the state. Their pleas went unanswered. They then complained to the authorities in Vienna. They argued that in Grabaz there were Hungarians (!) when they knew that there should only be Germans settled there. They pleaded with the central government to be allowed to settle there and if not there, in Puβta Pogarosch, where they seemed to know there was to be a new settlement. Their pleas focused on the need to raise their children.[2]

As we explored earlier, the reasons why peasants uprooted themselves from the German Reich and made the arduous trip to the Banat were multifarious. Throughout the eighteenth century, many peasants fled to escape the wars that periodically swept through the Rhine region. Others fled to escape harsh feudal levies.[3] At times, the government utilized recruiters who traversed parts of the Reich looking for potential settlers. Sometimes, the environment was a factor. A massive famine that hit parts of Europe in the late 1760s and early 1770s spurred migration. In addition to these large environmental and structural reasons that Germans migrated, there were also more personal ones. These are, of course, harder to detect, especially for the mass of Germans who left no written record. Some came as part of the army or from a desire for adventure. Others came looking for advancement in the administration. Every colonist had his or her own reasons for leaving the "known" and venturing to the Habsburg-Ottoman frontier.

With such a variety of potential settlers, the Habsburgs designed many of the settlement patents and ordinances regarding colonization to attract a certain "type" of colonist. As we have already seen, for many years this meant Catholic colonists, but there were also socioeconomic factors as well. Many of the calls for colonists included a means test, that is, the possession of a minimum amount of money in order to be considered for the official migration. These provisions were meant to ensure that only potentially loyal and successful colonists would make the journey and settle the region. Thus the settlement patents were meant not simply to populate the region (this could have been done more cost effectively using local people, as Joseph II noted), but to bring potentially successful *Europeans* and their culture to the Habsburg-Ottoman frontier. These expectations, and their supposed fulfillment, are reflected in the historical work on the German colonists, which is generally laudatory. Even into the late twentieth century, Germans were remembered in the region as industrious and honest.[4] This belief is reflected in almost all of the regions that experienced German colonization, most starkly in the Russian Empire.[5]

Unfortunately for government authorities, and these later historians, the colonists were not all able to meet their lofty goals. A combination of poor-quality settlers, harsh environmental conditions, and especially disease devasted the colonial communities. The government tried to address these issues with a stick and a carrot: a system of government oversight alongside education through schools and print culture. The biggest impact colonists made, at least initially, was in changing the material culture of the region. Villages and towns visibly demonstrated the colonial presence and served to highlight the differences between local and colonial culture.

Great Expectations: The German Colonists and the Government

In the 1720s, signs were good, and officials were upbeat. One of the first reports on German agricultural settlement in the Banat came in 1723, not long after Crausen's colonists were expected. Dated November 29, 1723, Governor Count Mercy and Cameral High Inspector von Rebentisch noted the existence of around seventeen settler villages, varying in size from fifty to 120 families. They reported that they had given the arriving colonists grain in exchange for the promise of repayment "of some thousands of Metzen" from increased agricultural production.[6] According to this report, disease was becoming less of a problem, a premature assertion, as we will see. Overall, the colonists were in good spirits in their new homes.[7] The administrators seemed grateful and excited to have them in the region. This was a promising start to the colonial effort.

While some early reports on the colonists recruited by Crausen were positive, later reports exposed deeply troubling problems for the administration. By the 1730s at the latest, the government recognized that the Germans were not going to be able to simply transplant themselves from the Reich to the Banat and make the region fertile and productive. A 1734 report on the state of the Banat provided a mixed assessment of the German colonists. It referred explicitly to the Germans who came with Crausen in the 1720s from "Mainz, Trier, Cologne . . . the Palatinate, Alsace, Hessen, and other areas along the Rhine." The report stated flatly and simply that those who did not die from disease helped improve viticulture, hardly a ringing endorsement of their ability to rework the landscape. It further chided them for adopting much of the locals' "negligent lifestyle." In particular, the author stated that the Germans' children were not learning to read and write and were being raised in "idiocy," though he did suggest that building schools could solve the problem.[8]

Complaints about the colonists' ability to reshape the region and its people continued into the 1750s. Impoverished German settlers were not uncommon, especially shortly after their arrival on the frontier. Many who found themselves in such situations had spent their money traveling to the Banat and were left with very little once they arrived.[9] An untimely sickness, which, as we will see in the next chapter, was not uncommon, could exacerbate the problem. Such people were unlikely to be the role models envisioned by some in the administration. In 1752, for instance, fifteen German Lorrainer families contacted the administration complaining that, because of rampant sickness, they were forced to survive on bread and water. While the authorities in Temesvar agreed to help them, they requested guidance from Vienna on what to do in the future with such poor colonial families.[10]

After hearing that the colonists were in such dire straits, the government in Vienna ordered the administration in Temesvar to ensure other incoming poor families had the necessities for survival. The administration replied with a list of these necessities, which could be obtained for 60 fl. per family. They needed shelter and animals (two horses and a cow). A plow could be shared among four families, dropping the price. They needed a wagon. Finally, they needed various smaller agricultural implements (a shovel, an axe, a harness and bridle for draft animals, a cutter, and a scythe).[11] They hoped that if the Germans were provided with the tools and materials necessary, they could avoid becoming impoverished.[12] Later experience belied this. The next year, 1753, the administration in Temesvar told Vienna that colonists now needed at least *150* fl. to set up their homesteads. Without this money, officials claimed there was a high likelihood that they would fail to establish themselves.[13] The situation at the military border later in the century was not much better. In 1782, the German border was considered the best furnished. The government first took care of the Germans, or at least those districts where there was going to be a preponderance of Germans. This strategy did not pay off in making the Germans better settlers. Only 60 percent were able to live without state assistance.[14] Such problems led Joseph II to dismiss German colonists as ineffective and to promote local people in their stead.

Government Oversight: An Enduring Tradition

The government responded to the problem of poverty by providing colonists with land and materials, though this support did come at a cost. The colonists may not have been serfs in the traditional sense of the word, at least until the Hungarian takeover, but they *were* tied to the land. The authorities in the Banat placed heavy restrictions on the movement of colonists. As early as 1733, the government instructed toll officials to stop any farmers who were trying to flee the Banat and report them to the district administration.[15] Throughout the entire period, colonists wrote to request permission to leave. As we saw, some requested permission to leave in order to go back to the German Reich and recruit. Others requested permission to return to their homes to collect inheritances. For instance, when three colonists from Mercydorf requested such permission, an official, in support of their application, mentioned that they would be leaving behind their wives and possessions. This was apparently not enough. Another official demanded a letter or some other proof of the inheritance before they would be allowed to leave.[16] Such requests to return home continued into the nineteenth century and indicate not only that governmental oversight continued but also that ties between the Reich and the Banat survived over a long period of time.[17]

The desire of Germans to permanently leave was a point of contention for the authorities. Already in 1724, colonists who had arrived only a year or two before were asking for permission to go back to their former homes. The administration even ordered the arrest of a colonist who wanted to leave and ordered the incident publicized for others to see. Two years later, local officials in Neu-Arad were informed that they were under no circumstances to allow German colonists to return home.[18] In 1753, the government in Temesvar wrote to Vienna for advice on just this point. They complained that settlers asked to be allowed to leave shortly after arrival in 1752. One imagines that they saw the conditions with which they were expected to contend and decided that they were better off where they had come from. According to the document, some migrants wanted to return to their relatives despite the fact that living conditions there were poor. Others were very sick.[19] Hungary was close and provided an enticing destination for some. When three German families from Saderlak attempted to flee there in late 1753, the government did not hesitate to order their return. The report on their flight further stated that any subjects from Banat found in Hungary were to be returned immediately.[20] That same year, the government instructed local authorities that no one was allowed to even move villages without official permission.[21] The problem of colonists wanting to return home continued throughout the century.[22] Some even argued that had they known they would end up in such a terrible situation, they never would have left, as their lives in the Reich offered more advantages than in the Banat.[23]

Sick, poor, and fleeing colonists were not what the government had envisioned. The problem of dissolute colonists became especially acute in the 1760s following the influx of deactivated soldiers and camp followers from the Seven Years' War. Many of them did not have the skills necessary to become successful agriculturalists. Although most of the later immigrants during the period were, according to one later author, "hardworking, job-seeking people," the individuals who had come earlier were prone to living poor lives and causing trouble. While such populations existed throughout the Banat, the soldier-colonists at Mercydorf were especially bad. Some had pawned the equipment and animals they had been provided and fled the area or used the money for "immodest activities." Others had allowed their animals to die or to be stolen due to ignorance and inattention.[24]

Observers and advisors proposed a number of solutions to the problem of unsuccessful agriculturalists. For example, the authorities suggested that future colonists be divided between artisans and farmers. This way, the authorities would know their skillset and thus to what kind of equipment or benefits they were entitled. If someone was neither a farmer nor an artisan, they should be told where to settle but should receive no benefits.[25] Some officials in Temesvar suggested not providing such extensive assistance. They specifically wanted to end the practice of providing colonists with cash.[26] Such proposals were designed to help improve the quality, or at the very least the profitability, of the colonial project in the Banat.

Importantly, the government inaugurated a system of Colonial Aufseher (colonial overseers) to supervise the colonists in their use of government funds and material.[27] These men were involved in ensuring the success of the colonial project and were an important, if often feared, part of colonists' lives starting in 1765. The "Instructions for Colonist Overseers" explained exactly what was expected of them.[28] First and foremost, the overseers themselves were to be respectable, pious, God-fearing Christians. As they were responsible for the moral behavior of the colonists, they were expected to be moral themselves. They were to encourage industriousness and work. They were to make sure the fields were planted on time and in the proper way. Cultivatable land was to be put to the best use while currently uncultivatable land was to be cleared and prepared. In Jarmatha, the overseer was to ensure that wine production proceeded apace and that the colonists did not drink their own product. They were to visit every village at least once per year and note the condition of the equipment, animals, and houses, and receive reports on each of the colonists from local officials. They were allowed to admonish or moderately punish colonists in certain situations, but more serious offenses, especially for drunkenness, gambling, and other offenses that distracted them from work, were to be reported to the district administrators for more severe punishment. They were also to note what was needed among the "hardworking, diligent" colonists and report this to the district administrator as well. Like other bureaucrats in the region, they were tasked with preventing the flight of colonists and participating in the discovery and return of those who had fled. They were to be the government's eyes on the ground and were expected to protect the government's investment in the colonists as well as the colonists' own well-being.

Once in place, overseers sent reports to the government on the state of the colonies and any issues that were relevant to their maintenance. In the late 1760s, for example, overseers reported an increase in animal theft, largely attributed to the Wallachs. They were quick to point out, though, that the Germans shared at least some of the blame. Many were still not caring for their animals properly. Some let their animals out in the morning and failed to watch over them or collect them at night. Some allowed local people to watch over them rather than doing it themselves or left their animals overnight with unknown people. The overseer suggested that Germans guilty of not tending to their animals correctly be given one or two months of hard labor building fortresses as punishment.[29] Apparently, even the watchful eye of the colonist overseers did not prevent some Germans from squandering their largesse.

In addition to the overseers, other government officials kept an eye on the German colonists and their activities. The colonial director, Neümann von Buchholt, was responsible for visiting the colonies from time to time to ensure that the government's will was being followed.[30] In the military border, officers also kept an eye on the colonists. In a 1778 report, for example, a company commandant in Pancsova reported colonist Martin Grösch for losing two oxen after the former noticed Grösch's absence from a church parade. He further reported that Grösch was cruel to his animals and thus was likely responsible for their disappearance.[31] While the colonists may not have been serfs, they were subjected to considerable restrictions and administrative oversight. The government had invested a lot of money into these projects and wanted to assure that it was not wasted.

Despite their reputation as industrious, accusations of malfeasance dogged German-speaking colonists all over Europe. Desertion was a problem in Russia. For instance, the residents of a village near Kaffa "were very poor and desponding." Faced with problems, residents fled, leaving "twelve families [there] . . . the rest having gone into service or to sea."[32] One traveler heard from a local that "most of the emigrants . . . were desirous of returning to their native country, could they but once discharge the obligations they had voluntarily contracted."[33] Some were terrible farmers. As one traveler put it, "The Crimea contains large colonies of Germans, who have been greatly favoured by government, and owe it to their own idleness and drunkenness, that they are not in the most flourishing circumstances." Given this, the government employed overseers to ensure a certain level of work and morality among the colonists, much as in the Banat. In Crimea, anyone who refused to do work whether out of laziness or drunkenness was flogged. Women could be flogged for "immoral conduct." Of course, not all Germans required such harsh treatment, and the situation improved over time. The succeeding generations of colonists had "habits and character . . . very superior to the above-mentioned."[34] Similar complaints about the treatment, or lack thereof, of animals were heard in the Sierra Morena in Spain. Some did not take care of their animals, and they were either lost or died. Others *claimed* their animals were lost when they had actually sold them. Some allowed their advances to be renewed despite not qualifying for them. Others simply did not improve their lands.[35] Again, the administration needed to provide careful, constant oversight to ensure that the venture did not end in failure.[36] German-speaking colonists did not have an innate ability to create wealth, whatever the proverb referenced at the beginning of the chapter might say.

How effective officials were in overseeing colonists and instilling them with a positive work ethic is uncertain. What is certain is that many of these officials, as we saw in chapter 1, were as corrupt or incompetent as some of their charges. One particularly egregious offender was the colonist overseer Martin Hirsch of Grabaz, whose name comes up in court records in the early 1770s. He was constantly in debt and being sued.[37] He was likely not much of a model for his charges to follow.

Despite, or perhaps because of, the extensive oversight, the German colonists were never afraid to petition the authorities for assistance. Throughout the 1750s, 60s, and 70s, colonists made numerous requests for money, equipment, and even the extension of privileges. In 1755, for instance, Johann Klemann and Michael Lillÿn petitioned the government in the name of fifteen households in Bruckenau for an additional free year. The government ordered an investigation. They wanted to know when the colonists arrived in the Banat, when they started planting, and whether or not they were of good "worth" and thus merited consideration.[38] Similarly, when Michael Blass of Beschenova requested sixty fl. to help the Lorrainer families there, the government wanted to know what kind of man he was.[39]

The idea of the "worth" of the supplicant was important in deciding whether they should receive help. When describing the plea of a newly arrived farmer in Jarmatha, the administrator saw fit to include the town mayor's (*Schulz*) judgment that he was a good worker and that he had already begun to build a house. The author even said that these facts made him "worthy" of help. Unsurprisingly, given these endorsements, the government in Temesvar ordered that he receive assistance in the form of loans, both financial and material.[40] Eventually, even "worthy" colonists found it hard to get government support. A report in 1774 made clear that only the "good landlords" among the recently arrived colonists would receive additional seed in the cases of accident or disaster. "Older colonists" (i.e., those who had been living in the Banat for more than three years) would receive only as much help as other local people did. They further ordered this information publicized with the plea that colonists should hold back some of their harvest for seeding next year. The government also urged colonists to put themselves in a good position through "hard work and industriousness," so they would not need any more government assistance.[41]

Much like the government, the colonists themselves also looked for "worth" in their fellow settlers when deciding whether to include them in their community. Those who did not possess it could be expelled from the village community. In Billiet, there was a "very dissolute colonist" that the village mayor sought to replace with a newcomer.[42] This makes perfect sense. Living on the frontier was difficult and dangerous. If one member of the village was unwilling to work, this could be disastrous for the collective. In this case, the village sought to expel a member seen as not useful and replace him with someone who perhaps had better qualities. In Rekash, both the government and the local community disliked Carl Barbi. Another "dissolute" individual, local administrators accused him of trying to pass himself off as a new colonist for the benefits despite the fact that he had been living in the Banat for twelve years.[43]

After the Hungarians gained control of the Banat and the treasury sold much of its land to private individuals, daily life was controlled to an even higher degree. Interactions with the authorities ceased to be based on the laws of a bureaucratic state and were now based on the whims of an individual lord. No longer was the emperor the sole landowner and lord. The decrees of 1774 and 1777, which had given peasants in the Banat ownership of their lands (*Eigentumsrecht*), were now largely meaningless. The new arrangement favored owners as Hungarian "feudal law" became the law of the land. Peasants, not knowing Joseph II's active role in their stunning reversal of fortunes, pleaded with the administration to protect them from their new owners.[44]

The incorporation of the Banat into Hungary represented the end of the earlier period of colonization. Prospective colonists no longer enjoyed the protections from duties and labor that had been afforded them. They now had to pay one gulden per house per year. They were also required to perform labor for their lord based on the amount and fertility of the land. One Session of good land equaled 104 days of robot per year while those who only owned a house were required to perform eight days. A portion of all crops was required to be given to the lord.[45] Taxes and their collection could be brutal even after the abolition of serfdom. Farmer Mathias Siebold related that when someone did not have enough money or grain to pay the taxes, the government came and took anything that moved in order to cover the bill.[46]

The situation in Mercydorf, one of the villages of ill repute cited above, illustrates both the good and the bad sides of private ownership. Count Johann Soro, fortress commander of Temesvar from 1767 to 1791, was the first owner. He was independently wealthy and invested money in the village. He apparently even sent soldiers from Temesvár to marry widows there. When Soro was replaced as commander in 1791, he decided to sell Mercydorf. The story goes that he initially offered the peasants of the village the chance to buy it for the discounted sum of 8,000 fl. Had they done this, they would have been "free peasants." Instead, they could not come to an agreement among themselves, forcing Soro to look elsewhere for a buyer. It was a fateful decision.

Baron Lo Presti de Fontana d'Angioli purchased the village.[47] According to local lore, he and his wife instituted a regime of corporal punishment. They both apparently loved to see people whipped. In the castle they built, they installed sixty marble plates with various numbers on them. A peasant who got in trouble was led to this place blindfolded; whichever plate one stood in front of represented the number of blows one received. One poor Romanian woman, not even from the village, was stripped naked, had a wet towel wrapped around her, and was released into the winter cold. She was dead in a few minutes. This treatment led the colonists to complain to Vienna, which initially seemed to help. The "Beating Baron" became milder but then sent recruiters to the village to take a son from every family for the army, telling the people that if they stopped their complaint against him, he would have their sons released. They had little choice but to comply.[48] How much of this is the truth and how much is exaggerated is hard to tell. Stories about the violence of the nobility appear elsewhere on the Habsburg frontier.[49] There was a certain "fairy tale" quality to the end of the story. According to Möller, the Baron's wife died, and his new wife was kind and helped him change his ways. In this new period, the accused appeared before a judge rather than the baron himself. Even if the story was fabricated or exaggerated, it still reflects the resentment the Germans of the Banat felt for the new noble class.

In the German villages surrounding Billiet, the representatives of the owner, the Bishop of Agram (today's Zagreb, Croatia), tried to demand extra labor from the peasants. In a particularly fruitful year, the prefect who represented the bishop wanted to enforce a new *urbarium* (the contract between lord and serf) that said that each household was required to send two men for four days per week during the harvest. According to one local informant, the village had a copy of the original *urbarium*; "many ha[d] read it carefully" and found that this new imposition was unjust. In it, each household was responsible for *one* man four days a week for two weeks then a two-week rest period during which no man could be summoned. The local elected official in charge of enforcing the new law went to the prefect and told him he would not do it. He attempted to resign, which the prefect accepted, but the local villagers reelected him, "declaring that they would obey no other."[50] What became of this volatile situation is unclear. Luckily for these Germans, they were literate and able to use the law to resist.

Overzealous lords after unification with Hungary and their treatment of the peasants were a main reason why many Germans initially supported Lajos Kossuth, the leader of the Hungarian Revolution of 1848. As we will see in the conclusion, the promise to eliminate serfdom struck a chord among Germans who had known a measure of freedom before 1780, a fact that remained in their communal memory.

Village Planning and Architecture

The government took an active role in shaping not only the colonists' lives, but also in shaping the material culture with which they interacted. The Europeanization of the Banat was something that was to occur both through changing and "bettering" the population and through changing the actual landscape. In the latter respect, the government had distinct ideas on how to change towns and villages to make them more "modern" and rational. Although rationalizing all villages was part of the government's overall plan, the authorities began the process with the construction of colonial villages. The design of the German colonial spaces set them apart from local people and further contributed to their sense of superiority, especially in the nineteenth century. It was also one of the most visible ways that the Habsburgs tried to impose Enlightened European forms on the region.[51]

Locals' housing had always been a source of derision. One simple type of house consisted of a hole dug into the ground and then covered with straw or tree bark.[52] Some Roma people lived in similar housing.[53] Soldier and traveler Johann Kaspar Steube gave a detailed description of a Wallach house in the late eighteenth century. First, four large trees were cut down to make the footprint of the house, a square or rectangle. They built up the walls using smaller trees. Windows were simply cut out of the wood and covered with a bladder or paper in the winter. They used cow manure and other "similar materials" to patch the holes between the wood. Better-built houses had wooden columns in each corner and in the middle of the house. Straw was used for roofs. Steube said that Wallachs needed "neither carpenters, fitters, nor nail smiths" to construct their houses. Only some got hinges from the Roma, who were often itinerant metalsmiths, for their doors. Houses generally had one room and an entryway kitchen. The chimney was constructed of mud-covered wood. Additionally, they had covered places to store grain and for animals as well space to weave and distill *rakia*, a fruit brandy.[54] As late as 1849, one British report said that some people still stored their grain in holes dug in the ground, "a remnant of Asiatic usages," though by that point they must have been in the minority.[55] Their villages had evolved without any central planning, thus they appeared chaotic and almost formless from a Western perspective. The system of fields was similarly irregular. There was not a standard size, and fields, woods, and grazing lands were often intermixed.[56]

The German houses and villages had a different look. Although some Germans initially lived in holes in the ground while their houses were built, this was not a common living space.[57] Instead, colonist houses consisted of three rooms: two general rooms and a kitchen.[58] Some dwellings were made of rammed earth. In these, two boards were placed parallel to one another. Soil was put in the space in between and tamped down. The process was continued until a wall was formed.[59] Such houses were common in areas that were not forested. In addition to rammed earth, other houses were made of unfired bricks (*ungebrannten sogenannten Koth Ziegl*). In areas where there were ample trees, especially in the upland region to the east, houses were constructed from wood. Some designers submitted blueprints to the government that contained plans for both wood and earth/brick houses. Such plans could then be used anywhere in the Banat, taking into account local conditions. Roofs were often made of straw or hay or sometimes boards. Some designs included a shed for a wagon and an animal pen. Other designs only had animal stalls.[60]

A lot of planning went into not only the individual houses but also the overall look and design of the German colonial villages, especially during the building boom in the 1760s and 1770s. Rational, enlightened values guided the layout and construction of these villages.[61] The first point of the "Main Population Instructions" of 1772 sums up the overall rational mindset of the planners. "Because geometric dimensions are the ground pillar on which the entire colonial business must be built, it is above all necessary that the entire land be surveyed accurately by certain engineers or 'earth measurers.'"[62] The authorities were not simply looking to populate the Banat but rather to intellectually possess it and integrate it into the rest of their European possessions. Measuring, mapping, numbering, and counting were all part of this wider goal of integration.

Maps of planned villages, such as the "Land Allocation of a Suggested

Ideal Village," showed the rational, geometric nature of the emerging order in the Banat. The village, a square checkerboard with a central plaza, was surrounded by grazing land for animals. Fields were numbered to indicate to which house they belonged.[63] These ideas were not merely confined to theory. They were often put into practice. For instance, Neudorf was designed in 1765 on a checkerboard pattern.[64] Guttenbrunn, while not a perfect square village, was rationally designed with equal rectangular plots that all faced streets.[65] The proposed colonial town "Franz- und Ludovica-Stadt" was designed in 1810 around a central square that had streets bordering the square on the north and south. The houses in this town were two stories, a relative anomaly among colonial architecture for the masses.[66]

The authorities were not content to have two styles of village in the region: the rational, geometric German village and the local "cluster village" (*Haufendorf*). They wanted *all* villages to conform to the rational, modern German colonial pattern. Official descriptions of villages often noted whether they were laid out in a geometric pattern or not.[67] Those that were not, largely older local villages, were often rebuilt along rational lines. In Kisfalud, the government razed the old housing after the local population was moved to make way for incoming settlers. They marked lots for one hundred new houses, erected new buildings, and dug wells for the incoming migrants.[68] The military border was no different. Villages there, both local and colonial, were organized along rational lines. In Sefkerin, for example, the authorities wanted to reorganize the Rascian village along rational lines. Thus, they forced the Rascians there to build a new village next to the old one. In other villages, the inhabitants were forced to tear down their old houses and build new ones on the same spot. In 1777, in Rascian Jabuka, for instance, the government forced the villagers to rebuild, using their own money and following plans for house type and location. They also had to pay for building churches. This was typical and was in stark contrast to the Germans' Catholic churches in the military border. The state covered their costs. In Opovo, for example, the authorities built a German schoolhouse and a Catholic church. They did not build a school or church for the Rascians, whom they fully expected would be living in the new village.[69]

In the civil Banat, when planning and building villages, designers attempted to make every settler equidistant from their fields.[70] Thus, those villagers with houses closer to the center had the nearer fields, those on the outskirts, the further ones. The new village designs incorporated the "three-field system" of agriculture that was to replace the old ley farm system (*Feldgraswirtschaft*). This was an ongoing process throughout the eighteenth and early nineteenth centuries. Many local villages were "checkerboard" patterned by Emperor Franz's reign (1804–1835). By 1850, even the small mountain villages had been remade along rational lines.[71]

The difference, especially in the early years before the standardization of all the villages in the Banat took place, appears to have been startling for Western Europeans. We must, of course, take these accounts with a grain of salt, but if we discount the value judgments the travelers made, as we should, they seem to have recognized real differences in design and layout. This is true not just in the Banat but everywhere that German colonists went. Joseph von Dorner noted that "[the German colonists'] nice villages certify a considerable prosperity." Given the "fertile region" and the "hard-working people [Germans]," Dorner was not surprised by their prosperity. Near Temesvár, he noted that the condition of the Wallach villages caused them to stand out compared to the German ones. While the "paltriness of the churches and houses [and] the pallid, sick look of the inhabitants do not make a favorable impression on outsiders," the colonists' villages were "beautiful," populated by "busy Germans."[72]

A. A. Paton was shocked and appalled by the differences between the villages, which he described in a narrative account of his travels in 1848. For him, "civilisation recommenc[ed]" when he entered the predominantly Banat German village of St. Miklos after traveling through southern Hungary. Houses were "well-built" and had "architectural pretensions." The German parts of villages on the Maros River had "neat farmyards, clean white-washed walls, green-painted Venetian window-blinds." In Csanad, the houses covered in ornamental plaster were "not, to be sure, in the best taste, but denoting industry, order, and easy circumstances." The Wallach and Rascian homes were worse, the Wallachs' "farmyards being in a most filthy and disorderly state." For Paton, the differences in material conditions were reflective of the moral and intellectual superiority of the German colonists.[73]

Traveler Johann Georg Kohl witnessed one of the old local villages *before* it was rebuilt. He described the "ruinous old hovels" of the Wallach village of Pechineska near Mehadia that the authorities had ordered destroyed to rebuild the town. Kohl commented that "these people had to be driven by the hand of authority to care for their own convenience and their own advantage."[74] Much as Paton, he also remarked on the "prettily painted in green and white" houses of the Germans along the road from Temesvár to St. Miklos.[75] An English traveler, John Paget, made a similar assessment. He declared that he could recognize one village as German occupied "from the superiority of its buildings, and from the large and handsome schoolhouse." He referred to a nearby local settlement as "a place formed only of the wooden hovels of Wallachs." He claimed a Scottish friend of his declared that "would to God our own people could enjoy the prosperity in which these peasants live" when he saw German villages in the Banat.[76]

The design of villages and buildings were not the only way that the Germans imprinted their culture on the landscape of the region. The naming of towns and villages also reflected certain beliefs about settlement. In places where villages were built for the incoming colonists, they often received a German name.[77] In the 1720s, the villages of Langenfeld (long field), Freudenthal (joyful valley), and Häuerdorf (hewer's village), among many others, were founded. There were also towns like Gottlob (God's praise). Towns were also often named after prominent Habsburgs or their officials. Salhausen was named after the commandant of Ujpalanka.[78] The village of Mercydorf was named after Banat governor Florimund Mercy. The Bulgarians' main settlement, most often known as Vinga or Vinka, was also known as Theresiopel. The proposed colonial town Franz- und Ludovica-Stadt, mentioned earlier, was named after Emperor Franz and his wife.

When the German colonists settled an existing village, it often lost its local name. Thus, the colonists took control both physically by occupying the village and intellectually by renaming it. It is unclear if the impetus for renaming came from the government or was the result of local colonist initiative, but the effect was the same; local Wallach and Rascian spaces became German spaces. Most obviously, the capital Temesvar was Germanized to Temeschburg, though interestingly, the original name (and the more Germanized variant Temeswar) appear much more frequently in the written record, even in government documents. The process of intellectually claiming what had been local land began very early in the colonial experience. Hedekut was a Wallach village near the Maros River. Sometime in the early 1720s, the Wallach residents were transferred to Gesseniz. In

1724, forty-five German colonist families replaced the transferred locals. A contemporary description of the village still called it "Hedekut" even after the takeover by the Germans. This same description mentions "some good spring sources."[79] The now-German village was renamed Guttenbrunn (good spring).[80] After the transfer of the locals from Kisfalud, the German name became Engelsbrunn (angel spring).[81] In addition to completely renaming places, the adjective *Deutsch* was used as a modifier in Deutsch-Skt. Peter, Deutsch-Karansebesch, or Deutsch-Rekas, for example, especially in places where Germans and local people lived close by one another. There were also hybrid names like Gross Becskerek (Great Becskerek) and Klein-Skt. Peter, that incorporated German and local names.[82] The most common hybrids used *Neu* (new) and *Alt* (old) to designate the German (new) from the local (old). All of these renaming practices had the effect of Germanizing parts of the landscape.[83]

Village design and upkeep is perhaps the most visible way that German-speaking colonists did initially fulfill governments' desires to remake and develop space. Importantly, this was the aspect of colonization, at least the design, in which governments took the most active role. Thus, this was not so much a triumph of the colonists but of the administration. Officials in Pennsylvania, William Penn included, had plans to settle incoming German migrants in a rational, enlightened manner, strongly resembling the plans executed in the Banat. Penn wanted a township system with centralized meeting houses and contiguous fields "divided in a regular fashion." Some later towns, like Chambersburg, Lebanon, and Gettysburg, were arranged on a grid or street-town patterns. The Pennsylvanian plan was significantly less successful as dispersed freeholders became the norm rather than regular villages of farmer-settlers.[84]

Colonial towns and villages in the Russian Empire highlighted the differences between the migrants and the neighboring Slavs and nomads, much as they did in the Banat. One traveler, who earlier had criticized the Germans for not working hard enough, remarked that "the cottages of the Germans are much better built than those of any other peasantry of the Crimea."[85] Another late nineteenth-century traveler mentioned the "white villages and clean German settlements."[86] Kohl noted the "stirring, active, prosperous German settlements" and that the German colonists provided "fresh milk, good bread, clean rooms, and other things which are generally looked for in vain in the Finnish and Russian villages."[87] According to Palmer, "Their [the Germans'] cottages are a complete contrast to the *izbas* of the Russian peasantry. They are solidly built and well-furnished."[88] The material culture of the German colonists was visible evidence of the changes authorities hoped to see.

Temesvar and Towns: Bastions of Germandom

While authorities could plan and execute "ideal" villages, often building them from the ground up, they did not have the same luxury when it came to towns. Unlike many of the villages in the region, the towns, and in particular the capital of Temesvar, were long established. Thus while the authorities could and did profoundly change these sites, they had to deal with an existing material culture to do so. Temesvar was an important city long before the eighteenth century and Habsburg rule. In 1316, the Hungarian king, Robert of Anjou, moved his capital there, hosting important guests and events such as tournaments. Much as it would be under the Habsburgs, Temesvár in the Late Middle Ages was a borderland, first with the Bulgarians and later with the Ottomans. As such, it was critical for imperial strategy, first and foremost as a site to rally armies for battle. In 1438, Johann Hunyadi made the city his residence and built a fortress to hold back the Ottoman advance.[89] Despite these efforts, Temesvár fell to the Ottomans in 1552. Even under Ottoman rule, the city retained prominence as the capital of an eyalet, an Ottoman administrative division. A seventeenth-century traveler, Heinrich Ottendorf, stated that there were eight mosques in the city, whose towers were visible parts of the skyline, and three smaller, poorly apportioned ones in the suburbs.[90]

In 1716, the army of Eugene of Savoy captured the city. At the time of conquest, the city was described as "average size[d]," whatever that might mean.[91] The same observer noted the extensive natural and manmade defenses, which made the Turks believe the city would be "unconquerable." In addition, the city had several suburbs, which also provided protection from an invading army, at least in theory. The region remained a potential geopolitical hotspot for the Habsburgs. As such, they undertook the construction of a new fortress in the town beginning in 1723. In 1738, during the war between the Austrians and the Ottomans, the inner city burned.[92] Throughout its history, war and conflict molded the city.

In changing the cityscape, the Habsburgs were merely following a well-established path. In the same way that renaming villages asserted ownership, changing the material culture of cities was a physical manifestation of a changed political reality. For instance, much as the Ottomans transformed churches in Temesvár into mosques when they took the city, reflecting the introduction of Islamic culture and values, the Habsburg authorities transformed mosques into churches, reflecting the reimposition of Catholic culture.[93] Likewise, the Turkish baths became the Rathaus, further highlighting Catholic Habsburg rule.[94] In 1753, a palace (*Palast*) was built for the civil-president of the Banat in the Cathedral square. It later became the county house (*Komitatshaus*) when control of the Banat went to the Hungarians.[95] Paton claimed that when he visited in the 1860s, there was nothing except a tombstone and the suburb of Mahalla to testify to the Turkish presence there.[96]

Under the first governor, Mercy, the city also experienced considerable economic growth. The construction of the Fabrik Vorstadt with its oil presses and textile manufactories represented a major development in the productive capacity of the town. Other towns also experienced similar, though more muted, developments. German and Greek trading societies formed in 1723 and 1725. The Bega Canal was finished in 1733, which helped to drain the swamps that surrounded the city.[97] Under Maria Theresia, efforts were made to improve the supply of potable water, though often people had to drink from the canal.[98] Increasingly clean water helped support an expanding population, which reached 6,718 in 1775.[99]

Much as the villages, the city was built along rational lines, and much as travelers praised the German villages, they likewise praised the city. According to one source, it was among the "handsomest and most regular towns in the whole Austrian Empire."[100] Having "mostly German inhabitants," according to a late eighteenth-century account, the streets were "broad and wide" and houses were built in the "Italian style."[101] Another later traveler described it as a "beautiful, regularly built, friendly city" with "beautiful, clean streets." He noted that anyone finding such a place "in such a distance from civilization" would be pleased.[102]

The Habsburgs also supported major construction projects designed to improve the city's cultural life. The first German schools were formed in Temesvar in 1717, with the Jesuits opening a Latin gymnasium there in 1725, which lasted until shortly after the Order was dissolved in 1773. Normal schools appeared in Temesvar, Pancsova, and Weisskirchen in 1774.[103] From the capital, schools spread through the Banat in the nineteenth century. In 1848, there were 349 Catholic (likely mostly German and some Hungarian), 181 Greek, 47 Lutheran, 15 Calvinist, and 12 Jewish schools in the Banat. By 1858, there were 529 Catholic, 595 Greek, 61 Lutheran, 22 Calvinist, and 43 Jewish schools. Seventy-one percent of boys and 41 percent of girls attended school. In 1859, there were two complete and three lower gymnasiums with 53 teachers and 1,098 students in the Banat.[104] The Catholic cathedral was begun in 1736 by the architect Emanuel Fischer von Erlach, though it was not finished until much later. Although a German theater had existed in the city since 1753, it was given a permanent home in 1776. By 1828, there was a German theater paper. Also in that same year, a Hungarian theater society was founded. A printing press arrived in 1769 with the first newspapers and calendars in 1771.[105]

The city was made a *Königliche Freistadt* or "Royal Free Town" by Joseph II in 1781.[106] This placed Temesvár among the most privileged urban settings. By the early nineteenth century, such towns were centers of German culture in Hungary. "Free Towns" paid taxes and answered to the treasury. They also had representation in the national Diet. All the towns collectively shared one vote. Residents of the free towns were "mostly non-Magyars, in the majority Germans." They were also largely agriculturalists who lived in towns rather than pure urbanites. Small cliques of influential citizens ran the towns, since only one-fourth of the residents were burgers and many of them took no part in government.[107] "Free Towns" existed in Hungary until 1870. In that year, Temesvár and Werschetz became "Independent Municipalities" equal to the existing Hungarian counties.[108]

The town continued to grow in the eighteenth century. In 1838, a casino opened and in 1846 a bank.[109] When Kohl visited the city in the 1840s, he described it as "one of the largest and best built in Hungary," noting that all such cities were "built by Germans or under German administration." That said, it was the home of the "Servian nobility" and most of the churches in the town were Orthodox. He estimated the population at about 20,000 inhabitants, while another source estimated "the population of the fortress [at] about 3,000; and that of the whole town, including the suburbs, [at] 13,000, besides the garrison." He also noted the terrible fevers and sicknesses that pervaded the town.¹¹⁰ The city remained 51 percent of German ethnicity in 1900, according to official statistics recording a resident's "mother tongue."¹¹¹

Newspapers: Government Organs of Progress and Development

Much as they were in the spread of education, cities were also integral in the creation of a local print culture in the later eighteenth century. As cities were physical manifestations of colonial power, so newspapers helped preserve the less material, more intellectual goals of Europeanization. German-language newspapers give us insight into the settlers' communal knowledge, or at the very least, what some ambitious printers wanted it to be. The Germans in the Banat, to say nothing of the other ethnicities, had very little access to locally-produced newspapers in the first three-quarters of the century. The only newspapers available until the 1770s were sent by post from Vienna, later from Pest and Pressburg (today's Bratislava) as well.¹¹² The first paper to be published in Temesvar, the *Temeswarer Nachrichten*, started in 1771 and had a short run from April to July. Two more newspapers had short runs in the 1780s: the *Temeswarer Zeitung* (1784) and the *Temeswarer Merkur* (1787). During the Napoleonic Wars, two more newspapers came into existence to provide information on the conflict: the *Temeswarer Wochenblatt* (1805) and the *Tagsbericht* (1809). To my knowledge, no examples of any of these papers have yet been found other than the *Temeswarer Nachrichten*. In the 1820s, the first periodicals printed in the region appeared, two of which dealt with the theater, indicating an increasingly educated and cultured segment of society in the capital. As the century proceeded, increasingly more newspapers were founded. By the 1850s, even some provincial towns had their own newspapers.¹¹³

The copies of the *Temeswarer Nachrichten* provide an interesting look into what its purveyors thought people in a Habsburg colonial town would be interested in.¹¹⁴ This newspaper was designed to inform readers about government policy and to encourage them to better their agricultural practices. There were official stories and ordinances from Vienna. For example, the first edition of the paper contained the full text of an ordinance meant to regulate fishing, especially on the Danube, something that would doubtless have been an important topic in the Banat. There were also releases from the Banat administration regarding local issues. For instance, the administration acknowledged that local wood sellers and millers were overcharging for their wares and promised to tackle these issues. Another article talked about the importance of the silk industry and encouraged people to undertake silk production. It even gave instructions on how best to get started.

Reflecting the goals of the government in integrating the region into the broader economy, the development of agriculture was a favorite subject not only of the newspaper writers but also within the wider enlightened literary culture. Many cameralists stressed the importance of farming in their works, especially that of "luxury" products like indigo and tobacco. As briefly noted earlier, Johann v. Klaniczay, the royal prefect in Werschetz, wrote a short book on growing olives in 1809.[115] Such tutorials were especially important in Hungary, which the Banat joined in 1779, as the Habsburg administration wanted it to be the agricultural center for the monarchy. These treatises touched not only on growing novel crops, but also on improving existing yields through crop rotation or the best practices in animal husbandry.[116] Newspapers were part of a wider effort to improve the population, and they reinforced and propagated agricultural as well as commercial knowledge. As we will see, in the nineteenth century, this purpose remained and became explicit in the names of the Banat's newspapers.

There were also advertisements for bookshops and estate sales. Both prove that there was an audience for a wide variety of books in Temesvar. There were books on agriculture, medicine, math, books to help kids learn, Greek-German grammars, a German grammar in French, sermons, and French translations including Diderot. The Enlightenment had a long reach. There was also an offer for a book that contained all the residents of Temesvar, including the address, age, religion, birthplace, "character," and profession of the individuals. This again highlights the central importance of religion in the minds of both the government and the people. They also covered more pedestrian information. Like newspapers for centuries afterward, it reported the lotto numbers.[117] A few weeks later, they announced the establishment of a local lottery.

While Francesco Griselini is typically credited with the first history of the Banat, the newspaper carried a multipart story that predates Griselini's by a number of years. Many of the elements that became part of the later histories were already visible. There was definite deference to the intelligence of the Habsburg authorities in settling Germans in the region.

The ethnoreligious hierarchy that had been constructed in the Banat was noticeable to the author of the article. While not extremely critical of the Wallachs, something that other authors certainly were, the author of the article did place them below the Rascians in his estimation (Rascians were "better mannered"). Like cities, the newspapers were showpieces for the authorities.

Nineteenth-century newspapers highlighted the continued centrality of agriculture in the lives of most of the region's residents. They also showed that the government and civic leaders were still interested in "bettering" the people. In the *Banater Zeitschrift für Landwirthschaft, Handel, Künste und Gewerbe* (The Banat journal for agriculture, commerce, crafts, and trade), which ran in the late 1820s, there were articles outlining the best practices for agriculture or advocating the diversification of crops and animals. There were articles on the three-field system and how to best use the ground. That such information still needed to be distributed indicates that the process of modernizing agriculture was still ongoing in the region. As one would expect, commodity prices were also listed. There were also articles on foreign trade, milling methods in Poland, ways to keep your cellar dry, bakers in Paris, a cure for baldness (cynoglossum officinale and pork fat or grease), among other topics. The journal catered to an audience that evidently had a variety of tastes outside their work, including intellectual pursuits. There was poetry and more articles on the history of the Banat (which bear the same hallmarks of previous and later attempts).[118] Both the eighteenth- and nineteenth-century newspapers ultimately had the same goals: to bring some high culture to the frontier and to encourage its development.

The Banat's colonists were a big expense for the government. As such, the government in Vienna and Temesvar tried to encourage their success. After it quickly became clear that colonists could not simply be transferred to the region and thrive, the government used a variety of tactics to encourage and support them. They hired overseers to look after their welfare. They built, and rebuilt, villages and towns for them. They encouraged education and the dispersal of advice in the form of newspapers and journals. The degree to which any of these strategies was successful is almost to impossible to evaluate from the existing records. What can be said with certainty is that the government tried, in various ways and with various degrees of urgency, to better the lives of the colonists over the course of the eighteenth century.

For the colonists themselves, the government played a dual role. The government was both coercive and potentially generous. Both strategies served the same goals: to keep the Banat populated and productive. From the 1720s forward, it was clear that without intervention, the colonies in the Banat would not survive, much less thrive. This was not a unique situation. German colonists in Russia and Spain also experienced problems establishing their colonies and were likewise encouraged, through oversight, to improve their lot. In the Banat, while the change in administration in the 1780s changed the methods of coercion and reward, the end goals remained remarkably similar. Rather than work directly to enrich the emperor, the colonists now worked to enrich their lord.

In the next chapter, we will look even more closely at the lived experiences of the colonists. How did they get on with their neighbors of varying ethnicity and religion? How did they make sense of and try to combat the natural forces like disease and weather that threatened their survival? As we will see, while the government attempted to help the colonists deal with the struggles they faced, the colonists developed their own ways of understanding and manipulating their situation for their own benefit. At times this involved leveraging governmental resources, but often they called upon their families and communities to support them in times of need.

5   Settler Culture

Frontier Problems and Solutions

> Because the region was marshy, it was very unhealthy.... At that time [1720s, 1730s], the Banat received the name "Grave of the Germans." Also here were attempts to better the circumstances.
>
> —*Felix Milleker, 1925*[1]

IN 1782, THE COLONIAL INHABITANTS of Albrechtsflur in the historic Banat wrote the county administration regarding the "wild animals" belonging to the village of Mokrin (likely Rascian) and the damage they had caused. The villagers contended that the animals damaged wine gardens, fruit trees, vegetables, straw, and corn stores. This forced them to buy straw to heat their homes and animal feed from other villages. The German colonists had sent two people who were "knowledgeable about their language" to complain but got nowhere. Finally, a government agent came to the village and observed the problem. He authorized the villagers to shoot the destructive animals, which they did. Later, two Rascians who had owned some of the now-deceased animals came to the colonists' village to complain. They demanded to see the skins and "confronted [the Germans] with much rudeness." The colonists, according to their own version, tried to be neighborly with them.[2]

If the government hoped that the colonists could be models for improved agricultural practices and a vanguard of Europeanization, then such incidents are illustrative of the difficulties the plan faced. As we have seen, the government was intimately involved in bringing German colonists from the Reich to the Banat and putting them into a position to be exemplars. They provided land and often housing, including other people's lands and housing. By the late Theresian migrations, they were given tools and animals among other important concessions. They attempted to encourage the colonists through oversight and education. In return, the Germans were to help rationalize and develop the region. The design of their towns, villages, and houses were to be beacons of a new order. While the administration tried to control every variable they could for the benefit of the colonists, there were certain realities of life on the frontier that remained beyond their grasp.

Life in the Banat was extremely difficult for many of the settlers. As the quote that started the chapter highlighted, early death was a constant threat, and a steady flow of colonists was needed to replace the dead. This was not, of course, unique. Throughout history, migrants have often had to contend with increased mortality.[3] German-speaking colonists in the peat bogs of the northern Reich likewise died in high numbers due to disease and malnutrition. In fact, the descendants of the northern German colonists and the Banat colonists retained the same romanticized, triumphal proverb: "Death to the first generation, need to the second, bread to the third." Despite the fact that the phrase was used by Germans in the 1940s to help Nazify the Banat and justify their dominance, the sources show that there is more than a grain of truth in the proverb's assertions of hardship.[4] Seventeenth-century immigrants to the Chesapeake Colonies in British North America who were lucky enough to reach twenty, most likely died before forty. We should also not forget that cities since ancient Mesopotamia have been bastions of disease and death. London, like the Banat, had a reputation as a "graveyard." It, too, required the constant in-migration to replace those who had died and to grow the population.[5] That said, and as the opening vignette illustrates, the rural, agricultural nature of the colonies made the challenges there of a different sort than those experienced by city dwellers. For instance, the weather was a constant concern of the largely agrarian German colonists in a way foreign to city dwellers, at least until food prices spiked.

Given the threats, the settlers had to come up with creative solutions to their problems. While relations with local people could turn violent and mistrustful, they could also be peaceful and cooperative. Colonists used a combination of religion, magic, science, and herbalism to explain and attack their most pressing concern, disease.[6] They addressed problems of old age and infirmity using land, children, and marriage to ensure stability. In this chapter, we will get to the ground level and explore the plethora of phenomena that influenced how colonists saw, understood, and interacted with the world around them. None of these solutions were novel, but they do highlight the fact that the colonists were not the Europeanizing force that many in the government, and many later scholars, hoped they would be. Instead, they were peasants trying to deal with the harsh conditions of an unknown land.

Colonists and Locals: Interethnic Relations

As with most colonizing groups, one of the first and enduring issues to confront colonists was their relationship with the people who already inhabited the region. When placed in close proximity, Germans and local people were often antagonistic groups and at times fought one another. As the introduction highlighted, most disputes centered on land and were based on differing conceptions of land use and agricultural practices. Over time, the actions of Wallachs toward settler communities during war increased distrust. Animosity on both sides may have been based on German feelings of superiority given their privileged position as colonists. Far from unidirectional, both Germans and locals were perpetrators and victims of violence and confrontation, though as a numerically smaller community, the Germans were more often on the losing end of such conflicts. This antagonistic relationship was especially problematic given that the Germans were to act as models for the local people.

Mistrust and confrontation were evident very early. The records are filled with incidents in which colonists and local people violently interacted. Unfortunately, it is in many cases impossible to know exactly what triggered these events. The details are spotty. Some colonists feared their low numbers put them at risk. Perhaps it was this fear that led the colonists to aggressive actions. In 1729, for instance, Germans and Wallachs in the villages of Petrillova and Csukits violently confronted one another. The German community was subsequently required to pay damages to an injured Wallach to end the dispute.[7] Relatively minor incidents such as this, and they were numerous, point to a fraught relationship between the colonists on the one hand and the locals on the other. Additionally, these were the incidents severe enough that they made it into the government's surviving official records. One can imagine that many more incidents occurred that did not rise to that level. Even Johann Kaspar Steube, an often-sympathetic observer, distrusted the Wallachs. He related that although he was ostensibly protected by Wallach guards, he never fully trusted them to protect him and thus slept with a loaded gun on his person.[8] The fact that he was both German and in the Habsburg military likely made him feel like a potential target. Intercommunal conflict continued into the nineteenth century. When the first German settlers appeared in the village of Schag in 1812, the local Wallachs resisted their arrival. In fact, they burned down their houses, forcing the settlers to flee.[9] This hot-cold conflict continued all the way until 1848.

Conflict was common in instances where German-speaking settlers encountered standing populations. For instance, colonists in British North America faced a Native American population that was, at times, helpful and accommodating and, at other times, distrustful and confrontational.[10] Similarly, a hostile population initially confronted the settlers on the Volga in the Russian Empire. Both the local nomadic Muslims and Buddhists, often known broadly as "Kirgiz" though undoubtedly including Kalmyks, as well as the Russian serfs, resisted German encroachment. In the early years of colonization, the nomads often raided villages. This largely ended by the 1770s though sporadic raids continued into the later eighteenth century.[11] In the Spanish-German village of La Parilla, local Spaniards set fire to German houses. Robbery was also a problem. The low quality of the settlers and their ever-decreasing numbers due to disease forced the Spanish government to use local Spanish-speaking colonists to bolster the number of settlers and ensure the survival of the towns and villages.[12] Germans feared the dilution of their numbers by local colonists, and there was even a rumor that they would be "robbed" of their lands after they had developed them.[13]

Germans in the Banat not only feared but also disdained local people. Their very ethnic identity could be used to insult. To call another German a "Wallachian whore" was a vile enough insult to land an old woman before a local court. She was sentenced to an hour in the *Geige* or Shrew's Fiddle, for this offense.[14] An important example of this superior attitude comes from one of the few colonial narratives we possess. Written by Johann Eimann, this work provides us with the experiences and impressions of a Reich German colonist and Habsburg state functionary in the 1780s. While Eimann was part of the movement to the Batschka, the region directly abutting the Banat to the west, many of the attitudes and ideals he described undoubtedly mirrored those in the Banat, especially given that by the time of his writing, both were under Hungarian control. To begin with, Eimann described his own impression of the hierarchy of the region. For him, the "hardworking" Germans were on the pinnacle. They were followed by the "hard-drinking" Slavs, the Hungarians, and finally, the poor Wallachians. Generally, the disdain for local people revolved around their agricultural abilities, or lack thereof. Eimann wrote a letter to the emperor in the name of his German community asking for the separation of the German section of the village from the Rascian. He argued that the Germans would be more useful and productive for the crown if they were separated. He complained that the Rascians did not know how to make butter or cheese. They did not want to live "orderly." They left their cows in pasture, leaving it to the Germans to bring them home and milk them. They let their animals run wild, to the detriment of the grasslands and the Germans' crops. He further argued that by simply looking at purely German villages, one could see that they were more prosperous. The colonists believed that mixing with the Rascians would only hurt them and cause them to be poor. Eimann, like many observers of his time and scholars writing on the region even into the twentieth century, believed that the Germans were simply better, more industrious farmers. Finally acceding to the Germans' demand, Emperor Franz allowed them to constitute their own village.[15]

Complaints about the agricultural practices of the local people, like the one that started the chapter, were a common occurrence. In addition to Eimann's complaints, J. G. Kohl talked about the Wallachs' "ill-attended cattle" in the Bella Reka valley and claimed that they were as mischievous as wolves and bears.[16] People also apparently destroyed crops, much to the consternation of some Germans. In the village of Marienfeld in 1826, Francz Erling and some of his neighbors complained that the inhabitants of Kikinda, likely Rascians, were responsible for damaging their cornfields. The local government wrote officials in Kikinda asking them to deal with the problem and prevent their residents from causing further damage.[17] Again, the sources make it hard to determine exactly why such incidents occurred. Were they the result of carelessness or maliciousness? Within the broader context, it seems likely a combination of both.

Given such incidents, officials and other regional observers throughout the eighteenth and nineteenth centuries often shared the Germans' feelings of superiority. The author of the 1734 report on the state of the Banat credited the German colonists with improving the state of viticulture in the region and with "animating" the Rascians to do the same.[18] When a number of Wallachs fled the area around Komlosch in the late 1770s, a local official in the region asked the government to settle "German people" there. According to him, they would both stimulate the local people to use their land better and they would provide more security for the region.[19] J. G. Kohl remarked that "[Germans] have introduced a better system of agriculture among the Russians, Poles, and Hungarians, and set an example of industry, care, and honesty which they would do well to follow."[20] A. A. Paton, a British traveler in 1848, was merciless in his comparison. He said that although the German colonists had an "unamiable, litigious spirit, which degenerates into avarice and [an] independence, which amounts to obstinacy, [the German] is morally, physically, and intellectually, the superior of the Roman [i.e., Wallach/Romanian]." Paton also noted that while German farmers employed Wallachs as servants, Germans rarely worked for Wallachs.[21] Such attitudes were likewise visible among the observers of Russian-German colonists.[22] This is all particularly interesting when set alongside the evidence of colonial ineptitude that was presented last chapter. While these beliefs may have existed in the minds of some colonists and observers, the situation on the ground did not always match the triumphal attitude.

Of course, not all interactions led to disdain, separation, or violence. In Paraputsch, for instance, differences between German and Rascian inhabitants, though "intense," did not lead to the division of the village.[23] In one tragic instance, colonists accidentally killed a Wallach shepherd while shooting at a cow. Rather than lead to intercommunal violence, the situation was resolved when the colonist responsible agreed to pay the family of the victim.[24] Religion also appears to have had some power to overcome ethnic differences. In Rekasch, the Rascians and Germans apparently worked together quite well. As we saw earlier, both ethnic groups in Rekasch were Catholic. In 1751, officials sent out a questionnaire asking if any subjects had issues with local administrators. Both the Germans and the Rascians responded that they had a problem with Martin Petrasko, an Orthodox official who lived in the town. They asked to have him transferred and replaced with a Catholic. The government was amenable to the request, especially because Petrasko also asked to be transferred.[25] In this case, Germans and locals were able to cooperate because of shared religious beliefs that dictated a common goal, the replacement of a "Schismatic" official with one who was religiously acceptable. The fact that the community was united in opposition to an "Other" also helped create solidarity. How far this cooperation continued, in terms of land use or intermarriage between the Rascian and German Catholics, is hard to discern.

There is further evidence that Germans and Rascians could cooperate, in this case when they shared economic or political goals. In 1767, leaders from the German and Rascian sections of Pancsova requested a *union* of their communities and their promotion to a "Military Community." This would have given them more autonomy. Perhaps unsurprisingly given its overriding policy of separation, the administration denied this request, though they used a property-based argument to dismiss the appeal. They renewed their attempts at unification in 1792–1793. This time their efforts were rewarded when on January 1, 1794, Emperor Franz agreed to unite German and Rascian Pancsova as a "Military Community." In so doing, the town gained more control over its own affairs. While the emperor appointed some of the higher officials, including the mayor (*Bürgermeister*), others were voted into their position. Half of the "lower employees" were German, and half were Rascian. This is particularly interesting given that in 1794, there were 433 Rascian families to 241 German.[26] In this case, economic solidarity and common political goals united the community. There was also the peaceful exchange of ideas over the long term. Historian Zoran Janjetović maintained that the Rascians slowly learned from and adopted the settled farming practices of the German colonists, though they were never as adept at it.[27] During the Serbian Revolt from 1803 to 1813, there was at least one incident in which the Germans showed their support for the Serbian cause. The Germans of Pancsova defended an Orthodox cleric, Arsenjević, who was transferred because of his public prayer in support of the insurgents in Serbia.[28]

Despite this evidence that colonists and local people *could* live together peacefully if they shared common goals, they rarely had to. Both of their own volition and that of the government, Germans tended to settle in ethnically and religiously homogeneous communities. In fact, one of the hallmarks of the German settlements in the Banat, and in the East in general, was their insularity. Until the nineteenth century, Germans largely lived either in mono-ethnic villages or in ethnically divided communities where certain areas were reserved exclusively for Germans. The notable exceptions to this general rule were larger towns, especially Temesvar, where Germans, Rascians, and Jews interacted to a greater degree.[29] In the early nineteenth century, Kikinda, an important Rascian town, had a recognized "German quarter."[30] Even in Temesvár, there were "German" and "Illyrian" sections of the suburbs as late as 1839.[31] The government was largely responsible for the ethnic homogeneity. While there was a certain desire on the part of some officials to have the Germans act as models for the local population, there was also a concurrent fear that the locals would negatively influence the Germans. To prevent this from occurring, officials wanted to keep the Germans separated from the local people as much as possible. As we saw, this impulse existed from the earliest mass movements of Germans and often involved the removal of local people to create the desired ethnic makeup.

This was not only government policy but also reflected the wishes of some migrants who specifically requested not to be settled near local people. David Ulrich and Wenzl Poliska, speaking on behalf of sixty Alsatians, requested to be settled together and separate from "other nations."[32] It was not only colonists and the authorities who pushed for separation. Some Rascians did not want to live with settlers either. In 1775, when colonists were brought to settle Baranda and Sakule, they wrote a letter requesting not to be "mixed" with these German settlers because of "differences of religion and morals."[33]

Alongside the dominant Rascian and Wallach ethnic groups, there were other groups in the Banat with whom the settlers interacted. Roma were traveling blacksmiths who made items necessary for homesteading like nails, knives, and other small iron tools and copper implements. Trade did not lead the Roma to like the Germans. In fact, according to a source cited in Kohl, while Roma got along with Hungarians and particularly with Wallachs, they "sympathize[d] least with the German," which, tellingly, Kohl took as a compliment.[34] Other itinerant merchants were generally "Greeks" (in general Orthodox Ottoman subjects) or Jews. Economic relations between these groups could be more complicated than simply buying and selling. In Lugos, Martin Reÿdinger and "a Jew named Hirschl" were the proprietors of a brew house.[35] Another Lugos Jew, Nathan Deutsch, asked the court to adjudicate a dispute between him and his partner, Mathias Keppel, regarding the purchase of a brewery.[36]

While business and agricultural interactions occurred, more personal connections were apparently rare. As many of these observations come from outside observers, we must maintain a level of skepticism. These observers, many of whom clearly believed in the superiority of German culture, may have not wanted to believe that Germans would associate, much less assimilate with a "lesser" group; their observations may thus have served to support their prejudices. That said, the existence of linguistic and cultural islands of Germanness in the Banat, Hungary, Russia, and the United States into the twentieth century proves that there was more than a bit of truth to their assertions of German-colonial insularity.

According to the sources, intermarriage was almost completely unknown in the eighteenth century. In fact, the government was unsure what to do about interfaith or interethnic marriages. In Carasova, for example, where Catholic and Orthodox Rascians lived near one another, the problem was acute. The administration in Werschetz was so concerned about the possibility of intermarriage between the two groups that they asked officials in Temesvar what to do about them.[37] When Kohl visited the region in the mid-nineteenth century, he commented that Germans and Wallachians *never* married. He quoted an inhabitant who said that in his village "they do come together to fight sometimes . . . but never to marry." He further stated that Germans also had similar prohibitions regarding Serbians and Hungarians, though were not so strongly policed.[38] Paget noted something similar. He said that the different groups "rarely intermarry." He also noted that although some Germans learned the Wallach language, Wallachs did not learn German.[39] In most cases, insularity was likely due to a combination of linguistic, cultural, and religious incompatibility as well as general antipathy. In the nineteenth century, at least in Temesvár, there is evidence of at least some amount of intermarriage. The graveyards in the city contain headstones from the late nineteenth century that seem to indicate that intermarriage occurred (as typical German names appear alongside typical

Rascian/Serbian or Hungarian names). Of the Germans' interactions with other settlers, there is even less to say. As we saw in the introduction, there were a number of Western European migrants to the Banat, including a number of French. It appears that by the nineteenth century, most French, Italian, and Spanish settlers had "Germanized."[40] Thus it seems likely that among colonists, widespread, peaceful interaction was the norm and that German language and culture eventually dominated the others.

The insularity of German-colonial culture was mirrored in the Russian Empire. According to outside observers, the colonists "evince[d] in their demeanor a dignified consciousness of their superiority to the Russian peasants around them."[41] Colonists would hire serfs as farm hands but would give them only menial jobs, after showing them very "carefully" what was to be done.[42] Given this sense of superiority, it is not surprising to hear that "they maintained their original nationality, so far as their religion and the use of their own language in their families are concerned." Settlers did not mingle or merge with the other Russian subjects but held fast to their language, culture, religion, social habits, dress, even hair and beard style.[43] They may have adopted some farming methods from the Russian peasantry, such as a type of plow or barn, but culturally, they were resistant.[44] This insularity continued into the twentieth century. An observer in the early 1900s remarked that while Germans felt that they and the Slavs "get on very well together . . . he [the German] would not change places with the Slav for anything in the world."[45]

In an exception to the rule, the German colonists in Spain assimilated rather quickly. Perhaps this is because the shared Catholic faith between the colonizers, standing population, and government served as a cultural bridge much as it had in parts of the Banat. The colonial patents themselves encouraged assimilation, something that did not happen in the Banat or Russian cases. Colonists were given the same rights as all other subjects. Priests who spoke German were only provided until the Germans learned Spanish, obviously something the government expected to happen.[46] The government required school-age Germans to learn Spanish from the outset of the colonial project. Already in the 1780s, German culture was in decline among the residents of the colonies in the Sierra Morena. Travelers to Santa Elena and La Carolina noticed that people in these supposedly German colonies could not speak German. They had blond hair and blue eyes but were completely "Hispanicized." This was part of the government's overall plan. No settlements had German names. All were Spanish. By 1781, the population of the region contained "many more" Spaniards than Germans. In 1834/35, the colonial areas were fully integrated into the surrounding provinces, ending their unique political status. By 1907, when the historian of the region Josef Weiss wrote his book, he claimed that the memory of the colonial endeavor in the region was very small indeed.[47] While in the Banat, Spaniards "became" German, in Spain, Germans "became" Spaniards.

Perhaps counterintuitively to people living in a nationalist age, there was no widespread solidarity among the Banat's colonists in the eighteenth century. This was especially true in periods of intense colonization when old and new colonists often competed for resources. For instance, the settlement patent in 1726 seemed to promise potential settlers that they would be given enough land for their children to settle.[48] Later, when the government was looking to place incoming colonists in 1765, the village of Periamosch was slated to receive ninety-two settlers. Since there was only enough room for thirty, the rest had to be settled in the neighboring village of Wariasch. There was a problem. Local administrators pointed out that the land belonging to Wariasch was already home to "150 old families excluding their many marriage-capable (*Heiratsmässig*) youth."[49] Any land given to the "new" colonists was land that was essentially taken away from the next generation. Another problem arose in Jarmatha. As we saw earlier, the authorities displaced the Rascians of this village to make way for incoming colonists. Due to a lack of housing, the government ordered old colonists to quarter new colonists over the winter. Later, there were questions about the new division of lands. The dispute got so bad that the newcomers requested administrative separation in 1768, much as other Germans did with local people.[50] Colonists were also involved in the court system, suing and being sued. In Mercydorf, one colonist sued another for the return of a wagon he felt was taken illegally.[51] In another case, a Hatzfeld colonist was being sued for a debt he owed a landlady.[52]

Apparently, the colonists, and other people in the Banat, could not always come together even in the face of disaster. The threat of fire was a communal problem. In 1773, the government released the "Fire Fighting Ordinance for the Temesvar Banat." This ordinance paints a grim picture of cooperation among people in the Banat. According to the author, experience had shown that the common people did not help one another out in cases of fire. Highlighting the lack of regional or ethnic solidarity noted above, if it was not a relative, they simply sat and watched the "sad accident." Sometimes, people even stole property during the uproar that accompanied such situations. To combat this apathy, the ordinance authorized government officials to round up townspeople and make them fight fires.[53] Solidarity among the Banat Germans came only later and, at least initially, largely existed inside the heads of nationalizing intellectuals.

Given the fractured nature of the Reich and the harshness of life on the frontier, it makes sense that many colonists saw settlement in the Banat as a zero-sum game. Whether competing against Wallachs, Rascians, or other Germans, settlers had to worry about their own best interests before those of outsiders, even outsiders who later generations would see as their ostensible "coethnics." While there are signs, even at this point, of an emerging shared settler culture, it took until the turn of the 1780s and 90s for this culture to become visible among the peasants themselves. Eimann was one of the first public cases of a German settler, of course an intellectual, declaring the existence of a settler community and describing its history. While such Banat-wide solidarity may have existed earlier, especially after the beatings the settlers took at the hands of the Ottomans and Wallachs in both Austro-Ottoman wars, Eimann's work was the first real expression of a solidarity extending beyond the local village community. Similarly, Griselini's history of the Banat and the history given in the *Temesvarer Nachrichten* around the same time point to some recognition of a shared settler culture. The rise of nationalism in general, and the ever-improving situation of the settlers themselves, allowed for ideas of a shared identity to come into being.

A Dangerous World: Climate and Disease

In addition to confronting the human element (both local and colonial), settlers had to deal with other, less personal dangers that threatened their lives and livelihoods. The climate was a constant concern. Most German colonists were farmers and, like farmers around the world, were intimately tied to the rhythms of nature for survival. Hail and violent storms wreaked havoc on agriculture.[54] Grasshoppers and locusts were recurring problems. Droughts brought terrible consequences. There was a major drought in 1795, leading to famine.[55] In 1838, a drought lowered the sales of grain by one-sixth, from six million *Metzen* to one.[56] Another drought in 1841 caused a newspaper writer to question whether the Banat had somehow drifted further south. He said he expected to look out the window and see "Moors."[57] In 1863, a major drought caused some farmers in Neubeschenowa (today's Dudeștii Noi, Romania) to trek to Serbia (Gladowa, today's Kladovo) with their animals (261 horses and 983 sheep) in search of relief. The village judge and notary had reported that there was hay and grazing lands there that could be exploited. This was no minor undertaking. The journey from Neubeschenowa to Kladovo is 244 kilometers. To their dismay, conditions in Serbia were no better, and the price of fodder for their animals was even higher. What they had been promised before they left did not match the reality they found. Many animals were lost on the trek back. The judge who organized the expedition was later tried for his "deceitful statements" regarding the conditions in Serbia. In 1874, the verdict fell in his favor. This caused one observer to remark that the courts "hang the small thieves and let the big ones free."[58]

More than droughts, though, floods, swamps, and standing water were ever present, especially in the early days of colonization. Three rivers formed the boundary of the region and many more crisscrossed the interior. The Habsburg efforts at hydrology were partly meant to help tame the rivers and streams of the region to prevent floods, encouraging agricultural and economic development. Floods destroyed villages. Colonists rebuilt some and sought to abandon others. Rebuilding could take years.[59] Floods also had an impact on the placement and design of towns and villages. After villages were destroyed, the authorities could move them and rebuild them along rational, geometric lines.[60] Floods also meant the creation and return of swamps.[61]

The swampy landscape was a perfect breeding ground for disease, the most feared problem for the German colonists in the Banat and a common problem for colonial ventures of the era. As we saw, the government sought to mediate one of the most feared deadly diseases, the plague, by instituting a quarantine system on the Ottoman border. The last outbreak of plague occurred during the Austro-Ottoman War of 1737–1739. An estimated one-sixth of the Banat's population perished as a result of the epidemic. The government employed drastic measures trying to control its spread, including the death penalty for breaking quarantine or hiding another's illness.[62]

Although after this point, the *Contumaz* system, or perhaps simply blind luck, was successful in keeping out the plague, the colonists had many other diseases with which to contend.

From the earliest days of colonization, various mysterious fevers (sometimes known as the "Banat" or "Theiss" fever) felled successive generations of newcomers.[63] Most observers blamed these "fevers" on the rivers, swamps, and areas of stagnant water in the Banat. When Johann Oswald's wife contacted the government about getting his payment for the colonists he brought to the Banat, she also opened a small window into the problem of morbidity in the Banat in the 1740s and 1750s. While trying to verify her claims about the number of colonists he led to the region, agents went to various villages looking to confirm the numbers. They also noted how many had died. Of the 558 individuals brought to St. Andrascher District in 1748/49, 138 (nearly 25 percent) were dead by 1753. In Werschetz and Gudiaz, three of thirty-seven (8 percent); in Csakover District, twelve of fifty (24 percent); and in Lipova, six of fifty (12 percent) were deceased. Though a small sample, this represented an overall death rate of nearly 23 percent within the first five years.[64]

There are many reports of sickness afflicting German colonial settlements in both government documents and in popular travel literature. In times of high migration, the reports of sickness in the archival record increase.[65] Much like the residents of New Orleans or colonial India, citizens of means often fled Temesvar to Lugoj during the summer to take advantage of a supposedly healthier climate and avoid the peak disease months.[66] Travelers reported the existence of such diseases into the nineteenth century, in 1830, 1831, 1836, 1838, and 1870. There were also outbreaks of cholera around the region.[67] In a report of the deaths from July 24, 1831, 331 of 462 (~72 percent) reported deaths were people under thirty years old. The youngest listed (one individual) was sixteen. Thus, the deaths of children were not taken into consideration in this list and would likely have made these numbers even more shocking.[68]

These diseases were often debilitating. In some towns and villages, 20 percent of the population died from disease, though those who survived appeared to have some sort of immunity.[69] In Rekasch, fevers in the summer of 1840 had at times rendered two-thirds of the German villagers of the area unable to work. In 1841, the "great majority of the population" of Temesvár had contracted the "Banat fever." Such fevers even affected populations in the mountainous regions, despite the belief that those areas were healthier.[70] In the aftermath of the 1848 Revolution, there was an outbreak of epidemic diseases, including cholera and typhus.[71] While most of the peasants who died in the Banat were forgotten, the region's diseases may have been responsible for the death of the most powerful man in the empire, Emperor Joseph II. While campaigning in the region in 1788, Joseph fell ill with a fever and never fully recovered.[72]

The Germans dealt with death and disease in a variety of ways. Certainly, prayer and religion were central to their understanding of how disease worked. After the plague in 1738–39, the survivors built a "plague column" (*Pestsäule*) in Temesvar in thanks for the lifting of the disease. Some may have believed that other supernatural forces, like curses or vampires, were responsible for death and disease. To combat these ills, they used folk medicine or "white magic" to help cure themselves, something explored in more detail below.

Importantly, the German settlers of the eighteenth century lived in a professionalizing world. The Enlightenment and Scientific Revolution touched even the frontier. Already in 1728, there was discussion of placing a doctor in Ujpalanka.[73] Trained physicians worked in tandem with more traditional healers, often to their chagrin.[74] In 1777, Frantz Hess, a doctor from Temesvar, asked that barbers be forbidden to practice medicine. He also put it in very cameralist terms: better doctors meant more healthier and productive subjects.[75] The government also began issuing certain licenses to practice medicine.[76] The Josephian settlement patent promised health care for sick colonists by building hospitals. In the Batschka, Eimann claimed that almost every new village had a hospital with experienced doctors and a pharmacy. Unfortunately for the colonists, the last one closed in 1789.[77] Such a pattern seems likely to have been the case in the Banat as well.

Not only were the plague and Banat fever a constant threat to colonists' well-being, but animal disease could also lead to disaster. Outbreaks of disease were common throughout the eighteenth century and could severely harm farmers' and herders' livelihoods.[78] Paralleling human health care, a new class of professional animal doctors became more prominent in the later part of the eighteenth century, alongside traditional white magic and herbalism. In 1788, for instance, the professor of veterinary medicine, Alexander Tolnäy, diagnosed the sickness affecting the animals in portions of the Banat as hoof-and-mouth disease and recommended a course of treatment.[79] By 1789, the government had opened a veterinary school in Pest and was training some district surgeons in the practice. In this same year, teachers of veterinary medicine from Pest came to the Banat to help with a disease outbreak.[80] In addition to using the latest science, officials also tried to cordon off animal disease much as they did human. For instance, when disease was reported in Hungary in 1754, the government banned the importation of horned animals into the Banat.[81]

A problem that warranted further scientific investigation was a kind of deadly mosquito, called *Kolumbatczer Mücke*, that harmed the animals. They were such a problem that doctor and naturalist Joseph Anton Schönbauer wrote a book on them in 1795.[82] These bugs generally appeared in spring near the Danube and wreaked havoc on people and animals. In 1783, and only in the areas under the auspices of the Mountain Department, the mosquitoes reportedly killed 20 horses, 32 foals, 60 cows and oxen, 71 calves, 130 pigs, and 310 sheep. The bites caused fever, cramps, and convulsions. The swarms also could plug up an animal's nose and mouth and suffocate it. To protect the animals, herders built smoky fires, and the animals grazed in the smoke. Schönbauer also provided a recipe for a salve using tobacco leaves, which may have proved effective, given that modern insecticides (neonicotinoids) like imidacloprid utilize a nicotine-like chemical. Empress Maria Theresia had sent commissions to the region to investigate the issue during her reign. According to Schönbauer, Wallachs believed the bugs emanated from the cave where the dragon slain by St. George was buried. They even tried to wall up the entrance to prevent them from appearing. It did not work. Siebold described them (he called them *Fliegen* or flies) as a problem as late as 1876. He claimed that in April of this year, the mosquitoes killed five cows and two foals.[83]

As the example of St. George and the dragon highlights, the calamities faced by the colonists and other local people demanded explanation, and often people turned to religion and the supernatural to find answers. Local people (especially Wallachs) appear to have had strong folk beliefs they used to explain death. The beliefs, and the reaction of both authorities and peasants, highlight the perceived role of German colonists in rationalizing the Banat. What is particularly surprising about supernatural reports is not the fact that they existed but rather the fact that local officials often took them seriously. In 1725, the administration ordered the exhumation of a suspected witch so that her body could be inspected. The administrator in charge of the disinterment later claimed that the witch was in fact a vampire! He asked the administration for advice on what would happen with the corpse that was now under watch. The same administrator apparently disinterred another suspected vampire almost a year later after some mysterious deaths in Lugos. After confirming that she was indeed a vampire by identifying a "known symbol," they decapitated the corpse with a shovel and burned the remains. Around this same time, the villagers of Babscha incinerated another "vampire." It is unclear whether he or she was alive at the time. In 1729, the administration ordered the Lipova authorities not to release a "magician" they had in custody pending further instructions. As late as 1753, local authorities reported the possibility that vampires (*Wampirs*) might be responsible for the deaths of thirty people in Klein Dikvan and twenty people in Rakasdia. Of course, there were voices of reason. In 1743, a doctor's report pointed out the falsity of one community's claim to having buried a vampire.[84] According to Johann Kaspar Steube, some Hungarians believed that the Wallachs themselves were vampires. He further related that when Wallachs buried their dead, all present would kiss the corpse. He said that enemies of the deceased kissed especially forcefully, hoping to prevent the dead from coming back as a vampire to torment them.[85]

In 1753, Georg Tallar, a doctor trained in Mainz and Strassburg, traveled to the Banat and Transylvania with the blessing of the administration and investigated the reports of vampirism with the intention of dismissing them. He claimed that it was not only Wallachs and Rascians who believed in these stories but also "reasonable peoples" of other ethnicities. Importantly, he mentioned that German colonists never reported a case of vampirism. Local people dealt with suspected vampires by disinterring them, cutting off their heads, driving stakes through their hearts, and burning them. While serving in the army, he had the opportunity to observe suspected cases in Transylvania and the Banat. Wallachs he interviewed claimed to have actually seen the vampire in their rooms and identified it as a certain dead man or woman. According to Tallar, these reports came from sick people who both lacked proper medical care as well as an understanding of what caused diseases. They used vampirism to explain their illness. He attributed their condition to their diet and religious fasting that was common among the Wallachs. That was why Germans, and also soldiers, never got the sickness and thus were never "victims" of Satan and vampires. He further noted that Germans and soldiers had better pastors, who prevented them from believing in such superstitions. In fact, he said that the Germans laughed at such myths and those who believed in them.[86]

The archival record attests to at least one report of vampirism that Tallar investigated in the course of his time in the Banat. In 1755 a report came to Temesvar that, after a spate of child deaths, local people in Vermesch Csakova District had disinterred a corpse believing it to be the vampire responsible for the deaths. Once again, administrators in Temesvar gave a certain amount of credence to the report and sent doctors out to the field to investigate. Tallar, here described as the Caransebecher District Surgeon, was part of this investigation. The team was to examine the body and the story and report any information back to the officials in Temesvar.[87] Their report is missing, but given Tallar's later skepticism, one must assume they debunked the claims.

The claims of vampires are interesting in two ways. First, they give us some insight into the minds of colonists and local people on the European frontier and how they interrogated and understood their world. Secondly, the stories serve as an example of the imposition of rationality in the Banat and the German role in it. The investigating doctor, Tallar, was a German physician specifically tasked with debunking the superstitious and irrational belief in vampirism. He also noted how the Germans were some of the few in the region who did not believe the claims. They, along with soldiers, were the bastions of rational thought in a sea of superstition, at least according to Tallar's report. Whatever the truth of the claim, the news would have pleased the Habsburg authorities.

It is hard to tell the degree to which the German colonists believed in the tales of vampirism, although they must have known that this folk tradition existed. There is also no doubt that certain colonists dabbled in the occult alongside their traditional religions. While most of this knowledge was passed orally throughout Europe, sometimes individuals would compile spells, incantations, prayers, and herbal treatments into a book. One such book appears in the Banat. The work's origin is mysterious, perhaps befitting a book of magic. It is a handwritten tome compiled by Johann Jacob

Freÿ. On the inside cover of the book, Freÿ related that on September 25, 1791, he traveled to Germany (*Deichlant*), the journey taking a little more than three weeks. He was "back" by December 19, though it is unclear where that was. The name "Thurschau" appears as a likely candidate for the location. Perhaps this is Thurgau, Switzerland, and perhaps Freÿ brought the book with him when he migrated to the Banat sometime in the late eighteenth or early nineteenth century. This is admittedly speculation. Freÿ described his book as a "copy" of one Georg Meichterer's "information of how during his lifetime the malevolence of the witches originated and was eliminated (*verbrand worden seÿed*)."[88] Despite questions about its origin, the book provides much needed insight into the beliefs and practices of at least some of the German peasantry in the Banat around the turn of the nineteenth century.

The book suggested an interesting mix of remedies drawing on Christianity, the occult, and herbalism. Following a recipe from Meichterer, for instance, Freÿ told how to counteract magic. To do this, he suggested creating a powder out of several herbs, including St. John's wort, common vervain, devil's-bit scabious, among others. If a person then carried this powder, no magic could harm them. It was also effective for protecting animals. The book is filled with both crosses as well as magic symbols. It has prayers to God and Jesus Christ as well as recipes for various powders and potions. One suggestion was a macabre use of "sympathetic magic." In the case of a weakening limb, the author advised going to the graveyard before sunrise and taking the leg of a corpse. This was then to be rubbed against one's own limb and magic words were to be spoken, finishing with "amen." Thankfully, the author did make clear that the leg should be put back when finished.[89]

This book provides insight into what most concerned German peasants at the time. If it was a major problem, especially one that they did not completely understand, they may have tried to tap supernatural resources to solve it. Most concerns are quite prosaic and mirror the problems we have encountered already. There are numerous remedies that deal with human disease, such as sore throats or eye problems. There are also remedies for animal disease or when animals are acting "strange," for instance, not eating or drinking. Given the problems with the health of people and animals in the Banat, the preponderance of such remedies is unsurprising. One section was titled "So You Had Something Stolen" and advised how to use the phases of the moon, wax, magical symbols, and prayer (!) to find the thief. The prayer implored God to make the thief confess his sins in church. While it is unknown how many peasants took advantage of such remedies, it seems likely that many colonist-peasants' world views did contain a mixture of Christian, occult, and natural forces similar to the one presented in the book and ultimately similar to the beliefs of other peasants in the region and throughout Europe. This certainly pushes back against Tallar's proposition that the German colonists were the only rational force in the region.

Marriage and Children: Frontier Social Security

Magic and religion were not the only ways in which Germans sought to combat the death, disease, and hardship that surrounded them. They also used more practical methods of dealing with these issues. For farmers, land and children were the two most important commodities of a successful survival strategy not only in one's prime of life but also as one aged. They were both items that could be exchanged for security. It was hard enough for able-bodied men and women to survive disease and hunger in the early years of colonization, but as people aged, these problems became even more acute. Farming was hard physical labor and at some point, it became difficult for an older person to work the land and provide food for themselves and their families. Marriage was often a key component to these "social security" strategies that sought to mitigate the effects of old age and promote effective land use.

The government had a history of supporting marriage among colonists, using both the carrot and the stick. Maria Theresia promised six gulden and six *Metzen* wheat to couples who married within three months of settlement. This promise made enough of an impact to be noticed by potential colonists. In Günzburg in 1767, single Germans on their way to colonize the Banat reportedly married in the hallway of the pastor's house.[90] Joseph II decreed that only married colonists were eligible to receive land and the accompanying material. This led many young men to marry during the migration. In 1785, in the middle of the Josephian migration, authorities in Vienna and Ulm reported 208 "colonial marriages."[91] The government saw marriage as integral to success in the colonies and promoted it as such.

Marriage, of course, occurred once migrants had arrived as well. In remote areas, intervillage, intraethnic marriage was very common. If nearby communities also contained Germans, then these could be outlets for marriageable individuals. This genetic diversity was not always large enough to ensure the health of the German communities. In Lindenfeld, settled between 1828 and 1833, there is evidence that the marriage pool became too small and led to minor genetic anomalies by the twentieth century.[92]

Many marriages were contractual, and the parties often produced a document outlining the terms of the marriage, a frontier "pre-nup." As the following review of marriage contracts will show, there was no single way in which marriage was contacted. Rather than relying merely on tradition, local and personal conditions dictated the nature of the agreement. A marriage contract was negotiated between the families of the groom and bride, who were often listed secondarily after their fathers, in which the terms that joined the two families were laid out. In some cases, the father of the groom gave the farm to the new family in exchange for certain concessions, usually relating to care in old age. For example, in the marriage contract between Peter Adam and Katarina Metzger, whose fathers were the main contracting parties, Adam's father gave the couple his farm, including the house, a full session of land in Niczkydorf, a garden, and all the accouterments of a working farm (the horses, a cow, the wagon, the plow, etc.). The contract stipulated that Peter and his wife had to take care of his parents until their death. What is perhaps most interesting about his particular contract is that even after having cared for his parents, Adam was still required to divide the worth of the farm between himself and his three siblings upon his parents' death. Providing security for his parents did not grant him outright ownership of the property. Eventually, the other children had rights to this inheritance.[93]

While Peter Adam paid for the farm upon his parent's death, when Peter Bürger married Anna Maria Mayerin, his father Anton *sold* him the farm for 1,800 fl. Mayerin's father agreed to pay 1,000 fl. He also provided his daughter with additional goods. This payment did not exempt the newly married couple from their obligation to care for the husband's parents in old age. For the first three years, Anton would live with couple and slowly cede control. After three years, the couple would have full ownership. Once Peter was the sole proprietor, he still had obligations to care for his mother and father.[94] He also took on the debts associated with the farm.[95] Adam Kathraÿn made a similar deal with his son, selling him the farm for 800 fl. He also included a clause that if he was "required" to remarry, his son and daughter-in-law would have obligations to his new wife as well.[96]

Not every family had a son on which the duties of caring for the parents could be bartered. In these cases, the marriage contract became an even more critical document between the bridegroom, acting in his newly created family's interests, and the father of the bride, seeking a level of security in old age. In a contract from 1804 between Bernhardt Wagner and Peter Verwanger, who was acting in the interest of his only daughter Anna, a quid pro quo arrangement was agreed upon. In exchange for the Verwanger farm, Wagner agreed to provide for Verwanger and his wife until their death. There was even a clause that allowed Verwanger to keep working the farm as long as he was alive, though a later clause indicated that he recognized the possibility that he might retire. Upon his death, the farm would pass to either his daughter or Wagner. He further secured two cows, grain, half of the hay garden, and fuel for the whole year for his wife should she outlive him. Perhaps most tellingly, Wagner kept the farm even if his wife died while her parents were still alive if he agreed to their upkeep.[97] The interests of the parents were at least equal to that of the daughter.

Similarly, Johann Katzler and his son-in-law Heinrich Reisser drew up a contract in which Reisser bought the farm with money provided by his foster father. In return, Reisser agreed to provide grain and oats to his father-in-law and his foster father for the rest of their lives.[98] Not only was the daughter not party to the contract, but her name was not even mentioned at all in the document. This was essentially a business agreement between men. This underlines the fact that the contract was intended chiefly for the protection of the parents in old age, rather than protecting their daughter in her new marriage.[99]

Given that Germans in the Banat practiced a modified primogeniture, these contractual marriages were a particular boon to the men who were not the oldest and who wanted to farm. The oldest son received the father's property for which he compensated the younger siblings in cash.[100] For instance, although Johannes Hoppauer was willed the farm, it was contingent on him paying 300 fl. to his sister Magdalena and his brother Christoph.[101] As a result of this system of inheritance, there were many young men looking for property. Marriage arrangements provided them with a way to get property. Not only that, but the farmland they received was not virgin soil that needed to be broken. They also often got animals and equipment in the deal. All in all, these marriage contracts were a form of "frontier social security" that benefitted both the old, who were guaranteed a certain level of care until their death through the work of the young, as well as the younger generation, who inherited the wealth of their elders while able-bodied and capable of improving and growing it.

As land prices rose and vacant land dwindled in the nineteenth century, the opportunity to own and work a piece of land grew scarcer, increasing the importance of an advantageous marriage. In the late eighteenth century, land was still affordable and available and as the basis of one's personal wealth, land ownership was essential to economic and social security. By the 1810s and 1820s, this was no longer the case. In 1788, a whole farm cost 300 fl.[102] In 1794, a house and a half session of land sold for 300 fl.[103] By the 1820s, land was much dearer. A house with a full session of land now cost at least 2,000 fl.[104] In 1833, land value had again almost doubled, a full session now being valued at 4,500 fl.[105] These numbers are, of course, to be interpreted with caution. Better land undoubtedly cost more, and it is hard to compare the fertility of the land based on the documents. Also, the prices do not account for inflation. That said, it seems reasonable to assume that land prices rose drastically as available, unoccupied land diminished.

By the nineteenth century, land prices had skyrocketed beyond what a simple laborer could ever hope to save. Although difficult to ascertain, it appears common laborers earned in the neighborhood of 50 fl. for one year's work in 1818.[106] A laborer earning this amount of money would have no chance of ever being able to become a landowner, except perhaps through an advantageous marriage. By this point, if one had squandered the opportunities and privileges offered at the time of settlement, little could be done to regain a strong socioeconomic position. Marriage provided such an opportunity, especially for sons who were not in line to inherit the family farm.

These contracts also further highlight the fact that the Banat was not a place of economic equality or ethnic solidarity. Contrary to the image often presented of the Germans of the Banat as all prosperous and industrious farmers, the truth is much more mundane. Germans in the Banat occupied all strata, from extremely wealthy landholding farmers to impoverished and indebted day laborers. Some German colonists were able to amass quite a bit of wealth in land and property. Estates worth nearly 10,000 fl. or more were not rare by the 1820s.[107] Most of this wealth was due to precipitous increase in the cost of land starting the early nineteenth century.

Individuals without children could also use their land to ensure they would be cared for in old age. This was done through quid pro quo arrangements among people with no blood or family ties. In what at first glance appears to be simply a contract for the sale of a farm, there are several interesting clauses and stipulations, not least of which is the fact that the "buyer" did not actually pay any money. The contract between Bernhardt Kint and his wife, Ana Marie, and Johannes Schung and his wife Magdalena was in fact the trade of property and goods for care in old age. Kint, at times referred to as *die Ältere*, gave his farm to Schung, including not only the land but also the implements and the debt, in exchange for two promises. First, that Kint and his wife would be able to live on the land until their deaths. Second, that until that time, Schung would provide them with food, hay, wood, and a spot for their cow. The contract further stipulated that should one of them die, their food ration would drop accordingly.[108] Thus land was not only important while a farmer worked it, but it could also be important in guaranteeing a certain level of security and stability following retirement, especially if the couple did not have children to take care of them.

While farmers could parlay their land into security as they aged, artisans had to use other strategies and assets to protect themselves and their families in the case of old age and death. While many craftsmen were able to work well into old age, they also used their unique societal position and privileges to maintain their status. For example, the ability to take on apprentices and host journeymen meant that masters were able to have the most physically demanding work done by others, thus extending their active working period. Even into the nineteenth century, the emperor was still providing charters to protect the interests of guilds and their members. In 1818, Franz I issued a charter regarding the rules and privileges governing guilds in Lugos, though given the printed nature of the document, it stands to reason that these rules also applied throughout the region, if not the empire as a whole. The privileges clearly protected the wives of masters who died. The wife was allowed, for example, to continue to operate her deceased husband's business. She could hire journeymen. If she remarried, her new husband had a fast track of sorts to becoming a master. Although required to perform the typical steps to attain this position, including time as a journeyman and the completion of a *Meisterstück* (masterpiece), he was guaranteed a position in the guild if he completed them. In one important way, though, the government hindered the security of the master's family:

it decreed that sons of masters had no more entitlement to positions as apprentices than did others. While perhaps a noble goal in the pursuit of a more meritocratic society, it is hard to image this being effective.[109] This is an important point of contrast between city and country. While country people relied on land and children for security, artisans in the city used statutory protections. Interestingly, both used legal frameworks, whether laws or contracts, to ensure that their interests and those of their families were protected.

Not all marriage contracts were solely about protecting oneself in old age. In fact, many contracts dealt with widows and widowers who were remarrying and who sought to balance their children's interests against those of their new spouses. It was also a way for the new spouse to protect themselves from the children in case of the death of their blood-related parent. A 1752 contract between Bantaleon Müller, a master carpenter from Temesvar, and Catharina Fuchsjägerin is interesting in a few respects. First, Fuchsjägerin appears to have been an orphan. Her foster father Thomas Jung, a master brewer, provided her portion of the "marriage wealth" of 150 fl., a sum matched by Müller. If Müller died, the money was to support Fuchsjägerin. If she died without issue, then Jung's money was to be returned to him. Müller also had a daughter, Anna Maria, from a previous marriage. The contract stated that her inheritance from the death of her mother and sister was held in the "orphan bureau" (*Waÿsen Amt*) in Ofen, and that in the future she had no further claims regarding their deaths. He further requested that if he should die without a will the 300 fl. in "marriage wealth" be divided equally between his wife, daughter, and any future children.[110] The marriage contract between Lorentz Klaus, a brewmaster, and Anna Maria Pfekin stipulated that his previous and future children were to have equal rights as inheritors, after each of his four existing children and the mother received 200 fl. that he promised them.[111]

Some situations were even more complicated. Both Johann Schneider and Anna Maria Schappert were widowed and had children. Their marriage contract combined concern for Schappert in her old age with the complicated inheritance issues involved in combining the two existing families. If Schneider proceeded his wife in death, whoever took over the farm, likely one of Schneider's children, though this is not explicitly stated, was required to care for her to a certain degree. She was to be given rights to a piece of land, animals, and hay "for life." The new farm owner was also to care for her fields. For her part, Schappert was to provide seed. She explicitly had the right to remarry, but the new husband was exempted from this help. In the case of her death, Schneider was the sole heir of everything brought to the marriage, likely to prevent her children from claiming a part of her wealth. This could have been seen as "payment" for taking care of her until her death. There was an interesting exception. Schappert's kitchenware was *not* inheritable by Schneider's children. Instead, they were for Schappert's daughters.[112] Schappert and Schnieder's contract sought to balance protecting the new wife in old age with the rights of both spouses' children to inheritance.

In addition to caring for the elderly, there was also a need to care for orphans. The harsh climate meant many men and women died comparatively young and often left children who had not reached an age where they were able to care for themselves. This fell first and foremost on family. In Elisabeth Hoppauer's will, this duty was to fall on her eldest son, Johann. In the event of her death, he was to care for his sister and brother until they reached their majority. The will also tasked him with providing for his mother and grandmother until their deaths.[113] As we have seen in the marriage contracts, an individual outside the immediate family often stepped in as a "foster father" and was often quite generous to his charges. The government released an ordinance in 1772 regarding the treatment of children who found themselves in such a predicament. It allowed men to choose a guardian for their children who were not of age or who had some handicap that would prevent them from effectively managing their inheritance. Women could appoint a guardian for their estates but could not appoint one for their husband's property. If no guardian was chosen, or if the chosen guardian died, the responsibility for management was passed on the next blood relative. First in line was the mother, but if she chose to remarry, then the responsibility passed to the next in the line and the mother was required to account for the whereabouts of her children's inheritance. In some cases, the authorities reserved the right to intervene and appoint someone.[114] As we saw in chapter 1, the government also sought to care for orphans by teaching them silk weaving.[115]

The Banat was a harsh place to live. From capricious officials to natural disasters, the German colonists faced a social and environmental landscape that was often unforgiving. While the end of Maria Theresia's reign heralded major changes in the German colonial society, it did not change the underlying structures of German life in the Banat. Settlers used a variety of means to combat death and disease. Even on the frontier, science and scientific inquiry gained influence over the lives of people throughout the eighteenth and nineteenth centuries. While the fields of human and veterinary medicine did exist, they were still developing and often unavailable or ineffective. As we already saw in chapter 3, religion was an essential part of everyday life. Although science and religion were factors in peasants' world views, local folk belief, which sometimes incorporated elements of the other two, was also strong. In addition, colonists designed various social arrangements, some backed by contracts, to protect their interests.

Despite hardships, colonists were expected to be the heralds of a new order of rationality in the Banat. Their towns and villages were visible signs of this transformation. Their supposed resistance to superstition also reflected this desire. As we have seen, this was a tall order. In fact, Habsburg policies that encouraged separation likely undermined their goals. Their fear that local people would somehow diminish or corrupt settler culture created a barrier between the supposed teachers and their pupils. As the opening vignette highlighted, mutual distrust was antithetical to the transfer of knowledge. In the next chapters, we will change perspective and explore how the two largest groups of local people (Rascians and Wallachs) reacted to the infusion of the German cultural element into the landscape. As we shall see, some accommodated the Habsburg government and its German settlers while others violently resisted the movement toward a more settled, centralized society in the Banat.

6 Local Responses to Habsburg Rule I

Migration and Unrest

> The Ujpalanka administration should arrest the residents of Kuschitz who stabbed the local mayor and imprison them until an investigation into the subjects' unrest occurs; in the meantime, a commando of fifteen men will be transferred to Kuschitz.
>
> —*Dispatch from August 8, 1752*[1]

IN THE MAJOR SURVEY of the Banat in the 1730s, then governor Graf Hamilton proposed ways to combat the lawlessness in the region. He feared the effects of the chaotic situation on commerce and on "well-minded subjects." He suggested the establishment of a militia to police the region. According to him, such a group should have knowledge of the local language, landscape, and culture in order to better track robber bands. They should also be able to trek into the mountains and sleep under the stars. He specifically said that German soldiers were not the best option for these types of missions. Highlighting the importance of religion to official ideas of loyalty, he suggested offering the *Catholic* Rascians of Carasova and Slatina freedom from the *Contribution* in exchange for their assistance in exterminating the threat of robbery. He also thought Rascian bishops and priests could do more to help prevent their followers from "the vice of robbery." For instance, they could excommunicate robbers, something that he felt would make a big impression on the religiously minded locals.[2] All in all, he advocated for the partial militarization of the Banat to defend it from an internal enemy. Shortly after his report was issued, this perceived internal enemy sided with an external enemy, the Ottomans, to wreak havoc throughout the Banat.

As we have seen, and will see again in this chapter, Habsburg officials and regional observers almost universally portray local people, particularly Wallachs, in a negative light. They are often described as wanders and criminals, likely to support whoever is more powerful. Whatever the truth of the portrayal of local people, this presentation served as the basis for policy as well as official and educated conceptions of the region and its people. As with any historical source, the truth value of these presentations can, and should, be questioned. What seems clear is that local culture in the Banat was notably, observably different from the rest of the monarchy. While our interlocutors may have used these differences to harshly judge the people they observed, we do not have to do the same. In the following presentation of the local people and their culture, I have tried to strip away simple prejudice and attempt to understand people's motivations. I am not interested in perpetuating negative stereotypes. That said, I am not willing to remove local peoples' agency to react to colonial impositions in a variety of ways from accommodation to resistance. In my reading, migration was not necessarily mindless "wandering." It could be a reasoned attempt to change or escape one's economic or social position. Violence could likewise be an understandable reaction to government pressure and dispossession. Unfortunately, we have few sources that can recover these people's authentic voices. Rather than doom them to silence, I have tried to read between the lines and reconstruct some semblance of their lives, much as I have done with the German colonists.

As we have seen, those colonists, along with strong governmental intervention, were intended to change the Banat from a chaotic "Eastern" to a settled European space. At times, this change was accompanied by violence and dispossession. At best, there was benign neglect. Each ethnic group reacted to this imposition in different ways. Some Rascians and Wallachs tried to use the change to their advantage and integrate themselves into the new system, often as frontier soldier-farmers. Others actively resisted the desired transformation, at times violently. Many tried to avoid interacting with the government and its agents, some deciding to pull up stakes and emigrate. The treatment of these ethnoreligious groups highlights the extraordinary way in which the government handled the colonists. Most importantly, it helps us understand exactly *why* the authorities felt the need to invite settlers to the region. Unlike the Spanish, who, as we have seen, integrated their settlers into the larger Spanish society, Habsburg ethnic policy was never about integration or assimilation. Rather, it paralleled settlement policy by building barriers between groups in an effort to define acceptable interaction.

Wallachs: A Bastion of the Traditional in the Modernizing Banat

The Wallachs were likely the most numerous people of the Banat at the time of conquest.[3] Many contemporaries believed that they were the remnants of the Romans who had colonized the area in antiquity.[4] The Habsburgs disliked them because, as a group, they appeared unwilling to Europeanize.[5] Most of the contemporary descriptions were derogatory. Unlike the Rascians, who were only rarely presented as "wanderers," this was a taint that many observers ascribed to the Wallachs both in the Banat and the surrounding region. They were also often described as having a predilection for crime and banditry. Finally, some observers highlighted the fact that they continued to live a traditional, subsistence-based existence in the face of an administration that wanted the Banat to become a modern, moneymaking province. It was from this fundamental conflict, between subsistence and profit, traditional and modern, that all other conflicts stemmed.

Trying to understand how the Wallach people lived is a difficult task given the biased nature of the contemporary sources. As a keen and sympathetic observer, Johann Kaspar Steube's impressions are particularly useful. Although not always positive in his assessments of local people, he did not simply resort to canned stereotypes when describing them. Steube presented the Wallachs as a hearty, stoic people. They jumped into the hottest springs, and then into the coldest pools in Mehadia, without any problem. When a violent thunderstorm frightened Stuebe, the local Wallachs were unfazed. Women went back to work within days of giving birth. Children, too, were hardy. They were not coddled but rather exposed to warm and cold water from three days old. They did not often get sick. Once, he witnessed a mass beheading of thirteen Wallach criminals. According to Steube, none of them feared death nor expressed remorse and three in fact recounted their crimes.[6] Others were long-lived, due to their fasting (apparently more than six months' worth) and their exposure to a harsh environment.[7]

Despite this relatively benign or even admiring description, there is evidence that much of what the Habsburg authorities did not like about the Wallachs was indeed based on observation rather than solely prejudice. Steube did not hide the fact that some Wallachs turned to banditry. For instance, he related that many started stealing at a young age and often joined robber bands headed by *harambascha* that lived in the mountains.[8] Another author blamed their religious leaders for much of the violence and theft, saying it was rare that even the clergy was not involved in crime. He further stated that the Wallachs attacked not only travelers but also towns and villages, where they extorted money or burned them down. In particular, one needed protection in the mountains. Here, robbers threatened villagers to keep them from cooperating with the authorities. The author also speculated that they were supported by the Turks, like modern proxy militias, or that at the very least the Turks did little to prevent them from using Ottoman land as a base. It should be noted that the assessment was not completely negative. In fact, the author went on to say that despite their roughness, they could be good soldiers and possessed a certain amount of industriousness. Interestingly, in both this account and that of Dorner, women are described as especially hardworking, though exploited by their husbands.[9]

There must have also been some truth to the widespread assertion that some were nomadic or seminomadic, especially preceding and in the early years immediately following conquest. When some local Wallachs were negotiating their transfer to other parts of the Banat, they mentioned that some in their community would be dismantling their houses and taking them with them.[10] It is hard to imagine that they would be dismantling brick or rammed-earth houses, the typical types for the sedentary population of the region. It seems much more likely that they were some manner of wood frame covered with straw or hides, like a yurt. On a map of Prädium Schumbul made in 1746, villages were represented as tents, indicating that such mobile villages were not unknown in the region.[11] They were often described as "herdsmen" or as having a propensity to wander in contemporary descriptions. How true this in fact was for the majority of Wallachs by the 1740s and 1750s is unclear. Regardless, the stereotype persisted into the twentieth century. A pamphlet clearly trying to advance Serbian claims to the Banat following World War I claimed that "from the very first, the Rumanians there [i.e., the Banat] have been a landless people, as most of them are to this day

[1919]."¹² For Habsburg officials, looking to build a new economy based on settled agriculture and manufacturing, their "unsettled" nature was a major detraction.

In the late 1770s, a mass movement of Wallachs out of the Banat was noted with alarm by all levels of the Habsburg administration and highlights official thinking on them as well as their own motives for moving. The migration involved eighty-one Wallachian families from "many villages" but was centered on the villages of Komlosch and Becskerek. Subjects had been fleeing since at least the summer of 1776. Some sold their animals, keeping only a horse and wagon to travel.¹³ By November 1777, these two villages were "half-empty," and the remaining inhabitants were openly talking about their plans to flee as well. While they told the administration they were only going to Transylvania to "visit friends" or pay off debts, there is evidence that at least part of the migration was driven by Habsburg policy. According to a report, some left because of land distribution and increased taxes. Others wanted to return to their "fatherland" to visit friends or begin a new life there.¹⁴ Much as with the colonists, the push factors of Habsburg policy and the pull factors elsewhere encouraged migration. This was not mindless wandering, as officials thought, but a calculated choice.

Also potentially creating pull factors for migrants, authorities suspected there were agents active in the region. To root them out, there was a proposal to pay twenty-five fl. per emissary turned in to the government. Few were found, though the postmaster of Komlosch was arrested for distributing false passes. There was another report of a woman and man dressed in "different Hungarian clothes" who distributed passes and assured locals that in Wallachia there was abundant land and low taxes.¹⁵ The government did its best to stop them, informing toll collectors and border guards to watch for them. They even placed thirty Hussars and an officer in the village of Komlosch to discourage further attempts to emigrate. Some were intercepted and returned.

The Banat Land Administration, attempting to deflect criticism about their oversight and handling of the situation, called on the old stereotypes of the Wallachs to aid them, arguing that such migrations were common. Dismissive of their agency, authorities argued that land distribution and taxes were not the true cause of emigration but rather it was the "in-born wanderlust of the Wallachs," their love of their homeland, and the machinations of emissaries.[16] Some officials even sought to completely dismiss any negative effects of this Wallach migration. They argued that most of the disappeared families were not "born" Banaters but rather had only moved to the Banat in previous years. They did not desire to practice agriculture. They had no possessions. Some were perhaps even animal thieves and robbers. In short, they were "dissolute people." Some Rascians who lived nearby had even paid out of their own pocket to move away from them. According to this line of reasoning, no good subjects had emigrated, and the state had lost nothing by their disappearance. In fact, since they left, fifty-three Bulgarian Catholic and 115 other Wallachian families had settled in the same region and were growing tobacco. Intriguingly, the author mentioned families who either returned or were caught trying to flee but does not seem to address the fact that he had just called them dissolute, worthless people. He only noted that the government needed to remain observant and watch for emissaries.[17] By playing on stereotypes of "bad Wallachs," this author sought to minimize the loss to the state.[18] This incident encapsulates much of the official perspective on the Wallachs. They were at best expendable, at worst a threat to the state. From the Wallachs' perspective, filtered through these official documents, it appears they were trying to make the best choices they could given the information they had, much as the colonists *to* the Banat had done.

Neither the authorities nor other observers recognized them as efficient or prosperous farmers, despite the near-legendary fecundity of the land. Rather than overproduce, they were content to subsist. This fact was vexing to authorities, including Joseph II.[19] One official remarked that they "by far surpassed even the Indians in laziness and indolence" because they had not exploited the agricultural possibilities in the Banat. They only cultivated a small field near their houses, growing a maximum of three *Metzen* Turkish wheat or corn.[20] Though they were not interested in growing more crops than they could use, Steube felt that this could have been easily done. Griselini's account supported this contention, and he was astounded that the Wallachs did not have enough "sense" to grow a surplus and use the money generated to buy goods to improve their lives.[21] We need to recognize these comments come from a Western tradition that prized economic development. Growth, and surplus, were key. Many Wallach peasants likely did not think like that, nor did every colonist, if we believe the sources. They appear to have been content to have enough to survive, and the fertility of the land enabled such a lifestyle. They only need to work as hard as necessary to accomplish this goal.

If we adopt this perspective, the other complaints advanced by outside observers make more sense. They may not necessarily be outright lies, but they assign a value judgment to the practices of people who did not share their values. Thus, according to the sources, Wallachs were neither conscientious farmers nor did they employ any advanced techniques. They did not protect their hay but rather allowed it to rot in the fields. They did not practice manuring, but the land was fertile enough to make this unnecessary. They did not plant fruit trees but rather used ones that sprung up from discarded seeds. Steube asserted that the only reason they tended the plum trees at all was to make *raki*, a potent schnapps, from the fruit to drink over the winter. When it came to the other major projects the authorities sought to establish in the Banat, Wallach contributions were a mixed bag. While they did not assist in the Habsburg attempt to create a silk industry, they did practice apiculture and labor in the rice fields. In terms of manufacturing, they had certain cottage industries, such as hemp weaving and glass blowing, and they did do some wood and masonry work.[22] Whatever the ultimate truth, the perceived lifestyle and culture of the Wallachs directly clashed with the Habsburgs' plans to make the region into a manufacturing and agricultural center. This conflict of interests led both to the importation of German settlers as well as the resistance of a large portion of the local population to Habsburg rule and to state-supported colonial encroachment.

In addition to bringing in outsiders to serve as examples, authorities, among them Joseph II, saw education as a way that they could change Wallach culture and make them more "useful" to the state.[23] They wanted to Europeanize them, making them rational, settled, obedient farmers. Starting in the mid-1760s, the government began to focus on improving education. Elementary schools were established in 1774. The focus was on religiosity and morality. While some officials wanted to use German as the language of instruction, the program was ultimately not intended to Germanize or Catholicize local people. Rather, it was to teach them "the virtues of hard work and obedience to the law." Thus, in the lower schools at least, the local languages served as the language of instruction. In order to promote attendance, religious instruction was to be in Orthodoxy and not Catholicism.[24]

From the 1780s at the latest, there was a school director specifically tasked with dealing with schools for local people. Though it is difficult to gauge how effective the education programs were, they were apparently mired in corruption as much else was, they were nonetheless a sign of the Habsburg desire to change the Wallachs and make them more productive subjects of the state.[25]

Violence in the Banat: Robbery and Rebellion

Not only were Wallachs accused of wandering and poor agricultural practices, they (and to a lesser extent Rascians) were also cited for a propensity toward robbery and general lawlessness. The reasons why the Wallachs and Rascians engaged in violent behavior were multiple. Most basically, they attacked those people and institutions that they believed had wealth they could take. This, of course, included the government and the colonists whom it sponsored as well as elites in the church and local government. There was also perhaps a cultural reason for robbery and theft by the Wallachs and Rascians. Among both groups, there was a distinctive culture of individuals who lived outside the bounds of society. Peasants often admired and feared *haiduk*s (robber-soldier peasants) in Serbia, similar to how peasants in Russia viewed Cossacks.[26] While they may have feared their incursion, or resented the retaliation heaped upon the community for their actions, local people nonetheless praised them in songs and poems.[27] In Transylvania, the Romanians placed the *haiduk*s in the same tradition as earlier fighters against the Muslim Ottomans. Historian Joseph Held said that "for many peasants, the highwaymen were now simply fighting another oppressor who happened to be either an Austrian official or a Hungarian nobleman."[28] This veneration, or at least understanding, of such bandits may go a long way to explaining why local people consistently were implicated in theft and robbery.[29]

As the veneration of the *haiduk*s and their exploits reveals, there were deep, structural grievances against Habsburg rule.[30] The authorities' generally harsh management of the local people, especially the Wallachs, had created an atmosphere of resentment. As we have seen throughout the book thus far, the Germans (administrators, soldiers, merchants, and settlers alike) were expected to be the proxies of Habsburg development plans in the region.[31] As the physical embodiment of Habsburg rule, which displaced local people and sought to disrupt traditional patterns of existence, the incoming German colonists were often on the receiving end of the Wallachs' frustration with the new system.[32] Rascians, especially later nationalists, disliked the privileges given to the German settlers. Some feared that the Habsburgs intended such privileges to help the Germans displace them economically. Serbian (Rascian) herders, in particular, feared, largely correctly, as it turned out, that German settlement would disrupt and eventually destroy their livelihoods.[33] Around the turn of the nineteenth century, the Rascians' resistance acquired a more nationalist character as many in the community began to agitate for an autonomous (or even independent) state. The desire for autonomy alternately made them pro- and antistate. In 1848, as we will see in the conclusion, achieving autonomy meant supporting the emperor while fighting the Hungarian state. Thus, resistance to "Habsburg rule" did not *necessarily* mean antipathy to the titular head of the royal house but could extend to his or her policies in the region or those implemented by the Austrian or Hungarian government. Regardless, Wallachs and Rascians did attack the foundations as well as the proxies and beneficiaries of the state (the colonists, state functionaries, nobles, clergy) and these actions should at least to some degree be seen as antigovernmental in nature. In a self-reinforcing circle, the attacks on the government convinced some administrators that local people could not be trusted and thus led to calls for more reliable subjects, that is, colonists.

In many cases, there were concrete reasons for the locals to resent the incoming Germans. As we have already seen, the government actively displaced Wallachs and settled their lands with colonists. While the government generally attempted to make the population transfers as painless as possible for the local people, there was still understandable resentment. In Sakelhas, for example, the locals felt that they were "robbed" of their newly built church that they left behind after their transfer to the Pradio Dorak. The government tried to calm them by promising to provide bricks and lime for a new church in their new village.[34] The Wallachs were also forced to perform menial labor duties for the Germans. Authorities required locals to build houses for the flood of incoming colonists in 1770, forcing them to assist in their domination.[35] In the metal works of the Banat's mountain districts, Wallachs made coal for the forges and did other menial labor as part of their feudal duties. They resented German foresters brought in to manage the woods.[36] This oppressive environment gave Wallach violence a political motivation beyond simple robbery. Even the supposedly loyal Rascians resisted Habsburg rule in 1752 (through outmigration), 1777, and 1808. Their political motives are much clearer than those of the Wallachs who joined the incoming Ottoman armies to plunder the Banat. While it is hard to know the exact motivations of the Wallachs, the Habsburg government certainly viewed this behavior as antistate and detrimental to the creation of a stable, productive society. Hence, they met this violence head on, even in cases, like the Wallach rebellions of the 1780s, where they accepted that many of their grievances were valid.

Even if some in the government later had sympathy for the Wallachs, officials in general neither liked nor trusted them. As discussed in chapter 1, there was a plan to remove the Wallachs from the mountains around Almas and Orsova and replace them with Catholic Germans, Croats, Uniate Wallachs from Transylvania, or Rusnaks (Rusyns). This plan came under a section entitled "Land-Security and Peace."[37] As we saw in chapter 3, officials transferred villages, often for security reasons. For much of the eighteenth century, the Habsburg authorities saw the Wallachs as an internal enemy. One author said that the Habsburgs could never expect loyalty from these "half-men" who, in his words, were "more animal than man."[38] The authorities could not trust them to live peaceably much less take part in the Europeanization of the region, a fact that encouraged colonial settlement.

Not all Wallachs, and likely only highly visible minority, violently disrupted Habsburg rule. Many more made their peace with Habsburg rule or actively aided them in the region. There is evidence that some worked *for* the Austrians spying on the Turks.[39] There were Wallachian border regiments that actively fought Turkish invasion, dying in service to the Habsburgs. A substantial segment of the Wallach population undoubtedly was more concerned with survival than with either colonial settlement or Habsburg rule. That said, the amount of violence attributed to the Wallachs throughout the century, whether through active rebellion, collusion with the Ottomans, or simple acts of murder and highway robbery, indicates that a segment of the local population was deeply unhappy with the new order imposed by the Habsburg authorities and consciously or unconsciously resisted it any way possible.

During times of war with the Ottoman Empire, resistance changed from isolated incidents of robbery to widespread and especially violent communal uprisings. As we saw in chapter 5, intercommunal conflicts occurred during peacetime as well, but the disappearance of authority in war alongside their small numbers meant that the settlers were often subjected to extreme violence as the most visible sign of Habsburg rule. During the Turkish War of 1737–1739, there were numerous incidents involving local people, especially Wallachs and Roma, attacking the Habsburg state, institutions, and proxies. To reiterate, their exact motivations are unclear. Their voices do not survive. Some may have been simple opportunists who took advantage of the chaos to enrich themselves. Some may have feared Ottoman violence if they did not cooperate. Individual motivations notwithstanding, the violence was directed at the state and the colonists and reflected resistance to Habsburg rule and their plans for the region. In 1738, there were reports of rebels, Turks, and "Tatars" invading the Banat from the surrounding mountains.[40] In Maidenbeck and Oravitza, the copper mines were destroyed and all of the inhabitants—likely German miners— murdered. A Colonel Picolomini, on his retreat from the area, reported that "he saw Peasants and Inhabitants of the Country flocking in Shoals, with weapons in their Hands, to aid them [the Ottoman army] in their cruel Designs." Other peasants attacked baggage trains.[41] A later article put the number of "Peasants, Wallachians, or Vagabonds" at four thousand with three hundred miners killed. Two pashas in command of six thousand soldiers supported these irregular troops from a distance.[42] An official report released after the war confirmed the contemporary newspaper reports. In it, the author described the "evils" undertaken by the Wallachs of the Almas and Orsova mountains. They not only offered guidance to the "enemy" but also were responsible for more "robbery, murder, plundering and the like" than the enemy himself.[43]

In response, some town and village residents tried to defend themselves. As planned, the government sought to use the Germans' existential fear to protect the Banat. In 1738, the central administration ordered that the German colonists be armed. In another case, the Lipova District administration asked that "district subjects" be armed in order to protect "hidden passages and the open streets" in 1737. An official was even sent to Temesvár to retrieve the materiel. The only report of peasants actually defending "hidden passes" is of twenty German men near the Maros River. More than a century later, when Kohl visited the region, he marveled at the fact that the government allowed *only* Germans to carry muskets. Wallachs and Rascians were prohibited. He attributed this to the "great confidence" that the government had in the Germans.[44]

Despite their arms, the Germans did not live up to the government's expectations and, like many other locals, fled in the face of the Ottoman incursion. This helped increase German populations in northern cities like Neu Arad. In Pancsova, inhabitants manned military positions after the militia had left the border in May 1737. It then became an important place for incapacitated soldiers. When the military left the town for Belgrade a second time in September 1738, many of the residents followed suit. The commander and his troops were ordered to return. A short time later, the army again left the town, chaos and violence ensued, and many of the remaining residents fled north, where some of the German families settled in Neu Arad. Imperial control returned in summer 1739 but not before the Ottomans set fire to part of the city.[45]

In addition to attacking German colonists and miners during times of war, local people also focused their ire on officials and notables. Given that these officials often demanded payment from the population, and many were Germans, this is perhaps unsurprising. For instance, bandits murdered and robbed a lower administrator named Mayer who oversaw collecting salt taxes. More interesting is the fact that robber bands also attacked coethnics. For instance, robbers murdered a mayor (*Knes*) whom the administration had sent to retrieve peasants who fled the war in late 1737. Robbers also threatened to kill any mayor who sought to deliver *Sarahorn* (?) to Temesvar. Religious buildings were not safe either. Robbers plundered a local monastery.[46] The situation in the Banat at this time was chaotic.

The authorities responded to these uprisings with swift retribution. Although the inhabitants of Almas claimed to have been coerced by the Turks into the uprising and asked for a pardon, officials found this explanation wanting. In retribution for their treason, a Colonel Halfrich came to the region "to exterminate the Inhabitants from the Face of the Earth, without distinction of Age, Sex or Condition. It [was] hoped this terrible Example will deter the rest of the Inhabitants of Temeswar from favouring the Designs of the common Enemy."[47] When a group of locals attacked Bavarian troops, the Bavarians tortured those they had captured for information regarding the whereabouts of their companions and booty.[48]

Despite the fact that by late 1738, many of the rebels had agreed to submit to Austrian rule and were asking for a general amnesty, there were still attacks. In January, "Vagabonds and Banditti" joined Turkish regulars in sacking forty villages near Temesvar and Arad as well as along the Marosch, all areas of heavy German settlement.[49] A dispatch from the administration in Lipova supports the newspaper's contention that the Wallachs were supporting roving bands of robbers throughout the Banat. They further mention the existence of *Hungarian* robber bands in the region during the war who were demanding horses and weapons.[50] When the Germans fled, the local people took advantage of their absence. In one case, the local people harvested the Germans' vineyards and sold the wine.[51] While peasants carried out most of the destruction, there was at least one case of a "Hungarian count" arrested in the Banat on suspicion of collusion with the enemy.[52] By May 1739, the government, through Count Wallis, was willing to again offer a "General Amnesty in Favour of the Vagabonds of the Bannat of Temesvar." Two chiefs agreed to lay down arms and received gold chains as rewards.[53] Again, this is supported by evidence from the dispatches in the region. In one from October 1738, the government offered pardons to two robber leaders (*Harambaschen*) and thirty of their followers in exchange for their good behavior and help in capturing other robbers over the six months.[54] Additionally, the authorities wanted the local village mayors to attempt to persuade "Serbians" who still held sympathy for the Turks to switch allegiance.[55]

As the above indicates, reports occasionally mentioned Rascians in connection to such unrest. In Lipova, there was a rebellion or "mutiny" as an observer termed it. The author attributed the uprising to the "careless and malicious" Rascians and other inhabitants who only had laziness to blame for their poverty in such a fertile area. The author further lamented that if only they were more like the Germans, they would have easier lives. Instead, the author complained that they did not recognize the mercifulness of their rulers and preferred to "remain idle in barbaric servitude than become happy through work." The author argued that the revolt needed to be severely punished in order to make an example of the rebels and to prevent other like-minded individuals from revolting. He pointed to a law that stated that rebellious subjects could be beheaded or, if the situation was less serious, beaten with a cane and exiled.[56]

In the postwar period, the government tried to ascertain who was guilty of siding with the enemy. This was a long process. In a trial in 1753, a villager accused a high mayor of having been a *harambascha* during the war, obviously in a ploy to gain sympathy for his case.[57] In 1755, another former rebel, the "Turkish sea-captain" Dragan Remeniack, tried to return to his home in the Banat. He had fled after the peace treaty was signed. Upon his return with his wife and children, he was arrested in Ujpalanka. Viennese officials were surprisingly forgiving. Crucially, they said that he could still take part in a general pardon they had offered. They ordered that he be released from arrest and allowed to settle "deep in the land," in his old village, Dikvan. That said, the Ujpalanka administration was to keep close watch on him and on the rest of the community and report any "suspicious behavior."[58] The fallout from the war lasted years after the fighting had stopped.

In war or peace, robbers did not only target Germans but rather anyone associated with the official hierarchy, including religious figures. They tried to extort money from a local priest, threatening to burn his property if he did not pay. Other robbers murdered an Orthodox priest. Targets for violence included judges, mayors, and local officials, some of whom were killed. The Habsburg military apparatus was also an obvious target. In 1747, robbers attacked a military settlement, tied up the watch, and killed the captain. There were also incidents of more generalized violence, such as a riot in 1752 caused by a tax hike. There was labor unrest "because of small earnings and low wages." The leaders were sentenced to hard labor but continued to foment rebellion and attack supervisors. The authorities then had them executed.[59] Not all officials were victims of bandits, though. Georg Staikovith, a high mayor in Ujpalanka, was "suspected of dealing with robbers" in 1770. He was specifically accused of accepting gifts from them. While some in the administration wanted him to lose his job and be arrested, one administrator simply wanted to admonish him and suggested moving him to a place with fewer robbers (!).[60]

In the late 1760s, officials recognized animal rustling as an acute problem in the Banat. Transferred Wallachs made especially good animal thieves in their former homes. They knew all the entrances and exits to their former villages. If they lived near the border with Hungary, they knew how to get the animals out of the country, making it easier to get rid of them. Officials realized this too. Colonial overseers alerted the government that "vagabonds," who did not want to work and used theft to support themselves, were concentrated in Wallachian and Rascian villages. According to reports, they were responsible for stealing large numbers of animals. The authorities attempted to make animal theft more difficult. They ordered the mayors of the local villages to report people there who lacked the proper papers. They wanted to have each village design a special sign for their animals (like a brand in the American West) that would alert authorities elsewhere of their origin. They also sought to limit the opportunities that Wallachs might have to steal animals. For example, they forbade Wallachs from offering to safeguard colonists' animals. They suggested searching the swamps for thieves. They also requested that the Hungarians, especially in those areas just over the border from the Banat, be on the lookout for stolen animals.[61] Some colonists also sought to recover their property. In one case, a colonist reported that he had seen a local in possession of his horse. The local, for his part, claimed the horse was his.[62] Despite the government's efforts, animal rustling remained a constant problem for German colonists and the government in the Banat.

In the 1780s, the Wallachs were again responsible for large uprisings. In 1784, open rebellion broke out among Wallachs throughout the Habsburg lands. The rebellion occurred despite the fact that Emperor Joseph II had taken far-reaching steps to improve the position of Wallachs in his realm.[63] In 1781, he had declared all residents of the Fundus, an area of southern Transylvania dominated by the German Saxons, had equal rights. Later decrees further sought to erode the traditional ethnic hierarchy in Transylvania. He also took steps to improve education. Perhaps most importantly, in 1783, he issued his first ordinance on the emancipation of the serfs. While it did not completely emancipate the Wallach peasants, it did allow them more autonomy than they had previously enjoyed.[64]

These steps did not calm the Wallach population. In fact, such limited freedoms may have further contributed to their discontent. In Transylvania, Horea (also Horiah or Vasile Nicola), Kloschka, and Krischan were the organizers of a 1784 rebellion that targeted the nobles. Horea was the recognized leader of the rebellion. Born a serf in 1730, he had worked constructing Orthodox churches. He also represented peasant interests. Numerous times (1779, 1780, 1782, 1783), he visited Vienna to present the complaints of the Wallach peasants to the court. When such actions failed to produce the desired results, unrest grew. Military recruitment in the summer of 1784 provided the spark that set off the rebellion. Many peasants wanted to join the military in order to be freed from serfdom. Opposition by the largely Magyar nobility delayed the planned conscription. On a march led by Krischan to a conscription center in Alba Iulia, Transylvania, nobles attempted to disperse them, leading to open conflict and the start of the rebellion.[65] The rebels felt that state officials and nobles were trying to deny promises of the emperor. In fact, Horea believed that the emperor would side with the peasants, restrain the military, and allow them to destroy the local nobles.[66] The rebellion did not remain confined to Transylvania but spread to the Banat and the area around Arad. In the Banat, 15,000 "mutineers" rose against the government and destroyed twenty villages. British newspapers reported that a Count Sales, an impostor wearing a "false star," had incited the Wallachs to rebel.[67] Undoubtedly, the rebels thought of themselves as "true to the emperor."[68] In all places, the rebels claimed that they were not fighting the government but rather their "masters," and to this end, they murdered noblemen and their families.[69]

To what extent the rebellion was a reflection of anti-Habsburg sentiment is unclear. The leaders were state serfs, thus the masters against whom they fought were ultimately state officials. In a sense, the revolt *was* anti-Habsburg as they were ultimately the party responsible for holding the nobility in check and enforcing the more progressive feudal relations that they recently propagated. In the end, though, the rebels and their demands were focused on local issues with the Transylvanian nobility. In an ultimatum delivered by the rebels in November, all four points related to noblemen, landowners, and feudalism. They wanted a leveling of society and the redistribution of noble land, that is, a complete dismantling of the status quo. There is no mention of the crown outside their implicit role in the system.[70] Whatever the rebels believed, the Habsburgs themselves saw the uprising as a challenge to their authority and put it down. Although the rebels enjoyed some initial successes, they could not withstand the power of the state. The leaders were caught in late 1784 and paraded in chains to prove their capture. In February 1785, they were broken on the wheel in front of 2,500 peasants from four hundred villages.[71] Although unsuccessful, the revolt highlighted the generalized dissatisfaction of the Wallachs with the feudal relations that spanned all the regions inhabited by them.

Joseph II was not content to merely quash the rebellion. He appointed a commission to explore the causes of the rebellion as well as oversee the execution of its leaders.[72] In 1785, the commission's report blamed everyone in the region. Local landlords were too harsh. Local officials were not enforcing the laws. The Wallachs themselves lacked "moral and religious training." Joseph acted on these suggestions and issued a second, more complete decree on the emancipation of the serfs. The major flaw with his decree was that it did not provide the serfs with land, the same problem that would later occur in the United States with slaves and in Russia with serfs. This meant that the landowner could still exert tremendous influence on the now-free serfs by controlling access to land. Joseph also continued to work to improve Wallach peasants' access to education.[73] According to Held, much of this work was for naught. He argued that following the revolt, Wallachs began to view each other, rather than the Habsburg state, as the best protector of their "well-being."[74]

Not long after the suppression of the Horea Uprising, the region was again wracked with violent upheaval. Renewed conflict with the Turks in 1788 came along with renewed rebellion among the local people of the Banat. Some observers deemed the Wallachians, "who spare nor sex, nor age, nor place, but kill, burn, and destroy every thing [*sic*] before them," even crueler than the Turks.[75] Given the eighteenth-century view of the Turks, this was quite a statement. According to a report in the *St. James's Chronicle*, the Wallachs hated the Germans, especially after the execution of the rebel leaders Horea and Kloschka. Accordingly, "The spirit of Revenge rankled in the Hearts of great numbers of them; and this Spirit received additional Strength from a Love of Plunder and Rapine." Thus when given the opportunity, they spread out throughout the region and took advantage of the war to wreak havoc.[76] Aside from those who aided the Turks or were involved in outright rebellion, there were also a number who used the chaos of war to rob and pillage without any definable goal other than enrichment.

The behavior of the Banat's Wallachs caused the emperor to order Captain Baron Capaun to remove their children from their care and place them in other families so they would be raised according to the "Principles of Submission, Honesty, and Fidelity."[77] The *Real-Zeitung* confirmed this report in December 1788. According to this story, not only were their children to be taken away, but Capaun was to hang any Wallach he captured on his expedition.[78] It appears that even the emperor, who only a few years earlier had proven one of their staunchest defenders by ending land seizures in the Banat and promoting Wallach rights in Transylvania, had reached his breaking point. Authorities hanged at least one group of Wallachs (fifty-five, including two priests) for their role in destroying and plundering German settlements.[79]

We see similar local reactions to colonial pressure in other places colonized by German speakers. A major rebellion had wracked the Russian Empire approximately fifteen years earlier (1773–1774) and had likewise targeted German-speaking colonists as representatives of the imperial establishment. The rebels, led by pretender-to-throne Emelian Ivanovich Pugachev, raged up and down the Volga attacking settlements and local notables. Historian Paul Avrich argued that the rebels, especially the Cossacks, had a "nativist hostility toward the German empress [Catherine]" and that Pugachev "promis[ed] to eliminate 'German' customs."[80] Thus while the rebels' ire was directed at Germanness in general, the colonists on the Volga were culturally connected to the source of their hatred and provided available targets, much as colonists in the Banat had. While sources implicate the Germans on both sides of the fighting, they undoubtedly were more victims than perpetrators of the violence that swept over the region.[81]

There was a similar set of reactions among Native Americans when faced with colonial pressure. There were instances of cooperation and collaboration. There was the potential for cross-cultural exchange. There were also instances of extreme violence.[82] Some of the indigenous people of North America likewise resisted the colonization of their lands. In an intriguing echo, Native Americans were accused of all sorts of atrocities from slave raiding to the desecration of corpses (i.e., scalping) both during times of war and ostensible peace. The authorities also unleashed incredible violence against the indigenous population in response to their resistance. In the aftermath of the Tuscarora War in 1711–1713, settlers burned Native Americans alive. A contemporary described "fatten[ing] [their] dogs with their carcasses" after the successful defense of a fort during the Cherokee War (1760–1761).[83]

In times of war, the Native American population, like the standing population in the Banat, might also engage in widespread communal uprisings opposed to settlement and dispossession. During the Revolutionary War, some groups, like the Mohawks led by Joseph Brant, sided with the British against the settlers. The War of 1812 coincided with Tecumseh's uprising, where again, groups of Native Americans sided with the British.[84] The Dakota War in Minnesota occurred in conjunction with the American Civil War.[85] As with the uprisings in the Banat, it is difficult to discern the exact reasons for the indigenous American violence, but it seems likely that it was largely due to the impositions (e.g., forced movement, loss of land, retribution, etc.) the colonial state put on the standing population that we have seen everywhere German-speaking colonists went.

Of course, not all local people resisted the Habsburgs during the war and, in fact, some performed very valuable service for the government. Much as the Ottomans used locals in the Banat to fight against the Habsburg authorities, the Austrian government used some local people, especially those who had fled from the Ottoman domains, as proxy fighters within the Turkish domains.[86] These so-called *freicorps* were made up of volunteers who agreed to perform raids inside the Ottoman domains. Koča Anđelković, an important leader, went into Serbia and recruited men to help fight the Ottomans and ease the Austrian invasion. He was responsible for capturing several cities in what is known as *Kočina krajina* (Koča's march). He was forced to retreat to the Banat but kept fighting. He was eventually caught and impaled, though the men he helped train were an important force in the First Serbian Uprising.[87] Thus, local people on both sides of the border used the chaos of war to agitate against their imperial rulers.

Once again, the years following this war saw an uptick in banditry as firm government control was reestablished. In 1794, robber bands stole seventeen wagons of goods and money from merchants returning from a yearly market. They robbed the post. The situation became so bad that the citizens of Pancsova took up arms against the bandits. They offered a reward of five hundred fl. for the head of one of the leaders, Lasar Dobrić. They also combined forces with the military battalion to drive the robber bands from the region. Although they were not successful in capturing any of the criminals, their efforts did force them to leave the region.[88]

The Wallachs, the most numerous population in the Banat, were not entirely willing to conform to the plans of the central government in the eighteenth century. The government sought stability, settled agriculture, and assistance against the Ottoman threat to the south. As we have seen, at least a portion of the Wallach population maintained a lifestyle that was at odds with these goals. Some Wallachs were mobile, and many were at least part-time herders. They practiced subsistence agriculture, which was at odds with the Habsburg's drive to produce for markets. When times of conflict came, the Habsburgs could not count on Wallach support, though there was some, and had to consider much of the population as enemy combatants or at least as opportunistic thieves. This impression of the Wallachs, one that has been persistent in the literature from the eighteenth century to the present, does appear to have some basis in fact. If we refuse to adopt the standards of Habsburg officials and their proxies in the region, Wallach life becomes understandable rather than condemnable. Far from being exceptional, migration ("wandering") and violence are common human reactions to social, cultural, and economic change and pressure. In fact, many of the German speakers had similar experiences of government oppression that caused them to emigrate to the Banat or, in the case of the Hauensteiner, to violently lash out against the authorities.

The Wallachs who did choose to resist the government had a ready population at which to vent their anger. The colonial population in their midst was the embodiment of the Habsburg regime and an easy target for robbery and violence, especially when society and order broke down in times of war. In addition, these Wallach rebels attacked other institutions and individuals associated with the state. While the colonists and government institutions may simply have been the easiest or most lucrative targets, it is hard to believe that these attacks were not at least in part a response to Habsburg policies that challenged and disrupted the traditional Wallach way of life.

As we will see in the next chapter, the Rascians had their own reasons to oppose and sometimes subvert Habsburg policy. While they were more privileged than the Wallachs, there were many Rascians who believed that either the privileges were not being upheld or that they did not go far enough. Much as the Wallachs, these Rascians likewise opposed the state through migration and unrest. Importantly for the Rascians, they had transimperial coethnics in the Ottoman Empire who were also dissatisfied with their position in the state. These two groups could, and did, work together, especially in times of crisis. Often, the Rascians also enjoyed the support of the Russian Empire, viewed by many as the protector of Orthodoxy throughout the world. By the end of the eighteenth century, we see an emerging modern national movement among the Rascians, led by Habsburg Rascian intellectuals. This movement heralded the emergence of a modern "Serbian" nation that would play a key role in the region's development and disintegration up into the twenty-first century.

7 Local Responses to Habsburg Rule II

The Making of Serbs out of Rascians

> Their [Rascian] proliferation is certainly desirable, and I believe that many would come over from the Turkish areas if one created good conditions for them.
>
> —*Habsburg emperor Joseph II*[1]

OF ALL THE LOCAL ethnoreligious groups, the Orthodox Rascians were the most important to the administration and thus were endowed with the most privileges. Their superior position had historical roots in the adoption of the Illyrian Privileges in the wake of the mass migration of Serbs to the Habsburg lands in the late seventeenth century. This migration solidified the region's place a "transborder region" straddling the Ottoman and Habsburg Empires.[2] Because of their importance in defending the southern border, the transimperial nature of the Banat's Rascian inhabitants made authorities anxious. In 1733, the government instructed local toll administrators to carefully watch Rascian and Greek subjects because they were known to collude with Turkish subjects to avoid taxes. They also helped smuggle goods in and out of the country.[3] In the war of 1737–1739, military officials were unsure how reliable the Grenzer would be and curtailed their direct involvement in hostilities. A revolt in 1735 had called their usefulness in fighting the Ottomans into question. Field Marshal Seckendorf said that they "prefer robbery, plunder, and stealing" to defense and advised against expanding their presence to new areas.[4] In the aftermath of the war, Court Advisor Kempf, an official expert on the region, pointed to the transimperial nature of the local population as a potential cause for disloyalty. In his opinion, they had connections on the other side of the border with whom they empathized and were not to be trusted.[5]

By the time of Habsburg conquest, Rascians had lived, one might even say dominated, the Banat since the sixteenth century. After Ottoman conquest in 1526, they moved to the region in large numbers. An area once populated largely by Hungarian speakers was "after 1552 . . . completely Serbianized."[6] These numbers were strengthened throughout the seventeenth century, most notably when the Ottomans forced a Habsburg retreat in 1690. Though the numbers are highly debated, Patriarch Arsenije III Crnojević led 60,000 to 200,000 Rascians into Habsburg territory, particularly the Batschka, to escape Ottoman domination.[7] Leopold I granted these Rascians, and specifically the Orthodox Church, certain religious and secular privileges (the *Diploma Leopoldinum*), which included freedom of religion, election of leaders, and for many, exemption from the jurisdiction of Hungarian nobles and magnates.[8] Although these privileges were most cited by Rascians in the eighteenth century, they were by no means the first accorded to them by the Habsburgs. In both 1520 and between 1578 and 1659, Rascians had received rights and privileges in the Austrian domains. In the earlier period in the military border, they "were granted modest land parcels, exemption from manorial dues, the right to elect their own military and judicial officials, and freedom of religion."[9]

The privileges, especially the *Diploma Leopoldinum*, helped cultivate an exceptionalist strain among the Rascians, especially when compared to the numerous Wallachs. Though constantly attacked and debated, the privileges remained in some form until 1769/1770.[10] The General Regulation of 1770 "completely changed the original Leopoldine Privileges." They now only applied to religious questions, and the church hierarchy was placed under state supervision.[11] As we shall see, another regulation released in 1777 further curtailed the scope of the privileges. Thus their importance lasted much longer than their effectiveness. Looking back at their history, one historian described the Serbs in 1848 as feeling as though they had come to the Habsburg domains not as "settlers but rather as a state with laws . . . a church, courts, and an army."[12] Their existence as a privileged group was visible throughout the period and became the foundation of an emergent national movement. While the government viewed their presence in the Banat as an overall positive, as Orthodox separatism then Rascian-Serbian nationalism grew, their transimperial connections became more and more concerning for the Habsburg and Hungarian authorities.

Rascians: Distrusted but Vital

The Rascians, because of the privileges bestowed upon them, were at the forefront of Orthodox religiosity in the Banat. Despite linguistic and ethnic differences, common religious ties often brought Rascians and Wallachs together.[13] By 1695, Serbian metropolitans were placing bishops over large numbers of Wallach adherents in the Banat and Arad. Serbian bishops in Arad consecrated Transylvanian Orthodox priests. In 1744, a Serbian monk named Visarion Sarai came to Transylvania from the Banat and began preaching against the church union. The Wallachs received him as a "saint" of sorts. His travels led to widespread unrest and backlash against the Uniate Church there. Hitchins argued that it was the abandonment of the union by local people following Visarion's travels that caused Maria Theresia to approve the establishment of a bishopric for the Orthodox and led the Habsburgs to "tacitly renounce the long-cherished dream of a complete church union of the Romanians."[14] The authorities eventually arrested him and banished him to a dungeon in Tyrol.[15] Around the same time, efforts to enforce the Uniate rite led Rascians to ask for Russian diplomatic intervention.[16]

While the privileges helped the Rascians secure a leading role among the Orthodox, they still had to contend with the fact that the government was Catholic, and it would protect Catholic prerogative. Although the following suggestions come from an undated, unsigned document, and thus may never have been implemented, they do give a clear idea of how at least some Habsburg officials viewed the correct relationship between Orthodox and Catholic.[17] Addressed at times to both Rascians and Orthodox in general, it sought to impose some new rules on the Orthodox Church, seemingly in violation of the privileges. These points were meant to "gird" the Catholic religion while not creating any "prejudice" toward the "Greek Ritual Rascians." For instance, if Orthodox people, even condemned criminals, wanted to utilize a Catholic priest for last rites, the document forbade anyone from preventing them from doing so. Conversely, if an Orthodox person hindered a Catholic in their employ from receiving last rites from a Catholic priest, they were to be harshly punished. If Orthodox children wanted to attend a German or Latin school, this was likewise not to be hindered. Orthodox pastors could not minister to Catholics. Only in exceptional cases could they baptize a child. Rascians who insulted Catholic belief were to be harshly punished. In cases of religiously mixed marriages, if either of the parents were Catholic, the children were to be raised Catholic. There were further protections for Orthodox clergy and laics who wanted to attend Catholic ceremonies, converse with Catholic religious, or convert.[18] The document makes quite clear that the Catholic faith was paramount and that Catholicism was going to be protected even to the detriment of the Orthodox. While the Habsburgs were often at pains to praise the loyalty and utility of the Orthodox Rascians, they were still clearly second-class subjects compared to Catholics.

The government released a similar set of guidelines in 1777, the "Regulations Concerning the Greek Ritual in the Banat."[19] This document was a follow-up to the General Regulation of 1770 that had curtailed the Leopoldine Privileges.[20] It was another attempt to delineate the boundaries of Orthodoxy and intercommunal relations. The regulations start by praising the loyalty and bravery the "Illyrians," as the Rascians were sometimes referred to, had shown in the past and promising to uphold the privileges extended since Leopold's reign if they remained so. Importantly, this document preserved *religious* privilege only, not political. In fact, the authorities explicitly forbade the bishops or metropolitan from presenting themselves as the "head of the nation." Only official congresses of the nation were tolerated. Others were deemed illegal. Schools were placed under state auspices. The Illyrians were given a press for their writings. This was done to help staunch foreign influence, especially Russian.

Even religious matters were regulated to a point. Active priests were exempted from the *Contribution*, military service, servitude, and corporal punishment. Some instructions were much more ambivalent, at least to modern eyes. They specified what the jurisdiction of the religious courts was ("spiritual matters") and assured Illyrians that they would be treated fairly in cases utilizing civil law. They stipulated that only Habsburg subjects could become priests. They banned the solicitation of priests from the

Ottoman domains. Monks from abroad needed to register, and local authorities were tasked with keeping a "watchful eye" on them. Authorities were also to keep an eye on Habsburg subjects traveling south to the Ottoman domains for religious reasons.

The government sought to further define the relationship between Orthodox and Catholics in this document. In areas where the groups lived side by side, the Orthodox were required to celebrate or at least refrain from working on Easter, Christmas, Pentecost, and Corpus Christi. The Orthodox were "by no means to celebrate" other Roman Catholic holidays, and they were to refrain from working or making noise while the Catholics were in church. The authorities further admonished Orthodox people to celebrate only those holidays approved by their church synod and included a list of these. In mixed villages, Orthodox were free to build one church, but the construction of a second required the approval of the Illyrian Court Department. Approval was also required for the construction of cemeteries. Interfaith marriages were "abuses" and were to be reported to either a Latin or a Greek bishop. Should an Orthodox believer convert to Islam, or the "Turkish Unbelief" in the government's parlance, they needed to be reported to both spiritual and secular authorities.

As both of these documents show, the authorities struggled to balance complete communal separation with the desire to convert Orthodox people to Catholicism. Especially in the earlier document, the government took pains to allow certain kinds of interactions between Orthodox and Catholics that could lead to conversions. It seems that as time passed, authorities cared more about separation and less about fostering interreligious dialogue that could lead to conversions to Catholicism. This trend mirrors the situation we saw in chapter 3. As time passed, authorities realized that conversion was more or less an impossibility and thus sought to deal with the religious reality in the Banat rather than fundamentally alter it. In response to this change in emphasis, the communal boundaries hardened. In 1753, the government ordered that no Orthodox believer could be buried in a Catholic cemetery.[21] By 1777, the authorities had banned interfaith marriages. Earlier, they were allowed provided the children were raised Catholic. In a way, the relative position of the Banat's Rascians dropped as the authorities gave up efforts to convert them. Rather than try to integrate them into the Catholic community by encouraging dialogue and interaction, by the end of the eighteenth century the authorities decided that they were unredeemable and best kept separated (spiritually and if possible physically) from the Catholic Germans.

Many Rascians were quite unhappy with the 1777 regulations. Before it had even been published, leading bishops had demanded that such an important change to their traditional rights be discussed at a national meeting (*Sabor*). The government ignored this request and simply released the regulations. This led to upheaval. Rascians, particularly angry over earlier regulations about funerals that sought to bring Orthodox rite closer to Catholic practice, organized violent protests. The Hungarian Chancellery advocated a harder line against Rascian claims to prevent further unrest. In Novi Sad and Werschetz, the local Orthodox population, inflamed by conservative priests, demanded that the government rescind the regulations. They threatened the Bishop of Werschetz as well as the clergy who sought to abide by the new laws. These protests continued for several weeks and were eventually put down by Grenzer.[22] Six were killed and twenty-six wounded.[23] There was also unrest in Temesvar. Around the empire, Orthodox in Buda, Pancsova, and Vukovar voiced their displeasure as well, though in a more peaceful manner. They aimed their criticism at both the Habsburg regime and the Orthodox hierarchy, if they did not advocate for changes. Some even expressed their willingness to die for the faith. These actions were effective. By early 1778, the government began to back away from the most contentious changes to keep the peace in the face of feared Prussian aggression.[24]

The regulations in both documents, especially those related to the interaction of Habsburg and Ottoman Rascians, indicate that the Habsburgs, for all their rhetoric about the value placed in the trueness and loyalty of the Rascians, did not really trust them to enjoy too much freedom of political and religious action. While they were undoubtedly trying to protect the legitimacy and supremacy of the Catholic Church and their own ruling house within their domains, the Habsburg administration was also suspicious of the interstate relations that were fostered by Orthodoxy and ethnolinguistic ties both to Russia and over the border in the Ottoman Empire. This was as true in the early days following conquest as it was in the period leading up to the handover to the Hungarians.

Throughout the eighteenth and nineteenth centuries, Rascian restlessness was driven in part by Hungarian intransigence to their desire for autonomy. The Hungarians did not like the special privileges the Rascians enjoyed as a result of the Leopoldine Diploma of 1690. From an early date, many Hungarians wanted to incorporate Rascians (especially those in the Batschka) into the Hungarian state and deny them any privileges beyond religious toleration. While the Hungarians believed that place of residence should determine who enjoyed the privileges, the Rascians believed they extended to any member of their ethnoreligious group wherever they might find themselves.[25]

For its part, the crown vacillated between supporting the Rascians' Leopoldine rights and acceding to the Hungarians' objections. The War of Austrian Succession highlighted this tension. On the one hand, the Rascians were an important source of manpower. In light of this, the crown established the Hofkommission in Banaticis, Transylvanicis, et Illyricis in 1745 to protect the rights of the Orthodox Grenzers (though the commission itself contained no Rascian members). On the other hand, the Magyars had been among Maria Theresia's strongest supporters during the war. She never forgot this aid and sought to make good on territorial adjustments she had promised them, to the detriment of the Grenzers' autonomy. When it became clear in the late 1740s that some lands that had traditionally been military border, and thus under the purview of Vienna, were to be transferred to Hungary, many Grenzer balked at the idea of living under Hungarian control.

The dissolution of the Theiss-Marosch (or Tisza-Máros) border led to conflict and flight. Following the gains of the Treaty of Karlowitz in 1699, this frontier began in Titel (in today's Serbia) and ran along the Theiss and Marosch Rivers to Transylvania. Szeged, which contained the Supreme Command, and Arad were the two main fortresses. Initially, it was home to 2,500 border guards. The gains of the Treaty of Passarowitz in 1718 moved the international frontier much further south, rendering the Theiss-Marosch border anachronistic. In exchange for Hungarian support, Maria Theresia agreed to abolish the border and incorporate much of the land into the Hungarian state.[26]

Grenzer began requesting permission to move from the region in the late 1740s as preparations were made to actualize the empress's plans. In early 1748, the district administration in Becskerek in the Banat reported on the availability of land there as per the request of higher officials. They needed to determine how much open land existed in the region to accommodate the expected influx of Grenzer from the Marosch border. On the land around Kikinda, for instance, which would later become a center of Rascian-Serbian culture, they reported sufficient ground for only twenty to thirty households "at present."[27] Later in 1748, a group of Grenzer petitioned the government regarding their status. Their land had recently been given to Arad County in Hungary, and they requested to remain military men and "in no way" wanted to be counted among the normal, *Contribution*-paying peasants. To this end, they left their homes and moved to the remaining land of the Marosch border. There they attempted to establish themselves again, though as officials noted, the entire Marosch border was to be dissolved. Authorities feared that if the Grenzer were not properly cared for, they would fall into poverty and be forced to beg to survive. To avoid this, officials sought to transfer some of the people from this region onto open lands in the Banat where they could be of use to the government and the military and, importantly for the Grenzer, they would not be subject to Hungarian rule. People who had permission to transfer were to be provided with passes from the Arad commando.[28]

Such requests continued over the next several years. When the official transfer of the Theiss-Marosch military district to Hungarian control in 1750 led to riots among the Orthodox Grenzer, who were adamant that their rights and privileges were being violated, the administration allowed them to move to the military border in the Banat. Some (50 out of 122 Grenzer officers) were more at ease with the transfer of sovereignty. They traded civilian status in Hungary for ennoblement and land.[29] Ultimately, the government's attempts to handle the displeasure of the Grenzer by transferring them within the monarchy were of limited success. This discontent with Habsburg rule made some Grenzer receptive to the overtures of Russian recruiting agents who had been active in the region for years. Some Rascians had previously gone to the Russian minister in Vienna to ask for permission to set up colonies in the Romanov lands. Initially, the Habsburg government was amenable to a limited out-migration of Rascians, allowing a group of three hundred to leave for Russia in 1751. Continued emigration caused them to adopt more drastic measures, including the 1752 Emigration Ban discussed in chapter 1.[30] "Several thousand" Grenzers eventually abandoned the Habsburg realms to try their luck in the southern Russian Empire (many in today's Ukraine).[31]

Much as the Rascians had a transimperial ethnic connection with the Ottoman Empire, they had a long-standing transimperial religious connection with Russia. In 1727, Russians played a key role in educating teachers and clerics in Belgrade and Karlowitz after the Habsburg government approved the establishment of Orthodox schools. These teachers taught in Russo-Slavonic, which became the official language of the Serbian Orthodox Church in the mid-eighteenth century. In addition, it became a literary language among the Rascians, at least for a time. The Russians were also responsible for the creation and importation of many books. The Habsburg government tried to counter this influence to varying degrees of success.[32] Similarly, Transylvanian Wallachs had appealed to the Russians for help maintaining their Orthodox faith. In 1751, for instance, a monk asked Empress Elizabeth during an audience to serve as the "protectress" of Orthodox adherents in Transylvania. Specifically, he hoped that Orthodox priests could be ordained in Russia and fall under the auspices of the Holy Synod of the Russian Church.[33]

Many of those who fled settled in the colonies of New Serbia (founded 1752) and Slavyanoserbia (founded 1754).[34] A desire to protect their Orthodox brothers, a need for settler-soldiers, and a desire to influence politics in the Balkans drove the creation of the South Slav colonies. Serb commanders ran the two colonies, and the Russian government gave them considerable autonomy. One, Khorvat, was a Habsburg Grenzer colonel who in 1751 agreed to recruit a Hussar and Pandur foot regiment for the Russians in exchange for land for the soldiers and a permanent appointment as a colonel for him.[35] The Serbs then agreed to serve as border guards, much as they had in the Habsburg domains. The Serb commanders were not particularly good administrators, especially Khorvat, who was eventually banished to Vologda, a town further in the Russian interior. By the mid-1760s, the Russians had withdrawn the autonomy of the colonies, and despite what the names seem to indicate, Serbs were never a majority in these areas.[36]

The Habsburg administration, both civil and military, tried to prevent the movement of Rascians out of the Banat. In October 1753, the General Command and the Banat Land Administration discussed how to prevent subjects from leaving the Banat and seeking service with a "foreign power."

The impetus for this was the movement of five Hussars who, traveling on official passes, made it to Vienna, where they sought passes to travel to Anspach or Württemberg. It appears that these individuals were part of a Hussar regiment that had recently been "reduced." Officials feared that the loss of employment caused them to seek an appointment in a foreign service. In response, the government ordered that all military personnel as well as "other Rascians and Wallachs" be denied passes to leave the Banat. Those who came to the General Command looking for a pass were to be asked why they wanted to leave and where they were going. This information was then to be reported the Land Administration, who would make the call on whether to issue the pass or not. They also informed district administrators as well as toll collectors not to allow anyone without an official pass to leave. Those without one were to be stopped and sent back.[37]

Such disloyalty made a profound impression on Maria Theresia. It was further evidence that only Catholics, or at the very least Uniates, could be trusted along the sensitive southern border. In the Croatian military districts, she wanted Orthodox Grenzer to accept Uniatism. In the Sichelburg District, the military authorities, with her blessing, removed the Orthodox clergy from power and established a Uniate bishopric. In 1754, a Uniate bishop was installed at the monastery of Marcsa, a central place to the Orthodox Grenzer that housed the original charters of privilege. By December, a revolt overtook the region because of this and other simmering grievances. In the end, the authorities agreed to remove the Uniate monks from the monastery but replaced them with Catholic Piarists (!).[38] Such blatant disregard for the religious privileges promised to the Orthodox must have increased their resentment toward the government.

Not only was there tension between the Rascians and the Habsburg administration but also between the Austrian and Russian governments. Although Maria Theresia had initially approved the release of one small group of migrants, she quickly sought to staunch any who wanted to follow. An official Russian request to recruit a Hussar regiment in early 1751/52 was denied. Not only was the migration depriving the Austrians of military men, but some authorities also saw it as an attempt by pro-Prussian elements to undermine the Austro-Russian alliance. They even sought to force the recall of the Russian ambassador who was promigration. In 1752, he was replaced with an ambassador more supportive of the alliance. While this settled down tensions for the moment, they rose again when more suspected recruiters were caught in 1754. The settlement of the northern Black Sea littoral also antagonized the Ottomans, complicating Austro-Russian relations as they contemplated the consequences of a possible war.[39]

Attempting to keep good relations with the Russians while preserving their own population, the Habsburg authorities agreed in 1754 to allow the parents and unmarried children of earlier migrants to leave.[40] This policy appears to have continued throughout the 1750s. One group of men, including a quartermaster, a corporal, and thirteen enlisted men, returned to the Banat in 1758 to retrieve their families whom they had initially left behind. The men were not exclusively from the Banat. Some were from towns and counties on the Banat's borders.[41] It does not appear that the Habsburg government tried to hinder them from reuniting with and repatriating their families to the Russian Empire. Their earlier order was reiterated. A note from 1759 allowed the returnees to take their wives, provided they left "willingly," and their unmarried children but no one else.[42]

Apparently, not all "deserters" to the Russian Empire were sufficiently impressed with the conditions there. Soldiers who had served in the Russian army and wished to return "home" came back to the Banat as early as 1756. The government greeted them with suspicion. They were placed under arrest as the government sought to ascertain the purpose of their return. Specifically, they wanted to know if they went willingly and during a time in which the government allowed some members of the "Rascian Nation" to emigrate. Alternatively, they wanted to know if they left "secretly," led by "emissaries" to join the Russian militia.[43]

One specific case is dealt with in depth in the archival record. When Damian Daskovich reentered the Banat sometime in January 1756 without a pass, he was treated as a Russian deserter or possibly a clandestine Russian recruiter.[44] He was immediately taken into custody. Daskovich was a fifty-seven-year-old Orthodox man from along the Marosch (the village of Nadlak) who had left for "New Serbia" three and a half years earlier. Apparently, he left his wife and grown sons, members of the border guard, when he moved and, in his own words, had returned to be with them "where [he] was born." He also said he had no desire to return to Russia. He claimed that his brother-in-law, a captain, had "seduced" him into moving with promises of money but had largely reneged. He had not been formally released from service but was told to go AWOL and that another person would take his place. Habsburg authorities were particularly interested in his traveling companions, also members of the Russian military. They were especially keen to know if they passed on any letters or messages to people on their trip or whether they were trying to recruit anyone. Daskovich said they had not. He further said that the only message he had been given to deliver was from his brother-in-law. He had asked Daskovich to greet his friends for him, let them know he was healthy, and tell them that "what he had sought, he had found."[45]

He was released more than a year later, in July 1758, after the authorities determined he was a "born subject," was not recruiting, and was not guilty of a crime against the government. Furthermore, the Russians had not requested his return. He was allowed to settle in Idvar, near Pancsova, with his wife and children. Despite releasing Daskovich, the government urged local officials to continue to keep an eye on former subjects who were returning to the Banat.[46] Daskovich's story is likely similar to that of many of the Rascians who left the Banat and sought their fortunes in Russia. He was convinced to leave because of promises of money but quickly became disillusioned and wanted to return home. His story would likely have been familiar to many of the German-speaking colonists around him as well.

Despite Daskovich's apparent innocence, the Habsburgs were right to fear clandestine Russian recruiters in their domains. With official requests denied, secret operations became the only option. Recruitment of new individuals to supplement and expand the colonies was a constant concern of the Russians. A retired Hungarian major of the Serbian Hussars, Ivan Filipovich, was just one important recruiter with Austrian ties. Other recruiters were freelancers looking for advancement. Recruiters could gain Russian military rank for the number of recruits they brought from the Austrian or Turkish domains. One hundred recruits, for instance, gave one the rank of captain. In New Serbia, it took three hundred recruits to gain the same rank. It took twice as many individuals if the settlers in question were nonmilitary.[47] In 1752, there were reports of recruiters spreading propaganda and leading Rascians out of the realm.[48] Sometimes suspected recruiters were caught and expelled. The authorities took Jacob Leonovsky and Joan Knezevich, both holders of Russian passports, into custody near Kikinda. Although they claimed to be simple travelers who were merely passing by the Theiss military villages, authorities accused them of being agents, took them to the border, and expelled them in 1754.[49] In December of the same year, a Lieutenant Mihaÿ Novakovich, also a Russian, was escorted to the Polish border.[50]

As we saw in the cases of the emigration of the 1750s or the riots following the 1777 ordinance, governmental interference in questions of politics or faith increasingly alienated the Rascian population and helped encourage anti-Habsburg and antihierarchical actions. They felt, in many ways correctly, that the privileges they had been offered at settlement had been undermined. With the transfer of sovereignty to Hungary, many German colonists would share their feelings. In the aftermath of the Austro-Turkish War from 1787 to 1790, relations between the government and the Grenzer were strained. Even though the Grenzer could not work their land due to the conflict, the government nonetheless demanded the yearly taxes.[51] The combination of resentment toward authorities (Habsburg and Hungarian alike) and the ideals unleashed by the French Revolution led to further unrest among the Rascians of the Banat.

The French Revolution: Rascians becoming Serbs

By the late eighteenth century, dissatisfaction with the status quo in the region had begun to change. It became more organized and focused (think of Horea's Rebellion discussed in the previous chapter), and further, it began to adopt a more national idiom. It was further a time of upheaval locally, internationally, and intellectually. The French Revolution and its ideals reverberated throughout Europe, and the Banat was no exception. For the Rascians, it acquired particular importance as it was part of the larger impact Francophilia had among the community's educated and prosperous members. Throughout the eighteenth century, some Rascians had sought out French language instruction for their children. Some went to universities in other parts of the empire and the German lands and were exposed to the language and culture there. Although the Habsburgs sought to prohibit the works of certain Enlightenment authors, soldiers from the Seven Years' War or other migrants to the region brought their books.[52] Thus, elite Rascian culture was attuned to French thought and able to access it.

This feeling of awe and respect for the French and their experiment came through in the "Speech to Open the Illyrian National Assembly" in

Temesvár in 1790.[53] The speech opened by discussing the reinvigoration of national rights and seemed to make slightly veiled, though extremely positive, references to the revolutionary events in France. In an interesting oratorical twist, the speaker appeared to reference the French Revolution and then turned the reference into praise for the way Emperor Leopold II (r. 1790–1792) helped reinvigorate the Illyrian nation.[54] The praise for Leopold was doubtless due to his championing the assembly itself, which had been resisted by Magyar elites.[55] Despite the constant references to Leopold as a good and true king, there were also many references to the "people" (*Volk, Nation*) and their rights, history, and uniqueness and their joining the ranks of other "enlightened nations of Europe." Further, the speaker claimed that the time had come when there was to be no tyranny, privileges were to be defended, and the demands of the subjects were to be secured.

The national congress asked for a number of radical changes in the status quo. They wanted the Banat to be made into an autonomous "Serbian" area. They wanted more self-government and more direct representation with the crown. They also wanted the Grenzer to remain under military authority. These suggestions must have frightened the Hungarian authorities. In response, they promised the Illyrians representation in the Hungarian parliament. While Leopold wanted to prevent Magyar-Rascian rapprochement, which would lessen his ability to influence events in the region, he was also bound to respect the promises made by Charles VI to return certain lands to the Magyar crown. To his representative at the meeting, he complained that the Hungarian situation did not allow him to decree anything concrete on the creation of an autonomous Serbian region. He further requested that his envoy do his utmost to dodge the question for the moment, though he claimed he would do "all the best" he could to help the Rascians. He privately promised them increased representation at court, something he delivered.[56]

The assembly produced important changes to how the Rascians in the Habsburg domains were governed. Authorities in Vienna created an "Illyrian Court Chancellery." This lasted only as long as Emperor Leopold and was disbanded in 1792. The Hungarians also accorded the Rascians more representation in the government. They were recognized as a "collective unit." Their notables also gained access to the Hungarian Diet. In exchange for these concessions, the Rascians had to give up their rights to autonomy given in 1690. Furthermore, their small number in the Diet guaranteed that their effect would be minimal. Ultimately, the fate of the Rascians in Hungary largely depended on the relations between Vienna and Budapest.[57]

At first, the Habsburgs viewed neither the French Revolution nor the corresponding identification of the Rascians with it, with too much apprehension. Both Joseph II and Leopold II viewed the revolution as an endorsement of their enlightened policies and did not believe such popular unrest would spread to their lands. In fact, the unrest they faced was from nobles opposed to change, not from commoners demanding it.[58] This changed in April 1792 when the Legislative Assembly declared war, starting a hot-cold conflict that lasted until 1815. The execution of Louis XVI and his wife, Empress Maria Theresia's daughter Marie Antoinette, in 1793 further highlighted the dangers of the revolution for the European status quo.[59] With the outbreak of war between the French and the Austrians, many Grenzer were sent to the front to fight for the Habsburg armies. At this point, the connection felt between the Grenzer and the French ideals of nationhood became extremely problematic. Many Grenzer resented their deployment away from their homes during the French Revolutionary Wars. Letters sent by Grenzer from the Netherlands, surreptitiously read by the Hofkriegsrat, revealed an "unabashed devotion" to the French ideals of freedom.[60]

By the early nineteenth century, events south of the border were also beginning to affect the Rascians.[61] The Serb Revolt in the Ottoman domains from 1804 to 1813 tested the Habsburg stomach for more war and caused them to increasingly question the loyalty of their own South Slav population. In Ottoman Serbia, Karadjordje, a former Austrian corporal, led an insurrection.[62] Although the Rascian-Serb community supported the uprising against the Ottomans, the Habsburg government, embroiled in the Napoleonic struggles though not currently at war, withheld most open support.[63] Karadjordje encouraged these feelings of solidarity between the Habsburg and Ottoman Serbs. In 1807, when the Serbs of Pancsova were building their new church, Karadjordje himself donated the material for the building. When an Orthodox cleric, Andreas Arsenjević, said a prayer of thanks for the material support, he was disciplined by the Orthodox hierarchy (he lost his job) and by the state (he was imprisoned). Only the intervention of Archduke Ludwig freed him.[64] The authorities were very much aware that the transimperial connections of Serbs were becoming ever more threatening to their control and the stability of the region.

As always, the Habsburgs had to balance Serb demands with Hungarian sensibilities and Russian aspirations. The Hungarians were especially afraid that the creation of a Serbian state to the south would rile up their own Serbian minority. As Turczynski put it, "In their [Hungarian] view, the Serbians were rebels, and the bandit raids that some Serbian rebels who crossed the border to steal cattle, food, and money to exchange for munitions, seemed symptomatic of the entire Serbian nation."[65] The Russians, for their part, moved troops into Serbia to help their coreligionists in 1810. Instead of openly supporting the rebels, the Habsburgs often simply turned a blind eye to the movement of money, men, and weapons from their subjects over the border. Though officially required to halt such transfers, border officials only sporadically enforced the law. The desertion of Austrian and Hungarian Rascians to fight the Ottomans was especially problematic for authorities. Not only did this represent a loss of manpower, but it also made the Ottomans suspicious of Habsburg motives. Some officials, especially in the military, wanted to offer direct support. Both Joseph Anton Freiherr von Simbschen, an expert of Serb society and culture from his years on the border, and his successor as the commanding general of the Slavonian border, Baron Johann von Hiller, both wanted to provide more aid to the insurgents.[66]

The tepid official policy of the Habsburgs was not enough to prevent local Serbs from countenancing and even attempting to join their coethnics to the south in some form of union. In 1804, Francophile and Orthodox Metropolitan Startimirović apparently approached the Russians asking for support in establishing a Serb state that would have encompassed not only the Serbian parts of the Ottoman Empire but those of the Habsburg Empire as well.[67] Startimirović's plan was to have a non-Habsburg Russian or Lutheran prince rule the new state, though the proposal never made it to Tsar Alexander I. The bishop of the Batschka, Jovan Jovanović, asked the metropolitan of St. Petersburg to support a Serb protectorate that included Habsburg territory. Even the Croatians, Slavs but not Orthodox, under Ljudevit Gaj, offered the tsar the "Crown of Illyria."[68] In 1807, authorities uncovered more plans to create a new state, though the details are sketchy. Historian Janjetović described it as a failed Habsburg Serbian plan to separate the southern Banat from Hungary and join it with Moldavia, Wallachia, and Serbia.[69] Local historian Felix Milleker mentioned a revolt planned for

May 10, 1807 that involved Serbs in Pancsova as well as similar, later (?) plans in Novi Sad and Weisskirchen. Authorities uncovered another rebellion in Pancsova and arrested the leaders.[70] To what extent these descriptions refer to discrete events and to what extent they refer to the more documented rebellion in 1808 or even Tican's 1807 rebellion in Syrmia, is unclear.

In 1808, a very visible uprising highlighted why the Habsburgs distrusted the transimperial Rascians, especially as their nationalist impulses grew. In that year, a mutiny occurred in the Wallach-Illyrian Regiment.[71] Led by an Orthodox cleric, Demetria Deak, the goal of the revolt, confessed at his trial, was to kill the Catholics of the region (almost exclusively Germans) and establish a Serbian empire.[72] The danger was greatest for the Catholics in Weisskirchen, a town near the southern border. There were even Ottoman-Serbian volunteers waiting over the border for the signal to invade. Deak also sought to incite the Wallachs to revolt, though this plan failed. After Habsburg officials discovered the plot, Deak attempted to flee to Serbia but was caught. While putting down the revolt, the authorities imprisoned the families of any householder not found at home. Originally sentenced to death, Deak's sentence was commuted. He later died in a Temesvár prison. The authorities also similarly punished a number of coconspirators, including lieutenants, a pensioned captain, another pastor, a deacon, and a merchant.[73] This incident represented a high point of armed Rascian-Serbian resistance to the state. Interestingly, the revolt took place at the military border, an area *not* under the control of the Hungarians but subject to Vienna's direct control. While much of the Rascian antipathy had traditionally been directed at the Hungarians, the national aspirations of the educated elite were now expanding beyond simple ethnic rivalries with Magyars or Germans to a desire to be free from all external control.

Both the Rascians and Wallachs bristled under Habsburg control, and both eventually resorted to violence in response. This is particularly interesting given the Rascians' often-privileged position. The Habsburgs initially needed and trusted the Rascians enough to grant them wide-ranging freedoms and autonomy in the late seventeenth century. Perhaps both sides believed their sojourn in the monarchy would be short and that they would return "home" after a resounding Habsburg victory in the Balkans, rendering the privileges null. This did not happen, and while the privileges gave Rascians a leading role in Orthodox affairs, that power raised suspicions among Habsburg administrators and particularly among the Hungarian elite. Ethnic and linguistic connections with Rascians in the Ottoman Empire and religious and cultural connections with the Russian Empire seemed to indicate the potential for divided loyalties. Evidence, from smuggling and collusion with their Ottoman coethnics to emigration to the Russian Empire, seemed to confirm many of the government's suspicions. As the government sought greater religious and political control, Rascians pushed back, particularly against the Hungarians, to protect their privileges. By the turn of the nineteenth century, sporadic collusion and emigration became much more serious as some elements of Rascian society sought the protection of the Russian tsar and independence from the Habsburg monarchy.

As we will see in the epilogue, the Revolution of 1848 again inflamed ethnic passion in the region, but in that case, the influence of nationalism became pronounced. It would be incorrect to say that all, or even a majority, of the Banat's residents were "nationalists" at this point. The role of religion, for instance, and the local community remained crucially important. Many residents simply wanted to keep their families safe and did not dream of some national victory. Still, there were some who did, and their voices got ever louder and more influential as the twentieth century dawned. In the end, it was German ultranationalists, calling themselves Nazis, who would arguably do the most to destroy the diversity that had defined the Banat since the eighteenth century. Their policies, and the aftermath of those policies, led to the demographic dissolution of the region, a dissolution that continues to this day.

Epilogue
The Banat Germans

1848 to the Present

DURING AND FOLLOWING THE Revolution of 1848, the Germans of the Banat petitioned the imperial government for their own autonomous region. On October 2, 1849, at a meeting in Bogarosch, leading Banat Germans from thirty-five communities drafted the so-called "Swabian Petition." The author of the document was the pastor of Bogarosch, Johann Nowak. The petition called for a German noble to lead them. They believed that "under his protection, our affairs, legal matters, and administration will be handled in the German language and according to German custom."[1] Germans centered in Hatzfeld also created a petition requesting more autonomy.[2]

The Swabian Petition is an important source for understanding how the leading Banat Germans saw themselves and their history in a time of growing nationalist sentiments among many peoples in the Banat and across the empire.[3] For instance, the Germans believed they were settled in the region "in order to transplant German industriousness and occupation to the, at the time, desolate, swampy, flooded, unhealthy, and almost completely depopulated Banat." In this document, the Banat Germans began constructing their own myths about why they were settled in the region. They were the leading lights who alone were able to develop an empty landscape. It went on to describe how the "German love of work" had conquered the Banat, though many of their "fathers" had "sacrificed" their lives and health to the "fight." The Germans claimed they had better schools, were more punctual with their taxes, were better able to bear burdens, and were less often responsible for crime than other "nations" in the Banat.

Despite their strong and hearty nature, they claimed to "respect and honor" the other nationalities in the Banat and would not want to take advantage of them. They stated that the Revolution of 1848 made them realize that they were not seen in the same way as the other nations were. They felt like an "unprotected orphan in the house of another national faction." The potential creation of a *Woiwodschaft* for the Serbs heightened their apprehension. If the emperor decided "to give the Serbs for the preservation of their nationality a *Woiwod*, the Romanians a *Capitain*, the Slovenes/Slovaks/Upper Hungarians their own *Oberhaupt*," then the Germans wanted a *Graf* (count) to represent their community.[4] They ended by saying that although they would rather live in a large state where there were only people "proud of their common Austrian nationality" rather than Hungarians, Bohemians, Poles, or Serbs, if other groups were "consolidating" their nation, then they wanted to do so as well. These "German speakers" formulated a new identity that, if not overtly tied to the "Germanness" asserting itself in the German Confederation, at least shows them conceiving of themselves as a unique regional group, Banat Germans. In so doing, they took the triumphal aspects of their history and ignored the tenuousness of their early years in the region.

As this epilogue will make clear, the drafters of the Swabian Petition were ultimately correct; as national feeling among other ethnic groups began to grow, the position of the Banat's Germans deteriorated. In a self-reinforcing circle, as the Magyars became more nationalist, so did the Serbs and the Romanians. They also sought to assimilate others into their nation (Magyarization). If that was not effective, these nationalists adopted the idea of compartmentalizing people through religion or ethnicity, which, as we have seen, was Habsburg policy in the eighteenth century, and took it to a violent end. As throughout the Banat's history, interethnic tension could become interethnic violence during periods of upheaval. It was generally, though certainly not exclusively, the ethnic Germans of the Banat who served as prime targets of violence and dispossession.

As the opening vignette shows, they were not immune from larger trends and sought ways to protect themselves. The autonomy and power many gained under than Nazis poisoned their relations with local people and led to retribution after the war. In the end, it was the convergence and interplay of local strains of nationalism, German ultranationalism (Nazism), and later national-communism, which drove the German communities (among others) out of the region and created the largely monoethnic states that comprise the historical Banat today. As we will see, many of the trends we saw in the eighteenth and nineteenth centuries (colonization, dispossession, compartmentalization, increasing nationalism) continued to play out well into the twentieth.

The Revolution of 1848 to World War I: Confused Loyalties

The period from unification with Hungary until 1848 was a time of increasing Hungarian social, governmental, and cultural assertiveness vis-à-vis both German-speaking colonists and Serbians (Rascians). Magyarization, the desire to unify the country around Hungarian language and culture, necessarily entailed assimilating the masses of non-Magyars. In the words of historian István Deák, Lajos Kossuth, a prominent politician and the man who eventually led the Hungarian Revolution, "held the assimilation into the Magyar nation to be the duty and the *summum bonum* of the country's national minorities." In 1842, Kossuth further stated that "in Hungary, Magyar must become the language of public administration, whether civil or ecclesiastic, of the legislative and the executive, of the government, of justice, of public security, of the police, of direct and indirect taxation and of the economy ... to accept less would be cowardice; to insist on more would be tyranny; both would be suicide on our part."[5] Not all Hungarians were on board with Kossuth's plan. In a prescient book published in 1841, one of his main rivals, István Széchenyi, warned that Kossuth's nationalist plans would lead to economic and ethnic conflict. In the years leading up to the Revolution of 1848, Magyarization was progressing fairly well in cities where Hungarians had taken hold of governments and were making inroads in the churches.[6] Unfortunately for their plans, the development of Hungarian nationalism coincided with and reinforced the development of Serbian and Romanian nationalism. The Germans of the Banat, perhaps the least nationalized group and the one that outwardly preferred to elevate loyalty to the sovereign over ethnic concerns, were caught in the middle of the maelstrom. These forces came into direct conflict in 1848.

The Revolution of 1848 in Hungary did not start out as a revolution demanding complete independence from the Habsburg crown. The initial impetus, at least from the perspective of the Hungarian leaders and Lajos Kossuth, was to defend what they felt to be the Magyar crown's traditional rights, not to overthrow the king and establish a republic. The wheels of revolution began turning following a March 3 meeting at which Kossuth gave a speech outlining Hungarian demands, which included sweeping changes to both the internal social order and external relations. On March 18, the Habsburg apparatus begrudgingly recognized the appointment of Count Batthyány as prime minister, thus endorsing, however tepidly, the new Hungarian government. The April Laws established a legal base for the redefined Hungary, creating a parliament and abolishing serfdom. The government created by this reform lasted six months. In September, Josip Jelačić, the ban of Croatia and a Habsburg appointee, invaded Hungary and precipitated a war between the Austrian forces loyal to the emperor and the Hungarians. On October 3, the emperor ordered the dissolution of the National Assembly and imposed martial law. This demand was rejected and on October 8, Kossuth became president and the so-called National Defense Committee, which Kossuth packed with his supporters, assumed executive control. It was not until April 14, 1849, that Kossuth formally deposed the Habsburg king and declared Hungarian independence.[7] What had been largely a Hungarian civil war now became a war between the Habsburg crown and the nascent Hungarian state.

In 1848, the revolutionary fervor affected the ethnoreligious communities of the Banat in many ways ranging from cooperation to violent conflict.[8] In the early days of 1848, for instance, the Germans and Serbs of Pancsova, in the Banat's military border, were *united* in their long-standing goal to gain more rights and freedoms for the city. In particular, no one in the town liked the military administration or bureaucracy. They wanted to be able to vote for their town leaders like the free cities in Hungary. On March 22, 1848, demonstrators stormed city hall, expelled the sitting military officials, and installed a new government, including a council that consisted of five Serbs and three Germans. Members of both groups also signed a petition outlining their grievances. They held unity banquets. Interestingly for later developments, one petition asked for the incorporation of Pancsova into Hungary proper. In fact, for a time in the early days of the revolution, the Hungarian flag flew over the city as a sign of the citizens' solidarity with the protestors in Vienna and Pest. Some members of the military resisted the move toward a more representative government and sought to reinstate military supremacy in the city.[9]

These feelings of solidarity with the Hungarians evaporated quickly. Serbian attempts to meet with Kossuth in early April failed. On April 8, he stated that "the true meaning of freedom is that it recognizes the inhabitants of the fatherland only as a whole. . . . The unity of the country makes it indispensable for the language of public affairs to be the Magyar language."[10] Apparently, Serbian autonomy was a dead letter in the new Hungarian state. Serbian riots occurred in Bečej in the Batschka and in Kikinda, where on Easter, people robbed and murdered the district senator Johann Csencitz.[11] Such events caused a strengthening of Serbian national feeling and by the end of the month, they no longer wanted unification with Hungary but rather increased separation from the state. In fact, a letter from Karlowitz, an Orthodox religious center, proposed an autonomous Serbian region (crownland) to include the Banat, Batschka, Syrmia, and Baranya. At a National Congress in May, which included representatives from the Principality of Serbia, this proposal received even more support. The Serbs declared the creation of the Vojvodina out of all southern Hungary. Stevan Šupljikac became the first *vojvod* (leader of the newly created polity). Joseph Rajačić became the Serbian patriarch. Shortly thereafter, the Hungarians began organizing troops in Segedin to combat the Serbs, who likewise began military preparations.[12] Initially, the army had 15,000 men and forty guns.[13] Claiming allegiance to the Habsburg monarch, the Serb revolt began in earnest on May 24.[14]

The Serbo-Magyar conflict highlighted many of the themes we have explored thus far. The Serbs continued their traditional opposition to Magyar impositions and forcefully countered their attempts to establish their own autonomous or independent state. Much as in their earlier rebellions, the Serbs combined both an ethnic and religious idiom in their resistance. This was personified in Metropolitan Rajačić, who entered Pancsova with a sword in one hand and a cross in the other. Already in mid-1848, there were an estimated 23,000 "insurgents" (meaning, in this case, anti-Hungarian forces) in the Banat.[15] Much as they had in the early years following conquest, some observers noted a connection between Protestantism and rebellion against the Habsburgs. As historian István Deák put it, "[Count György] Andrássy saw an unbroken line leading from the 'Protestant rebellions' of such seventeenth- and eighteen- [sic] century princes as Bocskai, Thököly, and Rákóczi to the 'Protestant Rebellion' of Kossuth."[16] Similarly, an alliance between the Hungarians and Ottomans, feared by the Habsburgs since the early eighteenth century, became a partial reality. Part of Kossuth's program included "seek[ing] an alliance with the Italian provinces and the provinces of the Ottoman Empire."[17] Also in 1849, Hungarian rebel (though ethnic Pole) General Bem tried to make an alliance with the Ottomans and asked for the protection of Hungarian refugees in Wallachia.[18] This gambit seems to have worked, at least initially. The Porte initially refused to allow the Russians access to the Banat.[19] Despite this initial setback, the Russians played a role in supporting the Serbs (and of course the Habsburg monarch) by entering the fray and helping crush the rebellion.

Much as in earlier times of upheaval, the Revolution of 1848 pitted the ethnic groups of the Banat against each other in interesting ways. While the Serbs were initially interested in the movement away from Austrian rule, Magyar intransigence on language autonomy forced the Serbs into the Habsburg camp.[20] It is often hard to tell if the Serbs were fighting *for* the Habsburgs or simply *against* the Hungarians. In addition, there were Serbs who fought *for* the Hungarians. The situation around Weisskirchen highlights the confusion. A German colonel, who reported to a Croatian general and was urged on by a Serb who worked for the Hungarian government, led a group of Polish lancers against Serbs *also* led by an Austro-German colonel. The leader of the Serbs persuaded the leader of the Poles to withdraw when he asked him "to think of his duty to the emperor and not of his duty to the king (the two were the same person)." There were even a few Germans on the Serbian side.[21] On the individual level, ethnic alliances were confusing indeed.

Using volunteers from Serbia and Bosnia, the Serbs fought the revolutionaries in southern Hungary.[22] In late 1848, the Serbian patriarch, fearing renewed Hungarian attacks, asked his transimperial coethnics for assistance. Serbian leader Alexander Karadjordjević complied and "several thousand" Serbs crossed the border.[23] Many of the recruits joined the counterrevolution because of the promise of plunder and thus the German communities of the Banat again became targets for aggression. In the Banat, the Serbs offered protection if the population remained quiet, destruction of their settlements if they did not.[24] In Tschanad, the Serbs who helped in the fighting were supposed to be rewarded with German houses. To identity who got what, the names of the "new owners" were written on the houses.[25]

Given this situation, it is hard to tell the extent to which the Germans supported the Magyar cause and the extent to which they were simply defending their homes and villages from Serb aggression. Kossuth, for his part, believed that both Germans and Romanians would side with the Hungarians against a common Slavic threat.[26] In addition to security, other Germans may have sided with the Hungarian rebels to protest serfdom and feudal dues.[27] Likely, many would have felt that they were *Kaisertreu*, that is, true to the emperor, regardless of whose side they fought.[28] A number took up arms with the Hungarians. Germans from Mercydorf and Bogarosch joined the Honvéd, the Hungarian national militia.[29] Regardless of their motivations, by 1848 the Germans of the Banat were no longer a group with unquestioned loyalty to the Habsburg government, if they had ever truly been one. By this point, they were much more concerned with their own communal problems and well-being than they were with acting as some sort of Habsburg proxies in the region.

Mathias Siebold, a colonist who wrote one of the few first-person accounts of the revolution from a German settler perspective, seemed pro-Hungarian, or at least in favor of the values that the Hungarians were promoting.[30] He described the new constitution, agreed upon by Emperor Ferdinand and the Hungarian nobility, as promoting "freedom, equality and fraternity." He praised the abolition of "robot and socage, laws which belong to slavery." During the revolution itself, Siebold, along with other Germans from around the region, took part in the defense of Werschetz and Weisskirchen when the Serbs attacked, remaining there from August 7–15, 1848.[31] In the pitched battle waged between Serbian and German forces there, Serbian spies infiltrated the Serbian families that remained.[32] Imperial troops (from the Temesvár General Command) had protected the town for a time, but when the commander refused to fight the Grenzer (he would only fight Serbs from the principality), they used the opportunity to attack the town. A Lieutenant Colonel Mayerhofer, later made a general, was "in effective charge" of the Serbs, in a way making them "imperial troops" as well.[33] Thus, all sides felt that they were loyal to the emperor, and the Germans of the town were simply caught in the middle of chaotic situation. After the German victory, those Serbs who had helped the besieging forces became victims of retribution.[34]

It appears that many Germans took part in the defense of the town, some even staying behind to help form a cordon to prevent further Serb advances. A later historian of Beschenowa estimated that a hundred villagers from there went to help defend the town of Weisskirchen as well, of which twelve remained behind after the fighting.[35] A similar incident happened in the village of Stamora. When German peasants in Morawitza heard that Serbian irregulars sought to plunder the village, they armed themselves and helped repel the invaders.[36] In Bogarosch, local leaders also organized men to fight the Serbs.[37]

Even in Pancsova, where there had been some measure of ethnic solidarity at the beginning of the revolution, the Serbs eventually decided they could not trust the Germans. More Serbs appear to have entered Pancsova on July 23, 1848, in response to the organization of a revolt by the Germans and the few Hungarians of the city. The Serbs took the leaders and important members of the community hostage, disarmed the non-Serbian residents, and threatened to kill anyone who resisted.[38] This incident occurred despite the fact that in July the Germans had taken an oath of allegiance to the emperor while promising to live in peace with the Serbs.[39]

As in previous conflicts, the Wallachs (with some now often calling themselves "Romanian") took advantage of the upheaval to attack German settlements. According to a report by the Hungarian treasury, the German villages of Bakovar, Niztkydorf, Darovar, Ebendorf, Moritzfeld, Freudenthal, Morawitza, Ritberg, and Liebling were especially affected. After the colonists fled, locals killed or stole animals, stole equipment, "wasted" their houses, and "ravaged" their fields. When the Germans returned, all they found was "barely livable houses."[40] Like the Serbs, the Romanians of the Banat sought to organize themselves politically. On May 16–17, 1848, they met in Lugoj, led by Eftimie Murgu, and demanded more freedom and autonomy. At a second meeting in Lugoj on June 27, 10,000 Banat Romanians oversaw three major policy declarations. First, they created a popular army. Second, they rejected Serbian control over the Romanian Church.[41] Finally, they adopted Romanian as the official language of their administration. The next year, they sought further recognition of their nationhood along with their coethnics throughout the empire.[42]

The town of Temesvár was key to the end of the revolution. In October 1848, a cadre of officers overruled their commander and declared the fortress would remain loyal to the Austrian emperor. Though often sieged, the fortress remained in Austrian hands throughout the revolution. Although there had been fighting in the region in 1848, by January 1849, the Hungarians had completely retreated from southern Hungary. On April 10, the decisive battle of the revolution was fought near Temesvár. Troops loyal to the Austrian emperor led by General Haynau defeated rebel troops led by General Bem. Following this battle, the rebel government fell apart and Kossuth fled the country, though sporadic resistance, especially in the fortress of Komárom, lasted into late summer and fall before finally subsiding.[43]

For their help in putting down the revolutionaries, the Serbs expected some sort of political recognition. Already in December 1848, the emperor "solemnly promised the Serbs a national self-government" in the area of southern Hungary then under combined Austro-Serbian control. By May 1849, some Serbs were reevaluating their position. They began to realize that not only was unification with the Serbian principality unlikely but also that the emperor's promise of more autonomy was likewise suspect.[44] After the war ended, they received at least titular recognition of this promise with the creation of the "Serbian Voivodship and Temeser Banat." This development represented the culmination of the demands for autonomy that stretched back to the National Congress of 1790. The region was constructed from the Batschka and Banat, ripped from Hungarian control as punishment for the insurrection. This creation only enjoyed a short existence, since the Austrians returned the region to Hungarian control in 1867.

Following the revolution, the relationship between the government and the Banat Germans changed. As we have seen, the German colonists were initially brought to the Banat to act as a settled, reliable, secure population. Their actions during the revolution proved to the governments in Vienna and Budapest that they were no longer impeccably loyal. In lists of suspected Honvéd members compiled in Gross Kikinda in 1850, German names appeared (though some of these were later listed as "unfit," indicating that they would not have been able to fight). In this admittedly small sample, seventeen of 111 individuals (15 percent) had recognizably German names or were explicitly identified as Germans.[45] Suspicions persisted in the years following the conflict. In a letter to the Kikinda mayor's office in 1853, authorities in Temesvár warned of "revolutionary proclamations" aimed at the "German Volk" and "German soldiers" being prepared by the chief of the German exiles in London. Apparently, this had been a problem for some time. The aim was to foment revolution among the German population. The local authorities were thus to keep a close eye for such materials.[46]

Tensions between the Serbs, Romanians, and Germans continued throughout the rest of the century. Among other local people, the Germans became negatively associated with the perceived "Germanizing" program of the government following the revolution. While there was tension, it did not spill over into any wide expressions of intercommunal violence, though politics could bring out the worst in people. In 1865, Romanians and Germans of Klein Becskerek, who supported rival candidates, fought one another during voting for the Landtag.[47] When the military border was disbanded the Germans celebrated the prospect of new rights as Hungarian subjects, while the Serbs and Romanians feared increased Magyarization.[48] In 1869 in Pancsova, Germans lost their seats in the town council as Serbs sought to consolidate their position ahead of the turnover. At the elections held on January 10, 1874, some Germans came to the polling places with flags in "German colors." This act, and others like it, concerned the Hungarian authorities enough that in February, they ordered that only Hungarian flags could be flown.[49] There were other traditional realms of nonviolent competition. Serbs and Germans, for instance, engaged in an economic rivalry.[50]

Migration remained a major issue in the region. By the later nineteenth century, the East itself became a place of German emigration rather than immigration as one-time settlers in the Banat and in Russia left for the United States. Around 1890, a number of residents from Weisskirchen left after phylloxera ravaged the wine industry of the region.[51] Especially between 1900 and 1907, many Banat Germans left for both North and South America. Some returned in 1908 due to a recession in the United States.[52] This movement of Germans abroad led Karl von Möller, a leading Romanian Banat German in the 1920s, to critically refer to the United States as "Dollarika."[53]

Although some people of the Banat sought prosperity overseas, others managed just as well at home. By World War I, reports indicated that the

German segment of the Banat's population was an economically important one.[54] According to a report prepared by the British for diplomatic use at the Paris Peace Conference, the Germans:

> formed a highly prosperous yeoman class, owning their own land, and are excellent farmers and most successful horse-breeders. They form a valuable asset in the economic life of the country, and contribute to its development and stability. Furthermore, whatever the result of the negotiations on the subject [on the dismemberment of the Habsburg Empire] may be, the rights of the German nationality in the new divisions would require some special guarantees if future unrest among so important a section is to be avoided.[55]

The *New York Times* reported that "up to the outbreak of the world war the Rumanians of the Banat belonged to the peasant, town proletariat, and other lower classes, and were in a backward condition, culturally and socially. The ruling and business classes and the intellectual classes were Germans and Magyars, who regarded the Rumanians with haughty contempt."[56] This impression is partially backed by statistics. By 1910, the Germans of Hungary had the lowest rate of illiteracy in individuals older than six (29.6 percent). This was even better than the Magyar rate (33 percent) and significantly better than either the Serbs (59.6 percent) or the Romanians (71.8 percent).[57] The famous observer and historian of Hungary, C. A. Macartney, declared that the Germans were a "particularly" important and wealthy segment of the Banat's population around 1918. He further claimed that Temesvár and "much of the country-side was thoroughly German" during the same period.[58]

While impressions of German prosperity were one thing, the reality, at least relating to land ownership, appears to be something else. By 1919, the Germans were a major segment of the population and were large landholders in the disintegrating Banat, though they did not own property out of line with their percentage of population. In Torontál County in 1910, Germans represented 26.6 percent of the population (158,312/594,343). In Temes County, Germans were 30.1 percent (120,683/400,910). In Krassó-Szörény County, Germans were 11.9 percent (55,883/466,147).[59] They held lands quite proportional to their population. In Torontál County, Germans owned 26 percent of the property. By comparison, Magyars owned 25.8 percent, Romanians 12 percent, and Serbs 31.2 percent. In Temes County, Germans had 29.2 percent, Magyars 27.3 percent, Romanians 27.7 percent, and Serbs

13.7 percent. Finally, in mountainous Krassó-Szörény, Germans had 2.5 percent, Magyars 41.8 percent, Romanians 50.1 percent, and Serbs 3.4 percent.[60] The reason for the discrepancy in property ownership in Krassó-Szörény is likely due to the fact that many of the Germans there were miners and likely did not own much property. It is also unknown how many "Magyars" were descended from German migrants given the intensive Magyarization that took place in the nineteenth century. If these "former Germans" had been included, it may have skewed the numbers to indicate a more dominant German role in land ownership.

World War I to World War II: The Division of the Banat

As important as 1848 and its aftermath were for the region, the demographic reality remained much the same. The aftermath of the next two wars, the World Wars, led to the political and demographic dissolution of the region. World War I swept away Habsburg sovereignty while World War II accelerated the ethnic homogenization. The national upheaval of the First World War and the promise of self-determination offered by Wilson's Fourteen Points affected the Germans of the Banat as it did many other groups. Some Germans advocated for the creation of a "Republic of the Banat."[61] Not all observers saw this as an attempt for autonomy or independence by a local population. Emile Dillon, a contemporary commentator, saw it as a play by capitalists in the West to gain control of "one of the richest unexploited regions in Europe." He claimed that Béla Kun, leader of the short-lived Hungarian Soviet Republic, had made a backroom deal with a "certain financial group" to keep the Allied armies from overthrowing him and give him a seat at the peace conference. These interests feared that if the Banat joined a Serbian or Romanian state, it would be very difficult to exploit the region. Thus, an independent state would be formed. The people behind this move were "obliging officers of the two armies, and behind them were speculators and concession-hunters." According to his narrative, the "easy-going inhabitants" did not take part. The French even offered protection for the nascent state.[62]

This episode is particularly confusing. Some sources claim the republic was largely a German idea. Others claim it was an agreement between a number of smaller ethnic groups, with the Romanians and Serbians largely abstaining. Historian Irina Marin described the affair as an effort to create an autonomous region under Hungarian control. According to her, there were Germans who were pro-autonomy within Hungary, pro-Serbia, and pro-Romania.[63] Historian Zoran Janjetović largely supports this version of events. He said that the main goal of the "Swabian Council" that met in Temesvár under the Socialist Otto Roth's leadership was the "integrity of a federalized Hungary." On December 8, the council called for a vote on the future of the region, autonomy for the Banat and Batschka, guaranteed minority rights, and representation at the peace conference. There were other "nationally conscious" Germans who wanted separation from Hungary. There were even ideas of an independent Banat. Most importantly for the Germans, they did not want the Banat and Batschka to be split.[64] This was not to be. Independence or autonomy for the Banat was a dead letter. Rather, at the peace conference, all sides (Romanians, Serbs, and Hungarians) claimed that the Germans would want to be under their rule.[65] For their part, the "Swabian delegation" at the peace conference requested Romanian rule over the Banat.[66] In the end, the Banat was unevenly divided between Romania and the Kingdom of the Serbs, Croats, and Slovenes, with a small wedge going to Hungary.

Much as in 1716, the end of World War I heralded major shifts in power in the region, which the city of Temesvár naturally reflected. In the introduction to his book on the history of the fortress of "Temeschwar," Anton Peter Petri bemoaned the loss of German culture in the Banat following the war. He related that in 1920, there had been a big fight in the city over the renaming of streets. In one meeting, a German said the community did not mind getting rid of all Magyar and Habsburg-related names but wanted to keep German ones. In response, the Romanian secretary replied that "in 40 to 60 years Temesvár will be a Romanian city. The Romanian people can not allow themselves to be led by their minorities, therefore we will do what we want here." As did the Ottomans, Magyars, and Habsburgs, so did the Romanians. Naming and material culture, especially in this region, was a sign of control and hegemony. This was true from the eighteenth century through today.[67]

Naming notwithstanding, relations between the German minority and the new nation-states were a mixed bag during the 1920s. In Yugoslavia, there were some initial expulsions in order to consolidate Serb–South Slav rule in their part of the Banat. They targeted mostly Magyars who resisted

Serb rule but undoubtedly some Germans fell victim as well. Much like the Habsburgs had two hundred years previous, the Yugoslav government used colonization to change the demography of the Banat. In this case, they moved Montenegrins and other South Slavs to predominantly German areas throughout the Vojvodina (the name for the region that included their part of the Banat and the Batschka).[68] Some non-Slavs responded by emigrating. Others resisted. Conscription led to an uprising of Germans in and around Kula in the Batschka in 1920. Eighteen were killed and forty wounded. Hungarian revisionism also remained a perceived threat. The fact that some Germans remained "Magyar-philes" even after the Serbs took control caused tension.[69]

In addition, the Yugoslavian nationalist group ORJUNA targeted Germans in the Vojvodina, bombing the editorship of the *Deutsche Volksblatt* in 1922, and returning in 1923. They also attacked Germans during the elections of 1923. In 1925, members of the SRNAO, a Serbian nationalist organization, attacked Stefan Kraft and Georg Grassl, notable Yugoslav Germans.[70] Such scare tactics might have had an effect. In the 1923 election, only 2.1 percent of votes cast (43,495) were for German parties, leading to eight of 313 seats. In 1925, their political fortunes worsened. Although they received more total votes, they received 1.9 percent of the votes cast (45,010), leading to five seats out of 315. Winkler attributed the weak showing, which he claimed failed to accurately reflect the number of Germans in the land, to "major difficulties," not only the "Germanophobic terror of the population" but also their scattered pattern of settlement.[71] Land reform also led to tension between the two communities, though most German farms were small enough to remain unaffected. Historian Valdis Lumans further argued that the Serbs, recognizing the importance of German agriculture, "refrained from applying the reform fully against them."[72]

Despite these problems, the authorities allowed the Germans of the Vojvodina a certain level of autonomy in schools, clubs, and newspapers in a bid to integrate them into the emerging society.[73] The Germans established the "Swabian-German Cultural Union" in Novi Sad in 1920, though it remained open only on the whim of the authorities and was closed and reopened twice.[74] They also enjoyed a significant financial upswing, which in turn caused other problems. Germans' success and wealth caused resentment among the poorer Serbs, especially following the Great Depression.

Some even believed that Nazi Germany was helping fund German land purchases. German businessmen and industrialists in the Vojvodina were in fact quite successful.[75] It appears that the Germans and their banks simply did a better job navigating the crisis, allowing them to use their credit to buy the land of indigent non-Germans.[76]

In Romania, relations were better. Although the Romanians did practice a degree of Romanization, the Germans were generally loyal subjects, and the Romanians were comparatively lenient rulers.[77] Germans (both Transylvanian "Saxons" and Banat "Swabians") hoped that the Romanian government would respect their cultural autonomy. The Karlsburg Declaration supported by Saxons, Transylvanian Romanians, and Banat Germans codified this hope, even though it was not initially ratified in Bucharest. Much as in Yugoslavia, Romanian Germans were quite successful. Also as in Yugoslavia, the Romanian authorities feared Hungarian revisionism and thus privileged the Germans, allowing them to create various clubs and entertainment organizations. Germans throughout Romania took advantage, and these groups eventually became infused with politics.[78] In 1922, Germans held a symbolic number of seats in the legislature (9/369 in the Abgeornetenkammer and 3/168 in the Senat). Of these, eight were Saxons in Transylvania, and four were Banat Germans. According to Winkler, based on their percentage of the population, the Germans should have had seventeen members in the Abgeornetenkammer and eight in the Senat.[79] In 1928, they had twelve seats in parliament and four in the senate.[80]

By the 1930s, the peaceful coexistence of the Germans and the Yugoslav and Romanian governments began to break down. Macartney, a contemporary observer of these events, described a change in German-Romanian relations around 1935, inspired by Germany's revitalization. He mentioned that although the Germans in the region were latecomers to nationalist ideology, "like mumps, it raged all the more fiercely when it came, and the worthy Swabians became so enthralled in the delights of building German Kultur in the far south-east as to become blind to almost any other consideration."[81] Particularly irksome was the Romanian attempt to convince and ultimately force Germans to learn the Romanian language.[82]

By the mid-1920s, the youth were organizing their own political movements.[83] In 1931, Germans returning from study in Germany began to bring the new, national-socialist ideology back to the Yugoslav Banat where it spread more readily among the younger generation than the older.[84] In Neubeschenowa, for example, "the national-socialist renewal movement" gained adherents in 1933.[85] These young Germans also organized paramilitarily.[86] At the outbreak of the war, the Yugoslav Germans became more enthralled with the national-socialist movement even while the Serbs generally supported the Allies. The government feared that the Germans might have more sympathy for Germany than for the Yugoslav state. In response, in the lead-up to the German takeover of Yugoslavia, both Serbs and Romanians in the Banat disrupted German political gatherings.[87]

There was some truth behind this fear. Membership in German paramilitary groups grew. A leader of the German community, Sepp Janko, began requesting weapons from Germany in 1940, ostensibly for the protection of the local German leaders but more likely in a bid to prepare the Germans to help in the event of war. At the end of March 1941, weapons were indeed smuggled in.[88] The authorities confiscated weapons, bicycles, and motorcycles from the Germans. They also identified Germans to be eliminated by their own paramilitaries should a conflict erupt. When Hitler decided to invade Yugoslavia, he used the mistreatment of the German minority there as one of his justifications. Once war was declared, German paramilitaries went to work, taking over villages and the military airport at Zemun. In the Banat, Germans gained autonomy by the Nazi takeover (though Reich Germans in fact led them).[89] This was not done, at least not completely, out of ethnic solidarity. Rather, Hitler believed German control of the Banat contributed to the security of Belgrade, the real prize.[90] In historical echo, "Germanness," the Banat, and security against internal and external enemies again became linked.

During the war, there was a high degree of intercommunal violence in Yugoslavia. Germans killed Serbs for a variety of reasons, from revenge to security. Educated Serbs were special targets. Others were made to perform forced labor. Banat Germans and Reich Germans alike participated in mass shootings and other war crimes. In the Banat, some Germans used their elevated position to dispossess Serbs and Jews. Germans also served in the military, ostensibly voluntarily but actually largely compulsory. Serbs and the Partisans attacked German villages in retaliation for the occupation and the Banat Germans' complicity.[91]

There were definite hierarchies among the Germans in the East when viewed from the Reich.[92] Many Reich Germans looked down on the Volksdeutsche. Some felt that they were not pure Germans and treated them as "second-class."[93] When the Nazis evacuated Bessarabia and Bukovina, for instance, authorities evaluated them to determine who should be "classified as racially and politically worthy." Of 93,548 Bessarabian Germans, about 80,000 received this distinction. Of the 43,568 from Bukovina, only about 23,000 did. Germans in Poland were evaluated for their "Germanness" and placed in one of four categories. Members of the first two groups were allowed to become Reich Germans. Members of the other two groups were sent to camps "to receive training in becoming better Germans." In German-controlled Serbia, a similar system existed. Here, admission to the highest category meant better rations while the Germans were in charge but particularly harsh treatment once they left.[94]

In Romania, the early years of the war saw increased recognition of German rights. The fascist Antonescu government finally approved the Karlsburg Declaration in a bid to please both local Germans and Hitler. In November 1940, the German minority was given even more official recognition "as a legal entity with public rights." They were allowed to display swastikas and Nazi flags alongside their Romanian ones, and their school system became considerably more independent. The Nazi Party of Romania became the Germans' sole political party. Andreas Schmidt, the appointed leader of the Romanian Germans, even had plans to turn the Germans in Romania "into an experimental field for a possible future SS state." Authorities in the Reich, including Hitler, encouraged the Germans to join the Romanian army, an ally they wished to support. The SS received Antonescu's permission to recruit Volksdeutsche in April 1943. By July, between 41,000 and 73,000 Germans from throughout Romania had volunteered, with 54,000 Romanian Germans in the Waffen-SS alone.[95] The Banat's Germans were the most hesitant to join and many deserted. An estimated 10 percent of the Romanian German population took part in the war either in the SS or in the German army.[96]

The major SS division in the region was the Seventh SS Volunteer Mountain Division Prinz Eugen, a Waffen-SS division, which a number of Banat Germans joined. Himmler, with Hitler's blessing, created this Waffen-SS unit following the seizure of Yugoslavia. It was intended to contain only Volksdeutsche. According to Lumans, the Waffen-SS was meant to contain "the peasant soldiers of a new racial order," a description oddly fitting for a group which had a long tradition of being "peasant soldiers." The lion's share of soldiers was from the Serbian Banat, but there were others from Romania, Hungary, and Croatia. The first commander was Arthur Phelps, a Transylvanian German. Voluntary enlistment did not succeed in filling the ranks, so by August 1941, the authorities made military service mandatory for local Germans, despite resistance from local notables like Janko. This unit performed counterinsurgency operations in Yugoslavia and the Balkans and "compiled a grisly record of massacres, torture, murder, and village burning."[97]

Postwar Retaliation: Expulsion and Dispossession

That violence, when combined with the Nazi loss, had a profound impact on the Germans communities of the historic Banat. The Germans of Yugoslavia faced much harsher treatment at the hands of Josef Broz Tito and his Partisans than did the Germans in the Romanian Banat. Many Yugoslav Germans fled. Estimates range from 60 to 80 percent of the population.[98] In September and October 1944, the Soviet Red Army occupied the Banat and the Batschka, placing 200,000 Volksdeutsche under Communist control. Between 27 and 37,000 Yugoslav Germans were sent to the USSR to perform reparations labor. When finished, they were sent to East Germany.[99] Both the Red Army and local people plundered German property. They arrested Germans who had openly cooperated with the Nazi regime. Many Germans, both those who had cooperated and those who had not, were executed. In November, Germans officially lost their civil rights.

Shortly after conquest until mid-1945, the Soviets and Partisans began concentrating Germans in camps and specific settlements. Many of these Germans were then "leased" to local non-Germans as laborers.[100] One of the most notorious was at Rudolfsgnad. The dead in the camps have been estimated between 10,000 and 48,000.[101] In addition, the partisans killed an estimated 8,049 after they took Vojvodina and another 2,599 who died en route to the USSR.[102] The government also expropriated 637,939 hectares from Germans throughout Yugoslavia (including outside of the Banat). The government asked the Allies to help expel 110,000 Germans in 1946.[103] Such plans helped reduce the number of individuals in Yugoslavia who identified as German. From 1948 to 1961, the number of German speakers plummeted from 321,821 to 11,471. By 1991, this number had further dropped to 3,873.[104]

The situation in Romania was a bit different. Perhaps around 100,000 Germans fled in 1944. Many of these appear to have come from northern Transylvania and the western Banat.[105] The Red Army captured others, around 75,000, and sent them to perform reparations in the Soviet Union.[106] These individuals were women between eighteen and thirty years old and men between seventeen and twenty-four. Even communists or veterans of the Romanian army were not exempt. Only if one had a Romanian spouse could one avoid this fate.[107] The new communist government expropriated the property of the German community. Romanian "colonists" began appearing in traditionally German villages. In Beschenowa, Macedo-Romanians (Aromanians) were placed in the village. By 1962, the once predominantly German village had 1,280 German and 1,200 Romanian residents.[108] Such settlement programs led to tension, especially when expropriated German land and property were given to incoming Romanians. A group sympathetic to the Communists known as the Ploughman's Front saw the folly in the policy. In one document they recognized that "by divesting the Swabians of their rights, we have jeopardized a most important productive resource. From the point of view of agricultural skills, the settlers [i.e., Romanians] are inferior because nobody made any selection before bringing them here. Some settlers are destroying goods and squandering farm equipment."[109] Settlement in the Banat had come full circle: Germans had displaced Wallachs, now Romanians were displacing Germans. The number of Germans did not drop as precipitously in Romania as it did in Yugoslavia. In 1948, there were still around 350,000 Germans in Romania.[110] In the Banat itself, the German population dropped from 223,167 in 1930 to 173,733 in 1956. Their percentage of the total population of the Banat fell from 23.74 in 1930 to only 14.53 by 1956.[111]

Their struggles did not end after the war and the immediate postwar period. When Tito and Stalin split, the Romanians, eager to keep in the USSR's good graces, decided to seal off the border between Yugoslavia and Romania. Beginning in 1951, a number of Germans, Serbs, and Romanians of the Banat became personae non gratae and were transferred to the Bărăgan Steppe.[112] In Beschenowa, for instance, authorities deported 170 Germans to the steppe, where nineteen died between 1952–56.[113] In Tomnatic (Triebswetter), the government targeted Germans as well as recent Romanian and Macedo-Romanian colonists for deportation.[114]

World War II and its aftermath were the end of large German settlements in the Banat. In Yugoslavia, this change occurred quickly, while in Romania, the dispossession and out-migration of the Germans lasted through the twentieth century. The ethnoreligious divisions and rivalries that went back to the first mass movement of Germans in the 1720s had been, for the moment at least, definitively solved. A strange synergy of virulent nationalism, communism, and total war destroyed the communities it had taken over two centuries to create. The titular nationals, the Romanians and the Yugoslavs, were now in complete political, economic, and demographic control.

In one of the final acts of the German story in Romania, they became political pawns under the Communist leadership of Nicolae Ceaușescu. In the wake of de-Stalinization, the Romanian minorities received more rights and recognition. As the economy began to disintegrate following failed industrialization projects, life again became more difficult. Looking for a means to secure more foreign currency, the regime decided to "sell" (ransom?) Romanian Germans to the West German government. In 1978, the Ceaușescu government agreed to send 12,200 individuals per year to the West, and German Chancellor Schmidt agreed to pay 8,000 DM per individual. The overall deterioration of the Romanian economy and society through the 1980s convinced many Transylvanian Saxons and Banat Germans there that their future lay in West Germany, and this led to another great emigration of Germans *out* of the East.[115] Although in the postwar period, the number of Banat Germans remained near 175,000, this number continuously fell throughout the second half of the century. While there were 118,271 Germans in 1977, by 1992, in the early post-Communist era, this number had plummeted to 38,826. At this point, they represented only 3.61 percent of the total population, a far cry from near 25 percent they represented before World War II.[116]

The memory of the Germans of the Banat was still strong among the local people even after the majority of them had left. Many looked back at the German cultural contribution with longing. Šević mentioned that some of his "old Banat Serb" interviewees in the late 1990s "would even now praise their former German neighbors, especially for their punctuality and tidiness."[117] Katherine Verdery noticed something similar among the Romanians of Transylvania. According to her, "Some Romanians say 'if it weren't for these Germans, we'd be as backward as hillbillies.' "[118] In my own experience, a twenty-something Romanian in Timișoara shared similar views. He told me that the Romanian Banat would have been better off remaining under Habsburg rule than it had been under rule from Bucharest. In fact, he wondered why people celebrated the day the Banat came under Romanian rule at all. Perhaps again coming full circle, in December 2014, a Transylvanian Saxon, Klaus Iohannis, was elected president of Romania.

Throughout their rule, the Habsburgs had a clear ethnic hierarchy in the Banat. On top were the Germans, and for most of the eighteenth century, Catholic Germans. Although tens of thousands of German speakers, among others, responded to the calls for settlement, the German presence only partially accomplished the goals of the planners. The colonists were loyal to the Habsburgs, though there were never enough of them to truly defend the region in times of war. In the early years of settlement, their communities would not have survived intact without continuous infusions of new colonists and government money. The evidence for their effectiveness as models for agriculture is sparse. Undoubtedly some were. The need for a system of colonial overseers indicates that many were not. As we have seen, this was the typical outcome for German-speaking settlers in the eighteenth century, whether in Banat, Russia, Spain, or North America. By the late nineteenth and early twentieth century, there is evidence that they were very successful businesspeople and farmers. Perhaps people wanted to read this success backward as though it was something that had always existed. Whatever their successes and failures, and however one wants to judge that, they did create new cultural traditions to deal with life on the frontier.

Next came the Rascians. While they were prized at times for their martial ability and loyalty to the dynasty, they were also distrusted because of their religion, their transimperial connections and later, their developing nationalism. By the early nineteenth century, there was potential for clashes with German colonists as nascent Serbian nationalist impulses were inflamed by events just over the border in Ottoman-controlled Serbia. The authorities never particularly respected the Wallachs. They were seen as a bastion of tradition that impeded the modernization of the region. Especially during times of upheaval (1737–1739, 1787–1790), parts of the community violently resisted Habsburg rule and attacked German bureaucrats and settlers as well as local people who were agents of the government. Although it seems unlikely that they would have preferred Ottoman rule, they at times resisted Habsburg political and religious domination.

This hierarchy was based on the subjects' perceived utility to the state. Informed by the state of the Banat at conquest and by cameralist thought, the government wanted two things: the creation of a productive economic region and security, in other words, Europeanization. From the government's vantage point, the local populations were unlikely provide either. In a vicious cycle, the more the state sought to impose oversight and a trusted German population, the more the non-German population of the region resisted, thus reinforcing the state's distrust of them. Stereotypes surrounding both communities, propagated by civil servants and outside observers, some of which that have survived until today, reflected the hardening of official attitudes vis-à-vis local people. As time went on, the demands of the people became clearer. From the chaotic Wallach rioting from 1737 to 1739 and generalized violence of the first three-quarters of the eighteenth century to the well-articulated demands of Horea in Transylvania and his adherents in the Banat, to the national aspirations of the Rascian Serbs in 1804 and 1808, the challenges to the status quo in the Banat became ever more organized and dangerous to the state's power there. The Germans, brought in to secure and develop the region, were caught between the state that supported them and the increasingly organized and articulate locals who resented their presence.

When combined with Habsburg ideas on demographic engineering, typified by the population transfers and ethnically homogenous communities, the ethnoreligious hierarchy was a potent force in the Banat and defined the "possible" for many people. As previous chapters have shown, the Habsburg authorities were keen to define how groups should interact with one another. When settling Germans, they were to be as removed from local people as possible. When defining religious prerogatives, Catholics were to be favored. They also used a system of privileges to promote groups they felt were important to the realization of their modernizing and Europeanizing plans. Although there is no "smoking gun" that the Habsburgs were pursuing an explicit Europeanizing and Catholicizing agenda, their policies indicate they were. Perhaps most interesting is that later nationalists would have recognized the authority's plans. They both believed that different groups could not live together in harmony and had to be separated into homogeneous communities. A difference in scale separated the Habsburg ethnic policy from later nationalist ones. By the end of the eighteenth century, both the Wallachs (through the creation and promotion of a Romanian identity) and the Rascians (through a Serbian one) turned to the ideas of nationalism to advance their rights within the monarchy. Both had tried other means (the Rascians largely through cooperation, the Wallachs largely through resistance) to extend their autonomy, and both paths had failed.

As this epilogue shows, many of the same issues we encountered beginning in the early eighteenth century following the Habsburg capture of the Banat continued well into the twentieth century. Ethnic and religious rivalries, not always violent, continued unabated. Following the Treaty of Trianon, the traditional hierarchy was inverted and Germans suffered in similar ways as had the titular nationals under the Habsburgs. Their political dominance was gone. They were now subject to expropriation and resettlement. "Foreign" elements, Serbs and Romanians, colonized their villages. In the end, though, modern nationalism increased the violence. Instead of mere resettlement, the Germans in some cases were expelled. Unlike in the Habsburg system, where there was a place for almost all religions and ethnicities if properly controlled, in the new national systems, minorities were subjected to extremes of the same techniques used by imperial powers. In the Banat, the problems and often solutions of organizing a multiethnic region remained the same, but the change in ideology from multiethnic empire to nation-state doomed the German communities.

Notes

Introduction

1. Like Galicia, the Habsburg Banat "belongs to the category of extinct geopolitical entities." Larry Wolff, *The Idea of Galicia*, 1.
2. Brown, *A Biography of No Place*, 1.
3. Pratt, *Imperial Eyes*, 8.
4. White, *The Middle Ground*, x.
5. Komlosy, "Habsburg Borderlands," 51.
6. Burke, *Popular Culture*.
7. As Brown stated, "Written evidence is evidence for the arguments of those who wrote the documents." While I find this contention a bit too cynical, there is truth in it that should cause us to be critical of our sources. Brown, *A Biography*, 13.
8. Pratt, *Imperial Eyes*, 60
9. Ibid., 12, 3.
10. Todorova, *Imagining the Balkans*, 80. In the nineteenth century, even British travel writing "became informative and knowledgeable, rising high on the comparative scale of European travelogues." Ibid., 89.
11. Todorova agrees. Ibid., 63–64.
12. Larry Wolff, *The Idea*, 4.
13. Burke, *What Is Cultural History?* Burke argued that while there have been studies on "memory," the literature on "social or cultural amnesia" is lacking. I hope that much of this work is read as a response to the historical amnesia regarding the region.

234 Notes to the Introduction

14. Born, Raspe, and Ferber, *Travels through the Bannat of Temeswar*; Griselini, *Aus dem Versuch*.

15. Kohl, *Austria*; Paton, *The Bulgarian, the Turk, and the German*; Paton, *Researches on the Danube*. Apparently, even some Hungarian officials in the mid-nineteenth century agreed with this position. Deák described a Hungarian official who, when arguing against Serb demands for more autonomy, questioned what would happen to the "German colonists who turned southern Hungary into an agricultural paradise" (Deák's words) if they came to power. Deák, *The Lawful Revolution*, 243.

16. Jordan, *Die kaiserliche Wirtschaftspolitik*. This amazing work is an in-depth exploration of the development of the Banat's economy, though even Jordan occasionally lauds the German colonists' contributions without much solid historical evidence.

17. Koranyi, "Reinventing the Banat," 101, 105–6.

18. Möller, *Wie die schwäbischen Gemeinden*. In his introductory words to Leo Hoffmann's work, Dr. Kaspar Muth summed up the feeling as follows: "A people, that does not have a history, is no people." Leo Hoffmann, *Kurze Geschichte*. Milleker, *Die erste organisierte deutsche Kolonisation des Banats*.

19. For example: Herrschaft, *Das Banat*; Zakić, "'My Life for Prince Eugene,'" 79–94.

20. Jivi-Banatanu, *The Banat Problem*; Horváth, *The Banat*; Pejin, "The Privileged District of Velika Kikinda."

21. István and Lang, *Gedenkstätten*; Baumann, *Geschichte der Banater Berglanddeutschen Volksgruppe*. Baumann's work was typical. He was born and worked in the region he wrote about before leaving for Austria following World War II. He was especially tough on the Wallachs/Romanians in his work, portraying them, not altogether wrongly, as inimical to German settlement. His book, like many in this genre, was published by a group of Germans who fled the region following the Second World War. It is highly elegiacal and triumphal regarding the German presence in the mountains of the Banat.

22. For a defense of the Banat Germans during this period by a leading SS commander, see Kumm, *Vorwärts, Prinz Eugen!*. Springenschmid, *Our Lost Children*; Wildmann, Sonnleitner, and Weber, *Genocide of the Ethnic Germans in Yugoslavia*.

23. For instance, Schünemann, *Österreichs Bevölkerungspolitik*; Kallbrunner, *Das kaiserliche Banat*; Lotz and Senz, *Festschrift für Friedrich Lotz*. Today, the Institut für donauschwäbische Geschichte und Landeskunde is an excellent source for the most up-to-date information regarding not only the Germans in the Banat but also all along the Danube. In particular, Josef Wolf has published

numerous articles and source collections on the region. He, too, has familial and cultural connections to the region. For a dated, though still useful, summary of the dissertations written on the Banat in the first two thirds of the twentieth century, see: Krischan, "Dissertationen über das Banat (1897–1967)," 203–21.

24. For a book on the complicity of German scholars in the Nazi regime throughout the East, see Haar and Fahlbusch, *German Scholars*.

25. Batt talked about this "paradoxical myth" in Batt, "Reinventing Banat." See also: Engel, foreword to *Kulturraum Banat*, 7. Neumann, *Multicultural Identities*.

26. James Koranyi also problematizes the idea of a "cosmopolitan Banat," though he largely focuses on modern events in Romania and Serbia. Koranyi, "Reinventing," 97–113.

27. Marin, *A Frontier Region*. There are a few article-length treatments that address the history of colonization in the region by Karl Roider (one with Robert Forest) alongside more focused articles by authors such as William O'Reilly, Sabine Jesner, and Benjamin Landais.

28. Batt, "Reinventing Banat," 180.

29. Only Catholics (and Orthodox, largely from the Ottoman Empire) were allowed to settle in the Banat until the 1780s. Even luminaries in the field are susceptible to such minor mistakes. Pieter Judson, for instance, says Jews were part of the colonizing program in the 1760s. Judson also refers to the Banat as part of Hungary, which likewise did not happen until the 1770s. Judson, *The Habsburg Empire*, 67. Likewise, Paula Sutter Fichtner writes that under Charles VI, "Temesvár Country" was part of Hungary. Fichtner, *The Habsburgs*, 119. Martyn Rady describes the Banat as "the reconquered part of Hungary." While true, this description hides the fact that the region was not officially united with Hungary until the 1770s and is thus misleading. Rady, *The Habsburgs*, 176. Beales, *Joseph II*, 2:173, 176, 198, also made similar claims for increased tolerance in the settlement of the Banat with Protestants in the later Theresian era. In *The Routledge History of East Central Europe since 1700*, the Banat receives only cursory attention and again the ability of Protestants to settle there is misstated. Brandy and Hajdarpasic, "Religion and Ethnicity," 186. Mistakes then creep into more synthetic works on migration. Hoerder, for instance, presents Habsburg policies as much more tolerant than they were, at least until Joseph II. Hoerder, *Cultures in Contact*, 285. Ingrao correctly notes the lack of religious toleration and provides the most in-depth and accurate discussion of the Banat, though still limited and scattered. Ingrao, *The Habsburg Monarchy*, 159.

30. AT-OeStA/FHKA NHK KaaleU BanaterA Akten 150B, f. 657–58.

31. For more on this complicated issue, see: Lotz, "Die französische Kolonisation," 132–78. In his article, he referred to any subject from France, whether German or French speakers, as "French colonists."

32. For a more exact breakdown of how the historical and modern meanings of these regions have changed, see Lotz, "Die französische Kolonisation," 135–36.

33. Ibid., 143–44. Stanglica claimed that most of the migrants from Lorraine were German speakers. Stanglica, *Die Auswanderung*, 44. Stanglica was also a Nazi and SS member who took part in the discussions related to the "Jewish problem." He was "hired in the Lublin district . . . as an expert for German migration history." As an ultranationalist, his conclusions should be suspect. Freund, "Palatines All Over the World," 165–66.

34. Other villages mentioned by Lotz that had a significant "French" presence were "Mercydorf, Triebswetter, Ostern, Gottlob, Segenthau, etc." Lotz, "Die französische Kolonisation," 133. Lotz mentioned that every "French" settlement had a "German street." Petri's collection of street names supports this fact. St. Hubert, Charleville, and Seultour all had a "Deutsch(e)-Gasse." Triebswetter also had a one. Interestingly, St. Hubert, Charleville, and Seultour, along with Reschitza, had a "Franzosengasse." Other towns and villages had streets named after Alsace (5), Lorraine (7), and Luxemburg (6). Petri, *Vom Aachenibrunnen*, 58, 62.

35. I will try here to make an educated guess for the number of possible French subjects and speakers who came during the high period of "French" movement between 1763 and 1772 based on a report describing the number of houses built during the time. This time also appears to be when the most "Lorrainers" and "Luxemburgers" would have migrated to the Banat (the other big period being in the early 1750s). From 1765 to 1772, the government constructed 3,731 colonist houses. Of these, 199 (5 percent) were in the "French" villages of St. Hubert, Charleville, and Seultour. If we include the other villages mentioned by Lotz (Triebswetter, Ostern, Gottlob, Segenthau), we must include an additional 525 houses, bringing the total percentage of houses in *new* villages with some French presence to 19 percent of the total. Between 1762 and 1772, 1,628 houses were built in existing colonist villages. In Mercydorf, the final village mentioned by Lotz, the government built 443 houses (27 percent). Thus, the villages mentioned by Lotz as having some French presence contained 22 percent of the houses built in the Banat during the period. To say a similar percentage of French subjects were among the migrants during this period, one would have to assume that *all* houses were occupied by French subjects, something that is undoubtedly untrue. In Mercydorf, for instance, the 443 houses were built in 1763,

long before the flood of French colonists who arrived during the famine years in the early 1770s. Most of the colonists in Mercydorf in this year would have been de-activated, likely "German," soldiers. If one makes a rough guess that half of the houses in all of these villages were settled by French, that would lead to an estimate of around 10 percent for this period. Even this number likely overestimates the total. Looked at another way, of the thirty-one villages founded during the period, three had "French" names. This also leads to an estimate of slightly less than 10 percent. Based on my research, I would estimate that somewhere between 5 to 15 percent of the colonists in the late Theresian migration were "French" subjects, likely toward the lower end of that estimate. An even lower number, then, were likely French speakers. The charts relating to house building are available in Tafferner, *Quellenbuch*, #152. When taken into account that this was likely the high point of French migration to the Banat, the overall percentage for the eighteenth century would be considerably less. Although at least partially settled during a period when Lorraine was not under direct French control (1740s and 1750s), of the 309 colonists Petri recorded having settled Neubeschenowa, seventeen (5.5 percent) were from Lorraine while ten (3.23 percent) were from Luxemburg. Petri, *Neubeschenowa*, 30. To give another example, in Weisskirchen, Milleker mentioned only two families whose origins appear to have been "French," Jeanplong and Massion. Milleker, *Kurze Geschichte der Stadt Bela Crkva*, 9.

36. Lotz noted something similar in the archival record. Lotz, "Die französische Kolonisation," 139–40.

37. This is, of course, not to say there was no mention. For instance, in Hübert (St. Hubert) the pastor Rocca (or Roka) asked for the government's help in getting the German catechism he translated into French through the censors. AT-OeStA/FHKA NHK KaaleU BanaterA Akten 154A, f. 391–92. Lotz also mentioned Roka. Lotz, "Die französische Kolonisation," 133. Here, the government also mentioned "German and French Lorrainians" in Mercydorf in 1755. AT-OeStA/FHKA NHK KaaleU ältere BanaterA Akten 52, December, f. 571/620.

38. A couple of examples from primary sources should help illustrate this fact. For instance, when Charles VI wrote to Landgraf Ernst Ludwig von Hessen-Darmstadt he said he wanted to make the lands recently conquered from the Turks a "bulwark of Christianity with German people" (*eine Vormauer der Christenheit mit Teutschen Leuten*). Tafferner, *Quellenbuch*, #47. In 1762, just before the start of the second major movement of Germans to the region, his daughter Maria Theresia ordered the use "as much as possible" of Germans in expanding the population and settling the land. Tafferner, *Quellenbuch*, #122. Although complaining about their ultimate utility, Joseph II mentioned the "settlement of

Germans ... in the Batschka and the Banat" (emphasis added). Tafferner, *Quellenbuch*, #173. Such examples could be multiplied many times over.

39. Lotz said they were all "fully Germanized" by 1830. Lotz, "Die französische Kolonisation," 134. Macartney, an important historian of Hungary, had this to say on the subject: "Not many of these freak minorities are to be found to-day [1937]. The Bulgars and Crassovans both exist (in the Roumanian Banat). The Cossacks died out, since it was part of their military tenets to eschew the unmanly act of marriage. The Italians and Catalans succumbed to the climate. The French villages ended by becoming Germanized, and are distinguishable to-day only by their surnames, by a few words which have survived in their local dialects, and by a slightly different style of domestic architecture." Macartney, *Hungary and Her Successors*, 384.

40. Smaranda Vultur, a scholar who has researched this topic in the postwar period, did an interesting study on the village of Triebswetter (later, Tomnatic) in the Romanian Banat that can help illustrate the fluidity of ethnic belonging among the French speakers of the Banat. The French villagers, who came in 1772, were so completely Germanized that according to the 1930 census, there were no French speakers in the village. Interestingly, a 1947 census noted 2,115 "French" in the village. Many of the "Germans" remembered their Frenchness once being German became dangerous. For instance, being "French" meant that they were spared deportation to the USSR after World War II. Some even used this ethnic identity to resist expropriation. By 1952, there were again no French in Triebswetter/Tomnatic. Vultur, "The Role of Ethnicity," 142–44.

41. Romanian historian Stefan Pascu, for example, believed that "the Habsburg goal, of course, was to Germanize and Catholicize the region." Pascu, *A History of Transylvania*, 145.

42. Schünemann, while admitting that theoretically, populationism was ethnicity blind, argued that the Habsburg use of German settlers was partially a means to consolidate their empire around German ethnicity. Schünemann, *Österreichs Bevölkerungspolitik*, 1–3. For a recent example, see O'Reilly, "Divide et Impera," 77–100. This could also be interpreted more insidiously. Serbian historian Jovan Pejin charged the Habsburgs with attempting to Germanize the people of the region. He further argued that this attempt was somewhat successful among the Serbian middle class. Pejin, "The Privileged District," 71.

43. Prinz Eugen von Savoy, "An den Kaiser. Feldlager vor Temesvár, 21. October 1716," in *Feldzüge des Prinzen Eugen von Savoyen Serie 2, Bd. 8 = Bd. 16*, ed. Ludwig Matuschka (Wien: Gerold, 1891), 157–62. "Ich habe indessen dem Interims-Commando anbefohlen, in dem oft widerholten neu eroberten Platze nichts als lauter deutsche Einwohner, wovon sich schon einige anmelden, anzunehmen, die Raizen und andere aber in der Palanka unterzubringen."

44. For a recent example, see Marin, *A Frontier Region*, 29. Also: Roider, "Nationalism and Colonization," 87–100; Roider and Forrest, "German Colonization," 89–104.
45. Schünemann, "Die Einstellung," 173–74.
46. Bailyn, *The Peopling*, 95–96.
47. Fata, *Migration*, 45.
48. Olin, "Cultivating an Orderly Society," 159–61.
49. Larry Wolff, *The Idea*, 7.
50. Brown, *A Biography*, 6–7.
51. Savoy, "An den Kaiser," 159–60.
52. Montagu, *The Complete Letters of Lady Mary Wortley Montagu*, 1:304.
53. Emperor Joseph II quoted in Hegedüs, "Joseph II," 141.
54. Griselini, *Aus dem Versuch*, 9, 10.
55. The exact phrasing was "unter dem türkischen Joche zu rohen Barbaren verwildert" (under the Turkish yoke gone wild to raw barbarians). Here, we see the animalization of local people, a common tactic. *Verwildern* can also mean "to go feral" or "gone wild." *Banater Zeitschrift für Landwirthschaft, Handel, Künste und Gewerbe*, Edition Nr. 6, July 19, 1827, 46. This mirrors a similar phrase in Griselini, likely the source of this history.
56. *Banater Zeitschrift für Landwirthschaft, Handel, Künste und Gewerbe*, Edition Nr. 5, July 15, 1827, 37.
57. Dorner, *Das Banat*, 48. This very nineteenth-century explanation of the history of the Banat and the Wallach people persisted well into the twentieth century. Julius Baumann argued that the Wallachs should have been happy that the Habsburgs freed them from Ottoman rule instead of resisting Habsburg rule. Baumann further argued that the Wallachs adopted a passive lifestyle to weather the constant wars that afflicted the region. According to his train of thought, this passivity then degenerated into laziness and primitiveness. Baumann, *Geschichte der Banater Berglanddeutschen Volksgruppe*, 26–27.
58. They were "tatsächlich eine gesellschaftlich und wirtschaftlich unterdrückte und verwilderte, leibeigenartige Bevölkerung." Evans, "Religion und Nation in Ungarn, 1790–1849," 36.
59. Paton, *The Bulgarian, the Turk, and the German*, 22.
60. AT-OeStA/FHKA NHK KaaleU BanaterA Akten 66, f. 390–91.
61. AT-OeStA/FHKA NHK KaaleU BanaterA Akten 66, f. 389–90.
62. Pratt, *Imperial Eyes*, 44, 147–48.
63. Griselini, *Aus dem Versuch*, 12, 13. Importantly, he was writing more than sixty years after the conquest. The "animality" of local people was a constant theme in many different observers' works. I will note (and have already noted) both in the text and in the footnotes the various occurrences of this phenome-

non. It helps highlight the fact that observers often denied the humanity of the local population. This further explains why authorities wanted to Europeanize and improve both the people and the landscape. The "animality" of cultural outsiders was a theme in European popular culture. Both Turks and Jews were at times presented as animals or in an animalistic fashion. Burke, *Popular Culture in Early Modern Europe*, 223.

64. Kaps shows how Habsburg language about the "Other" paralleled other empires and was likewise a means of justifying control, though he focuses on the province of Galicia. Kaps, "Orientalism and the Geoculture of the World System," 327.

65. See chapter 6 for more examples of how Habsburg officials and travelers viewed local cultures.

66. Frank, "The Children of the Desert."

67. Komlosy, "Habsburg Borderlands," 49–51, 64. According to Stefan Steiner, "Was die spanischen Habsburger in ihren Kolonien seit den ersten Städtegründungen verwirklichen konnten, das bot sich für die österreichische Linie mit der Rückeroberung Siebenbürgens und des Banats als Chance." Steiner, *Rückkehr Unerwünscht*, 143. Following Steiner, Timothy Anderson also highlights the similarities. Anderson, "Cameralism," 59, 66. O'Reilly also argues that this is an apt comparison for the Banat. O'Reilly, "Divide et Impera."

68. Thinking about the Banat in this way is especially important when examining the way Banat Germans viewed their own history. For a good introduction, see Veracini, *Settler Colonialism*.

69. Bailyn, *The Peopling*, 112, 120.

70. Rothenberg, *The Military Border*, 11.

71. Burke, *What is Cultural History?*, 83–84. Burke, too, argued that "ethnicity" is "regarded as flexible or even negotiable," though he described it as a counterweight to "tribe."

72. Wolf noticed a similar occurrence in his truncated study. Wolf, "Ethnische Konflict," 337–66. It is important to note that religion remained important throughout the nineteenth century, even as nationalism rose among many of the groups in the Banat. Many Rascian Serbs, for instance, rallied around religion as well as ethnicity and used their religion as an idiom of resistance against the Habsburgs and the Hungarians.

73. This situation lasted until the fall of the Habsburg monarchy, when it was partially inverted. The creation of nation-states in the region after World War I continued the process of segregation and differentiation championed by the Habsburgs in the eighteenth century though on a more dramatic scale. It also led to the replacement of Germans (and since the nineteenth century, Magyars

as well) at the theoretical pinnacle of society by the titular nationals, Serbs and Romanians.

74. All four of Manning's "Categories of Human Migration" (Home-community, Colonization, Whole-community, and Cross-community) existed in the eighteenth-century Banat. Manning and Trimmer, *Migration in World History*, 4–7.

75. Olin, " 'Flüchtlinge' oder 'Auswanderer'?," 45–47.

76. Gabaccia, "Historical Migration Studies," 47–49.

77. For more on this term and the overall connotations of "nation" in the region, see Landais, "Village Politics," 195–208.

78. Архив Војводине- Нови Сад (Arhiv Vojvodine, Novi Sad: hereafter AVNS), F. 11, Box 2, 1777, D. 231.

79. AVNS, F. 11, Box 2, 1777, D. 190. In another case, Joseph Kranz, from Siebenbürgen, wore "Hungarian pants" and spoke "Wallach, Hungarian, corrupt German, [and] Slovak." AVNS, F. 11, Box 135, 1789, D. 121.

80. Arhivele Naționale ale României, Direcția Județeană Timiș (hereafter ANRDJT), Fond Nr. 52, Inv. 1700, Nr. Nou 56.

81. Историјски архив Кикинда (Historical Archive of Kikinda, hereafter HAK), Fond 4, Document 893-I/1829.

82. AVNS, F. 11, Box 2, 1777, D. 226.

83. AVNS, F. 11, Box 3, 1778, D. 325.

84. AVNS, F. 11, Box 2, 1777, D. 271.

85. This was apparently the case in the Ottoman Empire as well. Regarding one collection of documents they used as a source base, authors Numan Elibol and Abdullah Mesud Küçükkalay stated that "they [Jews] were the only regional or ethnic group whose religious affiliation was always listed regardless of their place of origin." Elibol and Küçükkalay, "Implementation," 162.

86. HAK, F. 4, B. 11, D. 1242-I/1840. That said, in another document from 1816, one man was named "Lorenz Jud." Whether this was his actual name, or whether it was a description is unclear. HAK, F. 4, B. 2, D. 144–1/1786.

87. Rothenberg, *The Military Border*, 125.

Chapter 1: Conquest and Construction

1. Turkish saying circa 1663 in Ottendorf, *Budáról Belgrádba*, 105.

2. Clark, *Iron Kingdom*, 86–87; MacDonogh, *Frederick the Great*, 23–24, 319.

3. See, for instance, Davies, *Warfare, State and Society*; Sunderland, *Taming the Wild Field*.

4. Ringrose, *Spain, Europe, and the "Spanish Miracle,"* 172; Hauben, "The First Decade," 34–37.

5. See, for instance, Fenske, "International Migration," 333; Roeber, *Palatines, Liberty, and Property*; Knittle, *Early Eighteenth-Century Palatine Emigration*.

6. Dorner, *Das Banat*, 28–30. Dorner believed that everything came from Asia and reached perfection in Europe, even more reason to bring the "Asian" Banat into the European realm. "Asia" could also be a code word for backwardness. Even South America could be "Asiatic" to certain travelers if they were looking to disparage local people and culture. Pratt, *Imperial Eyes*, 183. Wolff notes that, like the Banat, Galicia was also a place where Europe and the "Orient" met in the mind of some observers. For one of the observers "Galicia minus the Germans equals Tartary." Undoubtedly many observers of the Banat would have crafted a similar equation. Larry Wolff, *The Idea of Galicia*, 47–49.

7. AVNS, F. 11, Box 131, D. 2463. Here the author referred to the Greek Non-Uniate Church as an "orientalische Kirche." "Temeswarer Wochenblatt." 24 July 1841. P. 367. Dorner, *Das Banat*, 204.

8. For an overview of the military situation and an excellent bibliography on pre-Habsburg Hungary, including the Banat, see Fodor and Dávid, *Ottomans, Hungarians, and Habsburgs in Central Europe*.

9. Finkel, *Osman's Dream*, 284–318.

10. Milleker, *Geschichte der Stadt Pančevo*, 14, 16.

11. This is the same Caraffa who oversaw the torture and execution of suspected plotters against the Habsburgs in Hungary following the conquest. Ingrao, *The Habsburg Monarchy, 1618–1815*, 85.

12. Osman Ağa, an Ottoman soldier, chronicled the brutality in the northern Banat in the 1680s. Ağa, *Der Gefangene der Giauren*. As late as 1752, Turkish subjects captured and imprisoned in Peterwardein, most likely for smuggling, expressed the conviction in letters home that they would be sold into slavery for their crimes. AT-OeStA/FHKA NHK KaaleU ältere BanaterA Akten 30, March, f. 258–63.

13. Davis, *Holy War and Human Bondage*.

14. Finkel, *Osman's Dream*, 318–28

15. Dávid, "The 'Eyalet,'" 113–18.

16. When Charles VI finally accepted that he would not win the throne in Spain, a number of Spanish soldiers who had served him were brought to Vienna. In 1734, after being assured by then-governor Graf Hamilton that there was enough free land, the suggestion was made to settle them in the Banat. Someone suggested that perhaps the Spanish could learn something from the Germans when they arrived. Another suggestion was to have those soldiers with a skill use that to earn money while others could be employed in the emerging manufacturing sector. AT-OeStA/FHKA NHK KaaleU ältere BanaterA Akten 8, f. 194, 794–800.

17. Roider, *Austria's Eastern Question*, 38–57.
18. *Daily Journal* (London, England), Saturday, August 13, 1726.
19. *London Evening Post* (London, England), January 24, 1741–January 27, 1741.
20. *London Evening Post* (London, England), February 17, 1741–February 19, 1741.
21. *London Evening Post* (London, England), October 15, 1741–October 17, 1741.
22. *London Evening Post* (London, England), November 17, 1741–November 19, 1741.
23. *London Evening Post* (London, England), February 17, 1743–February 19, 1743.
24. Hodson, "The Development of Habsburg Policy in Hungary."
25. Pálffy, *Hungary between Two Empires, 1526–1711*, 225.
26. Ibid., 225–26.
27. Jesner, "Making and Shaping a New Province," 59.
28. Prinz Eugen von Savoy, "An den Hofkriegsrath. Feldlager vor Belgrad, 21. Juni 1717," in *Feldzüge des Prinzen Eugen von Savoyen Serie 2, Bd. 8 = Bd. 17*, ed. Ludwig Matuschka (Wien: Gerold, 1891), 70.
29. Hegedüs, "Joseph II," 139.
30. Jesner, "Making and Shaping," 60. See also Jesner, "Personnel Management during Times of Crisis," 121.
31. Jesner, "The World of Work," 63, 64.
32. Ibid., 64–65.
33. Jesner, "Making and Shaping," 61–63.
34. Jesner, "The World of Work," 59, 71.
35. AT-OeStA/FHKA SUS Patente 65.5. This patent may have been released throughout the Austrian domains and not only in the Banat, but this is unclear.
36. AT-OeStA/FHKA SUS Patente 115.4.
37. AT-OeStA/FHKA SUS Patente 187.11.
38. Emperor Joseph II, quoted in Hegedüs, "Joseph II," 141.
39. ANRDJT, Fond Nr. 117, Nr. Nou 111, f. 3, 6–7.
40. Roth, *Die planmässig angelegten Siedlungen*, 26.
41. It is difficult to find any concrete information on the question of depopulation. For instance, historian Vojin Dabić maintained that "these accounts [which appear in military reports] enable one to assume with considerable certainty that most of the people living in Syrmia and the Banat settlements under Ottoman rule remained there after the establishment of Habsburg authority." According to his calculations, at the beginning of Habsburg rule, there were four inhabitants per square kilometer. He then went on to show, quite convincingly, that the total number of houses in the Banat dropped by one-third from 1717 to 1720. Thus, sometime between the onset of war and shortly after

conquest, many of the families in the region fled. This seems to support the contention that, at the very least, the region *appeared* depopulated. Dabić, "The Habsburg-Ottoman War of 1716–1718," 193–95.

42. Griselini, *Aus dem Versuch*, 9, 10.

43. The definition of cameralism is the source of much dispute and debate. Albion Small, for example, said "cameralism was not a theory and practice of economics but of politics." Small, *The Cameralists*, 3.

44. For an excellent review of this issue, see Wakefield, *The Disordered Police State*, 1–5. See also: Tribe, *Governing Economy*; Smith, *The Business of Alchemy*; Raeff, *The Well-Ordered Police State*.

45. The other two were Wilhelm von Schröder, *Fürstliche Schatz- und Rent-Cammer*, and Johann Joachim Becher, *Politischer Discurs*. Hörnigk, *Österreich über alles*, 13.

46. Ibid.

47. He himself largely ignores it, almost as though it were so obvious it required little elaboration.

48. Ibid.

49. Quoted in Fata, *Migration*, 41.

50. Schünemann, *Österreichs Bevölkerungspolitik*, 4.

51. Raeff, *The Well-Ordered Police State*, 70.

52. Wellenreuther, "Contexts for Migration in the Early Modern World," 17, 15.

53. Ibid., 13, 18.

54. Adam, *The Political Economy of J. H. G. Justi*, 191, 152.

55. Schünemann, *Österreichs Bevölkerungspolitik*, 8.

56. Ibid., 9–10.

57. ANRDJT, Fond Nr. 117, Nr. Nou 117, f. 1–2.

58. Griselini, *Aus dem Versuch*, 19.

59. Baumann, *Geschichte der Banater Berglanddeutschen Volksgruppe*, 6, 15. One must be careful with such claims of early German colonization, though this one is believable. There is a trend among certain early German scholars of the Banat to link the region's earlier "German" inhabitants, like the Goths, to the settlers of the eighteenth century. It is an attempt to make the region a historically "German" place and thus brush aside any claims that later German settlers were interlopers.

60. Born, Raspe, and Ferber, *Travels through the Bannat of Temeswar*, 79, 27, 61.

61. Baumann, *Geschichte der Banater Berglanddeutschen Volksgruppe*, 7–8.

62. Hoerder, *Cultures in Contact*, 280.

63. Olin, "Cultivating an Orderly Society," 162–63.

64. Jordan, *Die kaiserliche Wirtschaftspolitik*, 33–34.

65. AT-OeStA/FHKA NHK KaaleU BanaterA Akten 73, f. 655, 657, 661.
66. ANRDJT, Fond Nr. 302, Inv. 1613, Nr. Nou 5.
67. Knittle, *Early Eighteenth Century Palatine Emigration*.
68. Jordan, *Die kaiserliche Wirtschaftspolitik*, 34.
69. Baróti, *Adattár délmagyarország*, 103.
70. AVNS, F. 10, Box 10, D. 52.
71. Steube, *Von Amsterdam nach Temiswar*, 143.
72. ANRDJT, Fond Nr. 302, Inv. 1613, Nr. Nou 5.
73. Magyar Országos Levéltár (hereafter MOL), E303: a/, 13. U/, f. 29–30.
74. Roider pointed out the absurdity but also perhaps the necessity of this decision. Roider, *Austria's Eastern Question*, 76. For a more detailed exploration of the war, see Roider, *The Reluctant Ally*.
75. Roider, *Austria's Eastern Question*, 69–90. The surrender of Belgrade was a fiasco that arguably should never have occurred.
76. *London Evening Post* (London, England), July 15, 1738–July 18, 1738. Paula Fichtner explored the propaganda potential of Ottoman destruction in depth in her book on the evolution of Habsburg-Ottoman relations. While there is the possibility that both local reporters and newspapers exaggerated some Ottoman actions, it seems likely to me that most of these reports were based on actual occurrences. Even Fichtner did not argue against the veracity of the majority of reports. Instead, she argued that they were part of a wider narrative of fear of Ottoman domination that eventually became a popular dismissiveness and a scholarly curiosity as the military threat receded by the end of the eighteenth century. See Fichtner, *Terror and Toleration*.
77. *Daily Post* (London, England), Monday, October 16, 1738. Habsburg records also attest to attacks on monasteries. Baróti, *Adattár délmagyarország*, 5:28–29.
78. *London Daily Post and General Advertiser* (London, England), Wednesday, March 7, 1739. Similar activities (enslavement, hostage taking, burning of villages) occurred around Ujpalanka as well. Baróti, *Adattár délmagyarország*, 5:28–29.
79. Baróti, *Adattár délmagyarország*, 5:29.
80. Ibid., 144.
81. See chapter 6 for more details.
82. Baróti, *Adattár délmagyarország*, 5:27. Similar stories were reported around Lippa. Ibid., 84–85.
83. *London Daily Post and General Advertiser* (London, England), Tuesday, July 4, 1738.
84. Baróti, *Adattár délmagyarország*, 5:84–86, 144–45, 29.

85. *London Evening Post* (London, England), September 1, 1739–September 4, 1739.

86. AT-OeStA/FHKA NHK KaaleU BanaterA Akten 146A, f. 49.

87. Colonists were not the only group of former slaves in the Banat. A Rascian, who escaped slavery in the Turkish domains by ransoming himself, petitioned in 1770/71 to have two pistols and a watch that he took (stole?) from his former master returned to him or at least be monetarily compensated. ANRDJT, Fond Nr. 302, Nr. Nou 11, f. 74.

88. A number of excellent works have been written about the Habsburg military frontier. For example, see Roth, *Die planmässig angelegten Siedlungen*; Göllner, *Die Siebenbürgische Militärgrenze*; Rothenberg, *The Military Border in Croatia, 1740–1881*; Rothenberg, *The Austrian Military Border in Croatia, 1522–1747*.

89. Szakály, "Das Bauerntum und die Kämpfe," 251–71.

90. Fodor, "Das Wilajet von Temeschwar zur Zeit der osmanischen Eroberung," 37–39, 43.

91. Roth, *Die planmässig angelegten Siedlungen*, 28.

92. AT-OeStA/FHKA NHK KaaleU BanaterA Akten 66, f. 518.

93. Kallbrunner, *Das kaiserliche Banat*, 90–91.

94. Roth, *Die planmässig angelegten Siedlungen*, 29. An undated, unsigned plan that likely originated around this time called for the occupation of the frontier from Pancsova to the Wallachian border by Catholic Hungarians (!). They needed to be Catholic to ensure that they would have no "connection" with the local people there, a means to ensure loyalty. AT-OeStA/FHKA NHK KaaleU BanaterA Akten 66, f. 181–82. This plan likely faltered on the traditional suspicion of Hungarian influence in the Banat.

95. Hochedlinger, *Austria's Wars of Emergence*, 323.

96. Milleker, *Kurze Geschichte der Stadt Bela Crkva*, 15.

97. Interestingly, it took until 1770's Pest Contumaz Patent for the quarantine stations to be formally established. Rothenberg, *The Military Border*, 47.

98. Ingrao and Pešalj, "The Transitional Empire," 285.

99. AT-OeStA/FHKA NHK KaaleU ältere BanaterA Akten 30, February, f. 433, 434.

100. See, for example, Liulevicius, *The German Myth of the East*. For more on the construction of the East in Western minds, see Larry Wolff, *Inventing Eastern Europe*.

101. Steube, *Von Amsterdam nach Temiswar*, 120–25.

102. Hammer, *Geschichte der Pest*, 30. This was no ordinary smoke. Originally recorded in Vienna in 1713, it was described as "an excellent smoke against the

plague." It was also good for killing spiders and other poisonous insects. It was copied and brought to Temesvár in 1795 and was again copied in 1848. Someone obviously believed that this smoke was effective, and the recipe needed to be protected. The ingredients included lilac, juniper, elecampane, common rue, oak leaves, and fenugreek, among others. To give the mixture a dramatic edge, sulfur, which glows blue when lit, was an additional ingredient. All of these were ground into a coarse powder. ANRDJT, Fond Nr. 162, Inv. 780, Nr. Nou 4.

103. AVNS, F. 10, Box 1, D. 121.

104. ANRDJT, Fond Nr. 52, Inv. 1700, Nr. Nou 56. "Temeswarer Wochenblatt." July 24, 1841, 367.

105. ANRDJT, Fond Nr. 302, Inv. 1613, Nr. Nou 11, f. 40.

106. AT-OeStA/FHKA NHK KaaleU ältere BanaterA Akten 47, January, f. 234.

107. AT-OeStA/FHKA NHK KaaleU BanaterA Akten 161, f. 89.

108. ANRDJT, Fond Nr. 302, Inv. 1613, Nr. Nou 2.

109. At least Ingrao and Pešalj believe the border was effective in preventing the spread of plague out of the Ottoman Empire. Ingrao and Pešalj, "The Transitional Empire," 286. In an article on combatting COVID-19, Ingrao and A. Wess Mitchell reiterate this position. Mitchell and Ingrao, "Emperor Joseph's Solution to Coronavirus." It seems likely that the Ottoman military was not much deterred by the military border in Banat. When it came to war again in 1787, the German military border was quickly overrun. Both Pancsova and Weisskirchen were easily taken and later destroyed. The Deutsch-Banater Regimentskommando was moved to the Batschka while the German and Rascian population fled north. The population loss in the German-Banat Regiment was 13,331 while in the Wallachisch-Illyrischen Regiment it was 22,919. Roth, *Die planmässig angelegten Siedlungen*, 174.

110. Milleker, *Geschichte der Stadt Pančevo*, 32.

111. *Caledonian Mercury* (Edinburgh, Scotland), Monday, November 16, 1818.

112. AT-OeStA/FHKA NHK Banat A 138, f. 1106–7.

113. AT-OeStA/FHKA NHK Banat A 138, f. 1111.

114. AT-OeStA/FHKA NHK Banat A 138, f. 1111, 1112–13.

115. See Tafferner's note after #560. Tafferner, *Quellenbuch*, #560.

116. Adler, "Serbs, Magyars, and Staatsinteresse," 143. Fata, *Migration*, 59.

117. Hegedüs, "Joseph II," 142.

118. Tafferner, *Quellenbuch*, #565.

119. Fodor, "Das Wilajet," 32–33.

120. Hegedüs, "Joseph II," 143–52.

121. Tafferner, *Quellenbuch*, #597.

122. Deák, *The Lawful Revolution*, 4.

123. See chapter 4 for more detail.

124. To what degree Joseph believed in "Germanization" is up for debate.

125. Deák, *The Lawful Revolution*, 43–44.

126. Evans, "Religion und Nation in Ungarn, 1790–1849," 17–18.

127. Deák, *The Lawful Revolution*, 16, 20, 28, 35.

128. Milleker attributed the dissolution to the fact that the creation of a Serbian state pushed the Ottoman frontier to the south and the retreat of the plague threat. Milleker, *Kurze Geschichte der Stadt Bela Crkva*, 21.

129. It became part of Hungary in 1855. Hromadka, *Kleine Chronik des Banater Berglands*, 8.

130. Baumann, *Geschichte der Banater Berglanddeutschen Volksgruppe*, 36, 40.

131. Kohl, *Austria*, 306.

132. Möller, *Wie die schwäbischen Gemeinden*, 1:79.

133. Milleker, *Kurze Geschichte des Banats*, 26, 43.

134. AVNS, F. 11, Box 146, D. 1037.

135. AVNS, F. 11, Box 146, D. 1097.

136. *Banater Zeitschrift für Landwirthschaft, Handel, Künste und Gewerbe*, Edition Nr. 2, 5 July 1827, pp. 14–15.

137. Bright, *Travels from Vienna*, 237–38. A newspaper article on the attempt in 1810 stated that "little doubt is entertained of the complete success of this experiment." *Caledonian Mercury* (Edinburgh, Scotland), Thursday, November 15, 1810.

138. Klaniczay, *Nachricht*.

139. For thorough coverage of the war from the Austrian side, see Mayer, "The Price."

140. Milleker, *Geschichte der Stadt Pančevo*, 56.

141. Roider, *Austria's Eastern Question*, 169–89.

142. *Whitehall Evening Post (1770)* (London, England), November 11, 1788–November 13, 1788.

143. Milleker, *Kurze Geschichte der Stadt Bela Crkva*, 11.

144. Mayer, "The Price," 279.

145. *Morning Herald* (London, England), Monday, September 1, 1788. *General Evening Post* (London, England), September 18, 1788–September 20, 1788.

146. Smiley, "A 'Barbarous Law'?," 326–27, 331.

147. *General Evening Post* (London, England), February 5, 1789–February 7, 1789.

148. "Article VII, Definitive Treaty of Peace between the Emperor of Germany and the Ottoman Porte," in *The Parliamentary Register* XXXI (London: J Debrett, 1792), 106–7.

149. *General Evening Post* (London, England), January 12, 1792–January 14, 1792. Smiley confirms that payment of one hundred *kuruş* for returned slaves. Smiley, "A 'Barbarous Law'?," 332.

150. Smiley, "A 'Barbarous Law?," 325.

151. Böhm, *Geschichte des Temeser Banats*, 246–47.

152. Alternatively, the similarities could be due to common tropes of Ottoman captivity. If we had a better idea of the types of books available in the region at this time, we might be able to better untangle this potential contradiction. My interpretation assumes a limited opportunity for exposure to this type of captive narrative based on the few lists of books in the region I have seen. For more on harems and emancipation, see Davis, *Holy War and Human Bondage*, 223–52, 262–91.

153. *General Evening Post* (London, England), October 25, 1788–October 28, 1788.

154. *General Evening Post* (London, England), October 25, 1788–October 28, 1788.

155. *E. Johnson's British Gazette and Sunday Monitor* (London, England), Sunday, March 22, 1801.

156. *Glasgow Herald* (Glasgow, Scotland), Friday, June 8, 1821. *The Morning Chronicle* (London, England), Wednesday, April 24, 1822.

Chapter 2: Security and Loyalty

1. Lotz, "Johann Karl Reichard," 332, 342. As an appendix, Lotz included reprints of two letters written by the migrant Johann Karl Reichard to his friend Pastor Surdorff in Adelsheim.

2. AT-OeStA/FHKA NHK KaaleU ältere BanaterA Akten 31, f. 579.

3. AT-OeStA/FHKA NHK KaaleU ältere BanaterA Akten 31, f. 580a/583.

4. AT-OeStA/FHKA NHK KaaleU ältere BanaterA Akten 31, f. 580b.

5. The era described here corresponds with the second of five "periods of migration and cultural change" identified by Dirk Hoerder in his comprehensive survey of migration in the last millennium. Hoerder, *Cultures in Contact*, 3–5.

6. Livi-Bacci, *A Short History of Migration*, 29–30.

7. Some people are *forced* to migrate, slaves being the most obvious example. As we will see, the Habsburgs forced criminals and religious minorities to migrate to various parts of the empire, including the Banat. Hoerder noted "voluntary," "coerced" (like refugees), and "forced" (like criminals or slaves) migrants. All three types are recognizable in the Banat. Hoerder, *Cultures in Contact*, 15. Manning and Trimmer, *Migration in World History*, 7–8.

8. Harzig and Hoerder, *What Is Migration History?*, 62–64. While acknowl-

edging the diversity of migrants' experiences, Moch provides a largely economic explanation for migration over three centuries, though even here Moch recognizes many other factors that cause people to move. Not simplistic, Moch's focus on rural "proletarianization" and industry makes sense for Western Europe, especially migration within states. It is less effective in explaining migrations to the rural East, though Moch is clear that such migrations are "peripheral" to the work. Moch, *Moving Europeans*, 6–9, 17.

9. Wokeck, *Trade in Strangers*, 1–18.
10. Tafferner, *Quellenbuch*, #69.
11. Ibid., #71.
12. Gittermann, "German Emigrants," 190–91.
13. Wegge, "Eighteenth-Century German Emigrants from Hanau-Hesse," 233.
14. Tafferner, *Quellenbuch*, #78.
15. Ibid., #79, 186.
16. Ibid., #88.
17. Ibid., #132.
18. Ibid., #133.
19. The threat of the death penalty for recruiters, especially those who sought to recruit subjects for foreign military service, was common throughout the century. Intriguingly, I have not come across a case where the threat was carried out. From the few cases I have seen, the suspected recruiter was simply banished.
20. Tafferner, *Quellenbuch*, #166. This ordinance explicitly mentioned earlier ones related to migration in 1724, 1726, 1763, two in 1764, 1766, and the imperial edict of 1768.
21. Ibid., #105, 107, 118/119, 120/121, 141.
22. This seems an interesting turn of phrase that might leave open the possibility for continued migration to the Banat and Hungary. Both of these places, unlike Spain or Russia, do in fact have a "connection" with the Holy Roman Empire in the person of the Holy Roman Emperor.
23. Tafferner, *Quellenbuch*, #368.
24. Ibid., #148.
25. Schünemann noted that the agents quit open recruitment methods, such as newspaper ads, and instead continued recruiting in a more secretive manner. Schünemann, "Die Einstellung," 173–74. O'Reilly argued additionally that the Habsburgs stressed the connection between the Hungarian crown and the Reich to legally justify continued recruitment. His source on the matter is Schünemann, *Österreichs Bevölkerungspolitik*. O'Reilly, "To the East or to the West?," 283–84.

26. Bailyn, *The Peopling*, 10.
27. Moch, *Moving Europeans*, 87–88.
28. Schünemann, *Österreichs Bevölkerungspolitik*, 303–5.
29. Fata, *Migration*, 44–45.
30. Tafferner, *Quellenbuch*, #32.
31. For a number of early examples, see Tafferner, *Quellenbuch*, #34, 36, 42, etc.
32. Fenske, "International Migration," 333.
33. Knittle, *Early Eighteenth Century Palatine Emigration*, 24, 26, 27, 62–63, 141.
34. Ibid., 64–97.
35. Bailyn, *The Peopling*, 70. O'Reilly, "To the East or to the West?," 90.
36. Roeber, *Palatines, Liberty, and Property*, ix.
37. Leo Hoffmann, *Kurze Geschichte*, 9.
38. Kallbrunner, *Das kaiserliche Banat*, 18, 30–31. Baumann, *Geschichte der Banater Berglanddeutschen Volksgruppe*, 16–17. The Habsburgs referred to Wallach, Macedo-Slav, Bulgarian, and Orthodox Albanian traders as "Greek." In addition to shared religion, Greek became the lingua franca of commerce in southeastern Europe and many traders Hellenized over the course of the eighteenth century. Thus, the word "Greek" became synonymous with "trader" in many parts of southeastern Europe. The major exceptions to this rule were ethnic Serbs who eschewed a Greek identity, perhaps due to a mutual cultural enmity. That said, from the outside perspective, "all Orthodox merchants of the Balkans were frequently identified in Germany, Austria, and Hungary as 'Greeks.'" Stoianovich, "The Conquering Balkan Orthodox Merchant," 311, 291, 303–4, 290.
39. ANRDJT, Fond Nr. 117, Nr. Nou 111, f. 3, 11/14.
40. AT-OeStA/FHKA NHK KaaleU ältere BanaterA Akten 3, f. 410a/1–22.
41. AT-OeStA/FHKA NHK KaaleU ältere BanaterA Akten 3, f. 831 a/4–5.
42. AT-OeStA/FHKA NHK KaaleU ältere BanaterA Akten 3, f. 831 a/6–7, 1, 9, 10.
43. Hoerder, *Cultures in Contact*, 20. Wokeck supports this contention. Wokeck, *Trade in Strangers*, 26–31.
44. Lotz, "Johann Karl Reichard," 330–32. Letter from Amtsvogt Vock quoted in ibid., 331–32.
45. Ibid., 332.
46. AT-OeStA/FHKA NHK KaaleU ältere BanaterA Akten 4, f. 155 a/b.
47. After the four free years, the next three were staggered such that the colonist was expected to pay their full taxes only in the seventh.
48. "Seynd sie Familien in mehrbesagten Kayserl. Erb=Landen ganz und gar keiner Leibeigenschaft/ Frohn=Diesnsten/ Zinssen/ oder Pachten un-

tergeben, wie sie dann nicht weniger auch . . . Immediate einzig und allein Kayserlich/ keines weges aber eines Fürsten und Graffen oder sonstigen Privat-Grund=Herrn Unterthanen seyn und bleiben sollen."

49. Schrad, *Vodka Politics*, 79–83.
50. Tafferner, *Quellenbuch*, #74.
51. As it turns out, many did settle in the Banat.
52. AT-OeStA/FHKA NHK KaaleU ältere BanaterA Akten 8, f. 795.
53. AT-OeStA/FHKA NHK KaaleU ältere BanaterA Akten 7, f. 452a.
54. The requirement that colonists have two hundred fl. is rather unclear. Some secondary sources explicitly mention that this was a means test. Fata, "Einwanderung und Ansiedlung der Deutschen (1686–1790)," 151. Fata used Tafferner's transcription of the patent. O'Reilly, on the other hand, stated that "provision was also made for the purchase of horses and pigs." O'Reilly, "To the East or to the West?," 82. His source was Tinta, *Colonizările habsburgice în Banat. 1716–1740*, 149. Having seen the original document, the confusion is understandable. Initially, it appears to be saying that colonists will be *given* two hundred fl. Later in the document, it seems clear that they are in fact requiring potential colonists to *have* two hundred fl.
55. For a deep look into the practice of forced migration, see Steiner, *Rückkehr Unerwünscht*. Steiner discusses the *Wasserschub*, the Hauensteiner, and the Lutherans, covered in chapter 3.
56. Bailyn, *The Peopling*, 120–22.
57. As Moch points out, men were much more likely to end up in workhouses both because women were more often seen as "deserving poor" and were less likely to be seen as threats. Moch, *Moving Europeans*, 90–91. In the case of Australia, only one in seven convicts transported between 1788 and 1852 were women. Hughes, *The Fatal Shore*, 244.
58. AT-OeStA/FHKA NHK KaaleU ältere BanaterA Akten 16, March, f. 88–99.
59. AT-OeStA/FHKA NHK KaaleU ältere BanaterA Akten 31, f. 646–62.
60. In France, women with venereal disease were some of the few placed in workhouses. Moch, *Moving Europeans*, 91.
61. AT-OeStA/FHKA NHK KaaleU ältere BanaterA Akten 31, f. 646–62.
62. AT-OeStA/FHKA NHK KaaleU ältere BanaterA Akten 32, July, f. 15–36.
63. See chapter 5 for more on the importance of marriage practices.
64. Rees, *The Floating Brothel*.
65. Russell-Wood, *A World on the Move:*, 109–12.
66. AT-OeStA/FHKA NHK KaaleU ältere BanaterA Akten 31, f. 652.
67. AT-OeStA/FHKA NHK KaaleU ältere BanaterA Akten 33, September, f. 330–31.

68. AT-OeStA/FHKA NHK KaaleU ältere BanaterA Akten 43, March, f. 216–34.

69. The following discussion of the later years of *Wasserschub* is based on: Schünemann, *Österreichs Bevölkerungspolitik*, 78–88, except where otherwise cited. Schünemann's coverage of this topic is a bit problematic. In his introduction to the section, he talks about how the nationalizing Romanian and Yugoslav governments of the interwar period used the *Wasserschub* as a means to denigrate the Germans (i.e., they are the progeny of criminals). Writing in 1935, Schünemann seems intent on dispelling this charge in two sometimes-contradictory ways. First, he argues that most of the people sent on the *Wasserschub* were not really "criminals" in the first place. They were mostly everyday people who got caught up in the machinery and desires of the state. This interpretation ignores the early years of the *Wasserschub* (1740s and 1750s) completely, regarding which this contention is undeniably false. Whatever one thinks of the seriousness of the charges, it does appear these individuals broke the law. Second, he argues that they were never really integrated into the society in the Banat, mostly fleeing or dying. In order to mediate this bias, I have focused on his historical facts rather than his interpretations. In his 1940 work, *Deutsches Schicksal im Banat*, Karl von Möller also attacks the idea that the Banat Germans were descended from "beggars and . . . robbers." This opinion, apparently held by Viennese Germans as well, was attacked by the author who called it a "fairy tale." Interestingly, Möller argued that it was the presence of the Hauensteiner in the Banat that gave rise to the belief. Möller, *Deutsches Schicksal im Banat*, 8–9.

70. AT-OeStA/FHKA NHK KaaleU BanaterA Akten 68, f. 496.

71. AT-OeStA/FHKA NHK Banat A 104, f. 546–48.

72. AT-OeStA/FHKA NHK Banat A 108, October, f. 238.

73. Beales, *Joseph II*, 2:548–52.

74. The preceding and following synopsis is based on Luebke, *His Majesty's Rebels*.

75. Tafferner, *Quellenbuch*, #94.

76. A number of Protestants also called the fortress home in the 1750s while on their way to Transylvania.

77. Tafferner, *Quellenbuch*, #95–96. The preacher writing the letter noted that the rebels were "good Christians."

78. Ibid., #100.

79. Luebke, *His Majesty's Rebels*, 71, 78, 84. This is the only mention of the Banat, his focus being more on the incidents and importance of the event within German history.

80. Baróti, *Adattár délmagyarország*, 5:160.

81. AT-OeStA/FHKA NHK KaaleU ältere BanaterA Akten 48, f. 256. As for numbers, Luebke mentioned twenty-seven exiled families according to his sources in the empire. This lines up well with the Austrian sources that mentioned 110 individuals, including twenty-seven men, twenty-one women, thirty-three boys, and twenty-nine girls (though "boys and girls" included individuals in their twenties.) AT-OeStA/FHKA NHK KaaleU ältere BanaterA Akten 52, November, f. 54. Another earlier manifest listed twenty-four men, twenty-three women, and eighty-five children destined for "Transylvania." AT-OeStA/FHKA NHK KaaleU ältere BanaterA Akten 51, September, f. 295. Schünemann mentioned twenty-seven heads of household and 112 individuals. Schünemann, *Österreichs Bevölkerungspolitik*, 92.

82. AT-OeStA/FHKA NHK KaaleU ältere BanaterA Akten 48, f. 255–58. More on the Lutherans in Transylvania and the Habsburg religious hierarchy on the frontier appears in chapter 4.

83. AT-OeStA/FHKA NHK KaaleU ältere BanaterA Akten 49, May, f. 89.

84. AT-OeStA/FHKA NHK KaaleU ältere BanaterA Akten 51, September, f. 294.

85. Baróti, *Adattár délmagyarország*, 5:69.

86. AT-OeStA/HHStA RHR Passbriefe 15-2-28, Schmid, Johann Adam und Nikolaus Christ.

87. AT-OeStA/HHStA RHR Passbriefe 17-3-61, Vischbach, Mathias und Mathias Plesies. Petri, *Neubeschenowa*, 17.

88. Wokeck, *Trade in Strangers*, 31–33.

89. Manning and Trimmer, *Migration in World History*, 9–10.

90. For more on the agents and their role in the peopling of the Banat, see O'Reilly's dissertation.

91. AT-OeStA/HHStA RHR Passbriefe 12-2-59, Oswald Johann.

92. Petri, *Neubeschenowa*, 15–17.

93. AT-OeStA/FHKA NHK KaaleU ältere BanaterA Akten 36/1, f. 13–62. Wilhelm and Kallbrunner put the number at 900, 150 of whom were lost to other agents or landowners in Ofen. Wilhelm and Kallbrunner, *Quellen zur deutschen Siedlungsgeschichte*, III.

94. AT-OeStA/FHKA NHK KaaleU ältere BanaterA Akten 31, f. 295, 642–45, 850.

95. Ingrao, *The Habsburg Monarchy, 1618–1815*, 172–77.

96. Hoerder, *Cultures in Contact*, 278.

97. AT-OeStA/FHKA NHK KaaleU BanaterA Akten 146A, f. 207–9.

98. *Wienerisches Diarium*, Nr. 26, 31. March 31, 1764.

99. Roth, *Die planmässig angelegten Siedlungen*, 51, 55.

100. Ibid., 58.

101. Leo Hoffmann, *Kurze Geschichte*, 43, 50–51. Schünemann, *Österreichs Bevölkerungspolitik*, 262–65. AT-OeStA/FHKA NHK KaaleU BanaterA Akten 147, f. 30–47.

102. Wolf, *Quellen zur Wirtschafts-, Sozial- und Verwaltungsgeschichte des Banats*, 20–21.

103. The official English version of the manifesto can be found in Bartlett, *Human Capital*, 237–42. A German version can be found in Klaus, *Unsere Kolonien*, 22–26.

104. Wegge, "Eighteenth-Century German," 242, 247.

105. Brandes, "Einwanderung und Entwicklung der Kolonien," 55.

106. AT-OeStA/FHKA NHK KaaleU BanaterA Akten 150B, f. 1424–29. In his work, Weiss claimed that much of the largesse came from the monasteries and properties of the recently dispossessed Jesuit order. Weiss, *Die deutsche Kolonie an der Sierra Morena*, 87.

107. Barlett, *Human Capital*, 57.

108. AT-OeStA/FHKA NHK KaaleU BanaterA Akten 149B, f. 720–24.

109. AT-OeStA/FHKA NHK KaaleU BanaterA Akten 150B, f. 1276.

110. AT-OeStA/FHKA NHK KaaleU BanaterA Akten 150B, f. 1417, 1418, 1441, 1421/1431, 1415.

111. Tafferner, *Quellenbuch*, #145.

112. Ibid., #146.

113. Roth, *Die planmässig angelegten Siedlungen*, 92–93.

114. For a thorough recounting of the events that led to the end of the late Theresian migration, see Schünemann, "Die Einstellung,", 167–213.

115. AT-OeStA/FHKA NHK KaaleU BanaterA Akten 152/C, f. 1098–99.

116. AT-OeStA/FHKA NHK KaaleU BanaterA Akten 155A, f. 17.

117. AT-OeStA/FHKA NHK KaaleU BanaterA Akten 154A, f. 303–4.

118. AT-OeStA/FHKA NHK KaaleU BanaterA Akten 153/C, f. 1538.

119. AT-OeStA/FHKA NHK KaaleU BanaterA Akten 154B, f. 491.

120. AT-OeStA/FHKA NHK KaaleU BanaterA Akten 153/C, f. 1429.

121. AT-OeStA/FHKA NHK KaaleU BanaterA Akten 154A, f. 416.

122. AT-OeStA/FHKA NHK KaaleU BanaterA Akten 154B, f. 808.

123. AT-OeStA/FHKA NHK KaaleU BanaterA Akten 154B, f. 881.

124. AT-OeStA/FHKA NHK KaaleU BanaterA Akten 154C, f. 1255.

125. Pálffy, *Hungary between Two Empires*, 83–88, 187–94.

126. Kallbrunner, *Das kaiserliche Banat*, 27. Milleker, *Geschichte der Stadt Pančevo*, 22.

127. Baróti, *Adattár délmagyarország*, 5:5, 8, 27.

128. Ibid., 123, 25. This sometimes worked to the government's advantage. When a number of families moved out of Vrán for another village within the Banat in 1736, an enterprising administrator suggested settling the incoming Spanish families in the houses they had left behind. What became of this suggestion is unknown.

129. Ibid., 82–83, 28, 148. The Clementiner were Albanian Christians who lived in Bosnia. Mackenzie and Irby, *Travels in the Slavonic Provinces of Turkey-in-Europe*, 218.

130. AT-OeStA/FHKA NHK KaaleU ältere BanaterA Akten 9, f. 103, 125. He sent almost the exact same petition in September 1739. AT-OeStA/FHKA NHK KaaleU ältere BanaterA Akten 9, f. 1227.

131. AT-OeStA/FHKA NHK KaaleU BanaterA Akten 160, Konvolut 2, f. 39–40.

132. AVNS, F. 11, Box 133, D. 2623. The reason this story made it into the archives was that one of the emissaries, Stephan Stojan, was arrested. He apparently was too curious about the earthen-work battlements at a military position, which led to his arrest.

133. AVNS, F. 11, Box 135, D. 142/1789.

134. Milleker, *Geschichte der Stadt Pančevo*, 58–59, 76.

135. *The Morning Chronicle* (London, England), Friday, April 20, 1821.

136. Baróti, *Adattár délmagyarország*, 5:45, 46, 65, 66, 119. AT-OeStA/FHKA NHK KaaleU ältere BanaterA Akten 31, f. 100, 107.

137. Baróti, *Adattár délmagyarország*, 48, 51–52.

138. For example, when four to five hundred "wealthy" Rascian families wanted to settle in Neu Arad in 1723, the government hesitated. Before they would green-light the settlement, they wanted to know where these families had lived before and under whose rule. Baróti, *Adattár délmagyarország*, 5:65.

139. MOL, E305: c/, 8. 6/, f. 39–40.

140. Joseph II quoted in Bartenstein, *Kurzer Bericht*, XX.

141. Quoted in Schünemann, "Die Einstellung," 187.

142. Eimann, *Der deutsche Kolonist*, 48–49.

143. Leo Hoffmann, *Kurze Geschichte*, 74–75. Interestingly, Johann Eimann mentioned nothing about these criteria in his retelling of the Josephian migration. Eimann, *Der deutsche Kolonist*, 48–58.

144. Tafferner, *Quellenbuch*, #169.

145. Ibid., #180.

146. Elke Hoffmann, *Städte und Dörfer*, 326.

147. Horst Dieter Schmidt, *Ein verschwundenes Dorf im Banat*, 28–29.

148. Herrschaft, *Das Banat*, 134.

149. Möller, *Wie die schwäbischen Gemeinden*, 1:15. Möller mentioned a number of similar early examples of intra-Banat migration.

150. Elke Hoffmann, *Städte und Dörfer*, 127, 21–22, 76.
151. Roth, *Die planmässig angelegten Siedlungen*, 177–82, 228.
152. Ibid., 236–37, 247, 255–56.
153. Baumann, *Geschichte der Banater Berglanddeutschen Volksgruppe*, 34.
154. *Morning Post* (London, England), Saturday, October 12, 1793.
155. *Evening Mail* (London, England), October 9, 1793–October 11, 1793.
156. *Morning Post* (London, England), Tuesday, November 26, 1793.
157. *St. James's Chronicle or the British Evening Post* (London, England), January 4, 1794–January 7, 1794.
158. *Morning Post* (London, England), Monday, January 20, 1794.
159. *E. Johnson's British Gazette and Sunday Monitor* (London, England), Sunday, February 16, 1794.
160. Möller, *Wie die schwäbischen Gemeinden*, 1:23–24.
161. Tafferner, *Quellenbuch*, #598–600. Möller, *Wie die Schwäbischen Gemeinden*, 2:126–27.
162. Height, *Paradise*, 17. Roth, *Die planmässig angelegten Siedlungen*, 181–82.
163. Height, *Paradise*, 17.
164. Walker, *Germany and the Emigration, 1816–1885*, 111–14, 141–42. Moltke's quote is from ibid., 114. Scherling's quote is from ibid., 141.
165. Schünemann also notes these same two problems with the settlement figures he provides but argues that they can at least indicate the scale of the migration. Schünemann, "Die Einstellung," 169.
166. Jordan, *Die kaiserliche Wirtschaftspolitik*, 22. Kallbrunner more or less supported this figure. His was 15–20,000 for the whole "Mercyschen Kolonisation." Kallbrunner, *Das kaiserliche Banat*, 34. Möller estimated 15,000. Möller, *Wie die schwäbischen Gemeinden*, 1:9.
167. Roider and Forrest, "German Colonization," 92. This figure indicates that the number of Germans who came in the 1750s must have been significant. Most sources say that the early colonies were largely destroyed in the Austro-Ottoman War of 1737–1739. Möller estimated there were 25,000 Germans in 1760. Möller, *Wie die schwäbischen Gemeinden*, 1:11.
168. Schünemann, "Die Einstellung," 170.
169. AT-OeStA/FHKA NHK KaaleU BanaterA Akten 73, f. 661.
170. Hoffman, *Kurze Geschichte*, 89.
171. Winkler, *Statistisches Handbuch*, 104. By the late nineteenth century, Germans consistently represented between one-quarter and one-fifth of the population of the Banat. These numbers do not account for "Germans" lost to Magyarization, so the percentage of the population with colonial roots was likely higher.

Chapter 3: The Religious and Ethnic (Re-) Construction of the Banat

1. AT-OeStA/FHKA NHK KaaleU ältere BanaterA Akten 3, f. 1369.

2. This is today's Komárom, Hungary, and Komárno, Slovakia. Based on this and other documents, it appears to have been a holding or staging area for Protestants on their way to Transylvania.

3. This is an interesting way to view the "problem" of Protestantism. Every Christian (at least every Western Christian) was once Catholic. They only need to "return" to the fold to be totally reintegrated into Austrian-Habsburg society.

4. AT-OeStA/FHKA NHK KaaleU ältere BanaterA Akten 37, April, f. 118–124. For another case of Protestants found in the Banat, see AT-OeStA/FHKA NHK Banat A 108, September, f. 199–200.

5. Ibid.

6. Tafferner, *Quellenbuch*, #47.

7. This is a common interpretation. See, for example, Milleker, *Die erste organisierte deutsche Kolonisation des Banats*, 3. Ingrao also hints at this fact, though he focuses on the ethnicity (non-Magyar settlers) more than religion. Ingrao, *The Habsburg Monarchy, 1618–1815*, 115. Hitchins argued that the establishment of the Uniate Church was also a means to both expand the "true faith" and to undercut Protestant power, especially in Transylvania. Hitchins, *The Idea of Nation*, 21.

8. McNeill, *Europe's Steppe Frontier*, 142, 147.

9. Pálffy, *Hungary between Two Empires*, 203, 162–64.

10. In fact, Tököli was Rákóczi's stepfather though the influence of the former on the latter appears to be marginal. Pálffy, *Hungary*, 231–32, 234.

11. Wangermann, *The Austrian Achievement*, 42–44. Ingrao, *The Habsburg Monarchy*, 111, 115–17. Hitchins, *The Idea of Nation*, 27. Pálffy, *Hungary*, 231–39.

12. Roider, *The Reluctant Ally*, 131–33.

13. Anton Petri reprinted the "Anweisungen der Banater Landesadministration für den Temeschwarer Stadtmagistrat (vom 1.Januar 1718)" (the instructions of the Banat Land Administration for the Temesvar city magistrate). Petri, *Die Festung Temeschwar*, 76. Wolf, "Ethnische Konflict," 340. The prohibition was no longer in effect by 1739 at the latest. A census of non-Germans in the fortress of Temesvar from that year indicated that Rascians, Jews, Greeks, and Arnauts (likely Albanians, though it could be shorthand for various South Slav groups) were all living with there. There were *no* Wallachs listed. Magyar Országos Levéltár (MOL), E303: a/, 13., Zsidókra vonatkozó iratok, f. 7–12.

14. It is hard to tell if the plan to expel the Orthodox from the city of Temesvar was enforced. Some early documents seem to indicate that this was in fact done, but later sources seem to indicate that there were Orthodox living within

the city. Wolf, for instance, called the expulsion of the Orthodox inhabitants of Temesvar the "first official resettlement in the newly conquered region." Wolf, "Ethnische Konflict," 340. Other sources are much less clear. It is perhaps interesting to note that the Ottomans had done something very similar when they were in control of the city. According to Heinrich Ottendorf, a traveler to Temesvar in the 1660s, the residents of the city were all "Turks" while Christians lived in the suburbs. Ottendorf, *Budáról Belgrádba*, 105.

15. Fichtner, *Terror and Toleration*, 32–33, 54–55.

16. Jordan, *Die kaiserliche Wirtschaftspolitik*, 27. In subsequent years, a Rascian municipal council was established.

17. ANRDJT, Fond Nr. 117, Nr. Nou 108, f. 64.

18. See Hitchins, *The Romanians*, 200–205; Hitchins, *The Idea of Nation*, 22, 25, 29, 33.

19. Sometimes, the government specified either Uniates or Catholics for certain positions. AT-OeStA/FHKA NHK KaaleU BanaterA Akten 81, f. 1053.

20. ANRDJT, Fond Nr. 117, Nr. Nou 108, f. 10. An undated document likely written between 1716 and 1753 contained a similar appeal. In it, the author argued that the establishment of the Catholic religion would be greatly improved if Jesuits and other missionaries who traveled in the Banat spoke the local languages. MOL, E303: 11, Q/a, f. 30.

21. Hamilton's Bericht, "Chorographia Bannatus Temessiensis," 124–25.

22. Kallbrunner argued that already in 1717 officials were urged to accept the existence of Orthodox "schismatics" in the Banat. Kallbrunner, *Das kaiserliche Banat*, 19.

23. Tafferner, *Quellenbuch*, #122.

24. AT-OeStA/FHKA NHK KaaleU BanaterA Akten 152/A, f. 153.

25. Hamilton's Bericht, "Chorographia Bannatus Temessiensis," 65.

26. ANRDJT, Fond Nr. 117, Nr. Nou 130, f. 22. Hamilton's Bericht, "Chorographia Bannatus Temessiensis," 121.

27. AT-OeStA/FHKA NHK KaaleU BanaterA Akten 148, f. 211.

28. Kohl, *Austria*, 305.

29. Hambuch, "Nachwort," 2:332.

30. Macartney, *Hungary and Her Successors*, 384.

. Kohl, *Austria*, 305.

31. MOL, E303: I. a/, 9. E/a, f. 41.

32. Baróti, *Adattár délmagyarország*, 5:105, 108, 158.

33. MOL, E303: I. a/, 9. E/a, f. 42.

34. AT-OeStA/FHKA NHK KaaleU ältere BanaterA Akten 45, September, f. 8.

35. AT-OeStA/FHKA NHK KaaleU ältere BanaterA Akten 45, September, f. 1.

Notes to Chapter 3

36. AT-OeStA/FHKA NHK KaaleU ältere BanaterA Akten 49, May, 48–50.
37. Kallbrunner, *Das kaiserliche Banat*, 86.
38. Paxton, "Identity and Consciousness," 107, 112, 114.
39. Lotz, "Johann Karl Reichard," 327. Johann Schmidt, "Briefwechsel," 223–26. Tafferner, *Quellenbuch*, #47–51. Some of these documents were also reprinted in Schmidt's article.
40. Lotz, "Johann Karl Reichard," 328–29, 331.
41. Lotz indicated that these two people were one and the same, the pastor Johann Karl Reichard. Lotz, "Johann Karl Reichard," 340–41.
42. AT-OeStA/FHKA NHK KaaleU ältere BanaterA Akten 3, f. 1409–10. Also, Tafferner, *Quellenbuch*, #308.
43. Lotz, "Johann Karl Reichard," 334, 336–37.
44. Baróti, *Adattár délmagyarország*, 5:11, 15, 13, 14.
45. Hamilton's Bericht, "Chorographia Bannatus Temessiensis," 65.
46. AT-OeStA/FHKA NHK KaaleU ältere BanaterA Akten 3, f. 1366–67.
47. See description in chapter 1.
48. AT-OeStA/FHKA NHK KaaleU ältere BanaterA Akten 3, f. 1369–70.
49. He was advised by Christian Julius von Schierendorff that toleration of Protestants would help stimulate the economy. Schierendorff's pleas were ignored. His advice was not taken in any measurable form until the ascension of Joseph II. Wangermann, *The Austrian Achievement*, 44–45.
50. She did, however, protect the Orthodox Grenzers, who were important to the security of the region, from efforts to convert them when it was politically expedient for her to do so. Roider and Forrest, "German Colonization," 91.
51. Evans referred to a "late Counter-Reformation" that took place following the Habsburg conquest of Hungary until the Toleration Patent of Joseph II. Evans, "Religion und Nation," 16.
52. AT-OeStA/FHKA NHK KaaleU ältere BanaterA Akten 31, f. 646–62.
53. Bulgaria as such did not exist at this point, but this is the language used in the sources. I will follow their lead.
54. Hupchick, *The Bulgarians*, 75–78, 82.
55. Ibid., 79–82.
56. Ibid., 82–83.
57. AT-OeStA/FHKA NHK KaaleU ältere BanaterA Akten 10, February, f. 155.
58. AT-OeStA/FHKA NHK KaaleU ältere BanaterA Akten 15, February, f. 19–23.
59. AT-OeStA/FHKA NHK KaaleU ältere BanaterA Akten 28, July, f. 15–24.
60. AT-OeStA/FHKA NHK KaaleU ältere BanaterA Akten 30, February, f. 257.

61. *Beschreibung des Banats*, 46.

62. For instance, local authorities in Lugos denied a journeyman cobbler the right to settle there because he was a Calvinist. Baróti, *Adattár délmagyarország*, 5:162.

63. At the highest levels, some amount of religious dissension was apparently tolerated. August Jakob Heinrich Freiherr von Suckow, the commanding general in the Banat in 1739–1740, was a Calvinist. Due to his religion, the Jesuits refused to bury him, and he was subsequently buried in one of the bastions of the fortress. Petri, *Die Festung Temeschwar*, 83.

64. He was already on the authorities' radar in 1752. MOL, E303: I. a/, 9. E/g, f. 36.

65. AT-OeStA/FHKA NHK KaaleU ältere BanaterA Akten 38, June, f. 150–65.

66. Kallbrunner, *Das kaiserliche Banat*, 30.

67. AT-OeStA/FHKA NHK KaaleU ältere BanaterA Akten 37, April, f. 119.

68. For more, see Walker, *The Salzburg Transaction*.

69. AT-OeStA/FHKA NHK KaaleU ältere BanaterA Akten 37, April, f. 119.

70. AT-OeStA/FHKA NHK KaaleU ältere BanaterA Akten 37, April, f. 520.

71. AT-OeStA/FHKA NHK KaaleU ältere BanaterA Akten 32, July, f. 43.

72. AT-OeStA/FHKA NHK KaaleU ältere BanaterA Akten 37, April, f. 520–23.

73. AT-OeStA/FHKA NHK KaaleU ältere BanaterA Akten 40, September, f. 242–45.

74. Wilhelm and Kallbrunner, *Quellen zur deutschen Siedlungsgeschichte*, 315–21. This book contains lists of migrants. In this particular case, the list was compiled in the 1770s and listed the death years. This included only the head of households. One can imagine that children fared even worse.

75. Schünemann, *Österreichs Bevölkerungspolitik*, 100.

76. Tafferner, *Quellenbuch*, #123–25. As described in the introduction, several excellent scholars have misinterpreted this fact. See also Szabo, *Kaunitz and Enlightened Absolutism*, 337–38.

77. AT-OeStA/FHKA NHK KaaleU BanaterA Akten 146A, 207–9.

78. Jordan, *Die kaiserliche Wirtschaftspolitik*, 88.

79. AT-OeStA/FHKA NHK KaaleU BanaterA Akten 151B, f. 718.

80. AT-OeStA/FHKA NHK KaaleU BanaterA Akten 146A, f. 301.

81. AVNS, F. 11, Box 2, D. 153, 154.

82. Tafferner, *Quellenbuch*, #375.

83. Hitchins, *The Idea of Nation*, 112.

84. HAK, F. 4, D. 3955-I/1853.

85. Thiele, *Das Königreich Ungarn*, 102.

86. Tafferner, *Quellenbuch*, #998.

87. AT-OeStA/FHKA NHK KaaleU BanaterA Akten 148, f. 209.
88. Dumont, *The Military History of His Serene Highness*, 119.
89. Prinz Eugen von Savoy, "An den Hofkriegsrath. Feldlager vor Belgrad, 21. Juni 1717," in *Feldzüge des Prinzen Eugen von Savoyen Serie 2, Bd. 8 = Bd. 17*, ed. Ludwig Matuschka (Wien: Gerold, 1891), 70–71.
90. Petri, *Die Festung Temeschwar*, 6–9, 71–74.
91. Habsburg officials maintained the Turks (read Muslims) "emigrated." ANRDJT, Fond Nr. 117, Nr. Nou 108, f. 11. Ingrao and Pešalj put the number of Muslims expelled from the Banat at 100,000. Ingrao and Pešalj, "The Transitional Empire," 286. This expulsion, and the concurrent discrimination against the Jews, have even been compared to the Reconquista in Spain. O'Reilly, "Divide et Impera," 78.
92. Ağa, *Der Gefangene der Giauren*, 211–12.
93. Some of this ground has been covered by Wolf, "Ethnische Konflict," 337–66. He saw the transfers, correctly, in my opinion, as an effort by the Habsburg government to control and safeguard the Banat through controlling the distribution of people. He further noted that as religious affiliation became less crucial in determining loyalty after Joseph's institution of toleration, ethnic belonging increased in importance to the state.
94. Non-German names appear in reports on Moldova by the 1730s, thus it is hard to tell the exact extent of the population transfer.
95. AT-OeStA/FHKA NHK KaaleU ältere BanaterA Akten 3, f. 410a/1–5, 17–20.
96. See chapter 6 for more detail.
97. Kallbrunner, *Das kaiserliche Banat*, 81–82, 89–90.
98. AT-OeStA/FHKA NHK KaaleU ältere BanaterA Akten 15, February, f. 13–16.
99. AT-OeStA/FHKA NHK KaaleU ältere BanaterA Akten 16, August, f. 49–57.
100. AT-OeStA/FHKA NHK KaaleU ältere BanaterA Akten 49, May, 48–50.
101. Baróti, *Adattár délmagyarország*, 5:111.
102. MOL, E305: c/, 10. 8/, f. 38.
103. Tafferner, *Quellenbuch*, #904.
104. Ibid., #905. Petri, *Neubeschenowa*, 15–17.
105. Ibid., #909.
106. Roth, *Die planmässig angelegten Siedlungen*, 45–49. Roth speculated that this was done in order to keep costs under control. It was cheaper to put the veterans in already-built houses and have the dislocated Rascians build new ones. Similarly, the land was already broken, so they would be able to start

farming immediately. The numbers who chose to live in civil areas varied. In Ostrovo, Gaj, and Dobovac, not enough Rascians agreed to leave to even make it worthwhile to settle veterans. That was hardly the case everywhere. In Sefkerin 100/112, Jabuka 86/88, Deutsch-Pancsova 62/132, Serbisch-Pancsova 246/432, Starčevo 104/122, Omoljica 140/175, Brestovac 97/110, Pločica 71/90, and Kovin 195/257 refused to accept military status and were resettled (79 percent).

107. AT-OeStA/FHKA NHK KaaleU BanaterA Akten 147, f. 35.
108. AT-OeStA/FHKA NHK KaaleU BanaterA Akten 147, f. 22/63.
109. AT-OeStA/FHKA NHK KaaleU BanaterA Akten 147, f. 63.
110. AT-OeStA/FHKA NHK KaaleU BanaterA Akten 146B, f. 627.
111. Tafferner, *Quellenbuch*, #122. Jordan, *Die kaiserliche Wirtschaftspolitik*, 84–85, 73.
112. Even Hungarians could be targeted for dispossession. See: AT-OeStA/FHKA NHK KaaleU BanaterA Akten 147, f. 35–36.
113. AT-OeStA/FHKA NHK KaaleU ältere BanaterA Akten 3, f. 410a/ 17.
114. Wolf, "Ethnische Konflict," 353.
115. AT-OeStA/FHKA NHK KaaleU BanaterA Akten 147, f. 31–32.
116. Wolf, "Ethnische Konflict," 352.
117. ANRDJT, Fond Nr. 302, Nr. Nou 11, f. 13.
118. ANRDJT, Fond Nr. 302, Nr. Nou 10, f. 155.
119. ANRDJT, Fond Nr. 302, Nr. Nou 10, f. 261.
120. ANRDJT, Fond Nr. 302, Nr. Nou 10, f. 186.
121. This case is also a sad testament to the loss of archival material in the region. Some of the large, bound court books, which may have contained more information on this case, are missing from the archive. World War II, and the concurrent instability in the region, led to the loss of a lot of material, especially in then Yugoslavia.
122. AT-OeStA/FHKA NHK KaaleU BanaterA Akten 147, f. 32–33.
123. Wolf, "Ethnische Konflict," 350–53.
124. AT-OeStA/FHKA NHK KaaleU BanaterA Akten 147, f. 42. Sefdin was one of the "Wallach villages" that authorities wanted to transfer because of animal theft.
125. AT-OeStA/FHKA NHK KaaleU BanaterA Akten 148, f. 204–8.
126. AT-OeStA/FHKA NHK KaaleU BanaterA Akten 148, f. 216.
127. AT-OeStA/FHKA NHK KaaleU BanaterA Akten 153/A, f. 389–90.
128. AT-OeStA/FHKA NHK KaaleU BanaterA Akten 153/B, f. 958.
129. Tafferner, *Quellenbuch*, #150. See also Schünemann, "Die Einstellung," 205–6.
130. AT-OeStA/FHKA NHK KaaleU BanaterA Akten 154A, f. 44. Also ap-

peared in Tafferner, *Quellenbuch*, #151. Wolf reads this in a different way. He is relying on Tafferner's transcription, which is correct, but he interprets the document as the end of government-sponsored displacement. Wolf, "Ethnische Konflikt," 361. The pertinent extract: "Ist es aber . . . Ein Walachisch, oder Ratzisches Dorf, das überflüssige Gründe hat, *und ist selbes nicht mehr in Antrag von danen (unclear in original) weggeschoben zu werden*, so können die von diesem Orte zuschiebende National-Unterthanen dahin eingetheilet warden." Emphasis added.

131. Roth, *Die planmässig angelegten Siedlungen*, 109, 149, 151.

132. Joseph II quoted in Bartenstein, *Kurzer Bericht*, XIX. This quote appeared in the foreword of the book. The rest of the book was originally written by Bartenstein (d. 1767) as a tutorial for then–Crown Prince Joseph. Joseph made similar comments about the Wallachs in Transylvania. "The Wallachian subjects, beyond all doubt the oldest and most numerous inhabitants of Transylvania, are so overwhelmed with injustices, be it by the Hungarians or Saxons, and their existence is so pitiable, that it is astonishing that all have not run away. I am not surprised that their houses are ramshackle; how can it be otherwise when they are not sure of their possessions from one day to the next and when they are daily and even hourly at the beck and call of their masters?" Quoted in Hitchins, *The Idea of Nation*, 105–6.

133. Tafferner, *Quellenbuch*, #959.

134. Ibid., #173.

135. Wolf, "Ethnische Konflikt," 362–63.

136. Tafferner, *Quellenbuch*, #951, #986.

137. Elke Hoffmann, *Städte und Dörfer*, 402. According to the author, "The Germans stayed in Morawitza and were able, without hindrance, to live and work in peace. The peaceful work was only interrupted by natural disasters." This is a nice example of the sort of bias one finds in works on the Banat Germans by former Banat Germans and their progeny. Apparently, the irony of "peaceful living" following a forced migration was lost on them. Möller, *Wie die schwäbischen Gemeinden*, 36–37. This was far from the only case of intercommunal violence. See chapters 6 and 7 for additional cases.

138. Leo Hoffmann, *Kurze Geschichte*, 110–11.

139. In 1832 in Baratzhausen, for example, the lords of the village, the Armenians Johann, Martin, Franz, and Gregor Capdebo, settled Germans on the lands of local people who had failed to meet their obligations. Elke Hoffmann, *Städte und Dörfer*, 61–62. The German author argued that the people had left their lands willingly. She does admit, however, that the Romanian historians maintain the Germans expropriated the land.

140. AT-OeStA/FHKA NHK KaaleU BanaterA Akten 150B, f. 1423.

141. AT-OeStA/FHKA NHK KaaleU BanaterA Akten 150B, f. 1424–29.
142. Efron, Weitzman, and Lehmann, *The Jews*, 246.
143. Roeber, *Palatines, Liberty, and Property*, ix.
144. Knittle, *Early Eighteenth Century Palatine Emigration*, 24, 78.
145. From the English version of the 1763 manifesto found in Bartlett, *Human Capital*, 237–42.

Chapter 4: Expectations Fulfilled?
1. Möller, *Wie die schwäbischen Gemeinden*, 2:93.
2. Tafferner, *Quellenbuch*, #370.
3. Möller emphasized "Franzosen und Fron" (French and feudal duties) when talking about the reasons peasants were willing to migrate. Möller, *Wie die schwäbischen Gemeinden*, 2:11–36.
4. Verdery, *Transylvanian Villagers*, 65. Verdery noted that the idea of "paying like a German" still existed in Transylvania. The exact phrase, said by a tax collector, was "he [a Romanian] pays his taxes just like these Germans, one visit and you're done. Not like most of these other Romanians, whom you have to visit ten or twelve times before the whole tax is finally paid."
5. For Russia, see Fleischhauer, "The Nationalities Policy of the Tsars Reconsidered," pp. D1069–D1070, D1085. This idea is also discussed in Brandes, "Fragen an der Geschichte der Deutsche in Russland," 18.
6. It is unclear whether the document referred to the theoretical increase in production from the Germans and land or whether the Germans would actually be paying the government back in seed.
7. ANRDJT, Fond Nr. 117, Nr. Nou 117, f. 3.
8. Hamilton's Bericht, "Chorographia Bannatus Temessiensis," 65–66.
9. Tallar, *Visum repertum*, 34.
10. AT-OeStA/FHKA NHK KaaleU ältere BanaterA Akten 34, December, f. 283–84.
11. AT-OeStA/FHKA NHK KaaleU ältere BanaterA Akten 34, December, f. 291–92.
12. Though it appears they were expected to repay this money later.
13. AT-OeStA/FHKA NHK KaaleU ältere BanaterA Akten 37, April, f. 4.
14. Roth, *Die planmässig angelegten Siedlungen*, 168–69.
15. AT-OeStA/FHKA SUS Patente 65.5.
16. AT-OeStA/FHKA NHK KaaleU ältere BanaterA Akten 48, April, 33–34.
17. Istorijski arhiv u Pančevu (Историјски архив у Панчеву, Historical Archive of Pančevo, hereafter HAP), F. 4, Magistrat Municipalnog Grada Pančeva, 1794–1918, D. 1381/1808. HAK, F. 4, B. 7, D. 851-I/1829.
18. Baróti, *Adattár délmagyarország*, 5:8, 15, 71.

19. AT-OeStA/FHKA NHK KaaleU ältere BanaterA Akten 36/1, f. 329–30
20. AT-OeStA/FHKA NHK KaaleU ältere BanaterA Akten 38, f. 267.
21. Baróti, *Adattár délmagyarország*, 5:114.
22. Möller, *Wie die schwäbischen Gemeinden*, 1:25.
23. Tafferner, *Quellenbuch*, #580.
24. AT-OeStA/FHKA NHK KaaleU BanaterA Akten 147, f. 23/57, 37, 38/41. Similarly, the colonists in Blumenthal petitioned the government in the 1770s for replacement animals that had been lost to theft or bad luck. AT-OeStA/FHKA NHK Banat A 138, f. 758.
25. AT-OeStA/FHKA NHK KaaleU BanaterA Akten 147, f. 38/41.
26. AT-OeStA/FHKA NHK KaaleU BanaterA Akten 147, f. 28–29.
27. AT-OeStA/FHKA NHK KaaleU BanaterA Akten 147, f. 37–38.
28. AT-OeStA/FHKA NHK KaaleU BanaterA Akten 147, f. 376–79.
29. AT-OeStA/FHKA NHK KaaleU BanaterA Akten 151B, f. 748–50.
30. AT-OeStA/FHKA NHK KaaleU BanaterA Akten 155B, f. 338.
31. AVNS, F. 11, Box 3, D. 338.
32. Clarke, *Travels*, 436.
33. Macmichael, *Journey*, 60–61.
34. Holderness, *New Russia*, 160, 215–16.
35. Weiss, *Die deutsche Kolonie*, 88.
36. Hauben, "The First Decade," 39.
37. ANRDJT, Fond Nr. 302, Nr. Nou 11, f. 12, 52. ANRDJT, Fond Nr. 302, Nr. Nou 11, f. 70. These are just two examples of a number of cases against him for his indebtedness.
38. AT-OeStA/FHKA NHK KaaleU ältere BanaterA Akten 49, May, f. 38–39.
39. AT-OeStA/FHKA NHK KaaleU ältere BanaterA Akten 49, May, 26–27.
40. AT-OeStA/FHKA NHK KaaleU ältere BanaterA Akten 51, October, f. 534.
41. AT-OeStA/FHKA NHK KaaleU BanaterA Akten 155B, f. 334, 342–43.
42. AT-OeStA/FHKA NHK KaaleU BanaterA Akten 153/C, f. 1592.
43. AT-OeStA/FHKA NHK KaaleU BanaterA Akten 91, f. 125.
44. Hegedüs, "Joseph II," 146, 147, 149.
45. Leo Hoffmann, *Kurze Geschichte*, 72–73.
46. Siebold, *Deutsches Bauernleben im Banat*, 63, 68.
47. That the Lo Presti de Fontana d'Angioli family owned the village is a verifiable fact. *Oesterreichische Monatsschrift*, 290–92. His son, or perhaps grandson, was the creator of the "wooden railway system." Mercydorf was described as the "ancestral home" (*Stammsitz*) of his family.
48. This was apparently a common tactic. When a local peasant named Jakob Lui was caught saying that peasants ought to be free, the authorities wanted to

send him off to the army. They were unable to because he had land ("hatte . . . Grund und Boden"). Instead, they tied him to a nut tree on a hill as an example to others. Möller, *Wie die schwäbischen Gemeinden*, 2:123–27.

49. Larry Wolff, *The Idea of Galicia*, 23. In Galicia, travelers reported similar incidents involving nobles abusing commoners.

50. Paget, *Hungary and Transylvania*, 2:156–57.

51. See Weidlein, *Entwicklung der Dorfanlagen*.

52. Hamilton's Bericht, "Chorographia Bannatus Temessiensis," 64.

53. Dorner, *Das Banat*, 63.

54. Steube, *Von Amsterdam nach Temiswar*, 189–90.

55. *The Morning Chronicle* (London, England), Friday, September 20, 1839. Kohl, for instance, described grain barns, not grain holes. Kohl, *Austria*, 302.

56. Weidlein, *Entwicklung der Dorfanlagen*, 12.

57. Möller, *Wie die schwäbischen Gemeinden*, 1:93. Just north of the Banat in Deutschpereg, there were Germans wintering in holes in 1852 when they could not finish their stamped-earth housing in time. Möller, *Wie die Schwäbischen Gemeinden*, 2:44.

58. AT-OeStA/FHKA SUS KS, Rb 044.

59. Kohl, *Austria*, 332.

60. Both AT-OeStA/FHKA SUS KS, Rb 043/1–2 and AT-OeStA/FHKA SUS KS, Rb 077 contain plans for both wood and earth/brick houses. For other examples, see AT-OeStA/FHKA SUS KS, Rb 047, AT-OeStA/FHKA SUS KS, Rb 076.

61. For a recent article on the phenomenon, see Anderson, "Cameralism," 55–67. Anderson suggests that the rectilinear design may also have been easiest to use in order to meet the goals (e.g., equality of plot size) of the project's supervisors.

62. "Da die Geometrische Ausmasse die Grundsaule ist, auf welche das ganzen Ansiedlungsgeschäft gebauet werden muss, so wird vor allen nötig seÿn, dass das ganzen Land durch eigends dazu bestimmte Ingenieurs, oder Erd-Messer genau aufgenommen werde." AT-OeStA/FHKA NHK KaaleU BanaterA Akten 154A, f. 44. Although this passage was written after the end of the major period of building, it does a wonderful job summing up what had been the driving force throughout the period: measurement and rational planning.

63. AT-OeStA/FHKA SUS KS, L 079.

64. AT-OeStA/FHKA SUS KS, O 033. Another unnamed German colonial village had a similar design. AT-OeStA/FHKA SUS KS, O 031.

65. AT-OeStA/FHKA SUS KS, O 032.

66. AT-OeStA/FHKA SUS KS, L 170/1–2. A later "residence" also had a basement or cellar, though it is unclear if this was designed for colonists or for others.

AT-OeStA/FHKA SUS KS, Rb 404. The following images are available online at the Austrian Archives website: AT-OeStA/FHKA SUS KS, L 170/1–2, Rb 044, Rb 047, O 031, O 032, O 033, L 079, Rb 043/1–2, and Rb 077. The other images are available only at the archives themselves.

67. ANRDJT, Fond Nr. 117, Inv. 1575, Nr. Nou 233, f. 2, 13.
68. Möller, *Wie die Schwäbischen Gemeinden*, 2:91–92.
69. Roth, *Die planmässig angelegten Siedlungen*, 145, 161, 132–33, 109, 152.
70. Ibid., 91.
71. Weidlein, *Entwicklung der Dorfanlagen*, 12, 22.
72. Dorner, *Das Banat*, 60, 126, 129–30, 136.
73. Paton, *Researches on the Danube*, 2:31–32.
74. Even though this quote is from the nineteenth century, it reflects a very cameralist belief that the government needed to "police" the populace to ensure development and the subject's own "happiness."
75. Kohl, *Austria*, 283, 315.
76. Paget, *Hungary and Transylvania*, 2:154, 155. Elements of the preceding discussion of villages first appeared in Olin, "Cultivating an Orderly Society."
77. In these cases, it is often hard to know whether they were built on top of preexisting settlements or whether they were completely new villages.
78. Leo Hoffmann, *Kurze Geschichte*, 16–17.
79. MOL, E303: I. a/, 9. E/e, f. 77.
80. Leo Hoffmann, *Kurze Geschichte*, 15–16.
81. Möller, *Wie die Schwäbischen Gemeinden*, 2:91–92.
82. Leo Hoffmann, *Kurze Geschichte*, 15–18.
83. The new nation-states that came into being following the Treaty of Trianon nationalized place names in the Banat. There are numerous examples of this. Temesvar-Temschburg-Temesvár-Temeswar was Romanicized to Timişoara. Weisskirchen was Serbicized to Bela Crkva. These, much like the earlier German renamings, were an attempt to intellectually claim possession of place and landscape.
84. Lemon, *The Best Poor Man's Country*, 98–101, 142.
85. Holderness, *New Russia*, 161. Though she did go on to say that "they [the Germans] are low, and brutal in their manners, more especially the men, who appear the least civilized inhabitants of the Crimea."
86. Guthrie, *Through Russia*, 2:100.
87. Kohl, *Russia*, 438, 184.
88. Meakin described the German Hussite colony of Sarepta in the early twentieth century as "present[ing] a pleasing picture to the eye, with its paved streets, its sidewalks lined with poplars, and its reservoirs of pure sparkling

water. It seems to the traveler like a refreshing oasis amid the lonely wastes that form the Volga's bank for many a mile above it and below." Meakin, *Russia*, 22.

89. Milleker, *Kurze Geschichte des Banats*, 10–12
90. Ottendorf, *Budáról Belgrádba*, 103–4.
91. *Eigentliche Beschreibung der Vestung Temeswar* (Wien: 1716), 2.
92. Milleker, *Kurze Geschichte des Banats*, 22, 24.
93. Petri, *Die Festung Temeschwar*, 6–9, 71–74. At least one mosque in Temesvar had formerly been a Jesuit church. Ağa, *Der Gefangene der Giauren*, 18. *The Penny Cyclopaedia*, 174.
94. Petri, *Die Festung Temeschwar*, 6–9, 71–74.
95. Milleker, *Kurze Geschichte des Banats*, 25.
96. Paton, *Researches on the Danube*, 38
97. Milleker, *Kurze Geschichte des Banats*, 21.
98. Kohl, *Austria*, 309.
99. Milleker, *Kurze Geschichte des Banats*, 29.
100. Similarly, Josephstadt, a suburb inhabited by Germans, had "very broad, straight streets." *The Penny Cyclopaedia*, 173–74.
101. Büsching and Ebeling, *Erdbeschreibung*, 544.
102. Dorner, *Das Banat*, 127.
103. Milleker, *Kurze Geschichte des Banats*, 22, 28–29.
104. "Public Instruction in Hungary, Croatia, Slavonia," 175, 177, 178, 179.
105. Milleker, *Kurze Geschichte des Banats*, 22, 28, 38.
106. Milleker, *Geschichte der Städte*, 21. A different source says it was a "free city" already in 1742. Büsching, *Erdbeschreibung*, 544.
107. Deák, *The Lawful Revolution*, 7–8.
108. Milleker, *Geschichte der Städte*, 28.
109. Milleker, *Kurze Geschichte des Banats*, 38.
110. Kohl, *Austria*, 307–10. *The Penny Cyclopaedia*, 174.
111. Pădurean, "The Population of Timişoara," 66. "Mother tongue" is a problematic way to record ethnicity, but it gives us some ideas of the relative size of the German-speaking population.
112. The first newspapers published in the Banat in languages other than German did not appear until the 1850s (Serbian: 1851, Magyar: 1858, Romanian: 1872). There was one publication, the *Landes-Regierungsblatt*, that published mostly ordinances but did so in all four languages, from 1851 to 1860. Shortly after the Ausgleich in 1867, the newspapers became a key component in the Magyarization of the German population. Krischan, *Die deutsche periodische Literatur*, 10–12. The Jesuits did publish religious books in Romanian in the early 1700s in Nagyszombat to support the recently established Uniate Church. Re-

ligious texts for Orthodox Wallachs were often smuggled over the border from Wallachia. By the later 1700s, books on linguistics and history appeared. That said, the market for such books was incredibly small. In 1848, "there were perhaps 10,000 Romanians in Transylvania and the Banat and Crișana who could read and write out of a total population of about two million." More than half of these were priests or teachers. Hitchins, *The Idea of Nation*, 28, 58, 100, 146.

113. The first appeared in Gross Becskerek (1851), Lugos (1857), and Werschetz (1857). Krischan, *Die deutsche periodische Literatur*, 11. In Weisskirchen, the first paper appeared in 1868. Milleker, *Kurze Geschichte der Stadt Bela Crkva*, 20.

114. AT-OeStA/FHKA NHK KaaleU BanaterA Akten 73, f. 652–84.

115. Klaniczay, *Nachricht*.

116. Kosáry, *Culture and Society*, 184–88.

117. The winning numbers were 79, 4, 65, 44, 86. The winner received one hundred ducats.

118. *Banater Zeitschrift für Landwirthschaft, Handel, Künste und Gewerbe*, 1827–1828.

Chapter 5: Settler Culture

1. Milleker, *Kurze Geschichte des Banats*, 23.

2. AVNS, F. 11, Box 3, D. 70/1782.

3. Manning and Trimmer, *Migration in World History*, 8.

4. The phrase plays on rhymes in German (*Tod, Not, Brot*—death, suffering, bread). Hoerder, *Cultures in Contact*, 284–85; Zakić, *Ethnic Germans*, 193.

5. Bailyn, *The Peopling*, 100–101, 24–25, 53; Moch, *Moving Europeans*, 44–46.

6. Such a fusion of beliefs was common among the peasantry throughout Europe and earlier in the Banat. See Tóth, "Missionaries," 96, 98, 107–8.

7. For more incidents, see Baróti, *Adattár délmagyarország*, 5:8, 135, 70, 16, 148, 107. AT-OeStA/FHKA NHK KaaleU ältere BanaterA Akten 51, September, f. 77, 140.

8. Steube, *Von Amsterdam nach Temiswar*, 152.

9. Elke Hoffmann, *Städte und Dörfer*, 552.

10. Bailyn, *The Peopling*, 108–11, 114–17.

11. Khodarkovsky, *Where Two Worlds Met*, 227–34.

12. Hauben, "The First Decade," 39–40.

13. Weiss, *Die deutsche Kolonie*, 89.

14. ANRDJT, Fond Nr. 67, 1/1816, f. 21. In the Russian Empire, calling someone a "German" was a similar insult. "By the lower orders, the two races [Germans and German-speaking Jews] are regarded as almost identical, and *Ioudiéy* and *Niémietz* (Jew and German) are two of the most insulting expressions that

the peasants can use in their disputes among themselves." In one case, a serf stabbed a compatriot for daring to call him a "German." He was acquitted when "the magistrate admitted that the provocation was unendurable." Palmer, *Russian Life in Town and Country*, 159–60.

15. Eimann, *Der deutsche Kolonist*, 17–18, 126–29, 66.
16. Kohl, *Austria*, 294.
17. HAK, F. 4, B. 7, D. 789.
18. Hamilton's Bericht, "Chorographia Bannatus Temessiensis," 57–58.
19. AVNS, F. 11, Box 2, D. 281/1777.
20. Kohl, *Austria*, 323.
21. Paton, *Researches on the Danube*, 2:32.
22. See, for example, the work of anthropologist Annette Meakin: Meakin, *Russia*. Lady, *The Englishwoman in Russia*.
23. Weidlein, *Entwicklung der Dorfanlagen*, 34.
24. AT-OeStA/FHKA NHK KaaleU BanaterA Akten 68, f. 529–37.
25. Magyar Országos Levéltár (MOL), E303: I. a/, 10. 4269 (Kik), f. 10–11.
26. Unfortunately for them, the emperor dissolved all "military communities" in 1801. Milleker, *Geschichte der Stadt Pančevo*, 61–65.
27. Janjetović, "Die Konflikte,", 121–22.
28. Turczynski, "Austro-Serbian Relations," 203. It appears that Arsenjević said his prayer in support of the Serbs because Karadjordje donated material to build a church in the town. Milleker, *Geschichte der Stadt Pančevo*, 76. More on this incident and its context can be found in chapter 8.
29. As noted in chapter 4, a census of non-Germans in the fortress of Temesvar in 1739 indicated that Rascians, Jews, Greeks, and Arnauts were all living there, though no Wallachs. MOL, E303: a/, 13., Zsidókra vonatkozó iratok, f. 7–12.
30. Historical Archives of Zrenjanin, F. 3, Gross Becskerek City, B. 636 [4, 628], 1812–1817, D. 2/61.
31. In newspaper ads listing houses for sale, they were often advertised as located in the "German side" or the "Illyrian side" of the Fabrique Vorstadt. For example, see: "Temeswarer Wochenblatt." March 2, 1839. P. 64, 65.
32. AT-OeStA/FHKA NHK KaaleU BanaterA Akten 152/B, f. 628.
33. Hofkriegsrat, 1775-3-68, f. 1 in Roth, *Die planmässig angelegten Siedlungen*, 152–53.
34. Kohl, *Austria*, 280.
35. AT-OeStA/FHKA NHK KaaleU ältere BanaterA Akten 45, September, f. 395–96.
36. ANRDJT, Fond Nr. 302, Nr. Nou 11, f. 72.
37. AT-OeStA/FHKA NHK KaaleU ältere BanaterA Akten 50, July, f. 104.

38. Kohl, *Austria*, 315.

39. Paget, *Hungary and Transylvania*, 2:155, 154.

40. Kohl, *Austria*, 315. Kohl attributed this to the fact that "Romanic" people were more inclined to Germanize than become like locals. Stanglica, *Die Auswanderung*, 26–27. Stanglica made a similar point about the French, Italian, and Spanish settlers in Mercydorf. Möller was even more ambitious. He sought to Germanize the French residents of Orzydorf *before* they came to Banat. He claimed that the French last names were deceiving and that these people were in fact Germanic Franks and Burgundians. Even some Slavs apparently Germanized. In Ebendorf, the progeny of earlier Slovak colonists became "German." He pointed to names like Hubacek and Kolacek to prove Slavic heritage. Möller, *Wie die schwäbischen Gemeinden*, 1:99, 29. Also perhaps of interest here is the fact that, according to Konstantinos Koumas, writing in 1832, even the Greeks "in Austria" were forsaking the Greek language in favor of German. Clogg, "The Greek Merchant Companies in Transylvania," 166–67.

41. Palmer, *Russian Life*, 177.

42. Meakin, *Russia*, 26.

43. Palmer, *Russian Life*, 159, 176, 177. Lady, *The Englishwoman in Russia*, 299. Haxthausen, *Studies on the Interior of Russia*, 174.

44. Tooke, *View of the Russian Empire*, 3:141, 143. Mai, *1798 Census*, 130, 115. Though they were also credited with introducing a German plow.

45. Meakin, *Russia*, 20.

46. AT-OeStA/FHKA NHK KaaleU BanaterA Akten 150B, f. 1425–26.

47. Weiss, *Die deutsche Kolonie*, 95, 76, 98, 99, 100.

48. AT-OeStA/FHKA NHK KaaleU ältere BanaterA Akten 4, f. 155 a/b.

49. AT-OeStA/FHKA NHK KaaleU BanaterA Akten 147, f. 34.

50. Wolf, "Ethnische Konflict," 354–55.

51. ANRDJT, Fond Nr. 302, Nr. Nou 11, f. 52.

52. ANRDJT, Fond Nr. 302, Nr. Nou 11, f. 31.

53. AT-OeStA/FHKA SUS Patente 199.2.

54. Baróti, *Adattár délmagyarország*, 5:17.

55. Böhm, *Geschichte des Temeser Banats*, 308. On top of that, there was also a smallpox epidemic (*Pockenepidemie*). Milleker, *Kurze Geschichte der Stadt Bela Crkva*, 13.

56. Kohl, *Austria*, 263.

57. *Temeswarer Wochenblatt*, July 31, 1841, p. 378.

58. Siebold, *Deutsches Bauernleben im Banat*, 16–17, 51.

59. AVNS, F. 11, 1789, Box 148, D. 1256. AVNS, F. 11, 1782, D. 70.

60. In the case of Bukin in the Batschka, the placement of the village itself

was moved, and three contiguous "street villages" were combined into a single "checkerboard" village following a flood in 1812. Weidlein, *Entwicklung der Dorfanlagen*, 40.

61. Siebold, *Deutsches Bauernleben im Banat*, 14.
62. Hammer, *Geschichte der Pest*, 23, 69.
63. Griselini, *Aus dem Versuch*, 11.
64. AT-OeStA/FHKA NHK KaaleU ältere BanaterA Akten 36/1: Ältere Banater Akten: March 1753, f. 17, 19, 22, 23.
65. For the Theresian migration, for example, see AT-OeStA/FHKA NHK Banat A 138, f. 412–13, 445–46.
66. Born, Raspe, and Ferber, *Travels through the Bannat of Temeswar*, 57.
67. Möller, *Wie die schwäbischen Gemeinden*, 1:37, 34, 71, 83, 107, 63, 38.
68. HAK, F. 4, B. 8, D. 937-I/1831.
69. Leo Hoffmann, *Kurze Geschichte*, 23.
70. Kohl, *Austria*, 305–8, 278. Paton, *Researches on the Danube*, 2:24.
71. Siebold, *Deutsches Bauernleben im Banat*, 9.
72. *Morning Chronicle and London Advertiser* (London, England), Saturday, September 20, 1788. They reported that he was laid up in Temesvár barely able to continue on the campaign. Beales, in his splendid work on the emperor, attributed Joseph's death to tuberculosis "probably contracted during the campaign of 1788." According to Beales, Joseph mentioned his illness in a letter to Kaunitz in August after taking command of the army in the Banat. His health deteriorated from there. He left the Banat for Vienna on November 18, 1788. He died on February 20, 1790. Beales, *Joseph II*, 2:587, 572–74, 635.
73. Baróti, *Adattár délmagyarország*, 5:14.
74. Burke discussed how this struggle between professional and local healers represented the conflict between popular and elite understanding of the world. Burke, *Popular Culture*, 371.
75. AVNS, F. 10, 1777, Box 2, D. 31.
76. AVNS, F. 11, 1777, Box 2, D. 197. This was a license to practice optometry.
77. Eimann, *Der deutsche Kolonist*, 49, 57.
78. To mediate their losses, local officials in 1748 asked that people be able to skin the sick animals and send the hides to "Turkey." This plan was denied. Baróti, *Adattár délmagyarország*, 5:38, 39.
79. AVNS, F. 11, 1788, Box 131, D. 2435.
80. AVNS, F. 11, 1789, Box 134, D. 76. MOL, E305: c/, 10. 8/, f. 63.
81. AT-OeStA/FHKA NHK KaaleU ältere BanaterA Akten 45, September, f. 43–44.
82. Schönbauer, *Geschichte der schädlichen Kolumbatczer Mücken im Bannat*.

83. Siebold, *Deutsches Bauernleben im Banat*, 56.

84. Baróti, *Adattár délmagyarország*, 5:75, 135, 136, 50, 150. There are more cases. Another vampire was discovered in Sussanovezer in 1730 (140).

85. Steube, *Von Amsterdam nach Temiswar*, 180, 185.

86. Tallar, *Visum repertum*, 9, 10, 13–14, 22, 26–28, 33, 93.

87. AT-OeStA/FHKA NHK KaaleU ältere BanaterA Akten 51, September, f. 160–61. Elements of the preceding discussion of superstition and vampires first appeared in Olin, "Cultivating an Orderly Society."

88. It is unclear whether he copied just *this* section from Meichterer or the entire book. I tend to think that the book is a compilation from many different sources over a number of years rather than simply a copy of someone else's work. Also of interest, the word *verbrand* comes from the infinitive *verbrennen*. This would be the verb one would use to describe "burning" as in burning witches.

89. ANRDJT, Fond Nr. 52, Nr. Nou 97, f. 1–67.

90. Möller, *Wie die schwäbischen Gemeinden*, 1:105.

91. Lotz, "Donauschwäbische Kolonistenbrautpaare," 78, 79.

92. Horst Dieter Schmidt, *Ein verschwundenes Dorf im Banat*, 30, 105.

93. ANRDJT, Fond Nr. 709, 1/1809.

94. They got the "back part of the house," one-third of the house garden, twenty *Metzen* of grain per year, twenty *Metzen* of oats, one *Joch* of meadow, Peter's labor on "two *Joch* of purchased field," two *Klafter* of grain straw (*Frucht Stroh*), two *Klafter* of oat straw (*Haber Stroh*), one *Klafter* of straw (*Streu*), one hundred bushels of corn, the use of stalls, one-third of the poultry, and one-third of the eggs. If one of the pair died, the amounts of certain items shrank.

95. ANRDJT, Fond Nr. 99, Nr. Nou 30.

96. ANRDJT, Fond Nr. 67, 3/1827.

97. ANRDJT, Fond Nr. 709, 1/1804. In another similar case, Magdalena Kirchnerin gave her daughter and son-in-law the farm, equipment, and animals at the time of their marriage. The total value of the property was 3,886 fl. Although not explicitly said, it stands to reason that this was another quid pro quo arrangement where the son-in-law took over the farm but was expected to take care of his wife's family. ANRDJT, Fond Nr. 99, Nr. Nou. 22. Similar arrangements occurred in Western Europe. Moch, *Moving Europeans*, 36, 86.

98. ANRDJT, Fond Nr. 67, 2/1794. None of the men directly involved in the contract were able to sign their names. All made various crosses next to which someone wrote their names as well as *sein Handzeichen* (his sign). It is interesting that the signatories, for whom these contracts had major life-changing ramifications, were likely unable to read them.

99. Of course, not all marriage contracts contained provisions for caring for the elderly. The contract between Josef Hirsch and Magdelena Pelljung, for in-

stance, dealt largely with what the parents were to provide for the newly married couple (a small house, two cows, two beds, and some grain). Though even here there may have been an unspoken agreement that because of the land and material the couple received, they would care for the parents. ANRDJT, Fond Nr. 67, 6/1827.

100. Kohl, *Austria*, 330–31. Kohl said that the eldest son was only required to pay off other sons, but as the next example shows, women also had rights in certain places and at certain times. This type of arrangement also existed in Western Europe. Moch, *Moving Europeans*, 36–37.

101. ANRDJT, Fond Nr. 67, 2/1827.
102. ANRDJT, Fond Nr. 709, 1/1788.
103. ANRDJT, Fond Nr. 67, 1/1794.
104. ANRDJT, Fond Nr. 67, 1/1820, 1/1823.
105. ANRDJT, Fond Nr. 99, Nr. Nou 29.
106. ANRDJT, Fond Nr. 99, Nr. Nou 5, f. 4–5. Quote from an inventory of assets and debts of Connedus Schmidt: "Der Schmidt schuldet für die ganz Jährige Arbeit—50fl." Perhaps a person could work more than one farm and earn more money. This is unclear. Though from a hundred years earlier, Dabić put the average wage of a manual laborer at twelve kreutzer per day. Working 365 days a year, a worker would thus earn seventy-three forints. Dabić, "The Habsburg-Ottoman War of 1716–1718," 199.
107. ANRDJT, Fond Nr. 99, Nr. Nou 5, f. 6–7. ANRDJT, Fond Nr. 99, Nr. Nou 18.
108. ANRDJT, Fond Nr. 709, 1/1806.
109. ANRDJT, Fond Nr. 1045, Nr. Nou 30. Of course, sons often followed in their father's footsteps. In one case from the early nineteenth century, the government of Kikinda wrote a testament for the Tischlergesell Johannes Ehrhart in which they explicitly mention that his father was also a Tischler and Bürger in the town. HAK, F. 4, B. 2, D. 247-I/1805.
110. ANRDJT, Fond Nr. 117, Nr. Nou 155.
111. ANRDJT, Fond Nr. 117, Nr. Nou 195.
112. ANRDJT, Fond Nr. 709, 2/1822.
113. ANRDJT, Fond Nr. 67, 2/1827.
114. AT-OeStA/FHKA SUS Patente 224.2. The government was especially concerned with protecting individuals such as the deaf, blind, and mentally handicapped, who were seen as unable to care for themselves.
115. AVNS, F. 11, D. 1097.

Chapter 6: Local Responses to Habsburg Rule I

1. Baróti, *Adattár délmagyarország*, 5:48–49.
2. Hamilton's Bericht, "Chorographia Bannatus Temessiensis," 120–22.

3. Baumann argued that the majority of Wallachs in the Banat's mountain regions came between 1658 and 1737, when the loss of the Little Wallachia staunched the flow. According to him, it was only during this time that they became a majority in the uplands. Baumann, *Geschichte der Banater Berglanddeutschen Volksgruppe*, 13.

4. Dorner refuted this claim, relying heavily on an earlier scholar who surmised they were members of a later migrant group. Dorner, *Das Banat*, 49–52.

5. Hitchins mentioned a similar situation in Habsburg Transylvania and Bukovina. There, Habsburg rule "represented an intrusion by the West into the world of the patriarchal Romanian village." Hitchins, *The Romanians*, 198.

6. Peter Kolb, whose book on southern Africa was published in 1719, shared a similar story about a group of slaves executed for killing a European. Like the Wallachs, they were stoic when faced with a violent death. According to his account, they did not cry out or complain as they were tortured to death on the wheel. Pratt, *Imperial Eyes*, 47. Such stories may reflect some form of generalized "Othering" of non-Europeans as more stoic or hardened. It is hard to tell if this is meant as a compliment, or another way to deny non-Europeans humanity (i.e., they are emotionless, like animals awaiting slaughter).

7. Steube, *Von Amsterdam nach Temiswar*, 102, 132–33, 176, 177, 196.

8. Ibid., 174.

9. *Beschreibung des Banats*, 50, 51, 52, 53.

10. AT-OeStA/FHKA NHK KaaleU BanaterA Akten 148, f. 204, 215.

11. AT-OeStA/FHKA SUS KS, O 083. There was a long association of Roma people with tents, so perhaps the map was referring to a Romani settlement. See Achim, *The Roma in Romanian History*, 52.

12. Radonitch, *The Banat*, 9.

13. AVNS, F. 11, Box 1, D. 100/1777.

14. AT-OeStA/FHKA NHK KaaleU BanaterA Akten 161, f. 668, 680, 673–74, 681, 708–10.

15. Such fears had precedent. In the late 1710s, Mercy attributed the loss of the Banat's population to Transylvanian nobles who promised Banaters lower taxes on their estates. Dabić, "The Habsburg-Ottoman War of 1716–1718," 195.

16. AT-OeStA/FHKA NHK KaaleU BanaterA Akten 161, f. 668, 680, 673–74, 681, 708–10.

17. AT-OeStA/FHKA NHK KaaleU BanaterA Akten 161, f. 711–13.

18. Not only Wallachs were subject to such charges when they fled a region. According to the government, thirty-two residents of the Kikinda region, almost certainly Rascians, fled in the late 1770s because of "wantonness and malice." HAK, F. 3, B. 324, D. 25.

19. Bartenstein, *Kurzer Bericht*, xix.
20. AT-OeStA/FHKA NHK KaaleU BanaterA Akten 66, f. 389–90.
21. Griselini, *Aus dem Versuch*, 12.
22. Steube, *Von Amsterdam nach Temiswar*, 190, 191, 192, 193. Dorner seconded most of these claims. He was quick to add, though, that the Habsburg Wallachs were more civilized than those in Wallachia. Dorner, *Das Banat*, 53.
23. Bartenstein, *Kurzer Bericht*, xix.
24. Roider and Forrest, "German Colonization," 93.
25. For instance, in 1789 the administration heard "unending complaints" about teachers not being paid. They blamed the local officials for withholding the money. One report claimed that the problem was very widespread, especially in places where these officials collected the money to pay the teachers. AVNS, F. 11, Box 146, D. 1087/1789. See also: AVNS, F. 11, Box 134, D. 58/1789.
26. By the nineteenth century, some *haiduk*s were responsible for *stopping* robberies. Kohl, *Austria*, 295. Already in the 1770s, the government provided wages (*Lohnung*) to "county *haiduk*s" in Lugosch, Werschetz, and Caransebes. AVNS, F10, Box 2, D. 76, 85, 91.
27. Burke, *Popular Culture*, 62–63.
28. Held, "The Horea-Closca Revolt," 100.
29. Of course, this is not a specifically "eastern European" phenomenon, as Burke also pointed out in his book. He saw the praise of criminals as "wish fulfillment" that affected the popular imagination throughout Europe. In England, for example, there was Robin Hood. Burke argues that as peasants became more prosperous and were freed from serfdom, they became less likely to venerate criminals. Thus, the tradition lasted longer in the East than it did in the West. Burke, *Popular Culture*, 220–23. This interpretation is both supported and belied by the tradition in the United States. In the twentieth century, Bonnie and Clyde achieved a similar status in the United States. Oliver Stone's movie *Natural Born Killers* explored this phenomenon in the 1990s.
30. The Wallachs, for instance, had a history of fighting the Habsburgs since at least the 1680s, when they took part in the siege of Vienna. Finkel, *Osman's Dream*, 286. There were also uprisings of Wallachs along the borders of the Banat. In 1735, Pitr Seghedinat organized an uprising that eventually spread to Transylvania. It was both anti-Catholic and antifeudal in nature. The leaders were caught and executed. Pascu, *A History of Transylvania*, 145. It is quite difficult to find any scholarly literature on this revolt. Pascu referred to the unrest as occurring "in the Banat and around Arad." According to the town of Pecica's website (www.pecica.ro/), Seghedinat was from there. The town is located just over the Marosch River from the Banat proper, west of Arad. Resistance

to Habsburg rule, especially interference in Orthodox Church affairs, was also pronounced among the Wallachs of Transylvania. Many were especially keen to reject the union between the Catholic and Orthodox Churches promoted by the Habsburg administration. The 1740s and 1750s were particularly uneasy. Hitchins, *The Idea of Nation*, 63, 68. There was also much unrest among the Wallachs and Szekler border regiments in the 1760s, including a full-blown revolt among the Szekler that had to be put down with military force in 1763. Pascu, *A History of Transylvania*, 138.

31. This feeling continued in the 1920s. In describing the German position in the new Yugoslav state, Janjetović described them as "encumbered with the odium of the hated Habsburgs." Janjetović, "Die Konflikte," 153.

32. Wolf, "Ethnische Konflict," 343–45. Wolf noted this phenomenon as well. He also provided further evidence of the tense relationship between locals and incoming colonists. Pascu likewise argued it was Habsburg misrule and the influx of Germans that led to revolts among the Wallachs of the Banat. In particular, he pointed to the uprising between 1737 and 1739 as an example. Pascu, *A History of Transylvania*, 145.

33. Janjetović, "Die Konflikte," 120–21.

34. AT-OeStA/FHKA NHK KaaleU BanaterA Akten 148, f. 216.

35. AT-OeStA/FHKA NHK KaaleU BanaterA Akten 152/C, f. 1470.

36. Baumann, *Geschichte der Banater Berglanddeutschen Volksgruppe*, 19–20.

37. AT-OeStA/FHKA NHK KaaleU BanaterA Akten 66, f. 131.

38. AT-OeStA/FHKA NHK KaaleU BanaterA Akten 66, f. 390.

39. *London Chronicle* (London, England), August 18, 1789–August 20, 1789.

40. Naturally, the perpetrators tried to hide their identity. *London Gazette* (London, England), February 20, 1738–February 24, 1738. Baumann claimed that many Wallachs wore turbans to hide their true identities when the ravaged their ostensible homeland. Baumann, *Geschichte der Banater Berglanddeutschen Volksgruppe*, 25. This contention is supported by an anecdote told in the late eighteenth century: Prince Karl von Lothringen and Grand Duke Franz von Toscana came upon a group of Wallachs dressed as Turkish soldiers while out on a hunt. Responsible for "all kinds of violence," the leader of the group fell to his knees and begged for forgiveness before offering to lead them out of the area. *Beschreibung des Banats*, 27–28. There was a different report of robbers dressing like Hussars in 1738. Baróti, *Adattár délmagyarország*, 5:28–29. In 1771, robber victims claimed that "five robbers dressed as Turks" had committed the crime. AT-OeStA/FHKA NHK KaaleU BanaterA Akten 153/C, f. 1351.

41. *Daily Gazetteer* (*London Edition*) (London, England), Saturday, June 17, 1738

42. *London Evening Post* (London, England), June 24, 1738–June 27, 1738.
43. AT-OeStA/FHKA NHK KaaleU BanaterA Akten 66, f. 515.
44. Baróti, *Adattár délmagyarország*, 5:28, 83. Kohl, *Austria*, 316.
45. Milleker, *Geschichte der Stadt Pančevo*, 27–30.
46. Baróti, *Adattár délmagyarország*, 5:29, 27, 86, 28.
47. *London Evening Post* (London, England), July 25, 1738–July 27, 1738. Though this apparently did not halt the rebellion, as more rebels were reported coming from the area in 1739. *Daily Post* (London, England), Monday, February 26, 1739.
48. *London Evening Post* (London, England), October 26, 1738–October 28, 1738.
49. *Daily Post* (London, England), Monday, January 15, 1739.
50. Baróti, *Adattár délmagyarország*, 5:85.
51. Baróti, *Adattár délmagyarország*, 5:30.
52. *London Daily Post and General Advertiser* (London, England), Wednesday, June 20, 1739.
53. *Daily Post* (London, England), Monday, May 14, 1739.
54. Baróti, *Adattár délmagyarország*, 5:146.
55. Baróti, *Adattár délmagyarország*, 5:149, 30–31.
56. MOL, E303: I. a/, 9. E/e, f. 22–23. Unfortunately, the document is undated but comes from a fond that purports to contain documents from 1717 to 1753, but it seems likely that it is describing a situation that occurred during the 1737–1739 war. The author mentioned that the uprising "gives the neighboring enemy the opportunity to profit." He later mentions that the region "stands on the border of the archenemy."
57. Baróti, *Adattár délmagyarország*, 5:166.
58. AT-OeStA/FHKA NHK KaaleU ältere BanaterA Akten 48, March, f. 345–48.
59. Baróti, *Adattár délmagyarország*, 5:72, 25, 32, 99, 49, 50, 96. Pascu, *A History of Transylvania*, 147. Steube, *Von Amsterdam nach Temiswar*, 153.
60. AT-OeStA/FHKA NHK KaaleU BanaterA Akten 191, f. 902.
61. AT-OeStA/FHKA NHK KaaleU BanaterA Akten 151B, f. 746, 748–50.
62. AT-OeStA/FHKA NHK KaaleU BanaterA Akten 152/A, f. 371–72.
63. They were likely less "humanitarian" than enlightened, centralist realpolitik. For instance, Held argued that "the policies of the Habsburg administration in Transylvania were openly exploitative, representing an early colonial regime, throughout the eighteenth century." He went on to state that "the Habsburg rulers were not that much interested in easing the burdens of the peasants; they simply wanted to free them from landlord control in order to have them exploited by the state." Held, "The Horea-Closca Revolt," 96.

64. Hitchins, *The Romanians*, 205–14.
65. Edroiu, *Horea's Uprising*, 22, 60.
66. Held, "The Horea-Closca Revolt," 99, 101.
67. *General Evening Post* (London, England), December 11, 1784–December 14, 1784. Edroiu, *Horea's Uprising*, 60.
68. Russian peasants utilized the same political stance. The tsar was good, but his local representatives were bad. Held noted a similar phenomenon. Held, "The Horea-Closca Revolt," 94.
69. *General Evening Post* (London, England), December 25, 1784–December 28, 1784.
70. Edroiu, *Horea's Uprising*, 26–27.
71. Ibid., 23–24, 19–22, 52. *Allgemeine deutsche Real-Encyclopädie*, 5:401–2. Hitchins, *The Romanians*, 205–7. Hitchins, *The Idea of Nation*, 106.
72. Edroiu, *Horea's Uprising*, 54.
73. Hitchins, *The Romanians*, 205.
74. Held, "The Horea-Closca Revolt," 94.
75. *Morning Chronicle and London Advertiser* (London, England), Friday, October 17, 1788.
76. *St. James's Chronicle or the British Evening Post* (London, England), October 21, 1788–October 23, 1788.
77. *St. James's Chronicle or the British Evening Post* (London, England), November 25, 1788–November 27, 1788.
78. *Real-Zeitung auf das Jahr 1788*, 787.
79. Elke Hoffmann, *Städte und Dörfer*, 109. Perhaps referencing the same incident, Möller described the construction of seventy-two gallows south of Denta on which two hundred "robbers" were hung. He indicated the execution happened in 1790. Möller, *Wie die schwäbischen Gemeinden*, 1:37.
80. Avrich, *Russian Rebels*, 191, 239.
81. Koch, *The Volga Germans*, 99–103, 103–8. Koch related that Pushkin, in particular, blamed the German colonists for supporting Pugachev. Ibid., 100–101.
82. Hixson, *American Settler Colonialism*, vii–viii.
83. Bailyn, *The Peopling*, 113–17.
84. Hixson, *American Settler Colonialism*, 55–62, 71–75.
85. Carley cites the "realization of the young white 'warriors' had left for southern battlefields" as a reason for the uprising. Carley, *The Dakota War of 1862*, 5.
86. There were reports of "Turks" who helped the Habsburg armies by attacking supply trains in Ottoman territory. *Whitehall Evening Post (1770)* (London, England), May 1, 1788–May 3, 1788.

87. *Fourteen Centuries of Struggle for Freedom*, XXVIII.
88. Milleker, *Geschichte der Stadt Pančevo*, 70.

Chapter 7: Local Responses to Habsburg Rule II
1. Quoted in Bartenstein, *Kurzer Bericht von der Beschaffenheit*, xx.
2. Komlosy, "Habsburg Borderlands," 51.
3. AT-OeStA/FHKA SUS Patente 65.5.
4. Roider, *The Reluctant Ally*, 22.
5. AT-OeStA/FHKA NHK KaaleU BanaterA Akten 66, f. 518.
6. Pálffy, *Hungary between Two Empires*, 84–85.
7. The low estimate comes from Hochedlinger and the high estimate from Sugar, though it appears elsewhere as well. Hochedlinger, *Austria's Wars of Emergence*, 162. Sugar, *Southeastern Europe*, 222. Adler put the number at 100,000. Adler, "Serbs, Magyars, and Staatsinteresse," 117. Interestingly, Paxton noted that one thousand families fled Habsburg rule for their old homeland in 1702. Paxton, "Identity and Consciousness," 107.
8. Pálffy, *Hungary*, 189.
9. Paxton, "Identity and Consciousness," 103, 105.
10. Evans, "Religion und Nation in Ungarn, 1790–1849," 34.
11. Adler, "Serbs, Magyars, and Staatsinteresse," 138.
12. József Thim, a scholar writing in the 1930s and 40s, quoted in Evans, "Religion und Nation," 33.
13. These ties were long-lasting. Only in the mid-nineteenth century, with the rise of language nationalism, did they start to fray. In Weisskirchen, arguments about the language of the Orthodox service divided Romanians and Serbians in 1845. In fact, Milleker claimed that the language dispute caused the Romanians to take the Germans' side during the Revolution of 1848, which in Weisskirchen pitted Serbs against Germans (as we shall see in the epilogue). In 1850, the dispute led to the separation of the communities, and in February 1869, the communities completely severed their religious ties. The Serbs kept the church and school but paid the Romanians 11,431 fl., 17 kr. for their loss. The Romanians proceeded to hire their own pastor and construct a prayer house, though they did not have their own church completed until 1872. Milleker, *Kurze Geschichte der Stadt Bela Crkva*, 18, 20.
14. Hitchins, *The Idea of Nation*, 58–63.
15. Pascu, *A History of Transylvania*, 146.
16. Dyck, "New Serbia," 3.
17. Though I cannot say definitively, both the handwriting and the archival description of the fond ("Serbian Non-United Church, 1718–1729") seem to indicate a document created quite early following conquest. If correct, this indicates

that the Habsburgs were very interested in defining the relationship between the state religion and the mass of new Orthodox subjects from an early date.

18. Magyar Országos Levéltár (MOL), E303: 11, Q/b, f. 14–16.
19. AT-OeStA/FHKA SUS Patente 224.3.
20. Adler, "Serbs, Magyars, and Staatsinteresse," 140.
21. Baróti, *Adattár délmagyarország*, 5:114.
22. Adler, "Serbs, Magyars, and Staatsinteresse," 140–42.
23. Paxton referred to them as "Hussars" rather than Grenzer. Paxton, "Identity and Consciousness," 113.
24. Ibid.
25. The discussion of the Habsburg-Magyar-Rascian conflicts is based on the excellent article: Adler, "Serbs, Magyars, and Staatsinteresse," 116–47.
26. Hochedlinger, *Austria's Wars of Emergence*, 241, 318.
27. MOL, E303: I. a/, 9. E/c, f. 94–95.
28. MOL, E303: I. a/, 9. E/c, f. 47–48.
29. Paxton, "Identity and Consciousness," 106.
30. Dyck, "New Serbia," 3–4.
31. Bartlett, *Human Capital*, 19. Rothenberg, *The Military Border*, 29, 32–33. Paxton put the number at 2,200 families by 1760. Paxton, "Identity and Consciousness," 106.
32. Paxton, "Identity and Consciousness," 108.
33. Hitchins, *The Idea of Nation*, 67.
34. Dyck put the foundation date in 1751. Dyck, "New Serbia," 1–19.
35. Dyck, "New Serbia," 3, 6.
36. Bartlett, *Human Capital*, 19, 109, 114, 116.
37. AT-OeStA/FHKA NHK KaaleU BanaterA Akten 68, f. 219, 221.
38. Rothenberg, *The Military Border*, 32–38. It seems that similar actions must have taken place in the Banat, but I can find no direct evidence of them.
39. Dyck, "New Serbia," 4–14.
40. Ibid., 9.
41. AT-OeStA/FHKA NHK KaaleU BanaterA Akten 161, f. 69.
42. AT-OeStA/FHKA NHK KaaleU BanaterA Akten 161, f. 115.
43. AT-OeStA/FHKA NHK KaaleU ältere BanaterA Akten 53, January, f. 216/226.
44. AT-OeStA/FHKA NHK KaaleU ältere BanaterA Akten 53, January, f. 216/226. This document is most likely referring to Daskkovich, though here his name is listed as Damian Daczkow. He was arrested along with another deserter. The note also mentioned an additional six deserters whom authorities had taken into custody.

45. AT-OeStA/FHKA NHK KaaleU BanaterA Akten 161, f. 51–52.
46. AT-OeStA/FHKA NHK KaaleU BanaterA Akten 161, f. 7, 39.
47. Bartlett, *Human Capital*, 19, 62, 114.
48. Dyck, "New Serbia," 5.
49. AT-OeStA/FHKA NHK KaaleU ältere BanaterA Akten 45, October, f. 81. AT-OeStA/FHKA NHK KaaleU ältere BanaterA Akten 46, November, f. 93–105.
50. AT-OeStA/FHKA NHK KaaleU ältere BanaterA Akten 46, December, f. 303.
51. Bartenstein, *Kurzer Bericht*, xxv–xxvi.
52. Paxton, "Identity and Consciousness," 115.
53. "Illyrian" was another term referring to South Slavs and their lands. As we have seen, the Habsburgs used this term in an official capacity, e.g., Hofkommission in Banaticis, Transylvanicis et Illyricis. It is a reference with ancient origins, referring to the people who lived in the Balkans in the Greek and Roman eras. Napoleon likewise used the term after his conquest of parts of the Balkans. AT-OeStA/ HHStA Flugschriften 1790: Rede vor Eröffung der illyrischen Nazionalversammlung. Gehalten zu Temeswar. Im August 1790. These were heady times. That same year (1790), the nobles of Galicia released the *Magna Charta von Galizien: oder Untersuchung der Beschwerden des Galizischen Adels pohlnischer Nation über die österreichische Regierung*. Like the "Speech," the evidence of the influence of the French Revolution is clear. Larry Wolff, *The Idea of Galicia*, 36–40.
54. France, as such, was not mentioned once in the entire document. The references to a people who reclaimed their rights and threw off the nobility must refer at least in part to the French. The speech was rife with Enlightenment language and appeals to "reason" and "natural law."
55. Wandruszka, *Leopold II.*, 2:286.
56. Ibid., 2:287.
57. Adler, "Serbs, Magyars, and Staatsinteresse," 144–46.
58. Ingrao, *The Habsburg Monarchy*, 220–21.
59. Ibid., 222–42.
60. Bartenstein, *Kurzer Bericht*, xxv–xxvi.
61. Milleker, *Geschichte der Stadt Pančevo*, 75.
62. Captain Radič Petrović, another Habsburg deserter, became a mayor of Belgrade. A number of insurgents, including Karadjordje himself, ended up in the Habsburg domains when the revolt failed. The Austrians refused to extradite him to the Ottomans. Turczynski, "Austro-Serbian Relations,", 176, 184, 196–97.
63. Rothenberg, *The Military Border*, 102–4.

64. Milleker, *Geschichte der Stadt Pančevo*, 76.

65. Turczynski, "Austro-Serbian Relations," 200.

66. Though interestingly, given his pro-Serbian leanings, Hiller later proposed to close the border to Serbian refugees fleeing the war. Vienna denied this request. Turczynski, "Austro-Serbian Relations," 189, 175, 182, 180, 184, 190, 196.

67. Startimirović became metropolitan in 1790, the same year the speech regarding the rights of the Illyrians was given. Paxton, "Identity and Consciousness," 115.

68. For an in-depth analysis of the event, see Banac, "The Role of Vojvodina," 42–43. Kann and David, *The Peoples of the Eastern Habsburg Lands*, 282–83. Deák, *The Lawful Revolution*, 130.

69. Janjetović, "Die Konflikte," 122.

70. Milleker, *Geschichte der Stadt Pančevo*, 76.

71. Rothenberg, *The Military Border*, 107.

72. An early plot with a similar goal from 1768 occurred in Karlovac. The 1808 plot is all the more interesting because at least some Germans appear to have been sympathetic to the Ottoman Serbs. Turczynski, "Austro-Serbian Relations," 182–83, 203.

73. Vaníček, *Spezialgeschichte*, 3:296–98. Also in Böhm, *Geschichte des Temeser Banats*, 313–15.

Epilogue: The Banat Germans

1. Möller, *Wie die schwäbischen Gemeinden*, 1:72, 2:153.

2. Petri, *Neubeschenowa*, 66–67.

3. Reprinted in Herrschaft from a previous publication by Adam Müller-Guttenbrunn. Herrschaft, *Das Banat*, 142–46.

4. Interestingly, there appears to be a medieval precedent for this. In 1392, the Germans in Rékás "lived under their own *Grafen* [judge]." Whether or not the Germans in 1848 knew of this is unclear. Milleker, *Geschichte der Städte und des Städtewesens im Banat*, 8.

5. Deák, *The Lawful Revolution*, xvi. Quoted in ibid., 45. In the original document cited by Deák, the second phrase actually preceded the first. I followed his lead quoting them here.

6. Ibid., 41, 61.

7. Deák, *The Lawful Revolution*.

8. Ibid., 329.

9. Milleker, *Geschichte der Stadt Pančevo*, 105–8.

10. Quoted in Deák, *The Lawful Revolution*, 122.

11. When asked to further investigate this incident in 1853, the authorities replied that "in the community there are absolutely no notes" about the incident. In the turbulent year that followed, many documents were destroyed or simply not created, a fact attested to by the paucity of archival holdings in the region from those years. HAK, F. 4, D. 3935-I/1853.

12. Milleker, *Geschichte der Stadt Pančevo*, 108–10.

13. *Fourteen Centuries of Struggle for Freedom*, XXXV.

14. Deák, *The Lawful Revolution*, 128–29.

15. *The Newcastle Courant etc* (Newcastle-upon-Tyne, England), Friday, August 11, 1848.

16. Deák, *The Lawful Revolution*, 245.

17. Quoted in ibid., 260.

18. *Lloyd's Weekly Newspaper* (London, England), Sunday, May 13, 1849.

19. *Lloyd's Weekly Newspaper* (London, England), Sunday, May 20, 1849.

20. The Austrians, in their constitution issued on April 25, promised that "all peoples of the Monarchy are guaranteed the inviolability of their nation and language." Deák, *The Lawful Revolution*, 121.

21. Janjetović, "Die Konflikte," 123–24. Deák, *The Lawful Revolution*, xvii–xviii.

22. While the following will focus on Serb aggression, it is important to note that they also claimed to be victims of barbaric acts at the hands of the Hungarians. Metropolitan Rajačić claimed that the Magyars murdered women, children, and the elderly and desecrated churches. He further claimed that the Magyars disinterred and dismembered bodies, throwing them in wells or leaving them for animals to eat. Evans, "Religion und Nation," 13.

23. Milleker, *Geschichte der Stadt Pančevo*, 119. *Fourteen Centuries of Struggle for Freedom*, XXXV. These irregulars were eventually recalled, thanks to the work of Polish émigrés living in Serbia. Deák, *The Lawful Revolution*, 312.

24. Janjetović, "Die Konflikte," 125.

25. Möller, *Wie die schwäbischen Gemeinden*, 2:169–170.

26. Deák, *The Lawful Revolution*, 45, 78.

27. Möller stressed this point.

28. As Deák put it, "These power centers [in Vienna, Budapest, Innsbruck, Sremski Karlovci, around Radetzky, etc.] struggled for widely divergent objectives; but, at least in this period [spring and summer 1848], they unanimously and exclusively struggled in the name of the emperor-king." Deák, *The Lawful Revolution*, 109.

29. Möller, *Wie die Schwäbischen Gemeinden*, 2:126, 1:72.

30. Siebold, *Deutsches Bauernleben im Banat*, 7–8, 26, 68, 4. Toward the end

of his life, after increased, aggressive taxation and the loss of local men during the occupation of Bosnia-Herzegovina, Siebold was much more subdued. In fact, he said, "We can no longer cry, 'long live freedom!' but rather 'away with this freedom.'" Hans Diplich also briefly commented on this changed outlook in his introduction.

31. The travel involved was no mean feat. Today, it is 127 kilometers from Neubeschenowa (today's Dudeștii Noi, Romania) to Weisskirchen (today's Bela Crkva, Serbia).

32. Böhm, *Geschichte des Temeser Banats*, 338–57.

33. Deák, *The Lawful Revolution*, 141.

34. Janjetović described them as "pogroms." A similar situation almost occurred in Werschetz. Janjetović, "Die Konflikte," 125.

35. Petri, *Neubeschenowa*, 64.

36. Möller, *Wie die schwäbischen Gemeinden*, 1:38.

37. Ibid., 1:72.

38. Janjetović, "Die Konflikte," 124–25. Milleker referred to this incident but did not mention any uprising (planned or otherwise) among the Germans of the town. He later related that "the racial hatred, that at the time [1848] in other places degenerated to murder, is not to be observed in Pančevo, which exhibits a fine testimony to the intelligence of the leaders and the discipline of the people." He also quoted a Serbian priest and observer of the events of 1848 who noted that "Pančevo's Germans were opponents of the Serbian rebellion but no enemies of the Serbian people." Milleker, *Geschichte der Stadt Pančevo*, 114, 125–26. This all may be true, but I think it is worth noting that Milleker was writing shortly after Pancsova and other parts of the Banat had fallen under Serbian control following World War I. It was likely in his interest to promote peaceful interactions between the Serbs and the Germans.

39. Milleker, *Geschichte der Stadt Pančevo*, 112.

40. Möller, *Wie die schwäbischen Gemeinden*, 2:71.

41. Deák, *The Lawful Revolution*, 124.

42. Treptow and Bolovan, *A History of Romania*, 273–75.

43. Deák, *The Lawful Revolution*, 193, 270, 319–21, 325.

44. Ibid., 241, 270.

45. HAK, F. 4, B. 21, D. 2511-I/1850.

46. HAK, F. 4, D. 4157-I/1853.

47. Siebold, *Deutsches Bauernleben im Banat*, 22.

48. Janjetović, "Die Konflikte," 128.

49. Milleker, *Geschichte der Stadt Pančevo*, 146–47, 166, 169. Milleker said that the Serbs even toyed with the idea of taking the city over and resisting the Magyars à la 1848.

50. Janjetović, "Die Konflikte," 127.
51. Milleker, *Kurze Geschichte der Stadt Bela Crkva*, 26.
52. Petri, *Neubeschenowa*, 69.
53. Möller, *Wie die schwäbischen Gemeinden*, 1:13.
54. Janjetović, "Die Konflikte," 128.
55. Great Britain, *Transylvania and the Banat*, 40.
56. *Current History: A Monthly Magazine of the New York Times* 9, October 1919–March 1920, 428.
57. Winkler, *Statistisches Handbuch*, 542.
58. Macartney, *Hungary and Her Successors*, 274. Though here he did admit that Magyarization was taking its toll on the German community, especially its leaders.
59. Ibid., 104.
60. Winkler, *Statistisches Handbuch*, 420. Radonitch gave a more detailed breakdown by district, though only percentages rather than raw numbers. Radonitch, *The Banat*, 10–12.
61. Šević, "The Unfortunate Minority Group," 146.
62. Dillon, *The Inside Story of the Peace Conference*, 239–40.
63. Marin, *A Frontier Region*, 107.
64. Janjetović, "Die Konflikte," 130–32.
65. Macartney, *Hungary and Her Successors*, 394–95. Radonitch, *The Banat*, 14.
66. Janjetović, "Die Konflikte," 130–32.
67. Petri, *Die Festung Temeschwar*, 1–2. Petri put together two books that list various German names for streets and places. These books are simply lists of names, but they provide a great resource for German naming practice along the Danube. Petri, *Vom Aachenibrunnen*; Petri, *Von der "Abschiedsgasse."*
68. Komjathy and Stockwell, *German Minorities and the Third Reich*, 128–29.
69. Janjetović, "Die Konflikte," 129.
70. Ibid., 137–38.
71. Winkler, *Statistisches Handbuch*, 571–72.
72. Janjetović, "Die Konflikte," 131, 134, 135. Lumans, *Himmler's Auxiliaries*, 118.
73. Komjathy and Stockwell made the school situation sound much bleaker. They showed that throughout the 1920s, the Yugoslav government consistently tried to restrict education in the German language. They are not very precise as to where such activities were concentrated, so Šević's contention that things were better in the Banat and Batschka may also be true. Komjathy, *German Minorities*, 127. Lumans also maintained that while German relations with the Slovenes were bad, those with the Serbs and Croats were better. Lumans, *Himmler's Auxiliaries*, 118.
74. Šević, "The Unfortunate Minority," 147–48.

75. Although only 20 to 22 percent of the population, they "controlled a disproportionate share of industry, 40–45 percent. Key industries were from 60 to 80 percent controlled by Germans." Though, interestingly, only 8.6 percent of Germans were industrial workers compared with 14 percent of all adult males in the region. Komjathy, *German Minorities*, 129.

76. Janjetović, "Die Konflikte," 142–44.

77. Lumans, *Himmler's Auxiliaries*, 107.

78. Komjathy, *German Minorities*, 103–8.

79. Winkler, *Statistisches Handbuch*, 572.

80. Komjathy, *German Minorities*, 107.

81. Macartney, *Hungary and her Successors*, 340–41.

82. Komjathy, *German Minorities*, 110.

83. Ibid., 108.

84. Janjetović, "Die Konflikte," 145–48.

85. Petri, *Neubeschenowa*, 79.

86. Janjetović, "Die Konflikte," 136.

87. Komjathy, *German Minorities*, 139.

88. Ibid., 141.

89. Janjetović, "Die Konflikte," 150–52, 155–56.

90. Lumans, *Himmler's Auxiliaries*, 233.

91. Janjetović, "Die Konflikte," 157–61. The nationalities of war criminals cited by the Interior Ministry following the war are interesting. According to an initial report by the ministry, the criminals included 4,071 Reich Germans, 1,223 Austrians, 2,560 Volksdeutsche, 3,618 Italians, 3,325 Hungarians, 1,568 Bulgarians, 247 Albanians, 8,700 Yugoslavs, and 553 "others."

92. Zakić, *Ethnic Germans*, 3–7.

93. Komjathy, *German Minorities*, 143.

94. Lumans, *Himmler's Auxiliaries*, 173, 198, 234.

95. Ibid., 230.

96. Komjathy, *German Minorities*, 120–24.

97. Lumans, *Himmler's Auxiliaries*, 212, 235, 216. For a recounting of the events from a former commander of the unit, see Kumm, *Vorwärts, Prinz Eugen!*.

98. Swanson, "The Second World War," 357.

99. Ibid.

100. Janjetović, "Die Konflikte," 161–65.

101. The number 48,447 is also mentioned in the decidedly pro-German recounting of the events in Wildmann, Sonnleitner, and Weber, *Genocide of the Ethnic Germans in Yugoslavia*, 75. Swanson used the more conservative figure, 10,000. Swanson, "The Second World War," 357.

102. Šević, "The Unfortunate Minority," 154.
103. Janjetović, "Die Konflikte," 166–67.
104. Šević, "The Unfortunate Minority," 154.
105. Lumans, *Himmler's Auxiliaries*, 231–32.
106. Swanson, "The Second World War," 356–57. Lumans put the number between 60,000 and 65,000. He also said that the Romanians protested the deportations. Lumans, *Himmler's Auxiliaries*, 259.
107. Marin, *A Frontier Region*, 143.
108. Petri, *Neubeschenowa*, 79–80. For more on a similar situation in Triebswetter/Tomnatic, see Vultur, "The Role of Ethnicity," 145–48.
109. Quoted in Vultur, "The Role of Ethnicity," 147.
110. Lumans, *Himmler's Auxiliaries*, 259.
111. Batt, "Reinventing Banat," 179.
112. Marin, *A Frontier Region*, 149. Vultur, "The Role of Ethnicity," 141. Iordaci and Dobrincu put the number of deportees from the Banat at 44,000. Iordachi and Dobrincu, "The Communist Take-Over," 487.
113. Petri, *Neubeschenowa*, 79–80.
114. Vultur, "The Role of Ethnicity," 146.
115. Wagner, "Ethnic Germans in Romania," 137. Marin had the emigration occurring between 1973 and 1977. Marin, *A Frontier Region*, 160.
116. Batt, "Reinventing Banat," 179.
117. Šević, "The Unfortunate Minority," 155.
118. Verdery, *Transylvanian Villagers*, 65.

Bibliography

Archives and Collections

Историјски архив у Панчеву: Historical Archive of Pančevo, Serbia (HAP)
F. 4 Magistrat Municipalnog Grada Pančeva, 1794–1918

Историјски архив Кикинда: Historical Archive of Kikinda, Serbia (HAK)
F. 3 Archives of the District
F. 4 Gradski Magistrat Velika Kikinda

Istorijski Arhiv Zrenjanin: Historical Archives of Zrenjanin, Serbia
F. 3 Veliki Bečkerek, grad sa uređenim senatom

Архив Војводине—Нови Сад: Archive of Vojvodina—Novi Sad, Serbia
F. 10 Tamishka Zhupaneya
F. 11 Torontaler Komitat

Österreichisches Staatsarchiv: Austrian National Archives: Vienna, Austria
AT-OeStA/FHKA NHK KaaleU ältere BanaterA Akten 1–57: Ältere Banater Akten
(Selections including AT-OeStA/FHKA NHK Banat A 104 under new system)
AT-OeStA/FHKA NHK KaaleU BanaterA Akten 66: Banater Akten in publico-contentiosis, Temesvarer Banat, Landeseinrichtung (Nr. 12) und Miszellen (Nr. 14)
AT-OeStA/FHKA NHK KaaleU BanaterA Akten 68: Hofrat Kempfische Hofkommission, Berichte an die Hofdeputation in Banaticis und Verordnungen an die Banater Beamten

AT-OeStA/FHKA NHK KaaleU BanaterA Akten 73: Agenden des Departements in Banater Angelegenheiten und der Temesvarer Landesadministration
Including: AT-OeStA/FHKA NHK Banat A 138 (Under new system)
AT-OeStA/FHKA NHK KaaleU BanaterA Akten 81: Temesvarer Landgericht
AT-OeStA/FHKA NHK KaaleU BanaterA Akten 91: Distriktsverwaltung
AT-OeStA/FHKA NHK KaaleU BanaterA Akten 146–55: Deutsche Ansiedlung
AT-OeStA/FHKA NHK KaaleU BanaterA Akten 159–60: Militär-, russische, polnische, türkische, raizische und Zigeuner-Ansiedlung
AT-OeStA/FHKA NHK KaaleU BanaterA Akten 161: Emigration
AT-OeStA/FHKA NHK KaaleU BanaterA Akten 191: Deserteure und Räuberbanden
AT-OeStA/FHKA SUS KS: Kartensammlung
AT-OeStA/FHKA SUS Patente
AT-OeStA/HHStA RHR Passbriefe 15-2-28, 17-3-61, 12-2-59
AT-OeStA/ HHStA Flugschriften 1790: Rede vor Eröffung der illyrischen Nazionalversammlung. Gehalten zu Temeswar. Im August 1790.

Arhivele Naționale ale României, Direcția Județeană Timiș:
Romanian National Archives: Timișoara, Romania
Fond nr. 52: Colecția de documente din achiziții și donații
Fond nr. 67: Primaria Comuniei Gottlob
Fond nr. 99: Primaria Comuniei Lovrin
Fond nr. 117: Colecția de documente Muzeul Banatului
Fond nr. 162: Primaria Orasului Jimbolia
Fond nr. 302: Administratia Imperiala Regala Provinciala a Banatului
Fond nr. 709: Primaria Comuniei Nitchidorf
Fond nr. 1045: Colecția de documente a Muzeului de istorie și etnografie Lugoj

Magyar Orszagos Leveltár: Hungarian National Archives: Budapest, Hungary
E303: Landes-Administration in dem Banat Temesvár: 1716–1779
E305: Ungarische Kameral-Administration zu Temesvár: /1724/ 1779–1848 /1876/

Libraries
Austrian National Library: Vienna, Austria
Hungarian National Library: Budapest, Hungary
New York Public Library: New York, New York

Online Databases and Resources
The following databases were invaluable resources for research and at times as repositories of old and rare books.
Wienerisches Digitarium: Wienerisches Diarium and Zeitung (https://digitarium.acdh.oeaw.ac.at/willkommen/)
British Newspapers 1600–1950: British Library and the Gale, CENGAGE Learning
Google Books: (http://books.google.com/)
Hathi Trust: (http://www.hathitrust.org/)
J-Stor: (http://www.jstor.org/)
Town of Pecica: (www.pecica.ro/)

Published Primary
"Article VII, Definitive Treaty of Peace between the Emperor of Germany and the Ottoman Porte." In *The Parliamentary Register* XXXI, 102–11. London: J Debrett, 1792.
Ağa, Osman. *Der Gefangene der Giauren: die abenteuerlichen Schicksale des Dolmetschers 'Osman Ağa aus Temeschwar.* Translated by Richard Franz Kreutel and Otto Spies. Graz: Verlag Styria, 1962.
Banater Zeitschrift für Landwirthschaft, Handel, Künste und Gewerbe. 1827–1828.
Baróti, Lajos. *Adattár délmagyarország XVIII századi történetéhez.* Temesvár: Nyomatott acsanád-egyházmegyei könyvsajtón, 1900.
Bartenstein, Johann Christoph von. *Kurzer Bericht von der Beschaffenheit der zerstreuten zahlreichen illyrischen Nation in kaiserl. königl. Erblanden.* Frankfurt und Leipzig, 1802.
Becher, Johann Joachim. *Politischer Discurs von den eigentlichen Ursachen des Auf- und Abnehmens der Städt, Länder und Republiken . . . von dem Bauren- Handwercks und Kaufmannsstand derer Handel und Wandel.* Frankfurt, M.: Joh. David Zunner, 1668.
Beschreibung des Banats, der Walachey, Moldau und der Königreiche Servien und Bosnien, aus den besten Schriftstellern gezogen. Ein Beitrag zur nähern Kenntniss des Gegenwärtigen Kreigsschauplazzes. Leipzig: Carl Friederich Schneidern, 1789.
Böhm, Lénert. *Geschichte des Temeser Banats.* Leipzig: Otto Wigand, 1861.
Born, Ignaz, Rudolf Erich Raspe, and Johann Jakob Ferber. *Travels through the Bannat of Temeswar, Transylvania, and Hungary, in the Year 1770. Described in a Series of Letters to Prof. Ferber, on the Mines and Mountains of These Different Countries.* London: J. Miller, for G. Kearsley, 1777.
Bright, Richard. *Travels from Vienna through Lower Hungary: With Some Remarks on the State of Vienna during the Congress, in the Year 1814.* Edinburgh: Archibald Constable and Company, 1818.

Büsching, Anton Friedrich, and Christoph Daniel Ebeling. *Erdbeschreibung.* 2 *Zweyter Theil, welcher Ost- und West-Preußen, Polen und Litauen, Galizien und Lodomerien, Ungarn, die denselben einverleibten Reiche und Siebenbürgen, die Republik Ragusa und das osmanische Reich, enthält.* Hamburg: Bohn, 1788.

Clarke, Edward Daniel. *Travels in Various Countries of Europe, Asia, and Africa: Part the First. Russia, Tartary, and Turkey.* Philadelphia: Anthony Finley, 1811.

Current History: A Monthly Magazine of the New York Times. Volume 9, October, 1919–March, 1920.

Dillon, Emile Joseph. *The Inside Story of the Peace Conference.* New York: Harper & Bros., 1920.

Dorner, Joseph von. *Das Banat in topographisch, naturhistorischer Beziehung mit besonderer Berücksichtigung der Herculesbäder nächst Mehadia und ihrer Umgebungen: nebst einer ausführlichen Schilderung der Reise in die Bäder mit den Dampfschiffen und zu Lande, und einer Beschreibung der an den banatischen Donauufern vorkommenden Alterthümer.* Pressburg: Wigand, 1839.

Dumont, Jean. *The Military History of His Serene Highness Prince Eugene of Savoy . . . As Also of His Grace the Late Duke of Marlborough . . . and of His Serene Highness the Prince of Nassau-Friezland . . . Containing a Particular Description of All the Principal Transactions of the Last War . . . Together with Memoirs of the Life of Prince Eugene.* Translated by Paul Chamberlen. London: W. Rayner, 1736.

Eimann, Johann. *Der deutsche Kolonist oder die deutsche Ansiedlung unter Kaiser Josef II. In den Jahren 1783 bis 1787 besonders im Königreich Ungarn in dem Batscher Komitat.* Edited by Friedrich Lotz. 1820. Reprint, München: Verlag des Südostdeutschen Kulturwerks, 1965.

Great Britain. *Transylvania and the Banat.* London: H. M. Stationery Off, 1920.

Griselini, Francesco. *Aus dem Versuch einer politischen und natürlichen Geschichte des Temeswarer Banats in Briefen 1716–1778. Erschienen bei J. P. Krauss. Wien 1780.* München: Verlag des Südostdeutschen Kulturwerkes, 1969.

Guthrie, Katherine Blanche. *Through Russia: From St. Petersburg to Astrakhan and the Crimea.* Vol. 2. London: Hurst and Blackett, 1874.

Hamilton's Bericht. "Chorographia Bannatus Temessiensis sub auspiciis novi gubernatoris edita (1734)." In Wolf, *Quellen zur Wirtschafts-*, 47–127.

Haxthausen, August von. *Studies on the Interior of Russia.* 1843. Reprint, Chicago: University of Chicago Press, 1972.

Holderness, Mary. *New Russia.* London: Sherwood, Jones, 1823.

Hörnigk, Philipp Wilhelm von. *Österreich über alles, wann es nur will.* Edited by Horst Knapp, Hannes Androsch, Helmut Haschek, and Franz Vranitzky. 1684. Reprint, Wien: Edition Wirtschaft, 1983.

Klaniczay, Johann v. *Nachricht über die glückliche Verpflanzung der Olivenstaude aus Istrien in's Banat.* Temeswar, 1809.

Kohl, J. G. *Austria. Vienna, Prague, Hungary, Bohemia, and the Danube; Galicia, Styria, Moravia, Bukovina, and the Military Frontier.* London: Chapman and Hall, 1843.

———. *Russia.* London: Chapman and Hall, 1844.

———. *Travels in Ireland.* London: Bruce and Wyld, 1844.

Lady. *The Englishwoman in Russia.* 1855. Reprint, New York: Arno Press, 1970.

Mackenzie, G. Muir, and A. P. Irby. *Travels in the Slavonic Provinces of Turkey-in-Europe.* London: Daldy, Isbister, 1877.

Macmichael, William. *Journey from Moscow to Constantinople in the Years 1817, 1818.* London: John Murray, Albemarle-Street, 1819.

Mai, Brent Alan. *1798 Census of the German Colonies along the Volga: Economy, Population, and Agriculture.* Lincoln, NE: American Historical Society of Germans from Russia, 1999.

Matuschka, Ludwig. *Feldzüge des Prinzen Eugen von Savoyen Serie 2, Bd. 8 = Bd. 17.* Wien: Gerold, 1891.

———. *Feldzüge des Prinzen Eugen von Savoyen Serie 2, Bd. 8 = Bd. 16.* Wien: Gerold, 1891.

Meakin, Annette M. B. *Russia: Travels and Studies.* 1906. Reprint, New York: Arno Press, 1971.

Montagu, Mary Wortley, and Robert Halsband. *The Complete Letters of Lady Mary Wortley Montagu.* Vol. 1. Oxford: Clarendon Press, 1965.

Oesterreichische Monatsschrift für Forstwesen. Edited by Josef Wesseln. Wien: Verlag des österreichischen Reichsforstvereines, 1878.

Ottendorf, Heinrich. *Budáról Belgrádba 1663-ban Ottendorf Henrik képes útleírása.* Edited by Hermann Egyed. Budapest: Eggenberger, 1943.

Paget, John. *Hungary and Transylvania; With Remarks on Their Condition, Social, Political and Economical.* Vol. 2. London: J. Murray, 1839.

Palmer, Francis H. E. *Russian Life in Town and Country.* New York: The Knickerbocker Press, 1902.

Paton, A. A. *The Bulgarian, the Turk, and the German.* London: Longman, Brown, Green, and Longmans, 1855.

———. *Researches on the Danube and the Adriatic; Or, Contributions to the Modern History of Hungary and Transylvania, Dalmatia and Croatia, Servia and Bulgaria.* Vol. 2. London: Trübner, 1862.

The Penny Cyclopaedia of the Society for the Diffusion of Useful Knowledge. Vol. 16. London: Charles Knight, 1840.

"Public Instruction in Hungary, Croatia, Slavonia." *The American Journal of Education.* Edited by Henry Barnard. Vol. 17. New York: J. H. Schermerhorn, 1867.

Radonitch, Yovan. *The Banat and the Serbo-Roumanian Frontier Problem*. Paris: Ligue des Universitaires Serbo-Croato-Slovènes, 1919.

Real-Zeitung auf das Jahr 1788. Edited by Johann Heinrich Gross. Nurnberg: Aus dem Kaiserlichen Ober=Postamt, 1788.

Schönbauer, Joseph Anton. *Geschichte der schädlichen Kolumbatczer Mücken im Bannat, also ein Beytrag zur Naturgeschichte von Ungarn*. Wien: Alb. Ant. Patzowsky, 1795.

Schröder, Wilhelm von. *Fürstliche Schatz- und Rent-Cammer: ad augustissimum & invictissimum imperatorem Leopoldum I. principem triumphantem*. Leipzig: Gerdesius, 1686.

Siebold, Mathias. *Deutsches Bauernleben im Banat; Hausbuch des Mathias Siebold aus Neubeschenowa, Banat, 1842–1878*. München: Verlag des Südostdeutschen Kulturwerks, 1957.

Steube, Johann Kaspar. *Von Amsterdam nach Temiswar. Wanderschaften und Schicksale*. Edited by Jochen Golz. 1791. Reprint, Berlin: Rütten & Loening, 1969.

Tafferner, Anton. *Quellenbuch zur donauschwäbischen Geschichte: Mit einem chronologischen Quellenverzeichnis (Band I—V) und einer historiographischen Einleitung des Verfassers*. München: Meschendörfer, 1974–1995.

Tallar, Georg. *Visum repertum anatomico-chirurgicum, oder, Gründlicher Bericht von den sogenannten Blutsäugern, Vampier, oder in der wallachischen Sprache Moroi, in der Wallachey, Siebenbürgen, und Banat: welchen eine eigends dahin abgeordnete Untersuchungskommission der löbl. k. k. Administration im Jahre 1756 erstattet hat*. Wien und Leipzig: Johann Georg Mössle, 1784.

Temeswarer Wochenblatt. 1841.

Thiele, J. C. v. *Das Königreich Ungarn: ein topographisch-historisch-statistisches Kundgemälde, das Ganze dieses Landes in mehr denn 12,400 Artikeln umfassend*. Kaschau: J. C. v. Thiele, 1833.

Tooke, William. *View of the Russian Empire*. Vol. 3. London: T. N. Longman and O. Rees, 1800.

Wilhelm, Franz, and Josef Kallbrunner. *Quellen zur deutschen Siedlungsgeschichte in Südosteuropa. Im Auftrage der Deutschen Akademie und des Gesamtvereines der deutschen Geschichts- und Altertumsvereine*. München: E. Reinhardt, 1936.

Wolf, Josef. *Quellen zur Wirtschafts-, Sozial- und Verwaltungsgeschichte des Banats im 18. Jahrhundert*. Tübingen: Institut für donauschäbische Geschichte und Landeskunde, 1995.

Secondary Sources

Achim, Viorel. *The Roma in Romanian History*. Budapest: Central European University Press, 2004.

Adam, Ulrich. *The Political Economy of J. H. G. Justi*. Bern: Peter Lang, 2006.

Allgemeine deutsche Real-Encyclopädie für die gebildeten Stände. Vol. 5. Leipzig: Brockhaus, 1824.

Avrich, Paul. *Russian Rebels: 1600–1800*. New York: Schocken, 1972.

Bailyn, Bernard. *The Peopling of British North America*. New York: Knopf, 1986.

Banac, Ivo, John G. Ackerman, Roman Szporluk, and Wayne S. Vucinich, eds. *Nation and Ideology: Essays in Honor of Wayne S. Vucinich*. Boulder, CO: East European Monographs, 1981.

Bartlett, Roger P. *Human Capital: The Settlement of Foreigners in Russia, 1762–1804*. Cambridge: Cambridge University Press, 1979.

Baumann, Julius A. *Geschichte der Banater Berglanddeutschen Volksgruppe: ein Beitrag zur Geschichte des Temeser Banats*. Wien: Österreichische Landsmannschaft, 1989.

Beales, Derek Edward Dawson. *Joseph II*. Vols. 1 and 2. Cambridge: Cambridge University Press, 1987, 2009.

Brown, Kate. *A Biography of No Place: From Ethnic Borderland to Soviet Heartland*. Cambridge, MA: Harvard University Press, 2005.

Burke, Peter. *Popular Culture in Early Modern Europe*. Farnham, England: Ashgate, 2009.

———. *What Is Cultural History?* Cambridge: Polity Press, 2008.

Carley, Kenneth. *The Dakota War of 1862*. St. Paul: Minnesota Historical Society, 1976.

Clark, Christopher. *Iron Kingdom*. Cambridge, MA: Harvard University Press, 2006.

Davies, Brian L. *Warfare, State and Society on the Black Sea Steppe: 1500–1700*. London: Routledge, 2007.

Davis, Robert C. *Holy War and Human Bondage: Tales of Christian-Muslim Slavery in the Early-Modern Mediterranean*. Santa Barbara, CA: ABC-CLIO, 2009.

Deák, István. *The Lawful Revolution: Louis Kossuth and the Hungarians, 1848–1849*. New York: Columbia University Press, 1979.

Edroiu, Nicolae. *Horea's Uprising: The 1784 Romanian Peasants' Revolt of Transylvania*. Bucharest: Editura științifica și enciclopedică, 1978.

Efron, John M., Steven Weitzman, and Matthias B. Lehmann. *The Jews: A History*. Boston: Pearson, 2014.

Fata, Márta. *Migration im kameralistischen Staat Josephs II: Theorie und Praxis der Ansiedlungpolitik in Ungarn, Siebenbürgen, Galizien und der Bukowina von 1768–1790*. Münster: Aschendorff Verlag, 2014.

Fichtner, Paula S. *The Habsburgs: Dynasty, Culture and Politics*. London: Reaktion Books, 2014.

———.*Terror and Toleration: The Habsburg Empire Confronts Islam, 1526–1850*. London: Reaktion Books, 2008.

Finkel, Caroline. *Osman's Dream: The Story of the Ottoman Empire, 1300–1923*. New York: Basic Books, 2006.

Fodor, Pál, and Géza Dávid. *Ottomans, Hungarians, and Habsburgs in Central Europe: The Military Confines in the Era of Ottoman Conquest*. Leiden: Brill, 2000.

Fourteen Centuries of Struggle for Freedom. Edited by Idris Ćejvan. Belgrade: Military Museum, 1968.

Göllner, Carl. *Die Siebenbürgische Militärgrenze: ein Beitrag zur Sozial- und Wirtschaftsgeschichte 1762–1851*. München: Oldenbourg, 1974.

Haar, Ingo, and Michael Fahlbusch, *German Scholars and Ethnic Cleansing, 1919–1945*. New York: Berghahn Books, 2005.

Hammer, Anton Von. *Geschichte der Pest, die von 1738 bis 1740 im Temeswarer Banat herrschte*. Edited by Walther Konschitzky and Costin Fenesan. 1839. Reprint, Erding: Banat Verlag, 2011.

Harzig, Christine, and Dirk Hoerder. *What Is Migration History?* Cambridge: Polity Press, 2009.

Height, Joseph S. *Paradise on the Steppe: A Cultural History of the Kutschurgan, Beresan, and Liebental Colonists, 1804–1944*. Bismarck: North Dakota Society of Germans from Russia, 1972.

Herrschaft, Hans. *Das Banat; ein deutsches Siedlungsgebiet in Südosteuropa*. Berlin: Verlag Grenze und Ausland, 1942.

Hitchins, Keith. *The Idea of Nation: The Romanians of Transylvania, 1691–1849*. Bucharest: Editura ştiinţifica şi enciclopedică, 1985.

———. *The Romanians, 1774–1866*. Oxford: Clarendon Press, 1996.

Hixson, Walter L. *American Settler Colonialism: A History*. New York: Palgrave-Macmillan, 2013.

Hochedlinger, Michael. *Austria's Wars of Emergence: War, State and Society in the Habsburg Monarchy, 1683–1797*. Harlow: Longman, 2003.

Hoerder, Dirk. *Cultures in Contact: World Migration in the Second Millennium*. Durham, NC: Duke University Press, 2002.

Hoffmann, Elke. *Städte und Dörfer: Beiträge zur Siedlungsgeschichte der Deutschen im Banat*. München: Landsmannschaft der Banater Schwaben, 2011.

Hoffmann, Leo. *Kurze Geschichte der Banater Deutschen. Von 1717 bis 1848*. Temesvar: Druck der Schwäbischen Verlags-Aktien-Gesellschaft, 1925.

Horváth, Jenő. *The Banat: A Forgotten Chapter of European History.* Budapest: Sárkány, 1931.

Hromadka, Georg. *Kleine Chronik des Banater Berglands.* München: Verl. Südostdt. Kulturwerk, 1993.

Hughes, Robert. *The Fatal Shore.* New York: Knopf, 1987.

Hupchick, Dennis P. *The Bulgarians in the Seventeenth Century: Slavic Orthodox Society and Culture under Ottoman Rule.* Jefferson, NC: McFarland, 1993.

Ingrao, Charles W. *The Habsburg Monarchy, 1618–1815.* Cambridge: Cambridge University Press, 2000, 2019.

Ingrao, Charles, Nikola Samardžić, and Jovan Pešalj, eds. *The Peace of Passarowitz, 1718.* West Lafayette, IN: Purdue University Press, 2011.

Ingrao, Charles, and Franz A. J. Szabo, eds. *The Germans and the East.* West Lafayette, IN: Purdue University Press, 2008.

Iordachi, Constantin, and Dorin Dobrincu, eds. *Transforming Peasants, Property and Power: The Collectivization of Agriculture in Romania, 1949–1962.* Budapest: Central European University Press, 2009.

István, Márta, and Josef Lang. *Gedenkstätten der Donauschwaben in der Batschka, im Banat, in Syrmien.* Kikinda: Donauschwäbisches Archiv, 2010.

Jivi-Banatanu, Ioan. *The Banat Problem.* Cleveland, OH: Roumanian National League of America, 1920.

Jordan, Sonja. *Die kaiserliche Wirtschaftspolitik im Banat im 18. Jahrhundert.* München: Oldenbourg, 1967.

Kallbrunner, Josef. *Das kaiserliche Banat.* München: Verlag des Südostdeutschen Kulturwerks, 1958.

Kann, Robert A., and Zdeněk V. David. *The Peoples of the Eastern Habsburg Lands, 1526–1918.* Seattle: University of Washington Press, 1984.

Khodarkovsky, Michael. *Where Two Worlds Met: The Russian State and the Kalmyk Nomads, 1600–1771.* Ithaca, NY: Cornell University Press, 1992.

Klaus, A. *Unsere Kolonien: Studien und Materialien zur Geschichte und Statistik der ausländischen Kolonisation in Russland.* Translated by J. Toews. Odessa: Verlag der "Odessaer Zeitung," 1887.

Knittle, Walter Allen. *Early Eighteenth Century Palatine Emigration: A British Government Redemptioner Project to Manufacture Naval Stores.* Philadelphia: Dorrance, 1937.

Koch, Fred C. *The Volga Germans: In Russia and the Americas, from 1763 to the Present.* University Park: The Pennsylvania State University Press, 1977.

Komjathy, Anthony Tihamer, and Rebecca Stockwell. *German Minorities and the Third Reich: Ethnic Germans of East Central Europe between the Wars.* New York: Holmes & Meier, 1980.

Kosáry, Domokos G. *Culture and Society in Eighteenth-Century Hungary.* Budapest: Corvina, 1987.

Krischan, Alexander. *Die deutsche periodische Literatur des Banats: Zeitungen, Zeitschriften, Kalender 1771–1971: Bibliographie.* München: Verlag des Südostdeutschen Kulturwerkes, 1987.

Kumm, Otto. *Vorwärts, Prinz Eugen! Geschichte d. 7. SS-Freiwilligen-Division "Prinz Eugen."* Osnabrück: Munin, 1978.

Lemon, James T. *The Best Poor Man's Country: Early Southeastern Pennsylvania.* Baltimore: Johns Hopkins University Press, 2002.

Liulevicius, Vejas G. *The German Myth of the East: 1800 to the Present.* Oxford: Oxford University Press, 2009.

Livi-Bacci, Massimo. *A Short History of Migration.* Translated by Carl Ipsen. Cambridge: Polity Press, 2012.

Lotz, Friedrich, and Josef Volkmar Senz. *Festschrift für Friedrich Lotz.* München: Verlag des Südostdeutschen Kulturwerks, 1962.

Luebke, David Martin. *His Majesty's Rebels: Communities, Factions, and Rural Revolt in the Black Forest, 1725–1745.* Ithaca, NY: Cornell University Press, 1997.

Lumans, Valdis O. *Himmler's Auxiliaries: The Volksdeutsche Mittelstelle and the German National Minorities of Europe, 1933–1945.* Chapel Hill: University of North Carolina Press, 1993.

Macartney, C. A. *Hungary and Her Successors; The Treaty of Trianon and Its Consequences 1919–1937.* London: Oxford University Press, 1937.

MacDonogh, Giles. *Frederick the Great: A Life in Deeds and Letters.* New York: St. Martin's Press, 1999.

Manning, Patrick, and Tiffany Trimmer. *Migration in World History.* New York: Routledge, 2020.

Marin, Irina. *A Frontier Region in the Balkans: A History of the Banats of Eastern Europe since the Ottomans.* London: I. B. Tauris, 2012.

McNeill, William H. *Europe's Steppe Frontier, 1500–1800.* Chicago: University of Chicago Press, 1964.

Milleker, Felix. *Die erste organisierte deutsche Kolonisation des Banats unter Mercy, 1722–1726: aus Anlass der 200-Jahr-Feier der Einwanderung.* Werschetz: Verlag der Art. Anstalt J. E. Kirchner's Witwe, 1923.

———. *Geschichte der Stadt Pančevo.* Pančevo: Druck u. Kommissions-Verlag von Karl Wittigschlager, 1925.

———. *Geschichte der Städte und des Städtewesens im Banat.* Wrschatz: Druck und Verlag der Artistischen Anstalt J. E. Kirchner's Witwe, 1925.

———. *Kurze Geschichte des Banats.* Wrschatz: Druck und Verlag der Art. Anstalt J.E. Kirchner's Witwe, 1925.

———.*Kurze Geschichte der Stadt Bela Crkva (Weisskirchen) im Banat, 1355–1918.* Bela Crkva: Druck und Verlag von Peter Kuhn, 1927.
Moch, Leslie Page. *Moving Europeans: Migration in Western Europe since 1650.* Bloomington: Indiana University Press, 1992.
Möller, Karl von. *Deutsches Schicksal im Banat.* Wien/Leipzig: Adolf Luser Verlag, 1940.
———. *Wie die schwäbischen Gemeinden entstanden sind.* Vols. 1 and 2. Temesvar: Schwäb. Verl.-Aktien-Ges, 1923/1924.
Neumann, Victor. *Multicultural Identities in a Europe of Regions: The Case of Banat County*, Discussion Papers No. 34. Budapest: Collegium Budapest/Institute for Advanced Study, 1996.
Pálffy, Géza. *Hungary between Two Empires, 1526–1711.* Translated by David Robert Evans. Bloomington: Indiana University Press, 2021.
Pascu, Ștefan. *A History of Transylvania.* Translated by D. Robert Ladd. Detroit: Wayne State University Press, 1982.
Petri, Anton Peter. *Die Festung Temeschwar im 18. Jahrhundert. Beiträge zur Erinnerung an die Befreiung der Banater Hauptstadt vor 250 Jahren.* München: Verlag des Südostdeutsche Kulturwerks, 1966.
———. *Neubeschenowa: Geschichte einer moselfränkischen Gemeinde im rumänischen Banat.* Freilassing: Pannonia-Verlag, 1963.
———. *Vom Aachenibrunnen bis zur Zwölften Gasse: die Gassennamen der deutschen Siedlungen des vortrianonischen Banats: Versuch einer Sammlung und Sichtung.* München: Verlag des Südostdeutschen Kulturwerks, 1975.
———. *Von der "Abschiedsgasse" bis zum "Zwölfhaus": die Gassennamen in den ehemaligen deutschen Siedlungen der Batschka, Bosniens, der jugoslawischen Baranya, Kroatiens, Slawoniens und Syrmiens: Versuch einer Sammlung und Sichtung.* München: Verlag des Südostdeutschen Kulturwerks, 1980.
Pratt, Mary Louise. *Imperial Eyes: Travel Writing and Transculturation.* London: Routledge, 1992.
Rady, Martyn. *The Habsburgs: To Rule the World.* New York: Basic Books, 2020.
Raeff, Marc. *The Well-Ordered Police State: Social and Institutional Change through Law in the Germanies and Russia, 1600–1800.* New Haven, CT: Yale University Press, 1983.
Rees, Siân. *The Floating Brothel: The Extraordinary True Story of an Eighteenth-Century Ship and Its Cargo of Female Convicts.* New York: Hyperion, 2002.
Ringrose, David R. *Spain, Europe, and the "Spanish Miracle," 1700–1900.* Cambridge: Cambridge University Press, 1998.
Roeber, A. G. *Palatines, Liberty, and Property: German Lutherans in Colonial British America.* Baltimore: Johns Hopkins University Press, 1993.

Roider, Karl A. *Austria's Eastern Question, 1700–1790*. Princeton, NJ: Princeton University Press, 1982.

———. *The Reluctant Ally; Austria's Policy in the Austro-Turkish War, 1737–1739*. Baton Rouge: Louisiana State University Press, 1972.

Roth, Erik. *Die planmässig angelegten Siedlungen im Deutsch-Banater Militärgrenzbezirk, 1765–1821*. München: R. Oldenbourg, 1988.

Rothenberg, Gunther E. *The Austrian Military Border in Croatia, 1522–1747*. Urbana: University of Illinois Press, 1960.

———. *The Military Border in Croatia, 1740–1881: A Study of an Imperial Institution*. Chicago: University of Chicago Press, 1966.

Russell-Wood, A. J. R. *A World on the Move: The Portuguese in Africa, Asia, and America, 1415–1808*. New York: St. Martin's Press, 1993.

Schmidt, Horst Dieter. *Ein verschwundenes Dorf im Banat: Bevölkerungsbiologische Untersuchungen der böhmer-deutschen Gemeinde Lindenfeld*. Langenau-Ulm: A. Vaas, 1991.

Schrad, Mark Lawrence. *Vodka Politics: Alcohol, Autocracy, and the Secret History of the Russian State*. Oxford: Oxford University Press, 2016.

Schünemann, Konrad. *Österreichs Bevölkerungspolitik unter Maria Theresia*. Berlin: Deutsche Rundschau, 1935.

Small, Albion Woodbury. *The Cameralists: The Pioneers of German Social Polity*. New York: Burt Franklin, 1909.

Smith, Pamela H. *The Business of Alchemy: Science and Culture in the Holy Roman Empire*. Princeton, NJ: Princeton University Press, 1994.

Springenschmid, Karl. *Our Lost Children: Janissaries?* Milwaukee, WI: Danube Swabian Association of the U.S.A., 1980.

Stanglica, Franz. *Die Auswanderung der Lothringer in das Banat und die Batschka im 18. Jahrhundert*. Frankfurt a.M.: Selbstverlag des Elsass-Lothringen-Instituts, 1934.

Steiner, Stefan. *Rückkehr Unerwünscht: Deportationen in der Habsburgermonarchie der Frühen Neuzeit und ihr europäischer Kontext*. Wien: Böhlau, 2014.

Sugar, Peter. *Southeastern Europe under Ottoman Rule, 1354–1804*. Seattle: University of Washington Press, 1996.

Sunderland, Willard. *Taming the Wild Field: Colonization and Empire on the Russian Steppe*. Ithaca, NY: Cornell University Press, 2004.

Szabo, Franz A. J. *Kaunitz and Enlightened Absolutism, 1753–1780*. Cambridge: Cambridge University Press, 1994.

Tinta, Aurel. *Colonizările habsburgice în Banat. 1716–1740*. Timişoara: Facla, 1972.

Todorova, Marie. *Imagining the Balkans*. Oxford: Oxford University Press, 2009.

Treptow, Kurt W. and Ioan Bolovan. *A History of Romania*. Boulder, CO: East European Monographs, 1996.

Tribe, Keith. *Governing Economy: The Reformation of German Economic Discourse, 1750–1840*. Cambridge: Cambridge University Press, 1988.
Vaníček, Fr. *Spezialgeschichte der Militärgrenze aus Originalquellen und Quellenwerken geschöpft von Fr. Vaníček*. Vol. 3. Wien: K.K. Hof- Und Staatsdruckerei, 1875.
Veracini, Lorenzo. *Settler Colonialism: A Theoretical Overview*. Houndmills, Basingstoke: Palgrave Macmillan, 2010.
Verdery, Katherine. *Transylvanian Villagers: Three Centuries of Political, Economic, and Ethnic Change*. Berkeley: University of California Press, 1983.
Wakefield, Andre. *The Disordered Police State: German Cameralism as Science and Practice*. Chicago: University of Chicago Press, 2009.
Walker, Mack. *Germany and the Emigration, 1816–1885*. Cambridge, MA: Harvard University Press, 1964.
———. *The Salzburg Transaction: Expulsion and Redemption in Eighteenth-Century Germany*. Ithaca, NY: Cornell University Press, 1992.
Wandruszka, Adam. *Leopold II., Erzherzog von Österreich, Grossherzog von Toskana, König von Ungarn und Böhmen, römischer Kaiser: Band II: 1780–1792*. Wien: Verlag Herold, 1965.
Wangermann, Ernst. *The Austrian Achievement, 1700–1800*. London: Thames and Hudson, 1973.
Weidlein, Johann. *Entwicklung der Dorfanlagen im donauschwäbischen Bereich*. Stuttgart: Landsmannschaft der Donauschwaben in Baden-Württemberg e.V., 1965.
Weiss, Josef. *Die deutsche Kolonie an der Sierra Morena und ihr Gründer Johann Kaspar von Thürriegel, ein bayerischer Abenteurer des 18. Jahrhunderts*. Köln: 1907.
White, Richard. *The Middle Ground: Indians, Empires, and Republics in the Great Lakes Region, 1650–1815*. Cambridge: Cambridge University Press, 1991.
Wildmann, Georg, Hans Sonnleitner, and Karl Weber. *Genocide of the Ethnic Germans in Yugoslavia, 1944–1948*. Santa Ana, CA: Danube Swabian Association of the U.S.A., 2001.
Winkler, Wilhelm. *Statistisches Handbuch des gesamten Deutschtums*. Berlin: Deutsche Rundschau, 1927.
Wokeck, Marianne S. *Trade in Strangers: The Beginnings of Mass Migration to North America*. University Park: The Pennsylvania State University Press, 1999.
Wolff, Larry. *The Idea of Galicia*. Stanford, CA: Stanford University Press, 2010.
———. *Inventing Eastern Europe: The Map of Civilization on the Mind of the Enlightenment*. Stanford, CA: Stanford University Press, 1994.
Wolff, Stefan, ed. *German Minorities in Europe: Ethnic Identity and Cultural Belonging*. New York: Berghahn Books, 2000.

Zakić, Mirna. *Ethnic Germans and National Socialism in Yugoslavia in World War II*. Cambridge: Cambridge University Press, 2017.

Articles, Chapters, and Dissertations

Adler, Philip J. "Serbs, Magyars, and Staatsinteresse in Eighteenth Century Austria: A Study in the History of the Habsburg Administration." *Austrian History Yearbook* XII–XIII (1976–1977): 116–47.

Anderson, Timothy G. "Cameralism and the Production of Space in the Eighteenth-Century Romanian Banat: The Grid Villages of the 'Danube Swabians.'" *Journal of Historical Geography* 69 (2020): 55–67.

Banac, Ivo. "The Role of Vojvodina in Karadjordje's Revolution." *Südost Forschungen* 40 (January 1981): 31–61.

Batt, Judy. "Reinventing Banat." In *Region, State, and Identity in Central and Eastern Europe*, edited by Judy Batt and Kataryna Wolczuk, 178–202. London: Frank Cass, 2002.

Brandes, Detlef. "Einwanderung und Entwicklung der Kolonien." In *Russland*. Vol. 7 of *Deutsche Geschichte im Osten Europas*, edited by Gerd Stricker, 35–111. Berlin: Wolf Jobst Siedler Verlag GmbH, 1997.

———. "Fragen an der Geschichte der Deutsche in Russland." In Stricker, *Russland*, 13–20.

Brandy, Joel, and Edin Hajdarpasic. "Religion and Ethnicity: Conflicting and Converging Identification." In *The Routledge History of East Central Europe since 1700*, edited by Irina Livezeanu and Árpád von Klimó, 176–214. New York: Routledge, 2017.

Clogg, Richard. "The Greek Merchant Companies in Transylvania." In *Minderheiten, Regional-Bewußtsein und Zentralismus in Ostmittleleuropa*, edited by Heinz-Dietrich Löwe, Günther H. Tontsch, and Stefan Troebst, 161–69. Köln: Böhlau Verlag, 2000.

Dabić, Vojin. "The Habsburg-Ottoman War of 1716–1718 and Demographic Changes in the War Affected Territories." In Ingrao, Samardžic, and Pešalj, *The Peace of Passarowitz, 1718*, 191–208.

Dávid, Géza. "The 'Eyalet' of Temesvár in the Eighteenth Century." In "The Ottoman Empire in the Eighteenth Century." Special issue, *Oriente Moderno*, n.s. 18 (79), no. 1 (1999): 113–28.

Dyck, Harvey L. "New Serbia and the Origins of the Eastern Question, 1751–55: A Habsburg Perspective." *Russian Review* 40 (1981): 1–19.

Elibol, Numan, and Abdullah Mesud Küçükkalay. "Implementation of the Commercial Treaty of Passarowitz and the Austrian Merchants, 1720–1750." In Ingrao, Samardžic, and Pešalj, *The Peace of Passarowitz, 1718*, , 159–78.

Engel, Walter. foreword to *Kulturraum Banat: deutsche Kultur in einer europäischen Vielvölkerregion; [interdisziplinäres Symposion, Temeswar/ Timisoara, 23.-25. September 2004]*, edited by Walter Engel, 7–9. Essen: Klartext, 2007.

Evans, Robert J. W. "Religion und Nation in Ungarn, 1790–1849." In *Siebenbürgen in der Habsburgermonarchie: Von Leopoldium bis zum Ausgleich (1690–1867)*, edited by Zsolt K. Lengyel and Ulrich A. Wien, 13–45. Köln: Böhlau Verlag, 1999.

Fata, Márta. "Einwanderung und Ansiedlung der Deutschen (1686–1790)." In *Land an der Donau*, edited by Günter Schödl, 89–196. Berlin: Siedler, 1995.

Fenske, Hans. "International Migration: Germany in the Eighteenth Century." *Central European History* 13, no. 4 (December 1980): 332–47.

Fleischhauer, Ingeborg. "The Nationalities Policy of the Tsars Reconsidered—The Case of the Russian Germans." In "On Demand." Supplement, *The Journal of Modern History* 53, no. 1 (March 1981): D1065–D1090.

Fodor, Pál. "Das Wilajet von Temeschwar zur Zeit der osmanischen Eroberung." *Südost Forschungen* 55 (January 1996): 25–44.

Frank, Alison. "The Children of the Desert and the Laws of the Sea: Austria, Great Britain, the Ottoman Empire, and the Mediterranean Slave Trade in the Nineteenth Century." *American Historical Review* (April 2012): 410–44.

Freund, Wolfgang. "Palatines All Over the World: Fritz Braun, a German Emigration Researcher in National Socialist Population Policy." In *German Scholars and Ethnic Cleansing, 1919–1945*, edited by Ingo Haar and Michael Fahlbusch, 153–74. New York: Berghahn Books, 2005.

Gabaccia, Donna R. "Historical Migration Studies: Time, Temporality, and Theory." In *Migration Theory: Talking across Disciplines*, edited by Caroline B. Brettell and James F. Hollifield, 44–77. New York: Routledge, 2023.

Gittermann, Alexandra. "German Emigrants as a Commodity in the Eighteenth-Century Atlantic World." In *Globalized Peripheries: Central Europe and the Atlantic World, 1680–1860*, edited by Jutta Wimmler and Klaus Weber, 187–203. Woodridge, Suffolk: The Boydell Press, 2020.

Hambuch, Wendelin. "Nachwort." In *300 Jahre Zusammenleben: aus der Geschichte der Ungarndeutschen: Internationale Historikerkonferenz in Budapest (5–6. März 1987)*. Vol. 2, edited by Wendelin Hambuch, 331–37. Budapest: Tankönyvk, 1988.

Hauben, Paul J. "The First Decade of an Agrarian Experiment in Bourbon Spain: The 'New Towns' of Sierra Morena and Andalusia, 1766–76." *Agricultural History* 39, no. 1 (1965): 34–40.

Held, Joseph. "The Horea-Closca Revolt of 1784–85: Some Observations." In

Transylvania: The Roots of Ethnic Conflict, edited by John F. Cadzow, Andrew Ludanyi, and Louis J. Elteto, 93–107. Kent, OH: The Kent State University Press, 1983.

Hegedüs, Antal. "Joseph II und die Refeudalisierung des Banats." In *Österreich im Europa der Aufklärung: Kontinuität und Zäsur in Europa zur Zeit Maria Theresias und Josephs II.: internationales Symposion in Wien 20.-23. Oktober 1980*, edited by Richard Georg Plaschka et al., 139–52. Wien: Verlag der Österreichischen Akademie der Wissenschaften, 1985.

Hodson, Brian A. "The Development of Habsburg Policy in Hungary and the Einrichtungswerk of Cardinal Kollonich, 1683–90." *Austrian History Yearbook* 38 (2007): 92–107.

Ingrao, Charles W., and Jovan Pešalj. "The Transitional Empire." *Journal of Hungarian Studies* 27 (December 2013): 275–88.

Iordachi, Constantin, and Dorin Dobrincu. "The Communist Take-Over and Land Collectivization in Romania: Chronology of Events, 1945–1962." In Irordachi and Dobrincu, *Transforming Peasants*, 485–91.

Janjetović, Zoran. "Die Konflikte zwischen Serben und Donauschwaben." *Südost Forschungen* 58 (January 1999): 119–68.

Jesner, Sabine. "Making and Shaping a New Province: The Habsburg Banat and the Personnel Issue (1718–1753)." In *The Habsburg State-Wide and the Regions in the Southern Danube Basin (16th–20th Centuries)*, edited by Harald Heppner, Goran Vasin, Nenad Ninković, 57–70. Wien: New Academic Press, 2020.

———. "Personnel Management during Times of Crisis. The Austrian Banat and Austro-Russian-Turkish War (1736–1739)." *Истраживања* 27 (2016): 120–38.

———. "The World of Work in the Habsburg Banat (1716–51/53): Early Concepts of State-Based Social and Healthcare Schemes for Imperial Staff and Relatives." *Austrian History Yearbook* 50 (2007): 58–77.

Kaps, Klemens. "Orientalism and the Geoculture of the World System: Discursive Othering, Political Economy and the Cameralist Division of Labor in Habsburg Central Europe (1713–1815)." *Journal of World-Systems Research* 22, no. 2 (2016): 315–48.

Komlosy, Andrea. "Habsburg Borderlands: A Comparative Perspective." In *Borders in East and West: Transnational and Comparative Perspectives*, edited by Stefan Berger and Nobuya Hashimoto, 49–69. New York: Berghahn Books, 2022.

Koranyi, James. "Reinventing the Banat: Cosmopolitanism as German Cultural Export." *German Politics and Society* 29, no. 3 (Autumn 2011): 97–113.

Krischan, Alexander. "Dissertationen über das Banat (1897–1967)." *Südostdeutsches Archiv* 13 (1970): 203–21.

Landais, Benjamin. "Village Politics and the Use of 'Nation' in the Banat in the 18th Century." In *Forschungwerkstatt: Die Habsburgermonarchie im 18. Jahrhundert*, edited by Gunda Barth Scalmani, Joachim Bürgschwentner, Matthias König, and Christian Steppan, 195–208. Bochum: Verlag Dr. Dieter Winkler, 2012.

Lotz, Friedrich. "Die französische Kolonisation des Banats (1748–1773)." *Südost Forschungen* 23 (January 1964): 132–78.

———. "Donauschwäbische Kolonistenbrautpaare in Ulm und Wien. Ein Beitrag zur Herkunftsforschung der südostdeutschen Ansiedler." In *Festschrift für Friedrich Lotz*, edited by Josef Senz, 72–109. München: Verlag des Südostdeutschen Kulturwerks, 1962.

———. "Johann Karl Reichard (1700–1753). Der erste Banater evangelische Pfarrer nach der Türkenzeit. Ein Lebens- und Kulturbild aus der Frühzeit der Südostdeutschen." *Südost Forschungen* 22 (January 1963): 326–46.

Mayer, Matthew Z. "The Price for Austria's Security: Part I. Joseph II, the Russian Alliance, and the Ottoman War, 1787–1789." *The International History Review* 26, no. 2 (June 2004): 257–99.

Olin, Timothy. "Cultivating an Orderly Society: Physical and Mental Landscapes on the Habsburg's Southern Frontiers." *Austrian History Yearbook* 48 (2017): 159–72.

———. "'Flüchtlinge' oder 'Auswanderer'? Migration aus dem Osmanischen Reich in das Banat im 18. Jahrhundert." In *Aufnahmeland Österreich. Über den Umgang mit Massenflucht seit dem 18. Jahrhundert*, edited by Börries Kuzmany and Rita Garstenauer, 42–67. Wien: Mandelbaum, 2017.

O'Reilly, William. "Divide et Impera: Race, Ethnicity and Administration in Early 18th Century Habsburg Hungary." In *Racial Discrimination and Ethnicity in European History*, edited by Guðmundur Hálfdanarson, 77–100. Pisa: PLUS, Università di Pisa, 2003.

———. "To the East or to the West? Agents in the Recruitment of Migrants for British North America and Habsburg Hungary, 1717–1770." PhD diss., University of Oxford, 2001.

Pădurean, Corneliu. "The Population of Timişoara at the Turn of the 19th and 20th Centuries." *Romanian Journal for Population Studies* 16, no. 1 (2022): 61–74.

Paxton, Roger V. "Identity and Consciousness: Culture and Politics among the Habsburg Serbs in the Eighteenth Century." In Banac et al., *Nation and Ideology*, 101–19.

Pejin, Jovan. "The Privileged District of Velika Kikinda in the Serbian History, 1774–1876." In *The Austrian Military Border: Its Political and Cultural Impact*,

edited by Liviu Maior, Nicolae Bocșan, and Ioan Bolovan, 66–78. Iași: Editura, Glasul Bucovinei, 1994.
Roider, Jr., Karl. "Nationalism and Colonization in the Banat of Temesvár, 1718–1778." In Banac et al., *Nation and Ideology*, 87–100.
Roider, Karl A., and Robert Forrest. "German Colonization in the Banat and Transylvania in the Eighteenth Century." In Ingrao and Szabo, *The Germans and the East*, , 89–104.
Schmidt, Johann. "Briefwechsel zwischen Hessen, Kassel und Mainz über die Auswanderung." *Deutsch-ungarische Heimatsblätter* 2 (1930): 223–26.
Schünemann, Konrad. "Die Einstellung der theresianischen Impopulation (1770/1771)." In *A Bécsi Magyar Történeti Intézet évkönyve = Jahrbuch des Wiener Ungarischen Historischen Instituts*, edited by David Angyal, 167–213. Budapest: M. Történeti Intézet, 1931.
Šević, Željko. "The Unfortunate Minority Group: Yugoslavia's Banat Germans." In Stefan Wolff, *German Minorities in Europe*, 143–63.
Smiley, Will. "A 'Barbarous Law'? Capture and Liberation in the Russo-Habsburg-Ottoman War of 1787–1792." In *Eurasian Slavery, Ransom and Abolition in World History, 1200–1860*, edited by Christoph Witzenrath, 323–33. Burlington, Ashgate: Routeledge, 2015.
Stoianovich, Traian. "The Conquering Balkan Orthodox Merchant." *Journal of Economic History* 20, no. 2 (June 1960): 234–313.
Swanson, John C. "The Second World War and Its Aftermath: Ethnic German Communities in the East." In Ingrao and Szabo, *The Germans and the East*, 347–61.
Szakály, Ferenc. "Das Bauerntum und die Kämpfe gegen die Türken bzw. gegen Habsburg in Ungarn im 16.-17. Jahrhundert." In *Aus der Geschichte der ostmitteleuropäischen Bauernbewegungen im 16.-17. Jahrhundert*, edited by Gusztáv Heckenast, 251–71. Budapest: Akadémiai Kiadó, 1977.
Tóth, István György. "Missionaries as Cultural Intermediaries in Religious Borderland: Habsburg Hungary and Ottoman Hungary in the Seventeenth Century." In *Religion and Cultural Exchange in Europe, 1400–1700*. Vol. 1 of *Cultural Exchange in Early Modern Europe*, edited by Heinz Schilling and István György Tóth, 88–108. Cambridge: Cambridge University Press, 2006.
Turczynski, Emanuel. "Austro-Serbian Relations." In *The First Serbian Uprising*, edited by Wayne S. Vucinich, 175–206. New York: Brooklyn College Press, 1982.
Vultur, Smaranda. "The Role of Ethnicity in the Collectivization of Tomnatic/ Triebswetter (Banat Region) (1949–1956)." In Iordachi and Dobrincu, *Transforming Peasants*, 141–64.

Wagner, Richard. "Ethnic Germans in Romania." In Wolff, *German Minorities in Europe*, 135–42.

Wegge, Simone A. "Eighteenth-Century German Emigrants from Hanau-Hesse: Who Went East and Who Went West." *Continuity and Change* 33 (2018): 225–53.

Wellenreuther, Hermann. "Contexts for Migration in the Early Modern World: Public Policy, European Migrating Experiences, Transatlantic Migration, and the Genesis of American Culture." In *In Search of Peace and Prosperity: New German Settlements in Eighteenth-Century Europe and America*, edited by Hartmut Lehmann, Hermann Wellenreuther, and Renate Wilson, 3–35. University Park: Pennsylvania State University Press, 2000.

Wess, Mitchell, A., and Charles Ingrao. "Emperor Joseph's Solution to Coronavirus." *The Wall Street Journal*, April 6, 2020.

Wolf, Josef. "Ethnische Konflikt im Zuge der Besiedlung des Banats im 18. Jahrhundert. Zum Verhältnis von Einwanderung, staatlicher Raumorganisation und ethnostrukturellem Wandel." In *Migration nach Ost- und Südosteuropa vom 18. bis zum Beginn des 19. Jahrhunderts: Ursachen, Formen, Verlauf, Ergebnis*, edited by Mathias Beer and Dittmar Dahlmann, 337–66. Stuttgart: J. Thorbecke, 1999.

Zakić, Mirna. " 'My Life for Prince Eugene': History and Ideology in Banat German Propaganda in World War II." In *German-Balkan Entangled Histories in the Twentieth Century*, edited by Mirna Zakić and Christopher A. Molnar, 79–94. Pittsburgh, PA: University of Pittsburgh Press, 2020.

Index

Page numbers in italics indicate figures and tables.

Acts of Toleration, Joseph II, 10, 82, 104–5
Ağa, Osman, tragedy of, 106–7, 242n12
agriculture: experimentation in Banat, 45, 141–42; from subsistence to high-yield, 13, 17, 51; success of colonists, 125, 149, 222
Alexander I (Tsar), 206
American Civil War, 188–89
amnesia, social or cultural, 6, 233n13
Anđelković, Koča, *Kočina krajina* (Koča's march), 189
"animality" of local people, 15, 180, 239n55, 239–40n63, 276n6
animal rustling, Banat problem, 126, 184–85, 263n124
Anne (Queen), helping poor German Protestants, 118

Anticipation, repayment at later date, 71
April Laws, 212
Atanasie, Romanian Orthodox Bishop, 92
Austrians, 37; relationship with Russians, 45–46, 200–201; war between Ottomans and, 25
Austro-Ottoman War (1737–1739), 36, 47, 63, 83, 108, 156, 257n167; last, and political developments, 45–48
Austro-Turkish War (1787–1790), 203
Auswanderungsverbot (emigration ban), 54

Balkans, French and German literature on, 5
Banat: antecedents and early efforts at populating, 56–63; arduous

311

Banat (*cont.*)
    trip to, 120–21; cameralism and development, 27–36; Catholic, 111; centrality of, to security, 51; colonial populating of, 21–22; combating lawlessness in region, 171–73; controlling religious makeup by migration and conversion, 90–106; demographic dissolution, 1, 2; development of economy, 234n16; dumping ground for French POWs, 83; emigration from, 84; estimates of colonists in, 85–86; Europeanization of, 51–52; exclusive Catholic nature of, 104; German government standardizing movements of Germans to, 61–63; Germanization, Catholicization, Europeanization, 8–17; German migration to region, 21–22; hardships in, 170; history of, 2, 239n57; Hofkriegsrat approving large-scale movement (1721–1722), 58–61; Hungarian crown gaining, 41–45; important region for Habsburg authorities, 48; land transfers and mono-ethno-religious settlement, 106–18; last Austro-Ottoman War and political developments into nineteenth century, 45–48; name of, 1; newspapers, 140–42, 269–70n112; political dissolution, 1–2; prohibition of Protestant colonization, 102; religion, ethnicity and the state, 17–21; religion and ethnicity controlling settlement in, 89–90; renewed conflict and creation of military border, 36–41; reordering of society in, 5; settlers central to Europeanizing, 24; territorial dissolution, 1; transfer of sovereignty, 41–45; transplantation of Germans to, 48–49; treatment in English literature, 7; types of migration, 18–19; utility of history, 5–8; violence in, 178–89; violent conflicts, 25; vision for colonizing, 86–87; Wallachs as bastion of traditional in modernizing, 173–78; Wallach and Rascian settlers, 76–79; Wallachs' resistance to central government, 189–90

Banater Zeitschrift für Landwirthschaft, Handel, Künste und Gewerbe, (The Banat journal for agriculture, commerce, crafts, and trade), 142

Banat Germans: confused loyalties from Revolution of 1848 to World War I, 211–20; division of Banat from WWI and WWII, 220–26; during and following the Revolution of 1848, 209–11; illiteracy rates, 219; land ownership, 219–20; memory of, 228–29; migration, 218; postwar retaliation, 226–29; prosperity of, 218–19; relationship with government after revolution, 217–18

Banat Land Administration (Landesadministration), 28–29, 91, 175; care in transferring people, 111; General Command and, 199–200; shunning Uniate Church, 95

Bartenstein, tutorial for Crown Prince Joseph, 264n132

Batthyány, Count, appointment of, 212

Becher, Johann Joachim, cameralism thinker, 32–33
Binnenmigration, migration between villages, 82
Bishop of Constanz, migration resolution, 54
Bohemian Germans, settlement, 82
Bonnie and Clyde, 277n29
book of magic, 161–62
Brant, Joseph, leading Mohawks, 188
Britain, 56; colonists to North American colonies, 57–58; remoteness from Reich for recruiting migrants, 53
British North America: Chesapeake Colonies in, 145; German colonists, 147; German-speaking settlers in, 118
Buchholt, Herr Neumann von: colonial director, 126; proposal for resettling of village Monorat, 114
Bulgarian Catholics: Paulichaner and, 100, 101; treatment of, 77, 98–99
Bulgaro-Catholic settlement, Vinka, 108–9

Callugian (Orthodox) Monastery, 108, 114
Calvinists, 91, 102, 104, 139, 216n63
cameralism, 6; definition of, 244n43; development and, 27–36; early, 31; German, 32; sociopolitical theory of, 24; term, 30; theoretical and practical, 30–31
captive narratives, 47
Caraffa, Graf, command of imperial armies, 25–26
Carlsruher Zeitung (newspaper), 74
Catherine II, 23

Catholic Church, legitimacy and supremacy of, 196
Catholic Germans: civil rights of, 91; in ethnic hierarchy of Habsburg rule, 229
Catholicism: conversion, 88–89, 93–95, 97, 101–2, 104, 110; loyalty and, 10–12, 17, 100, 103–4, 108, 200; Paulichaners resisting conversion, 99; true belief of, 92
Catholicization: Banat, 8–17, 93, 177, 230; Hungarian territory, 90–91
Catholics: Bulgarians, 98–101; colonists being recruited, 71, 72; Protestants and, 87, 97–98; Rascians, 20, 94, 106, 149–50, 171; relationship between Orthodox and, 193–95
Catholics with Catholics, Habsburg policy, 83, 102, 105
Ceauşescu, Nicolae, Communist leadership of, 228
central Europe, migration in eighteenth-century, 52–56
"Central Population Instruction for the Banat," 115
Charles III, Spain, 23
Charles of Lorraine, 25
Charles VI, 10, 28, 29, 40, 91, 96, 204, 237n38; Spain, 242n16
Chesapeake Colonies, British North America, 145
children: removing, from Wallachs, 187; removal of, out of "Christian love," 104; settler culture of marriage and, 163–69; *see also* marriage
Christianity, 83; bulwark of, 89, 96; disease remedy, 162–63

314 Index

climate and disease, settler culture, 155–63
Collegium Theresianum, 33
Colloredo, Graf, calling for renewed colonization with Germans, 82–83
Colonial Aufseher (overseers): government inaugurating system of, 125–26; observing activities of colonists, 125–28
colonists: arduous trip to Banat, 120–21; artisans and farmers division of, 125; assessing "worth" of fellow colonists, 128–29; corporal punishment by "Beating Baron," 130; discontent of, 124–25; economic position of, 117–18; estimates of Central and Northern European, 85–86; expectations, 121, 122–23; expectations and fulfillment, 121–22; expense to government, 142–43; French-speaking, 9; German, and government, 121, 122–23; German, desire to permanently leave, 124; German-speaking, 8–9; government oversight, 123–31; government's system of Colonial Aufseher (overseers), 125–26; interethnic relations with locals, 146–55; overseers observing activities of, 125–28; petitioning authorities for assistance, 127–29; recruitment of specific type, 51–52; role of government for, 143; urbarium (contract), 130; vision for Banat, 86–87; Wallach and Rascian settlers, 76–79; *see also* settler culture
conquest (1683–1718), Ottoman, 24, 25–27

contracts, marriage, 164–69
Contribution (tax), 58; adjustment period, 114; freedom from, 71, 94, 171; peasants paying, 198; priest exemptions from, 194
conversion, controlling religious makeup through migration and, 90–106
corporal punishment, colonists, 130
Court Chamber (Hofkammer), 28, 42, 43, 82, 97, 111
Crassovans, 94, 238n39
Crausen, Johann Franz Albert: bringing colonists, 11; colonists recruited by, 122; payment scheme, 60; recruiter, 107; scouting of settlement sites, 58–60
crimes, people in shipments, 66
criminals: nationalities of war, 288n91; praise of, 277n29
"Crown of Illyria," 206
Csencitz, Johann, murder of, 213
"cultural beacons" (*Kulturträger*), Germans as, 3, 6, 13, 16, 121, 137
cultural life, Temesvar, 138–39
culture. *See* settler culture

Dakota War, Minnesota, 188
daughter colonies, 82
Deak, Demetria, goal of revolt, 207
decapitation, 46
deserters, bringing back, 76–77
Deutsche Volksblatt (newspaper), 222
Deutsch Jarmatha, community of German colonists, 112, 125, 128, 154
Deutschsanktmichael, Rauth recruiting for, 82
Diet of 1830, 44
Diet of 1832, 44

Diploma Leopoldinum, privileges of Rascians and Orthodox Church, 192, 194, 197
disease(s): animals, 158–59; Banat fever, 158; cholera, 158; cholera outbreaks, 157; mosquito *Kolumbatczer Mücke*, 159; plague, 156, 158; remedies for, 162–63; settler culture of climate and, 155–63; typhus, 158
Dorner, Joseph von, on German colonists, 134
dragon, St. George and, 159–60
droughts, climate and disease, 155–56
Duke of Württemberg, migration resolution, 54

Eimann, Johann: colonial narratives, 148, 155; on health care of settlements, 158; Josephian migration, 256n143
Einrichtungswerk des Königreichs Ungarn, 27, 28; no account of ethnicity in, 56
elderly care, settler culture, 169
Elizabeth (Russian Empress), 199
emigration, 32–33; Banat as place of, 84, 175–77, 197–203, 218, 228; edicts banning, 54–56
Engelshofen (Generalfeldwachtmeister), 29, 39
England, Dutch shipping colonists to, 57
Enlightenment, 80, 141, 158, 203, 283
epidemics, 83, 156; victims of French and Napoleonic Wars, 83–84; *see also* disease
Erlach, Emanuel Fischer von, architect, 139

ethnicity: communities, 19; controlling settlement in Banat, 89–90; importance for recruiting states, 118–19; religion, language and, 20–21; term, 18
ethnoreligious groups, Banat, 19–20
Eugen, Prinz, Waffen-SS division, 225
Eugene of Savoy (Prince), 10, 26, 106; army of, 137
Europeanization, 11, 13, 24, 48, 51, 140, 144–46, 173, 230; Banat, 8–17; civilizing mission, 13–14
Evangelicals, 97–98, 105; village of Franzfeld, 82, 84
expectations, colonists, 121, 122–23
Eyalet of Temesvar, 1, 26

Fabrik Vorstadt (Factory Suburb): cameralism in action, 34; construction of, 138
famine, Europe in 1760s–1770s, 74, 114, 121, 237
Fényes, Elek, statistics of, 94
Ferenc II Rákóczi's rebellion (1703–1711), 90, 214
feudal law, Hungarian, 129
Filipovich, Ivan, recruiter with Austrian ties, 202
First Serbian Uprising, 189
Florimund Mercy, 11, 38, 78, 97–98, 107, 108, 112, 122, 138; Habsburg monarchy, 6; village named for, 135
forced migrations, *Wasserschub* and Hauerensteiner, 63–68
France, enforcing migration ban, 53, 56
Franz (Emperor) (1804–1835), 11, 44, 134, 135; Military Community, 150

Franzfeld: Evangelicals in, 82; Protestant families, 84
Franz-Stephan (Duke of Lorraine and Duke of Tuscany), 11, 51
Frederick II, 23; Prussia, 70
Frederick William of Prussia, 23
"Free Towns," 139
free year concession, 50, 56, 62, 63, 58, 78–79, 82–83, 100, 101, 110
Fremaut, Maximillian, draining Banat's swamps, 35
French colonists, 8–9, 153, 272n40; "Emigrant Ecclesiastics," 83; estimates in Banat, 86, 236n31, 236nn34–35; villages, 238nn39–40
French goods, luxury, 32
French Revolution, 24; Rascians becoming Serbs, 203–7; wars, 45, 83
frontier social security, 165–66; settler culture, 163–69

Galicia, 13, 242n6; artificial Habsburg creation, 5
gender discrepancy, shipment of people, 65–66
General Evening Post (newspaper), 47
General Regulation of 1770, 194; Leopoldine privileges, 192
German(s): "cultural beacons," 6; industriousness and thrift, 10; Joseph II recruiting, 79–85; in language and culture, 9–10; term, 8, 9; transplantation to Banat, 48–49; *see also* German colonists
German Catholic Lorrainers, recruited for settlement in Banat, 50–52
German colonists: controlling and renaming villages, 135–36; desire to permanently leave Banat, 124; government and, 121, 122–23; houses and villages of, 132–37; locals resenting incoming, 179–80; miners, 83; narratives on, 146–49; population estimates of, 85, 86; Spain, 147, 153–54; *see also* Banat Germans; colonists
German Confederation, 210
Germanization, Banat, 8–17
German ultranationalism, 211
Germany: nationalist ideology, 223–224
government: assessing "worth" of colonists, 128–29; colonists petitioning for assistance, 127–29; expense of colonists to, 142–43; German colonists and, 122–23; inaugurating system of Colonial Aufseher (overseers), 125–26; maps of planned villages, 132–33; newspapers as organs of process and development, 140–42; oversight of settlers, 123–31; role of, for colonists, 143; towns as bastions of Germandom, 137–40; village planning and architecture, 131–37; *see also* Banat Land Administration
Grassl, Georg, attack of SRNAO members on, 222
Great Depression, 222
Great Northern War, 26
"Greek," Habsburgs use of, 251n38
Greek Catholics, 18; Catholicism, 3; Church, 16, 92; conversion to, 93; *see also* Uniate Church
Grenzer(s), 39, 41, 45, 110, 191–192, 200, 203, 204; abandoning Habsburg monarchy, 198–99; French Revolu-

tionary Wars and, 205; Orthodox, 197, 198, 200, 260n50; putting down unrest, 196; requesting permission to move, 197–98
Griselini, Francesco: on assessment of pre-Habsburg Banat, 30; comparing local people to pastoral peoples, 15; history of Banat, 141, 155; idea of Turkish yoke, 14

Habsburg authorities: on burdens of peasants, 279n63; controlling distribution of people in Banat, 262n93; Daskovich's experience and, 201–2; ethnicities and religions, 118–19; locals fighting against, 189; Rascians and Wallachs resisting, 207–8; Rascians as vital but distrusted, 193–203; on Russian and Spanish recruitment efforts, 72–74; tension between Rascians and, 200–201; violence in Banat, 178–89; Wallachs in response to modernizing Banat, 173–78
Habsburg monarchy: creation of nation-states, 240n73; Florimund Mercy, 6
Habsburg rule: ethnic and religious rivalries, 231; ethnic hierarchy during, 229–31; Europeanizing and Catholicizing agenda, 230–31; nationalism, 231; resistance to, 179–81
haiduks (robber-soldier peasants), 178
Hamilton, Graf: combating lawlessness in region, 171–72; free land, 242n16; on success of Germans, 62
happiness, Justi defining, 33
harambascha, mayor accused of being, 184; robber leaders, 183

Hauerstein, forced migration, 63, 67–68
head start, agricultural, 107
health care, settlement culture, 158–59
hemp production, 8, 35–36, 177
herbalism, 162
Hiller, Baron Johann von, aid to insurgents, 206
Hitler, Adolf, 225
Hofkammer, on colonization and settlement, 111–12
Hofkriegsrat, large-scale settlement near Arad and in Banat, 58–61
Holocaust, 7
Holy League, 25
Holy Roman Emperor, Joseph, 55
Holy Roman Empire (Reich), 2, 9, 10, 11, 49; Black Forest region, 67; Josephian migration of Germans from, 81; polities of, resisting draining populations, 53
Holy Trinity, doctrine of, 92
Horea Uprising, 185–87, 203
Hörnigk, Philipp Wilhelm von: development of Austrian lands, 32; *Österreich über alles, wann es nur will*, 31
"Hottentots," Khoikhoi of South Africa, 15
Hungarian(s), 6; Diet (1741), 42, 204; "feudal law," 129; gaining Banat, 41–45; Hungarian Academy of the Sciences, 44; "Hungarian Cameral properties," 81; Hungarian Revolution of 1848, 211–17; incorporation of Banat into, 129; Kossuth and, 131, 211–13, 215; offering free years for settlement, 50; religion in, 103–4; settlement in, 56–57

318 Index

identity, questions of, 19
illegal migrants, ordinance banning, 55
Illyrian, 194; term, 283n53
Illyrian Court Chancellery, 204
Illyrian Court Department, 195
imidacloprid, 159
Imperial Free Passes, 58
Impopulationspatent, decree for repeopling conquered regions, 56
interethnic relations, colonists and locals, 146–55
invalids, settlement of so-called, 71
Iohannis, Klaus, Romania president, 229
Italians, 8, 35–36, 153; estimates in Banat, 86

Janko, Sepp: on protection for German leaders, 224; resistance of, 226
Jarmatha, 125, 128, 154; confiscated land from Rascians, 112, 113
Jĕlacić, Josip, Hungarian invasion, 212
Jesuits, 92, 93, 94, 138; publishing religious books, 269–70n112
Jews, 20, 43, 58–59, 61, 91, 104, 151–52, 224; view in Banat, 93
Johann v. Klaniczay, 45, 141
Joseph II (Emperor), 2, 30, 42, 104; Acts of Toleration, 10; banning emigration, 55; death of, 158, 273n72; on education for Wallach culture change, 177; on forced migration, 67; future emperor, 74; Greek Catholics in Sabran after succession of, 109; *Königliche Freistadt* ("Royal Free Town") by, 139; lamenting Turkish form of government, 14; migration policy of no population transfer, 116; migration through early nineteenth century, 79–85; Patent of Toleration, 82, 104–5; reign of, 13; religious toleration, 18; resettlement policy at succession of, 116; response to rebellion, 186–88; reversal of peasant fortunes, 129; sole rule of, 87; steps aiming to improve Wallachs' position, 185–87; view of French Revolution, 205; on Wallachs and Rascians, 93
Jovanović, Jovan, on support for Serb protectorate, 206
Justi, Johann Heinrich Gottlob von, cameralist theorist, 33

Karadjordje's Revolt (1813), 78, 205
Karadjordjević, Alexander, Serbian leader, 214
Karlsburg Declaration, 223, 225
Kaunitz, Wenzel Anton: on punishing convicts, 67; settler patents, 73
Khoikhoi of South African, "Hottentots," 15
"Kirgiz," Muslims and Buddhists, 147
Kohl, Johann Georg: on Catholic Rascians, 94; on German agricultural system, 149; on Germanizing people, 272n40; on German settlements, 136–37; on intermarriage of Catholic and Orthodox Rascians, 152; on residents defending themselves, 181–82; settler interactions, 151–52; on Temesvar, 139–40; on Wallachs' cattle, 148; on Wallach village of Pechineska, 134–35

Kolb, Peter, on execution of slaves, 276n6

Kollonich, Leopold (Cardinal), 27; authoring decree for open-door policy, 56; Jesuits and, 92; on rebuilding Hungary, 96

Kolumbatszer Mücke, deadly mosquito, 159

Königliche Freistadt ("Royal Free Town"), Joseph II, 139

Kossuth, Lajos: Hungarian Revolution of 1848, 131; on Magyarization plan, 211–13; nationalist plan, 211–12; Protestant Rebellion of, 214; on siding with Hungarians, 215

Kovats, Kameralpräfekt Johann, on Roman Catholic settlers, 105

Kraft, Stefan, attack of SRNAO members on, 222

Kun, Béla, Hungarian Soviet Republic, 220

Kurzböck, Joseph von, on conversion to Uniate Church, 95

"Land Allocation of a Suggested Ideal Village," planned villages, 132–33

land ownership, Banat Germans, 219–20

"Land-Security and Peace" plan, 180

land transfers, mono-ethno-religious settlement and, 106–18

Leopold II (Emperor): Illyrian nation, 204; view of French Revolution, 205

Leopoldine Diploma (1690), privileges of Rascians and Orthodox Church, 192, 194, 197

Lippa administration: Crausen proposal, 107; Uniate Church, 94

Lobkowitz (Prince), 37

Lo Presti de Fontana d'Angioli (Baron), corporal punishment regime of, 130

Lorraine: German Catholics from, for settlement in Banat, 50–51, 56, 123, 128; source of migrants, 8–9, 11

Lotz, Friedrich, on French migrants, 9

Louis XIV (King), France, 90

Louis XVI (King), execution of, 205

Lutherans, 68, 91, 102–5; detention for faith, 88; Habsburgs expelling, 90; settlement in Banat, 96–97

luxury goods, 35, 45; creation of, 32; products, 141

Magyar(s), 18; dominance in Hungary, 44; Rajačić on, 285n22

Magyarization, 6, 21; "Germans" lost to, 257n171; land ownerships, 220; newspapers for, 269n112; policy of, 44; proponents of, 44; Revolution of 1848, 211; Serbs and Romanians fearing, 218

"Main Population Instructions" (1772), 132

Manifesto of 1763, promises of, 72

Marggräflich=Burgowisches Wochenblatt (magazine), 75

Maria Theresia (Empress), 7, 11, 27, 28, 29, 36, 41–42, 45, 118, 170; Catholic nature of Banat, 104; converting Orthodox believers, 93; death of, 79; on efforts to "Catholicize" Serbian Orthodox catechism, 95; Festetics' plan going against, 115; on forced migration, 67; halting

Maria Theresia (Empress) *(cont.)* recruitment, 74; investigating mosquito impact on animals, 159; on migrants if war breaks out in Poland, 77; potable water supply under, 138; settlement patent, 70; statement of, by government in Vienna, 50–51; succession of, 98; supporting marriage among colonists, 163; Theresian migration, 69–76; on threats to Wallach families, 110; Visarion's travels and, 193; welcoming Bulgarian Catholics, 101

Marie Antoinette, 205

marriage: contracts, 164–66, 168–69, 274n97, 274–75n99; government support of, 163; settler culture of, and children, 163–69

Mayer Amigo, Banat, 20

"means test," proclamation lacking, 71

memory, 6, 233n13

mercantilism, French economic system, 32

Mercy, Claudius (Governor), 34, 38, 96, 97; economic growth of Temesvar, 138; ordering removal of Wallachs, 107–8; Rascian Jarmatha, 112; rejecting Crausen's proposal, 107; settler villages, 122; village Mercydorf named for, 135, 154

Mercydorf, 124, 125, 129, 135, 154, 236–37n35

Metternich, Klemens von, on southeastern colonization, 85

migrants: legal and illegal, 55; Wallach and Rascian settlers, 76–79

migration: Banat Germans, 218; controlling religious makeup through conversion and, 90–106; eighteenth-century central Europe, 52–56; forced, of exiled families, 68, 254n81; forced, of Hauerstein, 67–68; forced, of *Wasserschub*, 63–67, 253n69; German, to Banat region, 21–22; Josephian, through early nineteenth century, 79–85; migrants against their will, 63–68; pull factors, 52–53, 79, 175; push factors, 52–53, 175; recruiting settlers, 53; Theresian, 69–76; types of, in Banat, 18–19

"Military Community," 150

Milleker, Felix, 144; on revolt plan (1807), 206–7; Serbian rebellion, 216, 286n38

mining, 31, 32, 34–35, 58, 108, 181; Protestant miners, 96–98

missionaries, Catholic, 93, 99

Möller, Karl von, United States as "Dollarika," 218

Moltke, Helmuth von, on German colonies along Danube, 85

multiconfessionalism, problem of, 102

multiculturalism, 6, 7

Murgu, Eftimie, Banat Romanians, 216

Muslims, 3, 89, 93, 99, 106–107, 118, 147, 262n91; Romanians against, 178; threats from, 91

Napoleonic Wars, 45, 83
nation, term, 18
National Congress of 1790, 203–4, 217
National Defense Committee, 212
Nationalist, term, 14, 19, 80

Native Americans, North America, 57, 147, 188–89
Natural Born Killers (movie), 277n29
Nazism, 6, 211; in Germany, 223; in Romania, 225
Nemanja, Stefan, monks moving bones of, 78
Neoacquistische Subdelegation, 28, 98
Newlanders, 69
New Serbia, 201, 202; colonies of, 199
newspapers: Banat, 269–70n112; government organs of progress and development, 140–42
New York Times (newspaper), 219
North America: immigrants to colonies, 57–58; Native Americans in, 188–89
Nowak, Johann, Swabian Petition, 209–10

occult, 162; disease remedy, 162–63
Orawitzer Oberbergverwaltung (Orawitza High Mountain Administration), 44
orphan care, 45; settler culture, 168–169
Orthodox Church: Diploma *Leopoldinum* privileges, 192, 194; monasteries seized, 108–9, 114–15; Patent of Toleration and, 104–5; Rascians and, 192–94; relationship between Catholic and, 195; Russian Empire and, 199; Uniates apostatizing and rejoining, 94–95
Orthodox inhabitants, 195–97; attempts at conversion, 91–95, 110, 200; Grenzers, 197; Religious intermarriage, 152; prejudice toward Greek Ritual Rascians, 193; Rascians, 18, 191–96; Wallach, 18
Österreich über alles, wann es nur will (Hörnigk), 31
Ostojić family, 82
Ottendorf, Heinrich, traveler on Temesvar, 137
Ottoman, conquest (1683–1718), 24, 25–27
Ottoman Empire, 2, 23, 25, 38, 78, 196, 241n85; Rascians and, 190, 208; resistance to, 180–81; spread of plague, 247n109; transimperial ethnic connection of Rascians, 199
Ottoman-Habsburg border, 40
Ottomans, 12, 89; aggression of, 2–3; detrimental effect of rule, 14; stories of civility, 47–48; threat of Muslim, 8; war between Austrians and, 25
Ottoman Serbia, 17; bringing back "deserters" from, 76–77; Rascians crossing to Banat, 77–78

Paget, John: on intermarriage of different groups, 152; traveler assessment, 135
Paris Peace Conference, 219
Pastorius, Franz Daniel, ethnic Germans in Philadelphia, 57
Patent of Toleration, Joseph, 82, 104–5
Paton, A. A.: comparing colonists, 149; narrative of travels in 1848, 134, 135; on Temesvar visit, 138; writing after conquest, 15
Paulichaner, 98–99; Catholic Bulgarians and, 100, 101; as *pavlikyani*, 99
Peace of Westphalia, 96

Penn, William, plans for Pennsylvania resembling Banat's, 136
Peter I, 23
Petri, Anton Peter: Banat Land Administration, 258n13; on loss of German culture, 221
Peyachevich, Georgi, Bulgarian Catholics rebelling under, 99
Phelps, Arthur, Waffen-SS division, 226
Philadelphia, ethnic Germans in North American colony, 57
Plague, 78; column (Pestsäule), 158; quarantine station, 40; quarantine stations, 40–41; smoke against, 246–47n102; spread of, out of Ottoman Empire, 247n109
popular culture, 4–5
Population Fund, 67
populationism, 21, 32–33
Prädium Schumbul, mobile villages of, 174
Pradium Beschenova, 100
Principality of Serbia, 213
prostitution, euphemism, women leading "wanton or dissolute life," 63–64, 67
Protestant families, Franzfeld, 84
Protestantism, problem of, 258n3
Protestants: Catholics and, 87; converting, 88–89; Magyars, 28, 89; migration to Hungary, 103; reconversion to Catholicism, 89; role of Catholic Banat in movement of, 102–3; view in Banat, 93
Protestants with Protestants, Habsburg policy, 83
pull factors, migration, 52–53, 79, 175
push factors, migration, 52–53, 175

quarantine station, plague, 40–41, 156

Ráday, Gaf Paul, settlement contract with peasant-colonists, 62
Rajačić, Joseph: on Magyars, 285n22; Serbian patriarch, 213
Rákóczi's rebellion (1703–1711), 90, 91
Rascian Nation, Pava Lasin and Pavel Ristin as, 20
Rascian(s), 7, 10, 11, 12, 14, 17, 21, 38, 39, 45; becoming Serbs during French Revolution, 203–7; Catholic, 94; confiscated land from, in Jarmatha, 112, 113; connection with unrest, 182; conversion from Orthodox to Catholicism, 195; culture, 4; description of, 17; *Diploma Leopoldinum* privileges, 192, 194, 197; distrusted but vital, 193–203; in ethnic hierarchy of Habsburg rule, 229; Jarmatha, 112; narratives on, 148–51; nationalism, 231; newspapers on, 142; opposing state through migration and unrest, 190; Orthodox, 18, 93, 191; Ottoman Empire and, 208; problem of Catholic and Orthodox, 152; as settlers, 76–79; Russian Empire and, 208; separation from Germans, 115–16; settler interactions, 151–52; term, 17; transimperial ethnic connection with Ottoman Empire, 199; transimperial religious connection with Russia, 199; violent behavior of, 178–79; Wortley Montagu describing, 14
Rascian-Serbian culture, 198
Real-Zeitung (newspaper), 187

rebellion, violence in Banat, 178–89
recruiting agents, 57, 60, 69, 107; German Catholic Lorrainers for settlement in Banat, 50–52; for North America, 54; for Russia, 199, 201–3; for Spain, 73; threat of death penalty for, 55, 250n19
Redemptioner System, 53
Refugees, 98, 214; modern term, 77; Wallach and Rascian settlers, 76–79
"Regulations Concerning the Greek Ritual in the Banat," government guidelines, 194
Reichard, Johann Karl, taking pastoral job, 96–97
Reich Germans, Banat Germans and, 224–25
Reichs-Oberpost-Amtszeitung (newspaper), 81
religion: controlling settlement in Banat, 89–90; importance for recruiting states, 118–19; language, ethnicity, and, 20–21; schools in Banat, 139; separating Catholics and non-Catholics, 105–6; uniformity in Banat, 103–4; unrest in Temerest and Sabran, 109
religious affiliation, Banat, 20
religious makeup, migration and conversion controlling, 90–106
Revertierung, convictions, 64
Revolutionary War, Native Americans, 188
Revolution of 1848, 21, 85, 208; Banat Germans during and following, 209–11; confused loyalties of Banat Germans from, to WWI, 211–20; language dispute, 281n13;

outbreak of cholera and typhus, 158
rice production, 8, 32, 35–36, 177
robbery: gallows for robbers, 280n79; *haiduks* (robber-soldier peasants), 178; Hungarian robber bands, 183; murder and highway, 180; rebellion and, in Banat, 178–89; spreading to uprisings, 180–82; targeting official hierarchy, 184
Robert of Anjou (King), Hungary, 137
Robin Hood, 277n29
Roma, 3, 65, 109, 115, 131, 181; settler interactions, 151
Roman Catholicism, 3
Romania, 6; Germans of, 227; recognition of German rights, 225; Yugoslavia and, 227–28
Romanian, nationalism, 211
Romanian Banat, 238n40
Romanian Germans, 225
Romanians, 6, 18, 174; Banat, 216–17; Catholic education, 92; Germans and, 223; language, 217, 281n13
"Royal Free Town," Joseph II, 139
Russian 1763 Manifesto, 72–73
Russian Church, Holy Synod of, 199
Russian Empire, 13, 17, 121, 147, 201; calling one "German" as insult, 270–71n114; calls for settlers (1763, 1763), 72; German-colonial culture mirroring, 153; German colonists left for, 84; Rascians and, 193, 196, 198–203, 206, 208; rebellion (1773–1774), 188; remoteness from Reich for recruiting migrants, 53
Russians: Austrians' relationship with, 36–37, 45–46, 73, 200–201, 214; religious tolerance of, 118

324 Index

St. George, dragon and, 159–60
St. James's Chronicle (newspaper), 187
Salinat (Bishop), Catholicism, 99
"Salpeter Wars" (1740s), 68
Schmerling, Anton von, on pacification of Hungary, 85
Schmidt (German Chancellor), 228
Schönbauer, Joseph Anton, book on *Kolumbatszer Mücke*, 159
schools: local people and, 177–78, 194, 199; Temesvar, 138–39
Schwarzenberg, Karl, 45
Scientific Revolution, 158
Second Treaty of Versailles, 70
Second World War, 3
security: controlling religious makeup by migration and conversion, 90–106; fleeing for, 77; land transfers and mono-ethnoreligious settlement, 106–18
Serbia, 15
Serbian nationalism, 211
Serbian rebellion, Pančevo, 216, 286n38
Serbo-Magyar conflict, 213–14
Serb Revolt, 205
Serbs, 6, 183, 192; Rascians becoming, during French Revolution, 203–7
Serb-South Slave rule, 221–22
settlement culture, intermarriage of groups, 152–53
settler culture, 144–46; caring for elderly and orphans, 169; climate and disease, 155–63; colonists and locals, 146–55; interethnic relations, 146–55; land prices, 166–68; marriage and children, 163–69; supernatural resources, 162–63; vampirism, 160–62
settler society and culture, creation of, 3–4

Seven Years' War (1756–1763), 8, 23, 70; conclusion of, 103
Shokatzes, Catholic Rascians as, 94
Shrew's Fiddle, 147
Siebold, Mathias: first-person account of revolution, 215; on government bill collection, 129; on mosquito problem, 159
Siege of Vienna, 57
silk, 32, 110, 141, 169; production in Banat, 45; textiles, 35
Simbschen, Joseph Anton Freiherr von, aid to insurgents, 206
slavery, 14, 26, 37–38, 46–47, 242n12, 246n87
Slavyanoserbia, colonies of, 199
Small, Albion, on cameralism, 244n43
Sobieski, Jan, 25
social security, marriage and children, 163–69
Sonnenfels, Josef, on benefits of population for state, 34
Soro, Johann (Count), Mercydorf village ownership, 129
Southwell, Sir Thomas, County of Limerick, 57
Soviet Red Army, 226
Spain: Charles VI, 242n16; German colonists, 147, 153–54; recruiters for settlers, 72–73; remoteness from Reich for recruiting migrants, 53
Spanish colonists in the Banat, 62, 153, 242n16, 246n128
Speckbacher, Josef, freedom fighters by, 83–84
SRNAO, Serbian nationalist organization, 222
Staikovith, Georg, mayor involvement with bandits, 184

Stanislavich (bishop of Nicopoli), 77
Startimirović, Orthodox Metropolitan, supporting Serb state establishment, 206
Steube, Johann Kaspar: assessment of Wallachs, 173–74, 176–77; distrust of Wallachs, 147; on Limony, 36; Wallach house description, 131; on Wallachs as vampires, 160
Suckow, August Jacob Heinrich Freiherr von, religious dissension, 261n63
Sun King, 90
Šupljikac, Stevan, as first *vojvod*, 213
Swabian Council, Janjetović on main goal of, 221
"Swabian-German Cultural Union," 222
Swabian Petition: author Nowak, 209; Banat Germans in, 209–10; drafters of, 210
swamps, climate and disease, 156–57
Széchenyi, István, on Kossuth's nationalist plans, 211

Tafferner, Andon, on actions of recruiters and migrants, 55
Tagsbericht (newspaper), 140
Tallar, Georg, on vampirism, 160–61
tax freedom, 80
Temesvar: bastion of Germandom, 137–40; community interactions in, 151; conquest of, 58; cultural life of, 138–39; plan for expelling Orthodox from, 258–59n14; religious schools in, 139
Temesvar administration: advocating for widespread displacement, 111; Bulgarians and Orthodox monks, 109; Catholic Bulgarians, 100

Temeswarer Merkur (newspaper), 140
Temeswarer Nachrichten (newspaper), 35, 85, 140, 155
Temeswarer Wasserschub (Temesvar water transport), 63–67, 253n69
Temeswarer Wochenblatt (newspaper), 140
Temeswarer Zeitung (newspaper), 140
textiles, production, 35
Theresian migrations, 69–76; on accommodating colonists in, 110–11; concessions for late, 145
Thirty Years' War, depopulation of, 32
Tican's 1807 rebellion, 207
Tito, Josef Broz, Germans of Yugoslavia, 226–227
Tököli, Imre, Hungarian leader, 90, 91
towns, bastions of Germandom, 137–40
transborder region, Banat, 2
transfer of sovereignty, Hungarians gaining Banat, 41–45
transimperial, local people as, 78, 190, 191, 192, 193, 199, 205, 207, 214, 229
Transylvania, 88, 89, 90; conflict at conscription center, 186; Lutherans expelled from Banat to, 97; migration, 175; organizers of 1784 rebellion, 185; Orthodox and Protestant, 102; Protestant, 111; Protestants to go to, 98; religion in, 103–4; relocating Wallach migrants, 109–10; Romanians against Muslim Ottomans, 178; Uniate Church in, 92; Wallach rights in, 187; Wallachs in, 264n132
Treaty of Karlowitz (1699), 26, 197
Treaty of Passarowitz (1718), 27, 197
Treaty of Sistova, 46
Treaty of Szatmár, 28, 91

Treaty of Trianon, 1, 231, 268n83
Trier, 53–54, 69, 122
Trinitarians, 47
Turks, 13–14, 30, 37, 47, 48, 91, 106, 181, 182, 187, 262n91; *see also* Ottomans
Tuscany, colonists from Lorraine, 51
Tuscarora War (1711–1713), 188

Ujpalanka administration, 184
"Uniate" Church, 3, 16, 92; converting Orthodox people to, 93–94; foundation of, 92–93; Wallach residents on border region, 110
Uniate Rascians, 18
United States, migration of Banat Germans, 218
urbarium, contract between lord and serf, 130
uti possidetis, principle of, 27

vampirism, Tallar on, 160–61
van Dorner, Joseph, on people of Banat as "behind" other Europeans, 14
villages: design and upkeep, 136–37; French movement, 236–37n35; German colonists controlling and renaming, 135–36; government planning and architecture of, 131–37; maps of planned, 132–33; placement of, 272–73n60; styles, 133
violence: animal rustling, 184–85; Banat, 178–89; banditry, 189; *haiduks* (robber-soldier peasants), 178; Horea Uprising, 185–87; Joseph II's response to rebellion, 186–88; local people resisting officials, 182; locals resenting incoming colonists, 179–80; Rascians in connection with, 183; robbery, 184; settlement process and, 119; Turkish War (1737–1739), 181; Wallachs in large uprisings, 185–86; war within Ottoman Empire, 180–81
Visarion Sarai (monk), 193
von Rebentisch, Cameral High Inspector, settler villages, 122
von Spinola, Christoph Roya, employ of Bishop of Passau, 31

Wallach families, relocating migrants, 109–10
Wallachs, 3, 7, 11, 12, 13, 15, 17, 37, 38, 39; bastion of traditional in modernizing Banat, 173–78; Catholic, 94; criticism of, 142; culture, 4; in ethnic hierarchy of Habsburg rule, 229–30; Evans describing, 14; mass movement out of Banat, 175–77; narratives on, 146–49; nationalism, 231; Orthodox, 18, 93; as settlers, 76–79; reputation of, 17; resistance to central government, 189–90; settler interactions, 151–52; Steube's assessment of, 173–74, 176–77; term, 17; in Transylvania, 264n132; Transylvanian, 199; uprisings along borders of Banat, 277–78n30; villages of, 134–35; violent behavior of, 178–80
Wallis (Count), government offering general amnesty, 183
wanderers, 77
War Council (Hofkriegsrat), 28, 58, 82, 107, 205
War of 1812, 188
War of Austrian Succession (1740–1748), 70
War of Polish Succession, 36
War of Spanish Succession, 26

wars: Habsburgs and Ottomans, 24, 26–27, 36–37, 45–48; of religion, 90
Wasserschub: migrants against their will, 63–68; partly as punishment, 64; Schünemann on, 253n69
Weiss, Josef, on German colonist in Spain, 154
Westernization, question of, 13
"White Spaniards," 47
Wienerisches Diarium (newspaper), 71
Wiener Zeitung (newspaper), 71
Wilson's Fourteen Points, 220
Woiwodschaft, potential creation of, 210
Wolff, Christian, on reasons for emigration, 33
women: convictions for *Revertierung*, 64; forced movement of criminals and predominance of, 63–64; integral in colonization and population plan, 65

World War I, 6, 7, 174; Revolution of 1848 to, 211–20
World War II, 6, 7, 15; Baumann on leaving for Austria, 234n21; division of Banat between WWI and, 220–26; Romanians and Yugoslavs, 227–28
Wortley Montagu, Lady Mary, describing Rascians, 14
Württemberger families, 82

Yugoslav Banat, national-socialist ideology, 223–24
Yugoslav Germans, national-socialist movement, 224
Yugoslav government, education and German language, 287n73
Yugoslavia, 6; Germans of, 226; Hitler invading, 224; intercommunal violence in, 224; Romania and, 227–28; seizure of, 225
Yugoslav Wars, 7

www.ingramcontent.com/pod-product-compliance
Lightning Source LLC
Jackson TN
JSHW080910161224
74479JS00001B/1